Painter's palettes are accessed through the Window menu.

Painter's Tools palette is shown below:

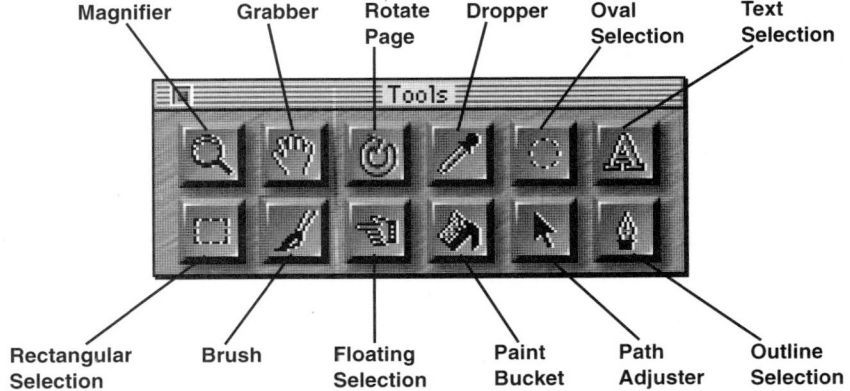

The options in the Controls palette change depending on the tool that is selected in the Tools palette. The name of the palette also changes depending on which tool is selected.

The Color Set palette allows you to change the primary and secondary painting colors by clicking on a swatch. See Chapter 2 to learn how to create your own custom Color Set palette.

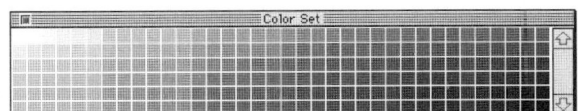

The Art Materials palette features five sub-palettes: Colors, Papers, Grads, Sets, and Weaves. These are discussed in Chapters 2 and 3.

The Brush Controls palette features five sub-palettes: Size, Spacing, Bristle, Looks, and Nozzle. These are discussed in Chapter 3.

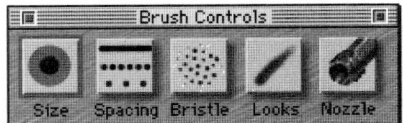

The Advanced Controls palette features five sub-palettes: Rake, Well, Random, Sliders, and Water. These are discussed in Chapter 3.

The Objects palette features five sub-palettes: Paths, Path List, Floaters, Floater List, and Sessions. These are discussed in Chapters 7, 8, and 10.

The Ultimate Guide to Fractal Design Painter®

**Adele Droblas Greenberg
and Seth Greenberg**

SYBEX®

San Francisco • Paris • Düsseldorf • Soest

Acquisitions Manager: Kristine Plachy
Developmental Editor: Steve Lipson
Editor: Doug Robert
Technical Editor: David Hendee
Book Designer: Suzanne Albertson
Chapter Artist: Lucie Živny
Desktop Publisher: Dina F Quan
Production Coordinator: Sarah Lemas
Indexer: Matthew Spence
Cover Designer: Joanna Gladden
Cover Illustrators: Daniel Ziegler and Eric Mendlow

Library of Congress Card Number: 95-68272
ISBN: 0-7821-1700-7

Manufactured in the United States of America

10 9 8 7 6 5 4 3 2 1

To our family, for their love and support

Acknowledgments

We'd like to thank everyone at SYBEX for helping make *The Ultimate Guide to Fractal Design Painter* such a clear, concise, and attractive book. We especially wish to thank Acquisitions Manager Kristine Plachy and Developmental Editor Steve Lipson for getting the project started, and asking us to write this book.

We'd like to express our special thanks and gratitude to our editor, Doug Robert, for his conscientiousness, patience, hard work, suggestions, and support.

Our thanks also to SYBEX Editor-in-Chief Dr. Rudolph S. Langer, Associate Publisher Carrie Lavine, Production Manager Jim Curran, Desktop Publisher Dina Quan, Technical Editor David Hendee, and Production Coordinator Sarah Lemas. Thanks also to Desktop Publisher Deborah Maizels for her help with screen-capture formats.

Thanks to everyone at Fractal Design, especially VP of Marketing Steve Guttman for his help and support. We'd especially like to thank Painter's principal developers: President and CEO Mark Zimmer, Chairman of the Board Tom Hedges, and VP of Creative Design John Derry. We'd especially like to thank both Mark and John for taking the time to explain some of the new features of Painter 3.1.

Thanks also to Quality Assurance Managers Michael Cinque and Karen Wagner; Manager of Tech Support Laurie Hemnes; Macintosh Technician Steve Rathman; Sales Managers Michael Popolo, David Roberts, and Jim Maslowski; PR Marketing Coordinator Daryl Wise; Poser Research and Development/Programmer Adam Croston; Production Administrative Assistant Kim Hinrichsen; and Production and Inventory Control John Prichett.

We'd also like to thank all of the artists who contributed their excellent work to the color inserts of this book.

We'd also like to express our thanks to Rich Green of SyQuest Technology for helping to streamline our production process. The SyQuest 270 cartridges we sent from coast to coast packed with our color files and black-and-white images always did the job reliably and efficiently.

We're grateful to Nancy Carr of Apple Computer who helped see to it that we could slip away from the cold weather for a few days to the warm weather in Florida, and still continue working—with an Apple Laptop 540C.

Thanks also to Deborah Vogel of Eastman Kodak for her assistance with the many Eastman Kodak digital imaging products.

We'd also like to thank our relatives, friends, and everyone else who helped along the way.

We thank the many corporations who graciously provided assistance: Adobe Systems, Alias Research, Alien Skin, American Databankers Corp. (ADC), Andromeda Software, CMCD Inc., ColorBytes, Cone Editions Press, Corel, Crystal Graphics, Digital Pond, Digital Stock Corp., Eastman Kodak, Elastic Reality, Electric Image, Gryphon Software, HSC Software, Hacker Art Books, Image Club, Macromedia, MicroFrontier, Nash Editions, Periwinkle Software, Pixar, RasterOps, Specular, Strata, SyQuest Technology, Valis Group, Virtus, Visual Software, and Xaos Tools.

Contents at a Glance

Contents

Chapter 1
Entering the World of Painter
1

Chapter 2
Working with Color
37

Chapter 3
Using and Customizing Brushes
73

Chapter 6
Cloning and Using Tracing Paper
173

Chapter 7
Working with Paths, Selections, and Masks
191

Chapter 8

Working with Floaters

239

Chapter 9
Creating Special Effects
275

Chapter 10
Recording and Playing Back Strokes and Sessions
343

Chapter 11
All about Making Movies
357

Chapter 12

Outputting Your Painter Work

389

Appendix
Using File Formats
403

Foreword

In mid-1991 I was working for Adobe Systems as the Photoshop product manager. Photoshop was about a year and a half old, and our main competition—Letraset's ColorStudio—was an interesting product. Despite a high price and inconsistent marketing, ColorStudio had a compelling set of features. Its Shapes annex, which gave the program a PostScript-based vector layer on top of its image editing tools, made it a kind-of SuperPaint on steroids. The program's authors, Mark Zimmer and Tom Hedges, were well known among the Mac cognoscenti, and were the seasoned authors of ImageStudio—the first microcomputer-based image-editing system. Despite the impressive success of Photoshop to that point, we considered it only a matter of time before Letraset got its marketing act together and gave us a run for our money.

Thus, you can imagine my delight when, at the 1991 Seybold Publishing show in San José, I spied a small booth in the lobby labeled Fractal Design Corporation, fronted by Mark Zimmer doing demos of his latest creation—a design program called Painter. I learned that Mark was focusing most of his attention on the new software which simulated natural media on the computer. Painter used image-editing technology, but aimed it at mimicking paints, charcoals, pencils, paper, and canvas, instead of color correction and prepress. Fractal Design Corporation was organized to promote and market Painter.

With Mark and Tom splitting their time between ColorStudio and Painter, I figured Painter's gain was ColorStudio's loss. Anything that detracted from progress on ColorStudio was probably a good thing for us at Adobe. So, when I saw Mark's demo at Seybold, I gave him some selfless words of encouragement. The rise of Fractal Design foreshadowed the floundering fortunes of Letraset, which nuked their applications software group less than a year later.

Over these last four years I've watched as Painter evolved from a simple application that faithfully reproduced traditional artists tools to a robust program that goes far beyond what is possible with physical tools. I think of Painter as a digital art supply store. Its wealth of brushes, paper textures, and other art materials, combined with the interactivity of the interface, encourages experimentation and fosters the happy accidents that are behind many remarkable pieces of art.

Upon joining the company in 1994, I found that much of the astounding realism of Painter can be traced to Mark's fanaticism about enabling human expression. He and John Derry, Fractal's Vice President of Creative Design (and digital artist extraordinaire), have an offsite facility known as The Wet Lab where they experiment with different art materials. On any given visit to The Wet Lab, you can find tubes of acrylics, canvases, colored pencils, silkscreening equipment and other supplies sharing the room with scraps of paper scrawled with cryptic mathematical symbols and obscure artistic references. This is where the real creation happens. No computers or telephones are allowed.

If Fractal Design stands for anything, it represents innovation, a new way of looking at things. We believe current tools for creating art on the computer have only begun to scratch the surface of what can be done. If you compare the kinds of looks and marks that can be made by traditional art tools you'll understand that we are still only at the very beginning of being able to realistically model their behavior. If you consider the kinds of *new* tools that can be created with the power of the desktop computer (tools that have no physical analogs), the potential of digital design seems immense. And whether it be recreating traditional tools digitally or developing new inventions, count on Fractal Design being there!

I've known Adele and Seth Greenberg since the time they were writing a book about Adobe Photoshop and I was the head of the Macintosh product support team at Adobe Systems. The relationship has carried over to my work at Fractal Design, and I consider the Greenbergs to be some of our best field testers. It is a tribute to their tenacity that they have been able to produce this book even as Painter itself was being developed for this new version. With a program as sophisticated as Painter, it's good to know that the Greenbergs are working to help users better understand the program.

Steve Guttman
Vice President of Marketing
Fractal Design Corp.

Introduction

Fractal Design's VP of Creative Design John Derry likens Painter to a small European shop. From the outside the shop looks quiet and unassuming. But once you enter it and begin looking around, a whole new fascinating and wonderful world opens up for you. The world is so enticing that, before long, you've spent many hours browsing and exploring.

The Ultimate Guide to Fractal Design Painter will help you explore the amazing world that Painter unlocks for you. The book is both an instructional guide and a reference, for both Mac and PC users. It is filled with numerous step-by-step tutorials and tips.

As you read through the book you'll learn the fundamentals of Painter as well as how to create paintings, special effects, and movies.

How This Book Is Organized

The book is divided into twelve chapters and one appendix. Chapters 1 through 3 are introductory chapters that guide you through Painter's fundamentals, and the basics of working with brushes and colors. Chapters 4 through 6 bring you to an intermediate level. Chapters 7 through 12 lead you through more advanced features of Painter.

◆ **Chapter 1: Entering the World of Painter** introduces you to the basic features of Painter. You'll explore Painter's menus and different palettes. You'll create your first image using the Calligraphy Pen and zoom in to see the pixels that compose your image.

◆ **Chapter 2: Working with Color** provides you with an understanding of color models, printable colors, and video legal colors. You'll learn how to use Painter's Art Materials :Colors, :Sets, :Grads, and :Weaves palettes to create colors, color sets, gradations, and weaves.

◆ **Chapter 3: Using and Customizing Brushes** provides a review of every one of Painter's numerous brushes and brush variants, and its Method Categories and Method Subcategories. You'll learn how to customize brushes, and use Painter's Image Hose brush. You'll also explore Painter's Art Materials :Papers palette and learn how papers and brushes interact with each other.

◆ **Chapter 4: Digitizing and Manipulating Images** examines how to digitize images using scanners, digital cameras, and video capture boards. You'll learn how to calculate the correct resolution for digitizing images, and how to resize, crop, scale, and rotate an image.

◆ **Chapter 5: Enhancing Images** covers color-correcting and enhancing images. You'll learn how to adjust the colors, tonal range, and lighting in an image, as well as techniques for sharpening and blurring images.

◆ **Chapter 6: Cloning and Using Tracing Paper** covers how to use Painter's cloning commands and brushes to retouch or duplicate images. You'll learn how to use Painter's Auto Van Gogh and Auto Seurat comands to add more painterly effects to a digitized image. You'll also learn how to trace over images, using Painter's Tracing Paper command.

◆ **Chapter 7: Working with Paths, Selections, and Masks** covers how to create and edit Painter's paths, selections, and masks. You'll learn how to use Painter's Outline Selection tool. You'll also learn how to use Painter's Drawing and Visibility buttons, and Painter's powerful Masking brushes.

◆ **Chapter 8: Working with Floaters** introduces you to Painter's floaters. You'll see how you can use floaters to paint more efficiently and create unusual blending effects between images and floaters. You'll also learn how to use Painter's Floater Mask Visibility and Image Mask Visibility buttons to create unusual composite effects when you blend floaters or floaters and background images together. Using floaters, you'll learn how to create drop shadows, embossed effects, and image fade-outs. At the conclusion of the chapter, you'll learn how to create your own nozzle files from floater groups, so you can generate your own custom effects with Painter's Image Hose brush.

◆ **Chapter 9: Creating Special Effects** takes you on a tour of the countless special effects you can create in Painter. You'll learn how to use Painter's Warp, Apply Surface Texture, Highpass, Blobs, Marbling, and a lot more. You'll also explore how third-party plug-ins and other programs can help you create startling and unusual special effects.

◆ **Chapter 10: Recording and Playing Back Strokes and Sessions** covers how to record and play back brush strokes to create unusual background effects. You'll learn how to turn on Painter's recording feature in a low-resolution file, so that you can later play back a painting session in high-resolution files.

◆ **Chapter 11: All about Making Movies** introduces you to Painter's exciting moviemaking features. You'll learn how to paint frame by frame to create your own movies, and how to create Image Hose nozzle files from your movies.

◆ **Chapter 12: Outputting Your Painter Work** covers how to output your work to an imagesetter, create color separations, and output your Painter movies to video. You'll also learn how to output your images to canvas, and other unusual substrates.

◆ **The Appendix: Using File Formats** introduces you to the different file formats you can use to import files into Painter or export files from Painter into other programs.

Conventions

Throughout this book we've used specific conventions to help you better follow the step-by-step instructions and learn Painter commands.

1. Text that you need to type appears in bold, as in "name this file **Art**."

2. Menu commands appear with the menu name followed by ➤, then the menu command name. When you see File ➤ Save, it means choose Save from the File menu.

3. Since almost every menu command in the Mac version of Painter is identical to the Windows version, we've created one book for both Mac and Windows users. In a few cases, however, Mac and Windows keyboard commands differ. In these instances, Windows-specific commands are provided in parentheses. For example, you might see, "to print, press Command+P (Windows users: Ctrl+P)." In general, the Mac's Command key corresponds to a PC's Control key, and the Mac's Option key corresponds to a PC's Alt key.

Entering the World of Painter

Welcome to the world of Fractal Design's Painter, a world of virtually limitless creative possibilities. When you paint with Painter, a whole new realm of digital art opens up for you. In just a few clicks and drags of the mouse, or strokes of your electronic stylus, you'll be able to paint as if using oils or watercolors and draw as if using chalk, charcoal, pencils, pens, felt pens, or crayons. You'll be able to paint with wet, dry, or drippy strokes, and even simulate the painting styles of Seurat and Van Gogh. Using Painter's "Image Hose" brush, you can even spray images across the screen as if you were the sorcerer's apprentice, painting with flowers or snowflakes or tennis shoes or what have you. And you can create frame-by-frame animation sequences using traditional "onionskin paper" techniques.

As you'll soon see, when you start using Painter your computer screen is transformed into an electronic canvas, and your worries about paint dripping or drying, ink clogging, and paper buckling will vanish. You'll no longer have to put up with the smell of thinner or turpentine or concern yourself with preserving your paint, paintbrushes, and materials.

But Painter is not merely a program that electronically simulates the painting process. It also allows you to edit images created in other programs and electronically transform them with fantastic special effects. You can scan images directly into Painter and trace over them. You can even "play" the images you create as simple "movies," by recording the brush strokes and then playing them back.

Undoubtedly, you're eager to dive right in and start turning your artistic vision into Painter magic. But before you begin, you need to gain a basic understanding of how Painter works and of the program's basic structure. This is especially important if you're used to working with a traditional paintbrush and palette, not a computer. Once you understand Painter's interface, using Painter will become as natural as using traditional media. That's the goal of this chapter. In it you'll tour Painter's powerful menus and palettes. Then you'll put your artistic skills into action by experimenting with Painter's Pen brush. At the end of the chapter, you'll use the Pen brush to create calligraphy over a digitized image to produce your first Painter project.

Before you begin your tour, you should have a basic understanding of the most important element in any Painter image: the **pixel.**

Understanding Pixels: Pixels versus Objects

When you paint with Painter, you are painting tiny squares called *pixels* (picture elements) on the electronic canvas. Images created in Painter are different from those created in drawing programs like Adobe Illustrator, CorelDraw, or Claris Draw. In drawing programs, you can *select* an object you have created (or imported or copied), and easily move it, change its color, shape it, or delete it. To some degree, Painter also allows you to work with objects in this way. But, by default, the entire Painter image "dries" on an electronic canvas of pixels just as paint dries on a real canvas, and the difficulty of dealing with dried paint, as you know, is ages old. For instance, what if Leonardo da Vinci thought he'd painted Mona Lisa's smile a little bit off-center? He couldn't just pick up her mouth and move it over; if he did, he'd rip a hole in his image. His only solution would be to repaint over the previous smile. When you create a painting in Painter, you're faced with much the same problem. Fortunately, Painter does provide multiple levels of "undo," and it does allow you to work in a floating layer, called a *floater*. (When an object is in a floater, it floats above the background pixels and can be freely moved around on screen, and be deselected and reselected.)

If you don't put parts of your image in floating layers, though, the pixels you paint are the same as paint that has dried on an actual canvas. To "delete" an area of the image, you'll usually paint over your old brush strokes with white (or with the image's background color)—just as a traditional painter would do.

Painter's ability to work with individual pixels makes it a tremendously versatile program. For instance, you can paint any of the thousands of individual pixels in an image with any one of over 16 million colors. You'll learn more about making sure you have the right colors and more about "floaters" in later chapters. For now, though, before you get started doing some simple painting and editing of pixels, take the next few minutes to save yourself some time (and possibly frustration) further down the road. Let's go over a few technical matters that can make working with Painter easier and more productive from the start.

● Optimizing Performance

When you start working in Painter, you'll want to work as efficiently as possible. Your first step in working efficiently with Painter is to ensure that your computer meets the program's minimum requirements.

Memory

The minimum system requirements recommended by Fractal Design are:

Macs	6 megabytes (MB) of RAM for computers with 68020 and greater processors
PowerMacs	8 MB RAM
PCs	8 MB RAM, and a 80386, 80486, or Pentium-based machine

256 Colors, or 16 Million?

As mentioned earlier, Painter can create over 16 million colors. Unfortunately, most computer systems won't allow you to view millions of colors right out of the box. Most provide only 256 colors. This is often referred to as *8-bit color*. If you are working with 8-bit color, you'll be able to use all of Painter's features, but gradations of color will not look as smooth as if your system could display 32 thousand or 16 million colors.

If you wish to view millions of colors on your screen, you'll need to upgrade your system to *24-bit color*, by adding a 24-bit video card or video memory.

> **Note** *If you don't wish to invest in a 24-bit video card, most Macintosh computers can be upgraded to approximately 32,000 colors by adding video RAM instead.*

Installing

Once you've ensured that your system meets Painter's minimum requirements, your next step is to install the program. This is a simple and automated procedure on a PC running Windows, and is almost as automated on a Mac. One extra step is required for Mac users, however: Since Painter does not automatically create a new folder on the Macintosh when you install it, if you're using a Mac you should create a new folder on your hard drive and name it **Painter 3**. Once you've created a folder, proceed to install Painter in that folder, as described in the Painter *User Guide*.

Changing Painter's Memory Allocation

Once you have installed Painter, your next step should be to decide whether to increase Painter's *memory allocation*. If you have enough memory, increasing the memory allocation will speed up many of Painter's chores.

By default, on the Macintosh, Painter's preferred memory allocation is set to 6 or more megabytes (MB) of RAM. This means that if 6 MB is available, Painter will use it. If Painter needs more memory than that, it automatically starts using free space on your hard disk to complete a task. Since

Painter works more slowly when it uses your hard disk instead of RAM, it is a good idea to allocate as much RAM as you can afford. What you can afford depends on how much you don't need for other programs. If you expect to be running only Painter when you're doing your art work, you can afford to allocate almost all of your system's RAM to it. Otherwise, you have to keep in mind that the RAM must be shared among all the programs you might be running.

> **Note** *For Macs: Even if you have 40 MB of RAM, Painter will not use any more than the 6 MB it is set to use by default unless you increase the allocation setting.*

Changing Memory Allocation on the Mac If you have a Mac and wish to change Painter's memory allocation, follow these steps:

1. If Painter is loaded, quit it now (you cannot change memory allocation while a program is running). To exit from Painter, choose File ➤ Quit (that is, choose Quit from the File menu).

2. Click once on the Painter icon located on your hard disk.

3. From the File menu, choose Get Info.

4. At the bottom of the Get Info dialog box, enter your desired Memory Requirements into the Preferred Size text field.

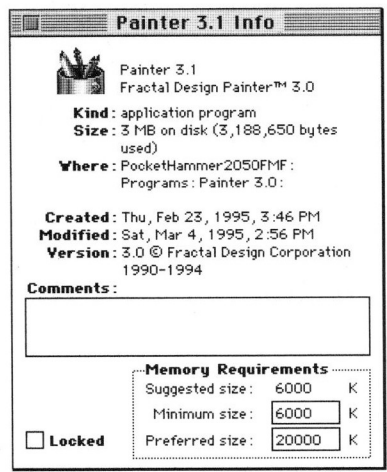

In this dialog box memory is measured in kilobytes (K), which are approximately a thousand times smaller than megabytes. Actually, a megabyte is 1,024 kilobytes, but for our purposes we'll calculate them simply as 1,000. To allocate 20 MB of RAM to Painter, therefore, type **20000**.

5. Close the Get Info dialog box by clicking on its close box.

The next time you load Painter, it will use the increased allocated memory if it is available.

Changing Memory Allocation on the PC On the PC, Painter's memory allocation can be set by choosing Edit ➤ Preferences ➤ Windows (that is, choose Preferences from the Edit menu, then choose Windows from the Preferences dialog box). If you will not be running other programs in the background while using Painter, choose the Maximum Memory For Painter option in the dialog box. This tells Painter it can use all the memory it can grab from your system. If you will be running other programs in the background while using Painter, choose the Half Memory for Painter option. This ensures optimum performance while other Windows programs are running.

Exploring Painter

Now that your system is set up, you're ready to start your first tour of Painter. To enter the world of Painter, launch the program by double-clicking on the Painter icon.

Painter 3.1

Once the program is loaded, its menu bar and four of its eight palettes appear on screen. Unlike many programs, Painter won't automatically create a new document when it loads. (You'll learn how to create a new document after you become familiar with Painter's menus and its palettes.)

Exploring Painter's Menus

Painter features seven pull-down menus, each providing a different set of commands and features.

File Menu

Like all Mac and Windows programs, Painter includes a File menu, which is primarily used for saving, opening, and printing files. In this menu, the New, Open, Close, Save, Save As, Page Setup, Print, and Quit (or Exit) commands work as they do in most Mac and Windows applications.

One extremely convenient option in the File menu is the Acquire command, which allows you to scan photographs and slides and digitize images from

File	
New...	⌘N
Open	⌘O
Close	⌘W
Clone	
Clone Source	▶
Save	⌘S
Save As...	
Revert	
Get Info...	⌘I
Acquire	▶
Export	▶
Page Setup...	
Print...	⌘P
Quit	⌘Q

digital cameras and videotape. The File menu's Clone command allows you to quickly duplicate images for retouching or to create special effects. The Clone command is covered in Chapter 6. The Get Info command lets you type any notes you want to make about whichever image you have active on screen.

Edit Menu

The Edit menu is primarily used for cutting, copying, and pasting different parts of images. For both Mac and Windows users, the familiar Cut, Copy, Paste, and Clear commands are found here. Commands for selecting are also in the Edit menu. One of the more interesting of these is the Magic Wand, which allows you to select image areas according to their color. The Preferences submenu offers choices that allow you to change interface settings to help you customize the program so it's tailored specifically for your individual use. This is also where you turn to tell Painter how many Undo levels to keep available, and which hard drive to use when it needs more "virtual" memory.

Edit	
Can't Undo	⌘Z
Can't Redo	⌘Y
Fade...	
Cut	⌘H
Copy	⌘C
Paste	▶
Clear	
Select All	⌘A
Deselect	⌘D
Reselect	⌘R
Drop	
Mask	▶
Magic Wand...	
Publishing	▶
Preferences	▶

Effects Menu

The Effects menu is your gateway to special effects. Here you'll find a variety of commands that can help you create drop shadows, distort images, and invert an image's colors. The Effects menu also allows you to rotate, flip, and scale images (or selected areas of an image). If you have other companies' special effects "plug-ins" (such as Adobe Gallery Effects, Kai's Power Tools, KPT Convolver, Xaos Tools' Paint Alchemy and Terazzo, Andromeda Software Series 1 and 2, Alien Skin Textureshop by Virtus and Alien Skin Black Box, and Knoll Software's CyberMesh filters), you can access them from the Effects menu. Special effects are covered in Chapter 9.

Effects	
Apply Surface Texture...	⌘/
Glass Distortion...	⌘;
Orientation	▶
Fill...	⌘F
Tonal Control	▶
Surface Control	▶
Focus	▶
Esoterica	▶
Objects	▶
Plugin Filter	▶

Canvas Menu

The Canvas menu allows you to change the size of your painting area (the *canvas*). If necessary, you can also use the Canvas menu to resize your image. The Grid Options command, which allows you to change the color and size of Painter's *grid*, will be demonstrated later in this chapter, where you'll see how you can use the grid to help ensure that you are painting along a horizontal or vertical line. The Canvas menu also allows you to change the color of your paper or to turn Painter's Tracing Paper option on or off. Tracing Paper is covered in Chapter 6.

Canvas
Resize...
Canvas Size...
Wet Paint
Dry   ⌘Y
Tracing Paper ⌘T
Set Paper Color
View Grid   ⌘G
Grid Options...
✓View Annotations
Annotate...

Tools Menu

The Tools menu provides a variety of different options for a broad range of subjects. The Movers submenu allows you to create and edit new *libraries,* which are repositories for brushes, paper textures, weaves, and gradations that you expect to use frequently or only with certain projects. You can also name each of the items within the library according to your needs. Once a library is created, you can load it into a palette for quick access to everything you stored in it. You can also use the Tools menu to create three-dimensional textures and weaves. Textures and weaves are covered in Chapters 2 and 3.

Tools	
Movers	▶
Brushes	▶
Selections	▶
Image Hose	▶
Gradations	▶
Textures	▶
Patterns	▶
Record Stroke	
Playback Stroke	
Auto Playback	
Record Session	
Playback Session...	
Session Options...	

One of the more interesting options in the Tools menu is the Record Session command, which allows you to record your strokes—keystrokes as well as brushstrokes. After you've recorded your strokes, you can click on the Playback Session command, sit back, and watch the recorded strokes being played back on screen. These Session options also allow you to record the strokes you use to create a painting in a low-resolution file and then play it back in a high-resolution file. This can speed up your work if you don't have a fast computer. For more information on using the Session options, see Chapter 10.

Movie Menu

Use the Movie menu to create *animation* in Painter. As you'll learn in Chapter 11, Painter allows you to specify how many frames you want in your movie, then create your images one by one in each of the frames. Later, if needed, you can add frames to the movie. If you work in advertising, you should consider using this feature to create animated storyboards.

Movie
Add Frames...
Delete Frames...
Erase Frames...
Go To Frame...
✓Clear New Frames
Insert Movie...
Apply Session To Movie...
Apply Brush Stroke To Movie
Set Grain Position...
Set Movie Clone Source...

Window Menu

The Window menu allows you to open, close, and arrange Painter's eight palettes. (Each palette is described later in this chapter.) You can also use the Window menu to zoom in and out as well as to switch from one open painting to another.

> **Note** *Now that you've toured Painter's menus, your next step is to create a new document so that you can explore the Painter document screen and Painter's versatile palettes.*

Window	
Hide Palettes	⌘H
Clean Up Palettes	
Zoom In	⌘+
Zoom Out	⌘-
Zoom To Fit Screen	
✓Tools	⌘1
✓Brushes	⌘2
✓Art Materials	⌘3
✓Brush Controls	⌘4
✓Objects	⌘5
✓Controls	⌘6
✓Advanced Controls	⌘7
✓Color Set	⌘8
Screen Mode Toggle	⌘M
✓Untitled-1 @ 200%	

● Practice: Creating Your First Electronic Canvas

Before electronic painting programs came along, an artist's first step was to choose the appropriate-size canvas. As you might expect, the document work area in Painter is also called the canvas. Your first step is to specify its width and height. You can enter these values in pixels, inches, centimeters (cm), points, picas, and columns (columns are two inches high and two inches wide). Complete the following steps to create a new canvas so you can start painting.

1. To create a new document (canvas), choose File ➤ New. The New Picture dialog box appears.

The settings you'll see in the New Picture dialog box are either the default settings or the settings last used.

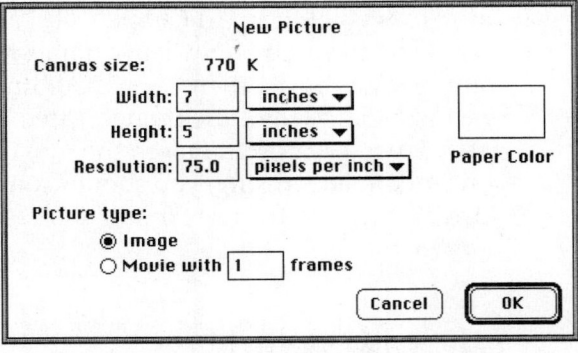

2. Since most of us are most familiar with inches, change the units for the Width and Height pop-up menus (referred to as drop-down menus in Windows programs) to inches if they aren't already showing inches.

3. Now type **7** in the Width field and **5** in the Height field.

4. Don't leave this dialog box yet—we'll get to the other settings in a minute.

Note *This canvas size of 7" by 5" will be large enough for you to create the calligraphy exercise later in this chapter.*

Your next step will be to enter the *resolution* you want. Resolution is the number of pixels in an image, measured in pixels per inch (*ppi*). Deciding the proper resolution to use is extremely important, particularly if you will be outputting your image on a commercial printing press. Usually the greater the number of pixels in an image, the sharper it is and the smoother the transitions in color. Choosing the proper resolution for printing will be covered in detail in Chapter 4. For the time being, though, it's important to be aware of a few basic facts about image resolution.

If you are creating practice images, or if your images will be viewed on a computer monitor, Painter's default setting of 75 ppi should be adequate. The primary reason for choosing an image resolution of 75 ppi is that this is the resolution of most 12- to 14-inch monitors. If your monitor can only display 75 pixels per inch, choosing a higher resolution won't make the image on screen look any better. Keeping the image resolution set to 75 ppi will also help keep the size of your files small. High-resolution files consume more memory, and can be quite cumbersome to work with. Your best strategy is to never make the image resolution higher than necessary.

If you expect to output your work to a commercial printer, however, you should work with a higher resolution—generally, twice the screen frequency of the final output device (these topics will be presented in detail in Chapter 4). When working at higher resolution, don't be deceived by the size of the image on screen. If you create an image 2″ by 2″ at a resolution of 300 ppi, the image will be 8″ by 8″ on your 75-ppi screen, though it will still print at 2″ by 2″. At first this seems a bit bewildering. To understand why the image enlarges on screen, you must remember that your monitor is always displaying approximately 75 pixels per inch of *screen*. If you set the resolution to 300 ppi, four times as many screen pixels are needed to display one inch of your *image*, so it takes four times as many inches as well.

> **Note** *If you will be printing images on a commercial printing press, the general rule for digital images is to use a resolution that is twice the screen frequency that will be used for printing (see Chapter 4). For this example, though, we'll set the resolution to 75.*

5. If the resolution is not set to 75 ppi in the New Picture dialog box, set it to that now.

After setting the resolution, your next consideration is to set the background color of your canvas.

6. For this exercise, leave the Paper Color set to white. (If the rectangle or *swatch* above the words Paper Color is not white, click on it to choose a background color for your canvas. When you click on the swatch, the Apple Color Picker or Windows Color dialog box appears. By clicking or entering numbers in this dialog box, you can set the color you desire.)

Your final decision in the New Picture dialog box is whether to create an image or a movie. In this chapter you'll learn how to create an image. (In Chapter 11 you'll learn how to create movies.)

7. If the Image radio button isn't selected, click on it now.

8. Click OK to create and open your first electronic canvas.

Exploring the Painter Window

After you've created a new canvas, your screen will look like Figure 1.1. Although Painter incorporates standard Mac and Windows interface elements that allow you to move, resize, scroll, and zoom in and out, it's important to note several invaluable window features that are unique to Painter.

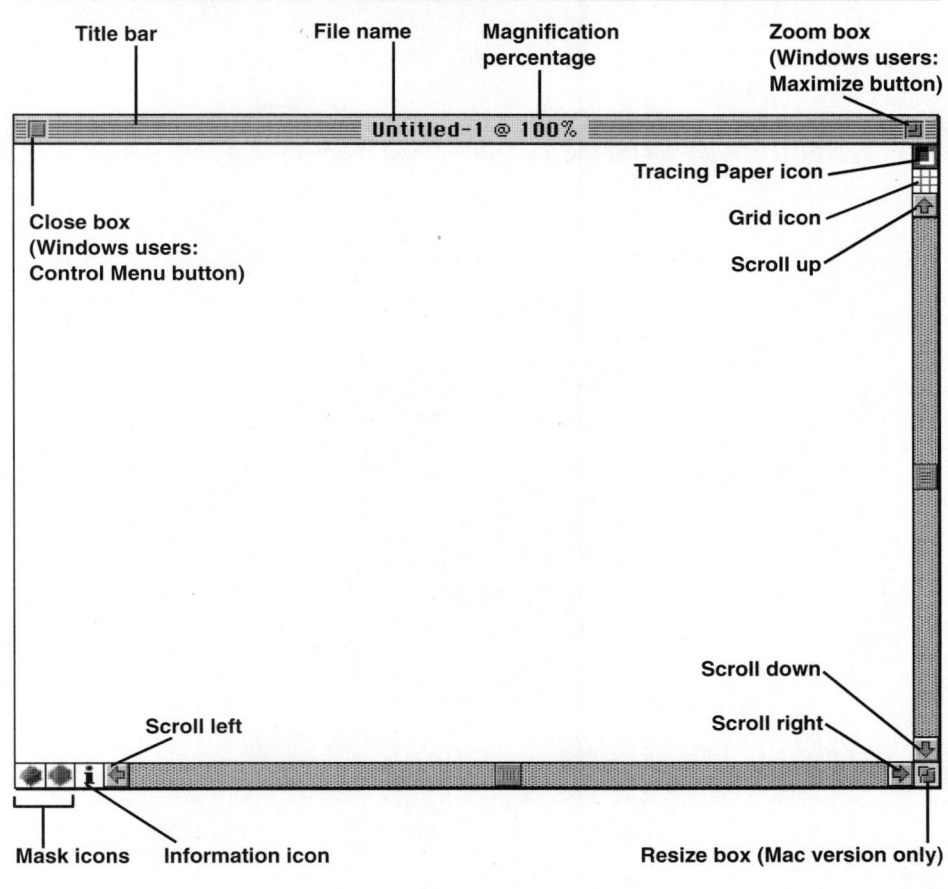

FIGURE 1.1: The Painter window

Notice that Painter's title bar not only includes a file name but also a magnification percentage. A 100 percent size indicates that you are viewing your image at its actual size. A 200 percent magnification would indicate that the image on screen is two times its actual size.

Situated in the top right corner is the Tracing Paper icon. This handy feature, which works in conjunction with the File menu's Clone command, allows you to paint over an underlying image. When Tracing Paper is applied, you trace over the cloned image without affecting the original. You'll learn how to use tracing paper in Chapter 6.

Below the Tracing Paper icon is the Grid icon. Clicking on this icon drops a grid of horizontal and vertical lines over your document window. As you work, you see the grid through your image. Later in this chapter, you'll have a chance to use the grid and to set grid options in the Canvas menu.

In the lower left corner appear two mask icons. A mask allows you to protect part of your image, and keep other areas unprotected so that they can be edited. In many respects, using a mask is like painting over an image with a stencil. The two mask icons are actually both pop-up menus. Click on either of the two icons, and a trio of mask choices pop up on screen. The second trio of icons allows you to pick exactly how you want your mask to appear on screen, the first trio allows you to pick how your mask protects image areas. When a choice is made in the pop-up menu, the mask icon changes to indicate the current setting. For a detailed explanation about using masks, see Chapter 7.

The bold letter **i** in the lower left corner of the screen provides information about your image. Clicking on the **i** opens up a window that displays your image's dimensions and its resolution.

Your next stop on your Painter interface tour is its *floating palettes*.

Exploring Painter's Palettes

Exploring Painter's floating palettes is like visiting an enormous art supply store where all the brushes, paint, chalk, paper, and paint buckets are magically within arm's reach. Since open palettes always float above your image, they provide quick access to Painter's most commonly used features. For instance, one click in the Brushes palette and you can switch brush strokes; one click in the Art Materials palette and you can change painting colors.

Although each palette provides different options, most share common attributes. All palettes can be opened or closed by clicking on the palette's name in the Window menu. When a palette is opened, a check mark appears by its name in the Window menu.

A palette can easily be repositioned on screen by clicking and dragging its title bar. As you work through this book, you'll be using each one of Painter's powerful palettes, and sometimes have two or three palettes on screen simultaneously. For the next few pages we'll present an overview of each palette available in Painter. We'll start with the items available through the Brushes palette, because it typifies certain features you'll find in some of the other palettes.

The Brushes Palette

The Brushes palette allows you to pick from one of Painter's 18 electronic brushes. In Chapter 3 you'll see that the contents of the Brushes palette extend beyond the inventory of the brushes section in an art supply store. Variants of electronic pens, felt pens, chalk, and airbrushes can all be found in the Brushes palette.

Like many of the other palettes, the Brushes palette features a drawer handle that, when clicked on, opens a drawer with more brushes. The palette also includes several pop-up menus. These allow you to specify exactly how the brush will create its stroke and how paint will be applied. At the end of this chapter you'll have a chance to pick a brush from the Brushes palette and paint with it. For a detailed explanation of each brush in the Brushes palette, see Chapter 3.

Figure 1.2 shows the Brushes palette. Notice the title bar, used for moving the palette; the close box, used to close the palette; and the zoom box, which allows you to expand or contract the palette (not applicable for some palettes). In Figure 1.2a you can see that the Brushes palette's title bar not only includes the name of the palette but the name of the currently selected option in the palette. In Figure 1.2a the selected palette tool is the Pen tool. The pop-up list below the icons provides a list of variants for the currently selected option. The Pen variant currently operative is the Scratchboard Tool.

Close box   Name of palette   Item selected in palette   Zoom box

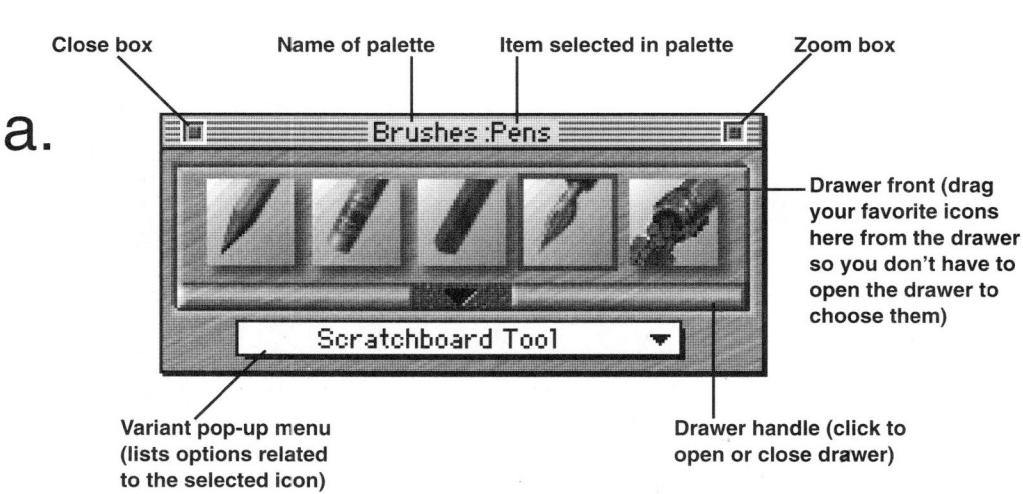

a.

Drawer front (drag your favorite icons here from the drawer so you don't have to open the drawer to choose them)

Variant pop-up menu (lists options related to the selected icon)

Drawer handle (click to open or close drawer)

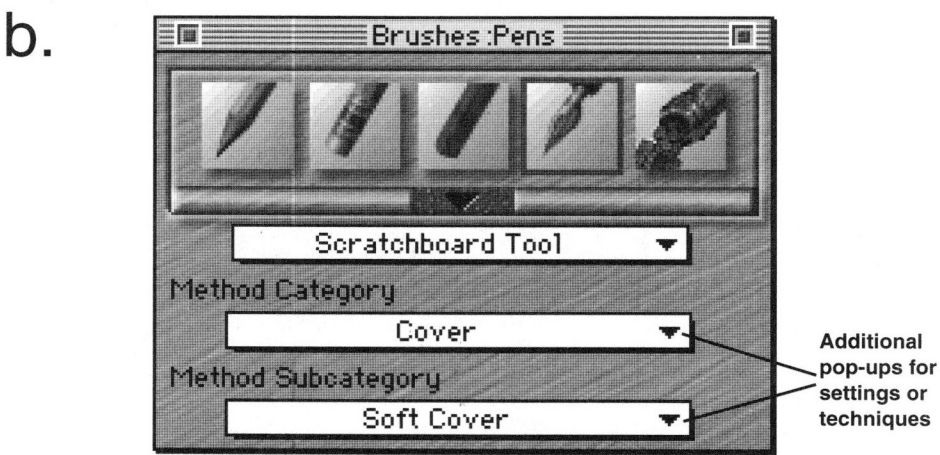

b.

Additional pop-ups for settings or techniques

FIGURE 1.2a and b: The Brushes palette (a) condensed, with the drawer closed; (b) expanded with the drawer closed

C.

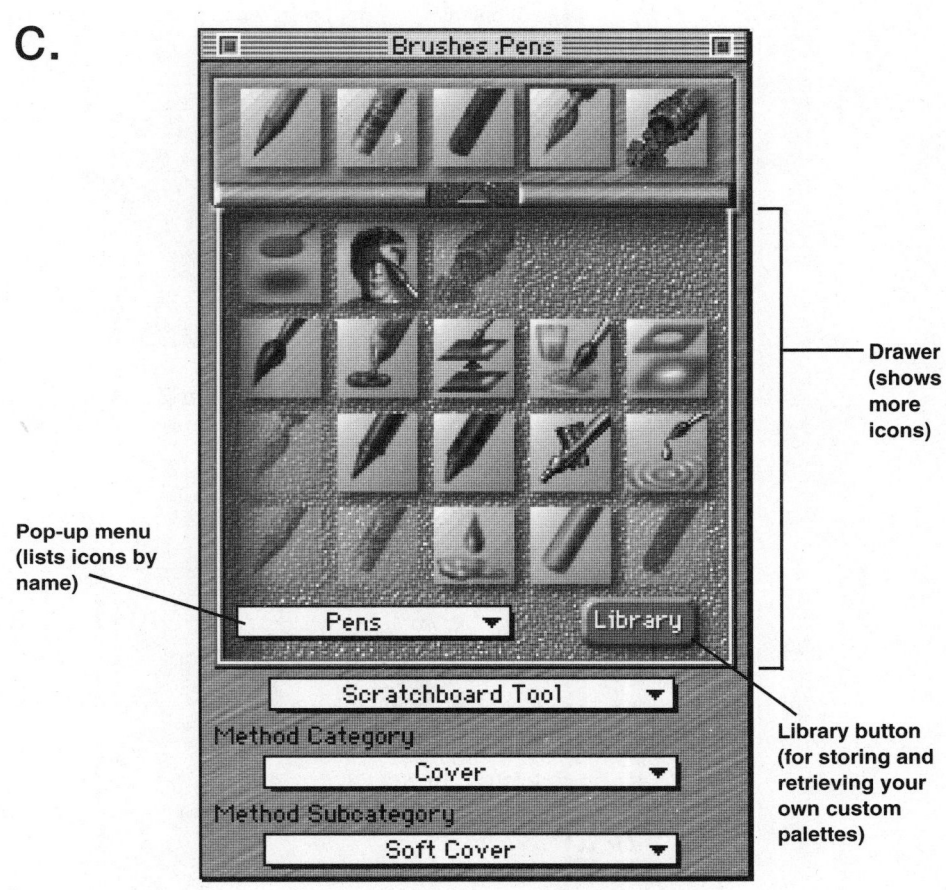

FIGURE 1.2c: The Brushes palette expanded with the drawer open.

Most palettes can operate in two modes: condensed and expanded. The expanded mode takes up more screen space, but shows extra palette options. By default, Painter's palettes first open in a condensed mode. To see a palette in its expanded mode, click on the zoom box, in the upper right-hand corner of the palette. Figure 1.2a shows the condensed version of the

Brushes palette. Figure 1.2b shows an expanded version of the Brushes palette, showing more pop-up menus.

Most of the palettes also feature a drawer handle. When you click on the drawer handle, Painter pops open the drawer, providing access to more palette options. Figure 1.2c shows the Brushes palette expanded and with the drawer open. To choose one of the drawer items, you merely click on it. After you click, one of the icons in the drawer front is replaced by the item you clicked on. You can also click on a drawer item and drag it to replace one of the icons on the drawer front.

If you want, you can *lock* icons on the drawer front so that they do not change. To lock an item on the drawer front, click on the icon and hold the mouse button down until a tiny green dot appears under the icon. Painter allows you to lock every item but one on the drawer front.

The Tools Palette

The Tools palette sets the mode you are in. Click on the Brush tool, you're in a painting mode; click on a selection tool, and you can select image areas to cut, copy, or paste. Each time you select a tool in

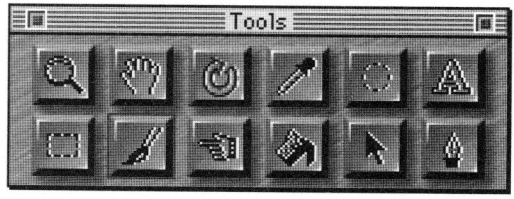

the Tools palette, the occupants of the Controls palette change, allowing you to change specific options for the selected tool. Each tool has a specific purpose, as described in the following paragraphs.

The Magnifier Tool The Magnifier tool is Painter's telescope, allowing you to zoom in to examine intricate work areas in your image. To activate this tool, either click on it in the Tools palette or press **M** on your keyboard. When the Magnifier is activated, clicking on your image magnifies the image area that you clicked on. After you click, Painter displays the magnification percentage in both the title bar and the Controls palette. If you click and drag over an area with the Magnifier tool, the area you clicked and dragged over is enlarged. You can also reduce magnification by pressing the Option key (Windows users: the Alt key) and clicking in your image with the Magnifier tool.

The Grabber Tool The Grabber tool allows you to scroll in your image without clicking and dragging on the window's scroll bars. The Grabber is very handy when you want to scroll diagonally up and down. If your canvas is off-center, clicking with the Grabber tool anywhere within the Painter window centers the window. When the Grabber is activated the Controls palette allows you to set the zoom level as it does when the Magnifier tool is activated.

> **Tip** *If you press the spacebar with any tool but the Text Selection tool activated, the tool's cursor changes to the Grabber cursor.*

The Rotate Page Tool As its name suggests, the Rotate Page tool allows you to rotate your canvas. This tool was added to Painter 3.0 so you could rotate the canvas (for the same reasons you might want to rotate a sketch book). When the Rotate Page tool is selected, you can set the angle of the rotation in the Controls **palette.**

> **Tip** *If you press the spacebar and Option key together (Windows users: if you press the Alt key) with any tool but the Text Selection tool activated, the tool's cursor changes to the Rotate cursor.*

The Dropper Tool The Dropper tool allows you to sample colors on screen. To select this tool, either click on it in the Tools palette or press **D** on your keyboard. When you click the Dropper tool over an image, color readouts appear in the Controls panel indicating the color values of the pixel that you clicked on, and the primary painting color changes to that color. For more information about working and understanding color in Painter, see Chapter 2.

The Oval Selection Tool The Oval Selection tool allows you to create elliptical selections. Use this tool to copy or cut circular selections in your image. To activate this tool, either click on it in the Tools palette or press **O** on your keyboard. When this tool is chosen, the Controls palette displays the width and height of the selection, and other Controls palette readouts indicate the top right and bottom left position of the selection on screen. The Oval Selection tool can also be used create a mask. For more information about masks, see Chapter 7.

The Text Selection Tool The Text Selection tool allows you to create text on screen. It's called a selection tool because it creates an outline of text which can be filled with color. To select this tool, either click on it in the Tools palette or press **T** on your keyboard. When this tool is selected, you can then go to the Controls palette to choose the size, font, and *tracking* of the text. Tracking controls the spacing between letter.

The Rectangular Selection Tool The Rectangular Selection tool allows you to create rectangular selections. Use this tool when you wish to cut or copy rectangular areas in your image. To select this tool, either click on it in the Tools palette or press **R** on your keyboard. When this tool is chosen, the Controls palette indicates the width and height of the selection as well as the top right and bottom left position of the image on screen. If you move a selection with the Rectangular selection tool, the selection turns into a floater. A floater allows you to place part of your image in a layer that can be moved and edited independently of the underlying image. Floaters are covered in Chapter 8.

The Brush Tool The Brush tool allows you to paint using one of Painter's electronic brushes. To activate the Brush tool, click on it in the Tools palette. You can then paint with the currently selected brush in the Brushes palette, or change brush options in the Brushes palette. When the Brush tool is selected, you can set painting opacity, paper grain, and choose a Draw Style (Freehand or Straight Lines) from the Controls palette. You can also press **B** on your keyboard to paint with freehand strokes or press **V** to paint with straight line strokes.

The Floating Selection Tool The Floating Selection tool turns a selection into a *floater*. This places a selection into a layer and allows you to move the selection and apply special effects to it independently of the underlying image. To select this tool, either click on it in the Tools palette or press **F** on your keyboard.

The Paint Bucket Tool The Paint Bucket tool is used to fill a selection, an image, a mask, or a cartoon gel. When the Paint Bucket is selected, the Controls palette provides a variety of filling options for the Paint Bucket. For example, you can also use the Paint Bucket to fill with the current color, a clone source, a gradation, or a weave. To select this tool, either click on it in the Tools palette or press **C** on your keyboard.

The Path Adjuster Tool The Path Adjuster tool allows you to edit the *paths* created with the Outline Selection tool. Paths, which are discussed in Chapter 7, are wire frame shapes that can be turned into selections or masks. To activate this tool, either click on it in the Tools palette or press **A** on your keyboard.

The Outline Selection Tool The Outline Selection tool allows you to create paths. The paths can be created in three different modes: Freehand, Straight Lines, and *Bézier Curves* (see Chapter 7). This tool functions somewhat like the Pen tools in Adobe Illustrator, Photoshop, and Macromedia Freehand. To select this tool, click on it in the Tools palette then choose a Draw Style (Freehand, Straight Lines, or Bézier Curves) from the Controls :Outline Selection palette. Press **H** on your keyboard to activate the Outline Selection tool and the Freehand draw style. Press **L** on your keyboard to activate the Outline Selection tool and the Straight Lines draw style. Press **P** on your keyboard to activate the Outline Selection tool and the Bézier Curves draw style.

The Controls Palette

The options in the Controls palette change depending on the tool that's selected in the Tools palette. In addition, the name of the currently

selected tool appears in the title bar of the Controls palette. For instance, when the Magnifier

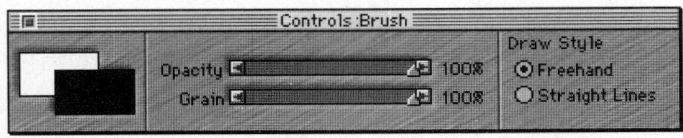

tool is activated, the Controls palette allows you to choose a magnification percentage, and the Controls palette title bar reads Controls :Magnifier. When you select the Brush tool, the Controls palette allows you to change the opacity of the painting color. Depending on the style of the brush, the palette also allows you to choose how much "paper grain" appears in a painted stroke.

The Art Materials Palette

The Art Materials palette allows you to choose colors, create customized color palettes, and pick papers, gradients and weaves. In many respects the palette is actually four palettes in one. Clicking on any one of the four icons at the top of the palette completely changes the palette contents.

For instance, clicking on the Colors icon changes the palette into a large color wheel with which you can pick painting colors. Clicking on the Papers icon turns the palette into a drawer full of paper grain options.

One of the most convenient features of the Art Materials palette is that it allows you to drag the top icons off the palette to create what are essentially sub-palettes. When you drag one of the icons off the palette, a sub-palette is created on screen. In the title bar of the sub-palette is the name of the icon that you clicked and dragged on. This is more helpful than you might at first think, because it allows you to keep different Art Materials options on screen at the same time. For instance, by clicking on the Colors icon and dragging it out of the Art Materials :Papers palette, you can display the Colors palette as a sub-palette while still keeping the drawer full of paper grains open in the Papers palette. (In the title bar of the sub-palette containing the color wheel, you'll see the words Art Materials :Colors.)

For more information about the Art Materials palette, see Chapter 2. (Picking colors using the Art Materials palette is covered in Chapter 3.)

> **Note** *In palettes that allow you to create break-away sub-palettes, you can only create the sub-palette by dragging an icon that is not already activated.*

The Brush Controls Palette

The Brush Controls palette allows you to the customize the currently selected brush. Clicking on one of the icons at the top of the palette completely changes the entire palette to provide options for the selected icon. The palette's options allow you to change a brush's size, spacing, bristle, look, and *nozzle*.

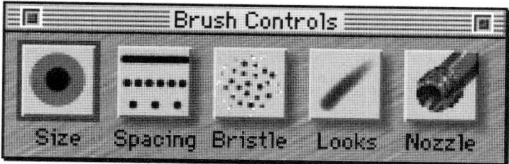

Painter's nozzle control allows you to customize the Image Hose brush, which provides an effect of spray painting with a pattern or digital image.

For instance, you can paint with shamrock and coin shapes. Like the Art Materials palette, the Brush Controls palette allows you to drag the top icons off the palette so that the different sub-palettes can be accessible at the same time. For more information about the Brush Controls palette, see Chapter 3.

The Advanced Controls Palette

The Advanced Controls palette provides even more control of specific brushes than the Brush Controls palette provides. For instance, by access-

ing the Sliders options, you can change the way a brush paints according to how fast or what direction you drag your mouse or stylus. The Advanced Controls palette also allows you to alter brush

components such as bristle angle and how much paint is replenished before each paint stroke.

Like the Brush Controls and Art Materials palettes, the icons at the top of the Advanced Controls palette can be dragged off their home palette. This allows different options in the palette to be accessible at all times.

The Objects Palette

The Objects palette allows you to rename and reorder selections, floaters, and paths. A floater is like a floating selection or a layer on screen that can

be accessed at any time from the Objects palette. By clicking on an icon at the top of the palette, you can choose whether to control paths, floating objects, or recorded sessions.

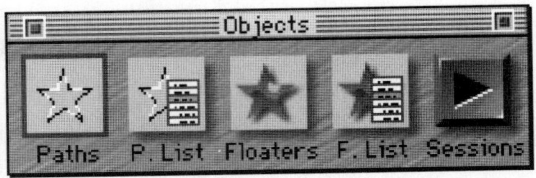

As with the Advanced Controls palette, the icons at the top of the Objects palette can be dragged to create sub-palettes.

The Color Set Palette

The Color Set palette allows you to pick a painting color from a palette of preset colors called a *color set*. (You create color sets in the Art Materials palette, not in the Color Set palette.)

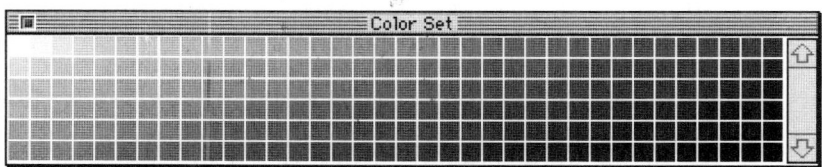

Note *Now that you've had a chance to familiarize yourself with the Painter document window, menus, and palettes, you're ready to paint! Try this simple exercise, using Painter's elegant calligraphy brush.*

Practice: Using the Calligraphy Brush to Paint Your First Picture

Undoubtedly, the easiest way to start learning Painter is to dip a brush into some paint and start creating some simple brush strokes.

In this section you'll learn how to choose a brush from the Brushes palette. In the exercise, you'll test the Calligraphy variant of the Pens brush. You'll also learn how to pick options that determine exactly how the brush will paint. After you've had a chance to create calligraphy, you'll zoom in to examine how Painter paints the tiniest image elements, pixels.

Before you begin, you should have a file 7 inches wide by 5 inches high open on the screen, as we created earlier in the chapter. If you don't, choose New from the File menu to create the new file.

1. Your first step is to choose a brush from the Brushes palette. If the Brushes palette isn't open, choose Brushes from the Window menu to open it.

2. To access all of Painter's 18 brushes, the drawer in the Brushes palette must be opened. If you don't see all 18 brushes on screen, open the

palette drawer by clicking on the drawer handle (the bar with the triangle, in the middle of the palette).

Tip   To conserve screen space, it's often a good idea to close palettes you don't need. To complete the Calligraphy exercise, you need to have the Brushes, Controls, and Tools palettes open on screen; you may close any others. To close the palettes you don't need, click on each palette's close box.

3. To use the Calligraphy brush variant, you must select the Pens brush. To select Pens, click on the Pens icon in the Brushes palette. Alternatively, you can select it by name, by clicking on the pop-up menu inside the drawer, and selecting Pens from that. After you select Pens, its icon appears on the drawer front and Pens becomes the active brush.

After you've made your choice, you can conserve screen space by closing the Brushes palette drawer. To close the drawer, click on the handle.

4. Just below the drawer is another pop-up menu filled with variants for the currently selected Brush tool, i.e., a variant menu for the Pens brush. Click on the variant pop-up menu, and note the choices.

When you selected Pens in the Brushes palette, Painter loaded the Calligraphy option as one of the choices in the variant pop-up menu. The variants you see now appear only when Pens is selected. Before proceeding, choose Calligraphy from this list of choices.

5. Your next step is to choose a painting method from the Method Category pop-up menu.

Note   The Method Category and Method Subcategory pop-up menus will not appear in the Brushes palette if the palette is condensed. If you don't see either pop-up menu in the Brushes palette, expand it by clicking on the zoom box in the top right-hand corner of the Brushes palette.

The Method Category pop-up menu controls how your brush strokes are applied. For example, you can choose to have paint color *build up* one stroke at a time by choosing Buildup in the Method Category pop-up menu. In this example, however, we need to have the paint *cover up completely* any existing colors under your stroke.

To select this type of painting method, choose Cover from the Method Category pop-up menu.

6. When you picked Cover from the Method Category pop-up menu, the Method Subcategory pop-up menu below it changed to provide options for the method chosen. Click on the Method Subcategory pop-up menu to observe the choices. (In Chapter 3, you'll learn what effect each subcategory option produces.) For this exercise, choose Soft Cover.

Soft Cover uses *anti-aliasing*, a technique that blurs the jagged edges of pixels to smooth the edges of your image. Later, when you zoom in to view the actual pixels that Painter uses to create your calligraphy, you'll see how anti-aliasing softens the edges of brush strokes.

> **Note** *Once you've set your option in the Method Subcategory pop-up menu, you've completed all the settings you need in the Brushes palette. Your next steps are to change the Opacity setting in the Controls palette and to make sure that the Draw Style option in the Controls palette is set to Freehand.*

Using the Controls Palette to Set Opacity

Opacity controls how transparent or light the painting color appears (depending on the Method Category chosen). If your painting color is not 100 percent opaque and the Method Category is set to Buildup, Wet, or Eraser, you'll be able see through the color as you paint, as if it were translucent. In the following steps you'll lower opacity slightly so that you'll be able to see a darkening of colors if you cross one stroke of your calligraphy over another.

1. If the Controls palette isn't open, open it by choosing Controls from the Window menu.

2. Opacity is set by clicking and dragging on the Opacity slider control. If you click and drag to the left you lower opacity. If you click and drag to the right you raise opacity. Set the Opacity to 80% by clicking and dragging on the horizontal slider control.

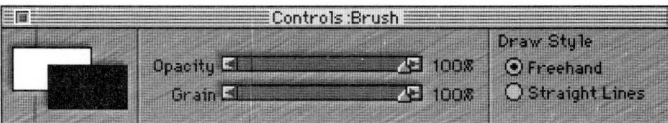

Note *Changing the Grain slider in the Controls palette will have no effect on your painting. Had you chosen one of the Cover Grainy method subcategories rather than the Soft Cover option, the slider would change the paper grain effect in your painting.*

3. To use the calligraphy brush variant, you want to be able to draw in Freehand mode, so check to see that the Draw Style option in the Controls palette is not set to Straight Lines. If it is, change it to Freehand.

Note *Now you are ready to start experimenting with the Pens Calligraphy variant.*

Creating Calligraphy

For your first brush strokes, try painting your first name with the Pens calligraphic brush variant.

Start by positioning the pointer in the left side of the screen. When you're ready to start, click and drag. As you drag, you'll see a calligraphic brush stroke following your mouse or stylus. As you paint, try to keep your motion slow, steady, and smooth. Continue painting until you've painted each letter. Note that the color of the paint will either be Painter's default (black) or whatever was last used. You'll learn how to change colors in Chapter 2.

If you make a mistake, you can erase your last brush stroke by choosing Undo from the Edit menu. By default, Painter is set to 5 levels of undo. You can change this setting in the Undo Preferences dialog box (discussed at the end of this chapter).

As you work, you may wish to return to previous letters to fine-tune your work. The easiest way to do this is to switch to the Eraser option in the Method Category pop-up menu. When you choose Eraser in the Method Category pop-up menu, the Method Subcategory automatically switches to Soft Paper Color. This means that Painter is erasing by painting with the paper color; in this case white.

With the Eraser option set, your pen variant is still set to Calligraphic. This means that the eraser whites out with the same brush stroke that you painted with. When you're finished be sure to set the Method Category back to Cover, and the Method Subcategory back to Soft Cover.

Tip *If you are planning to use calligraphic effects often, you may wish to purchase a stylus tablet. When you work with a stylus, you have more control over the letters you create. If you are using a stylus, each time you start Painter, you can set Painter to adjust the pressure you apply to the stylus. To set the stylus pressure, choose Brush Tracking from the Edit ➤ Preferences submenu. When the dialog box opens, use your stylus to create a brush stroke using the pressure that you would normally use when painting.*

When you've completed creating your name, save your work by choosing Save from the File menu. When the Save dialog appears, type **My Name** (Windows users: **MyName**) in the Save Image As field. When you save a file in Painter, you will normally save the file in Painter's default file type (RIFF). If you plan to use the image in another program such as Photoshop, you can click on the type menu and choose the appropriate file type. Painter's different file format options are discussed in detail in the appendix. If the Type pop-up menu is not set to RIFF, click in the menu and choose it now. The file will automatically be compressed to save disk space.

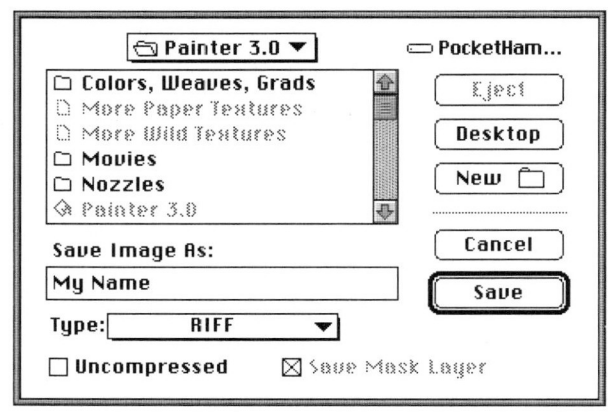

Note *To erase your entire image and start again, choose Edit ➤ Select All, then choose Edit ➤ Clear. To remove the selection marquee, choose Edit ➤ Deselect. Another way to erase everything is to double-click on the Rectangular Selection tool and press Delete on your keyboard.*

In the next section, you'll zoom in to examine the pixels that comprise the calligraphy you just created.

Examining Pixels

When you paint in Painter, the painting process occurs because you are changing the color of the tiny squares called pixels. By taking a look at the individual pixels that comprise an object, you'll gain a better under-standing of how Painter creates images. It will also help you understand the infinite possibilities for editing images that Painter provides.

Since the pixels that make up your image are very small, you'll need to zoom in to see them. The easiest way to zoom in to a particular image area is to use the Magnifier tool.

1. To activate the Magnifier tool, move the mouse pointer over the Magnifier in the Tools palette, then click on it.

2. Next click and drag over the first letter in your name, which you created in the previous section. Immediately Painter zooms in. To zoom in to see the individual pixels in the image, you'll need to increase the magnification to the maximum percentage Painter al-lows, 1200 percent. Click on the Zoom Level pop-up menu in the Controls :Magnifier palette and choose 1200%.

Tip *Whenever the Magnifier, Grabber, or Rotate Page tool is activated in the Tools palette, you can change the zoom level in the Controls palette.*

Tip *You can zoom in by choosing Window ➤ Zoom In or by using the key-board shortcut: Command+plus (Windows users: Ctrl+plus). Later, you'll zoom out by pressing Command+minus (Windows users: Ctrl+minus) or Window ➤ Zoom Out.*

After the image is magnified, you should see the jagged edges of your cal-ligraphy, as shown in Figure 1.3. If you don't see the jagged pixel edges, you may need to reposition the image on screen. The best way to reposi-tion the image is to activate the Grabber tool.

3. To activate the Grabber tool, click on it in Tools palette. Then move the pointer over your image. The mouse pointer changes to a tiny hand. Next click and drag the grabber hand icon over your image. As you drag, the image will move in the direction you drag.

When the image is in view, you'll finally see how the calligraphy is com-posed of the pixels, or tiny squares, that we've been talking about. When you apply a brush full of color in Painter, you're actually coloring in these tiny squares. Since the resolution of your image is 75 pixels per inch, each

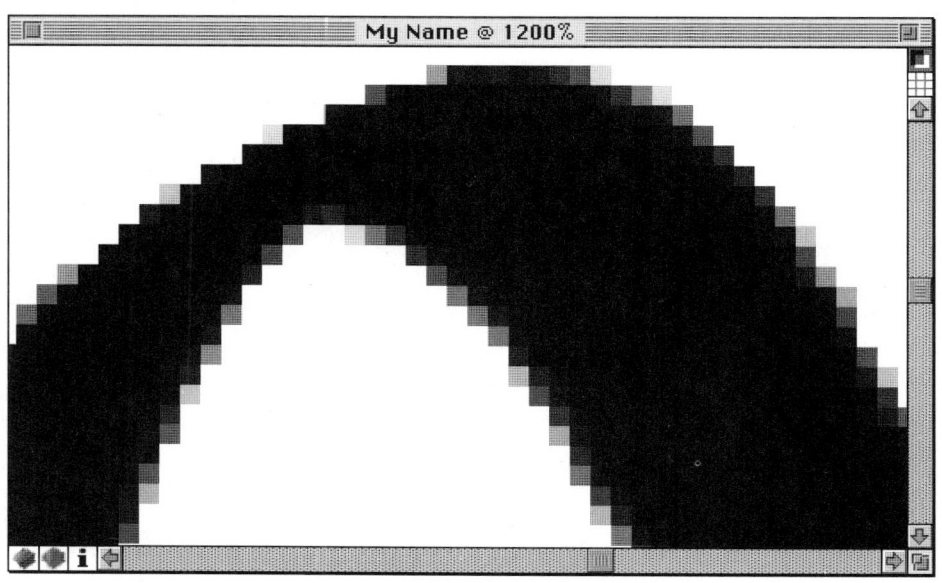

FIGURE 1.3: Magnified view of pixels created by Calligraphy Pen

linear inch of the image on screen is comprised of 75 pixels. Thus, every square inch of your image is comprised of well over 5,000 pixels.

Notice that along the edge of the calligraphy the color of the pixels is very light. This is the anti-aliasing, referred to earlier, that you can have Painter apply to your strokes to make your calligraphy look smoother.

Editing Pixels

One reason that Painter packs so much power into a brush stroke is that it can change the color of any one pixel in an image. This means that even if you paint with a thick drippy brush, you can return to your image and fine-tune the brush strokes to perfection. It also means that you can take all the pixels in an image, jumble them together into unusual combinations, or displace the pixels in your image to create startling special effects.

Painter provides several methods for editing images one pixel at a time. Since Pens should still be activated in the Brushes palette, the easiest way for you to edit pixels is to switch to the Single Pixel Brush variant. In the

Brush variant pop-up menu, change from Calligraphy to Single Pixel. Next click in the Method Category pop-up menu to change the Method Category to Eraser. The Method Subcategory should be set to Soft Paper Color. Now move the mouse over any painted area in your calligraphy and click. Assuming you're still viewing your calligraphy at 1200 percent, one of the pixel squares turns white. Click and drag to see the effects of editing several pixels at a time.

Now zoom back to see how large the pixels appear when you view them at 100 percent magnification. To zoom to 100 percent, select 100% in the Controls palette or double-click on the Magnifier tool. After you've zoomed back to 100 percent, the white dots are barely noticeable.

The foregoing simple example is an indication of exactly how precise you can work when you begin to paint and edit. After painting an image, if need be, you could zoom in and fine-tune or change the colors on a pixel-by-pixel basis to ensure that the final image has exactly the artistic effect you desire.

If you'd like, try using the Single Pixel variant to create unusual effects in the calligraphy on screen. Using the Single Pixel variant, you could edit the edges of the text, or create tiny moth holes in it.

Using Save As and Revert

When you're done experimenting, save your work by choosing the Save As command in the File menu. By choosing Save As, you can give your pixel editing experiment a new name. After you save the document with its new name, your original image (My Name, or MyName on the PC), still remains on your disk unchanged.

If you're unhappy with the special effects you created and wish to start editing your original calligraphy, you can quickly return to the original version of your file by reopening it or choosing File ➤ Revert. The Revert command closes the file on screen automatically and reopens the last saved version of your file.

When you've finished working with your image, you can remove it from the screen by choosing File ➤ Close. If you'd like to continue working with the calligraphic brush and paint over something besides a white canvas, proceed to the next section to create a Bon Voyage greeting card.

Practice: Creating a Bon Voyage Card

One of Painter's most intriguing features is its ability to digitize images and to open images created in other programs. This allows you to mix photographic images and painting on one Painter canvas.

In this section you'll open a digitized image and then use a grid to guide you as you use your calligraphic skills to create the Bon Voyage card shown in Figure 1.4.

FIGURE 1.4: The Bon Voyage project

Opening and Browsing Images

Before you begin creating the Bon Voyage card, you need to open a digitized image. If you don't have an image to use, you can use the Sailboat image in Painter's Tutorial folder.

To open a picture, choose File ➤ Open. Use the mouse to navigate into the correct folder. Open the folder by double-clicking on it or by clicking on the Open button. To see a preview of the images in the folder, click on the Browse button. Clicking Browse opens a tiny art gallery of the images in the selected folder. Beneath each image are its title, dimensions, and resolution. To open the desired image, click on it.

Using a Grid

When you're creating calligraphy on screen, it's sometimes difficult to prevent the letters you create from veering up or downhill. The best way to keep yourself on a straight path when creating any artwork is to use Painter's *grid*.

1. To place the grid on screen, click on the grid icon in the upper right corner of the Painter window. Horizontal grid lines that look very similar to graph paper immediately appear over the screen.

2. To make the grid easier to use when creating Calligraphy, you can widen the space between the lines, as well as remove the vertical lines. These options are available in the Grid Options dialog box. To open the Grid Options dialog box, choose Canvas ➤ Grid Options.

Grid Options

Grid type: [Rectangular Grid ▼]
Horizontal Spacing: [12] [pixels ▼]
Vertical Spacing: [12] [pixels ▼]
Line Thickness: [1] [pixels ▼]

Grid Color: [ ]   Background: [ ]
☐ Transparent Background

[Cancel] [OK]

3. First remove the vertical lines from the grid by changing the Grid type. From the Grid Type dialog box, choose Horizontal Lines. Now the Grid shows only horizontal lines.

4. To change the spacing between the lines, set the Vertical Spacing to
75 pixels (so you can work with a grid comprised of lines one inch
apart in an image with a resolution of 75 pixels per inch).

If you'd like to change the measuring units from pixels, click on the
pop-up menu to the right of the Vertical Spacing field and choose
inches, then set the value to 1 (instead of 75!).

5. If you wish to change the color of the grid lines, click on the white
swatch next to Grid Color. This opens the Apple or Windows color
picker. Click on the color of your choice.

With the grid on screen, begin painting the word *Bon* of Bon Voyage. Use
the grid lines as a guide to ensure that you are creating your letters on a
straight line.

When the grid is on screen, it appears over your image as if you've placed
tracing paper with grid lines over the image. This causes the image to be
seen at a 50 percent opacity. If you want the grid to remain but appear as
if it was on a sheet of clear plastic acetate rather than tracing paper, open
the Grid Options dialog box and select the Transparent Background option. Your image will appear at its normal opacity, but you'll still be able
to see the grid.

Work carefully as you paint. Remember, when applying paint in Painter,
it's as if your paint is drying on an electronic canvas. This means that you
just can't click on the letter you created to delete or move it. If you do
make a mistake, immediately choose Edit ➤ Undo. If you can't undo the
mistake, you have to paint over your mistake just like you would in the
real world of paints and canvas. If you wish to start the whole session
again from scratch, choose Revert from the File menu.

> **Tip** *If you set the Painting method category to Masking, you can paint a
> mask on screen with the Calligraphy brush. Afterwards, you can edit and per-
> fect the mask before filling it with color. To learn more about Painter's mask-
> ing brushes, see Chapter 7.*

If you're happy with your creation, choose File ➤ Save, and name your image **Bon Voyage** (Windows users: **BnVoyage**). Once the file is saved,
you'll be able to revert to this version of the image if you make a mistake
with it later.

Now proceed to carefully paint the word *Voyage* over your image. Once again, correct any mistakes by immediately choosing Edit ➤ Undo. If you need to return to the previous, saved version of the file, choose File ➤ Revert.

When you've completed your Bon Voyage card, don't forget to save your work again by choosing File ➤ Save. Your next step is to print your card.

● Printing

Painter's printing options are simple and straightforward. To print your image, choose Print from the File menu. If you are printing to a color printer, choose the appropriate radio button. If you are outputting to a black-and-white laser printer, choose the Black-and-White option. Notice that the Print dialog box also allows you to print *separations*. If you choose this option, Print divides your image into its color components so that plates can be made for printing. For more information about printing separations, see Chapter 12.

● Customizing Painter

Before proceeding to the next chapter to learn about color, you may wish to make a few changes to Painter to customize the program so it is tailored specifically for your needs and your system. Customization of Painter is primarily handled through its Preferences menu.

Changing the Paintbrush Cursor

While creating calligraphy in the previous section of this chapter, you un-doubtedly noticed that Painter's paintbrush cursor did not change when you picked the Calligraphy brush variant. No matter what brush you pick, the icon remains a colored triangle. At times you may wish to change the color of this triangle or change its angle. If you are working in intricate areas, you can also change the brush cursor to the width of a single pixel.

To change the paintbrush cursor, choose File ➤ Preferences ➤ General (that is, from the File menu, choose Preferences, and from the Preferences submenu, choose General). In the General Preferences dialog box, you can make changes to the default painting icon by changing the options in the

Drawing Cursor section. Click on the color you want by clicking on a swatch. To change the direction of the triangle icon, click on one of the Orientation radio buttons. If you wish to use the 1-pixel-wide icon, click on the Single Pixel radio button.

General Preferences

Drawing Cursor:

Cursor type: ⦿ Triangle
○ Single pixel

Orientation   Color

Floating selection pre-feather [16.0] pixels
☒ Indicate clone source with cross hairs while cloning
☐ Disable automatic sync to disk
☐ Draw zoomed-out views using area-averaging
☐ Display warning when drawing outside selection

Default Libraries:

Brushes: **Painter Brushes**
Paper Grains: Paper Textures
Paths: Painter Paths
Floaters: Painter Portfolio
Color Set: Painter Colors
Temp File Volume: PocketHammer2050...▼

Color Palette Type
⦿ Color Ring+Triangle
○ Hue Slider+Triangle
○ Red-Green-Blue

[Cancel]   [OK]

Before closing the dialog box, proceed to the next section to learn how to change Painter's Temp Volume setting.

Changing the Temp Disk Setting

As Painter carries out your commands, it may need more memory than your system has available in RAM. When this happens, Painter turns to your hard disk and uses free disk space as a work area. The disk that Painter uses for this is called the *Temp File Volume*. If you have more than one hard disk connected to your computer, you should change Painter's temp disk to the fastest and emptiest hard disk available. The Temp File Volume setting is found in Painter's General Preferences dialog box (File ➤ Preferences ➤ General).

In the General Preferences dialog box, reset the Temp File Volume setting by choosing the appropriate hard disk in the pop-up menu. When you've completed your changes, close the dialog box by clicking on the OK button.

Changing the Levels of Undos

Painter allows you to set multiple "undo" levels. This means that you can experiment and need not worry that only your last keystroke or brushstroke can

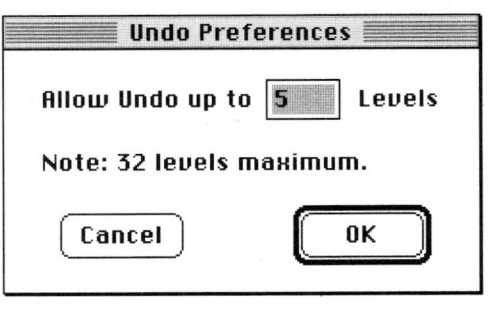

Undo Preferences

Allow Undo up to [5] **Levels**

Note: 32 levels maximum.

[Cancel]   [OK]

be undone. Painter allows up to 32 levels of undo/redo changes. The default setting is 5 levels.

If you wish to change the undo levels, choose Edit ➤ Preferences ➤ Undo. In the Undo Preferences dialog box, enter the desired number of undo levels.

> ***Warning*** *The higher the level of undos, the greater the disk space used. Also, be especially careful if you have multiple documents open and set to high levels of undo: Painter must keep track of all the undos for all the open documents.*

Wrapping It Up

Now that you've taken an introductory tour of Painter and learned the basics of how Painter creates images, you're ready to proceed to the next chapter to learn how to choose colors and create gradients and weaves.

Working
with Color

Color can wake up a tired landscape, add passion and intrigue to a somber portrait, and add zest to a quiet, dull still life. It can set the mood in an image and evoke sensations. It can create the content in an image, and control the lighting and the reflection of lights.

To all artists, choosing the correct color is vital to conveying the intended artistic vision. In a sophisticated computer graphics program like Painter, choosing colors can present a challenge quite different from picking colors in the traditional art world. You won't see the words Burnt Sienna, Cadmium Red, or Titanium White anywhere in Painter's Colors palette, let alone paint tube icons labeled Emerald Green or Prussian Blue.

In Painter, as in programs like Photoshop and Photostyler, colors are chosen using a color *model*. A color model divides a color into the components that make it distinct, such as its hue, brightness value, and intensity, or the proportions of Red, Green, and Blue light that comprise it. Colors are then picked choosing the numerical values of the components, or by visually picking the components with a mouse or stylus.

This chapter focuses on how to pick and use colors with Painter. As you read through this chapter, you'll explore and learn to pick colors using the Hue, Saturation, Value and Red, Green, Blue color models. After you learn how to choose colors, you'll learn how to create a custom color palette, called a *color set*. This will allow you to create your own versions of Burnt Sienna and Emerald Green and to search for them by whatever name you want to give them.

You'll also have a chance to create a variety of beautiful gradients, where one color gradually blends into another, and learn how to change the colors of Painter's weaves and apply them to your image.

● Understanding Color Models

Physicists created color models to provide a consistent means of defining color. Why do you need a consistent means of describing color? Well, assume you wish to add yellow to brighten up a landscape scene. You decide to add a bright yellow. But how bright? How do you quantify the actual brightness in the color? By using a color model to describe color, you can assign consistent numerical values to the components of colors, so colors can easily be replicated and described.

The *Hue, Saturation, and Value (HSV)* color model is considered to be the most intuitive color model, because it is founded upon how the human mind perceives color. It is also Painter's default color model.

The first aspect most artists perceive in a color is its *hue*—its color component, such as red, green, or blue. In technical terms, hue is created when a wavelength of light is reflected from an object or transmitted through objects. A color's *saturation* describes how strong the hue is. Saturation can also be considered the amount of gray in a color. A color's *value* represents *brightness* defined in terms of how light or dark the hue is.

The easiest way of understanding the relationship between hue, saturation, and value is to open up Painter's Art Materials :Colors palette and begin picking colors.

Picking Colors Using the Color Ring and Triangle

Picking colors using Painter's HSV color model is quite simple, primarily because Painter allows you to pick each color component visually. The HSV color model is represented by a *color ring* and *triangle* in Painter's Art Materials :Colors palette. If the Art Materials palette is not on screen, open it now by choosing Art Materials from the Window menu.

As mentioned in Chapter 1, the Art Materials palette is essentially four palettes in one. In order to display the Colors palette, the Colors icon at the top of the palette must be selected. When the icon is selected, the last-used color palette is displayed.

By default, the Colors palette has a color ring and triangle, as shown in Figure 2.1. If the palette on screen does not display a color ring, somebody has changed the palette in the General Preferences dialog box.

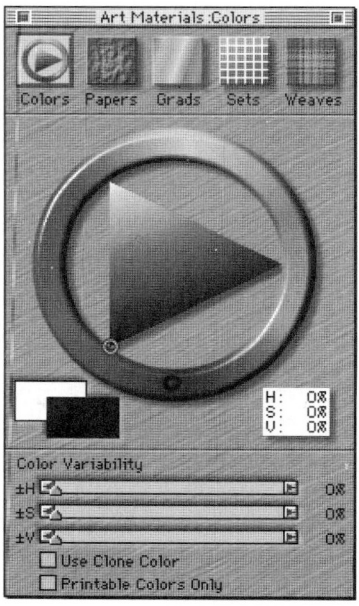

FIGURE 2.1: The Colors palette expanded

Note In order to follow along with this discussion, the Colors palette should show the color ring and triangle. If you don't see them, reset the palette by selecting Edit ➤ Preferences ➤ General. In the General Preferences dialog box, click on the Color Ring + Triangle radio button in the Colors Palette Type group, then click OK.

Tip Remember, the Colors palette can be separated from its home in the Art Materials palette by dragging the Colors icon off the Art Materials palette. This allows you to keep the Colors palette handy while you're painting. (Note, though, that you can't separate a palette when it's the active palette. First you would have to click on another icon at the top of the palette, then drag the Colors icon away from the Art Materials palette.)

Before you begin choosing colors, notice the two overlapping rectangles in the lower left corner of the Colors Palette. When the front rectangle is selected (that is, when a black frame appears around it), you can change the *primary* painting color in the Colors palette. The primary color is the color that flows on your canvas when you paint. (The back rectangle is the *secondary* color. It can be used when creating gradients and when setting the color of multicolored brush strokes).

If the front rectangle isn't selected, select it now by clicking on it.

Changing Hue, Saturation, and Value

Once the Colors palette is open on screen and the primary painting color rectangle is selected in the palette, you're ready to start picking colors. To pick a color, you click on the color ring to choose a hue and click in the triangle in the center to pick the saturation and value of the hue.

Assume you wish to create a bright red color. You'd start by selecting a red hue. To pick a red hue, move the pointer over a red color on the circle, then click. A small circle appears over the hue that you clicked on, and the H percentage (hue) in the lower right corner of the palette changes. (If the categories are set to R, G, and B instead of H, S, and V, click on them—that will switch them to H, S, and V. You'll learn about RGB later.) A red hue should read approximately 34 or 35%. You can change the hue by dragging on a different color in the circle. Notice that no white, black, or gray appears in the hue ring. That's because they are not technically considered "colors" in this color model. You'll learn how to create white, black, and gray later by altering saturation and value.

When you picked the red hue, you may have noticed that the color inside the triangle changed. The triangle now allows you to choose the saturation and value for the red hue. Notice that the triangle shows a light red toward the top of the triangle, a darker red toward the bottom, and a rich intense red toward the right.

To set the color's value, you click and drag up or down in the triangle. As you drag, a tiny circle indicates your current position in the triangle. Dragging up lightens the color, dragging down darkens it. Try clicking and dragging up in the triangle now. As you drag, notice that the V percentage (value) increases. The higher the value, the lighter the color; the lower the value, the darker the color. No matter what hue you choose, if the value is set to 100%, your color will be white.

Now try changing the color's saturation by clicking and dragging to the right within the triangle. The further right you drag, the greater the saturation (the intensity) of the red. If you drag to the left, you decrease the saturation—and make the color more gray. If you set both S and V (saturation and value) to 0%, you create black. Release the mouse when the saturation percentage in the HSV readout is at least 90%. Notice that the primary painting color rectangle displays the bright red color that you've chosen.

> **Note** *Once you've picked your color, you're ready to paint. If you'd like, choose the Brush tool from the Tools palette and try painting a few strokes with the calligraphic pen you used in Chapter 1. Before you test the color, first create a new file, set the Brushes palette to Pens, the variant to Calligraphy, the Method Category to Cover, and the Method Subcategory to Soft Cover.*

Understanding the Color Ring

Before continuing to explore more options in the Colors palette, you should take a moment to analyze the color theory behind Painter's color ring. Understanding the relationship among the colors in the ring can help you paint more effectively.

Painter's color ring is based on the traditional color wheel in which the three colors red, green, and blue are equidistant from one another. Similar colors appear near each other, and the *complement* of each color appears directly across from it on the wheel. A color's complement is the color most unlike it. The complements of red, green, and blue are, respectively, cyan, magenta, and yellow.

Try dragging around the ring with the mouse. As you drag, notice that the color in the primary painting rectangle gradually changes from one color to another. Notice also that colors near each other on the ring are similar in hue. If you want to paint with harmonious colors, pick colors close to each other on the ring. To create contrast, pick a color on the opposite side of the ring. For instance, if you wish to paint yellow flowers and want to create contrast between the flowers and the vase, you could paint the base blue, the complement of yellow.

Although the HSV color model was designed to provide a consistent means of picking color, it only allows you to pick one color at a time. The real world of painting isn't so rigid. A dab of oil, acrylic, or watercolor might include more than one hue, saturation, and value. Painter provides for this by allowing you to vary the color in a brush stroke.

Changing Color Variability

The bottom of the Colors palette features three sliders that allow you to vary the hue, saturation, and value of your brush strokes as you paint on the electronic canvas. Use these Color Variability sliders to add a bit more variety and interest to the colors you're working with. (If you don't see the variability sliders, your palette is not expanded. To expand it, click on the zoom box in the top right corner of the palette.)

By dragging the ±Hue slider to the right, you add hues to a brush stroke. Initially, the added hues are those closest to the one chosen in the color ring; the farther you drag to the right, the more colors you add from farther away. Dragging the ±Saturation slider varies the saturation as you paint. Dragging to the right increases the variability. Dragging the ±Value slider increases the variability of the value of the painting color. This means that the value varies as color is applied.

To see how the primary color can vary as you paint, try dragging each of the ±Hue, ±Saturation, and ±Value sliders to the right. Notice that the primary painting color rectangle previews the change in color. Now try painting a stroke to see how the color varies as you paint.

Note *Before proceeding to the next section, make sure that the ±H, ±S, ±V sliders are set to 0%.*

Using the RGB Color Model

Note *Although most artists prefer working with the HSV color model, you may wish to use the Red, Green, Blue (RGB) color model, particularly if you are very familiar with other painting and image-editing applications. Some programs, most notably Adobe Photoshop, use RGB as their default color model.*

When your computer generates colors it creates them by lighting up red, green, and blue phosphors that light up the pixels on your monitor. By combining different components of red, green, and blue light, your computer can create over 16 million colors in any pixel on screen. This is the basis of the RGB or Red, Green, Blue color model.

To many artists, picking colors by choosing red, green, and blue components is more difficult than using hue, saturation, and value. For instance, assume you want to create orange. How much red, green, and blue do you need to create orange?

Nonetheless, a knowledge of using the RGB color model can prove helpful, particularly if you will be using *process colors* to print your work. When images are printed on a commercial printing press using the four-color process, colors are created by overlaying different percentages of cyan, magenta, yellow, and black inks. As mentioned earlier, cyan, magenta, and yellow are the complements of red, green, and blue. Although Painter does not allow you to edit colors using the *CMYK system* (Cyan, Magenta, Yellow, and Black—the K stands for Black), you can indirectly adjust the amount of cyan, magenta, and yellow in a color by adding and subtracting different amounts of red, green, and blue. You'll learn how to do this after you switch to the RGB Colors palette.

In order to switch to the RGB Colors palette, you must change the color palette type in the General Preferences dialog box (Edit ➤ Preferences ➤ General). After the dialog box opens, click on the Red-Green-Blue option in the Color Palette Type group. Click OK to close the dialog box. Immediately the color ring and triangle in the Colors palette are replaced by red, green, and blue slider controls.

Note *Make sure that the ±H, ±S, ±V Color Variability sliders are set to 0; otherwise the colors will not be solid colors.*

The RGB Colors palette allows you to choose colors by dragging the R, G, and B sliders, whose values range from 0 to 255. When all three sliders are set to 0, black is created. As the values of the sliders increases, color is added. When all three sliders are set to 255, white is created.

Note *Each slider provides 256 (2^8) settings. The permutation of the three settings in combination (2^8 red × 2^8 green × 2^8 blue) gives a total of 2^{24}, or 16.7 million, possible colors.*

Try creating a pure red by first dragging the R (red) slider to 255, then drag the G (green) and B (blue) sliders to 0. Notice how the primary color rectangle gradually grows redder as you reduce the green and blue levels.

To create green, set the G slider to 255 and the other two sliders to 0. To create blue, set the B slider to 255, and the other two sliders to 0. If the values of all three sliders are equal, gray is created: darker toward the 0 end of the scale, whiter toward the 255 end. By setting all colors to 255 and subtracting one of the RGB colors, one of the complements of RGB is created. When both the R and G sliders are set to 255 and the B slider is set to 0, yellow (the complement of blue) is created. When both the R and B sliders are set to 255 and the G slider is set to 0, magenta (the complement of green) is created. When both the G and B sliders are set to 255 and the R slider is set to 0, you produce cyan (the complement of red).

The relationship between the colors red, green, and blue and their complements cyan, magenta, and yellow means that you can use the RGB sliders to add or subtract cyan, magenta, and yellow to any color. For example, you can…

◆ add magenta to a color by adding equal amounts of red and blue or by subtracting green.

◆ add yellow to a color by adding equal amounts of red and green , or by subtracting blue.

◆ add cyan to a color by adding equal amounts of green and blue, or by subtracting red.

Working with Printable Colors

The printable color spectrum is based upon the *CMYK* (*Cyan, Magenta, Yellow, and Black*) color model. When an image is printed on a commercial printer press, color is produced from four inked printing plates, one for each of the CMYK process colors. By overlaying the inks, the printable range of colors is created. The range of colors in a color model is referred to as *gamut*. Like the HSV and RGB gamuts, the CMYK gamut comprises millions of colors. But the CMYK gamut is smaller than either the HSV or RGB gamut. Many bright saturated colors cannot be reproduced on a commercial printing press. This means that you can't reproduce all the colors you can create on your monitor. For the computer artist, this can present problems. If you're not careful, the colors in a printed image won't look like the colors used to create the image on screen.

Fortunately, Painter can change the colors on your screen so that they do not fall beyond the printable colors gamut. Painter provides two ways to avoid painting beyond the boundaries of the CMYK gamut. The first and easiest is to select the Printable Colors Only check box at the bottom of the Art Materials palette. Once the check box is selected, you can only choose colors that are within the printable color gamut.

> **Note** *If you wish to see the difference between printable and nonprintable colors, choose the brightest red, green, or blue you can create in the Art Materials :Colors palette, then paint a few brush strokes. Next select the Printable Colors check box in the palette. Paint and compare the difference between the bright color and its printable counterpart. The printable color will be duller, or less saturated.*

The second method of restricting Painter to printable colors is helpful if you've forgotten to use the Printable Colors Only option when painting, or if you decide after you've created your image that you want to output your on-screen image to a commercial printing press. You can change all the colors in an image to printable colors by choosing Printable Colors from the Effects ➤ Tonal Control submenu. This opens the Printable Colors dialog box, which provides a preview of your image with printable colors enforced. To convert your image to printable colors, click OK. After you click OK, Painter changes the colors on screen to their nearest printable equivalent.

Working with "Video Legal" Colors for Best Video Output

The final stop for Painter images is not always a commercial printing press or a computer screen. Sometimes it's a video monitor connected to a VCR (videocassette recorder). The gamut of television colors is not as broad as the RGB or HSV gamut. If your final output will be a videotaped presentation, Painter offers a way for you to ensure that your video presentation's colors will match the colors in your painting as shown on your computer monitor: Painter can change its colors so that they match those that would appear on American or foreign television (two different standards).

To change the colors in your image so that they conform to those allowable on television, choose Video Legal Colors from the Effects ➤ Tonal Control submenu. In the Video Legal Colors dialog box, choose either NTSC or PAL from the System pop-up menu. NTSC is the American standard; PAL is the standard used in most foreign countries. Click OK to activate the changes.

Working with Color Sets

As you begin to work with different colors, you may grow tired of constantly recreating the colors you use the most. You'll probably want to store your colors on a palette so you can access them again and again. To satisfy this need, Painter allows you to maintain groups of frequently used colors in a *color set*, a group of colors that appear in the Color Set palette. Once you create a color set, the colors can be tagged with a name and chosen from the palette by clicking on the color. Before we show you how to create your own color set, take a look at Painter's default color set.

> **Note** *If you wish to reset the Art Materials palette back to the HSV color model, open the General Preferences dialog box by choosing Edit ➤ Preferences ➤ General. Reset to the default color palette by choosing Color Ring + Triangle in the Color Palettes Type group.*

To view the Painter's default color set, choose Window ➤ Color Set. A long rectangular palette filled with a 180 tiny color swatches opens on screen. (To choose a color from this palette, simply click on the color swatch you want. Immediately the primary painting color in the Colors palette changes to that color.)

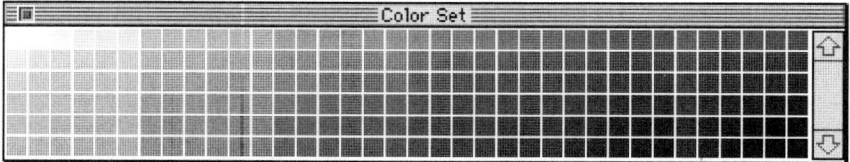

Loading a Color Set Library

Color sets make choosing colors easier and they can help you retain a consistent color scheme in an image. Painter provides several color sets that provide harmonious colors. For instance, Painter includes color sets for earth tones, muted tones, and pastels. Color sets, however, are not loaded from the Color Set palette; instead, they are accessed from the Art Materials :Sets palette.

To load a color set, first click on the Sets icon at the top of the Arts Material palette. This displays the Art Materials :Sets palette and its options as shown in Figure 2.2. To load a color set, click on the Library button in the palette. This opens a dialog box from which you can pick color sets stored on disk. Painter's color sets lie in the Colors, Weaves, Grads folder on the Mac, and in the Supplies directory on a Windows PC. If you like, try loading a new color set now; otherwise proceed to the next section to learn how to use the Pantone® Color set.

FIGURE 2.2: The Sets palette expanded

Using the Pantone Color Set

Many times Pantone Spot colors are used to reduce the cost of a color print job. In a spot color job, money is saved because, typically, only one or two colors are used. Spot colors are also used when you want to add a "fifth" color such as a metallic or silvery color that is beyond the CMYK color gamut. Using a fifth color, however, is more expensive than a four-color job.

When a spot color is created, the print shop mixes different inks and uses the resulting color in a printing plate. This is quite different from the four-color printing process where countless colors can be created by overlaying cyan, magenta, yellow, and black inks.

If you will be outputting your Painter files to a commercial printing press and need to output spot color, you'll find Pantone spot colors to be one of Painter's most valuable color sets. This color set can also help you predict how your colors will look when printed.

One problem with creating color images on the computer is that your screen colors will never perfectly match the colors of the printed page. Using Pantone *spot colors* makes color matching easier because you can pick the colors to use from a *swatch book*. The swatch book shows how the color looks when printed. When you choose a Pantone color, your commercial printer matches the color based upon the Pantone color in the same swatchbook.

Assume that you wish to use a light blue Pantone color in your image. You find Pantone 305 in a swatch book, and decide that it is the light blue you wish to paint with. Here are the steps for changing the primary color to Pantone 305.

1. In order to load the Pantone Color library, the Art Materials :Sets palette must be open on screen. If it isn't, choose Window ➤ Art Materials. When the palette opens click on the Sets icon at the top of the palette.

2. Click on the Library button in the Sets palette.

3. Locate the Pantone Colors library by opening the Colors, Weaves, Grads folder (Windows users: the Supplies directory). Then, double-click on the Pantone Colors file. Instantly the Color Set palette changes to display Pantone colors. (If the Color Set palette is not open, open it by choosing Window ➤ Color Set.)

Once the Library is loaded, you can now direct Painter to search for the color you wish to use in your image.

4. To find the Pantone color you want, click on the Find Color button in the Art Material :Sets palette.

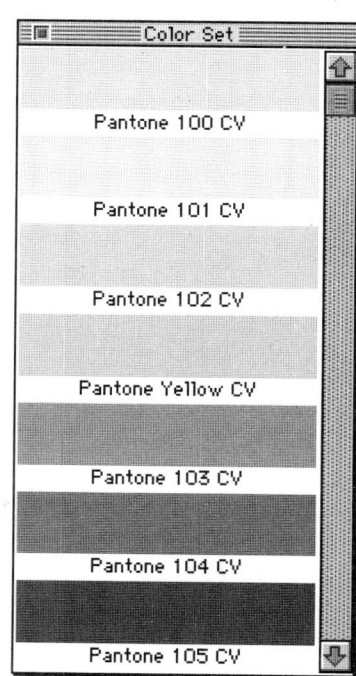

5. In the Find Color dialog box, enter the name of the color you wish to search for. For this example, you should type **Painter 305**. Then click the Search button. After Painter finds the color, click OK. The primary painting color is now set to the Pantone 305.

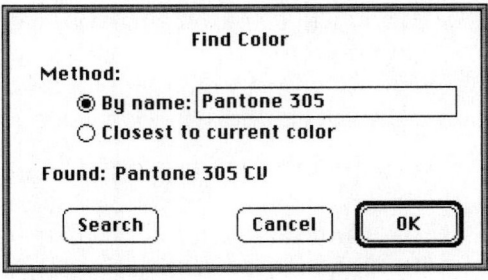

Note Even if the Art Materials :Colors palette is closed, you can still view the current primary painting color by opening the Controls palette and selecting the Brush tool from the Tools palette.

After you've picked the color you need, you may want to return to the default color set. If so, click on the Library button in the Art Materials :Sets palette. After the Open dialog box appears, locate the the Painter Colors (Windows users: Painter.PCS) file, then double-click on the file to open it.

Note You will learn how to print spot colors in Chapter 12.

Note Pantone's Macintosh ColorDrive software allows you to create custom palettes that can be exported to both Mac and PC versions of Painter. The program helps insure that you can obtain consistent colors across different applications.

Creating a Color Set from a Digitized Image

One of the best ways of keeping your favorite colors handy is to create your own color set. You can even create a color set that uses colors from an existing image or from an image that you are creating.

Note You can create as many color sets as your hard drive can store.

To create a color set using colors from an image, you first need to open the image. If you don't have an image to use, load the Mission file from the Painter Tutorial folder.

1. With the image you want already open, click on the New Set button in the Art Materials :Sets palette. Notice that the Current Color Set field now displays the word *Untitled* and that the padlock in the middle of the palette becomes unlocked. The unlocked padlock indicates that the color set can be changed.

   Now use the Dropper tool to click on a color in your image so that you can add it to your new color set.

2. Activate the Dropper tool in the Tools palette by clicking on it.

3. Move the Dropper tool over a color in your image and click the mouse. Notice that the primary color displayed in the Controls palette and in the Colors palette changes to that color.

4. To add this new primary color to your new color set, click on the Add Color button in the Sets palette. Notice that the color is now added to the Color Set palette.

5. Repeat steps 3 and 4 a few times to add more colors from your image to the Color Set palette.

   Note *To delete a color in your color set, click on the color in the Color Set palette and click on the Delete Color button in the Art Materials :Sets palette.*

After you've added a color to the Color Set palette, you can name a color by double-clicking on it in the Color Set palette. Try double-clicking on one of the colors that you created, and typing a name in the Name field. You'll be able to use this name when you learn how to annotate an image later in this chapter. You can also use the Find button in the Art Materials :Sets palette to find a color by its name.

When you've finished adding and deleting colors to your new color set, you may want to view the colors in the Color Set palette in a different order, other than the one they were created in. Read on to see how.

Adjusting a Color Set Using the Sets Palette

When the Art Materials :Sets palette is expanded, a set of buttons and icons appear that allow you to change the color order, swatch size, and row-to-column setup. If the Color Set palette is not expanded, click on the palette's zoom box to do so.

The color set can't be edited if the Color Set palette is locked. If you need to unlock the current color set, click on the padlock in the Art Materials :Sets palette. (To lock the color set, click on the padlock again.)

To change the order of the colors in a color set, click on one of the Sort Order buttons in the Sets palette. The buttons allow you to sort by Hue Luminance and Saturation. (Luminance is a measure of a color's brightness.) For instance, click on the HLS button. The colors in your color set are now arranged by Hue. Hues with the lowest percentage in the color ring come first in the palette. To sort by Luminance, click on the LHS button. To sort by Saturation click on the SHL.

Painter also allows you to change the size of the color set's swatches, and how they are arranged in the color set window.

By clicking in the Color Square Size icons you can change the width and height of the color swatches. Clicking the left or right arrow allows you to increase the width one pixel left or right. Clicking on the double arrows doubles the width or height. Take a moment to click once or twice on the right arrow, then the down arrow, to change the width and height, respectively, of the swatches in your color sets.

Clicking on the Color Set Size icon allows you to change the number of rows and columns in your color sets. Essentially, this provides you with a means of resizing the Color set palette so that you can see the colors arranged in the manner you wish. Clicking on the right arrow adds columns, clicking on the down arrow adds rows. If you click on the double right arrows, the number of columns is doubled. Clicking on the double down arrows doubles the number of rows.

Now that you've created a color set, you may wish to annotate your image with the names of the colors in the color set.

Annotating Colors

Annotating an image allows you to tag the colors in it by name. When you annotate a color in an image, Painter draws a line from the color in the image to the place you decide to display the color's name, as seen in Figure 2.3.

FIGURE 2.3:   Painter's Annotate command allows you to tag colors by name. Artwork by Beatriz Droblas.

Follow the steps below to annotate an image.

1. Open the image you wish to annotate. Next open the color set you want to use to label the colors in your image. (If you'd like, just use the image and color set you used in the previous sections.)

2. Choose Annotate from the Canvas menu. The Annotate dialog box appears.

3. Click on the color you want to annotate and drag to where you want the name of the color to appear. As you drag, a line appears from the point where you clicked on the color to where you released the mouse. At the end of the black line is the name of the color that you named in your color set. If the color does

not yet have a name in the Color Set palette, you will only see an asterisk at the end of the black line.

Note *If you want to delete an annotation, the Annotation dialog box must be open. Click on the color label, then press Delete on your keyboard.*

4. When you are finished annotating, click the Done button on screen.

When you wish to hide the annotations, click on View Annotations in the Canvas menu. The check mark disappears from the View Annotations menu item, and the annotations disappear from the screen. To see the annotations again, simply choose View Annotations again from the Canvas menu.

Closing and Saving a Color Set

Once you have finished working with a color set, you can save it to disk by clicking on the Library button. Clicking on the close box triggers an on-screen alert inquiring whether you wish to save the changes to the current color set. Click on the Save button. This opens another dialog box where you can enter the color set's name. After entering a name, click Save to save the color set.

Working with Gradations

Now that you've learned the different ways that you can pick and create colors, you're probably eager to create beautiful effects with them. Certainly one of the easiest ways to produce striking color effects is to create *gradations.*

Painter's color gradations allow you to create beautiful and exquisite blends from one color to another. Gradations can be used to create lighting effects, interesting backgrounds and other special effects. In this section you'll learn how to create gradations, customize gradations, and create a gradation library.

Before you can create a gradation, you must first click on the Grads icon at the top of the Art Materials palette. This displays the Art Materials :Grads palette.

Painter boasts a tremendous assortment of gradations. You can create a gradation that simulates anything from a crimson sunset to the colors in the color spectrum. Five of Painter's gradation patterns are visible on the front of the Art Materials :Grads palette drawer. To access all of the gradations, as shown in Figure 2.4, open the drawer by clicking on the drawer handle.

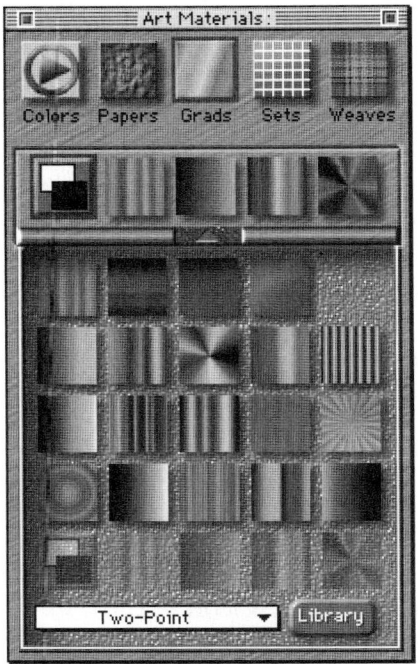

FIGURE 2.4: The Grads palette with the drawer open

Choosing Gradations

Figure 2.4 shows the variety of gradation patterns provided in the gradations drawer. Each gradation has a name, which appears in the palette's pop-up menu. To see the names of the gradations, click on each gradation. Names such as *Crimson Sunset, Golden Sun, Earth Tones,* and *Spectrum* should provide you an idea of the effects available.

Picking Colors for the Two-Point Gradation

The "two-point" gradation is one of Painter's most versatile gradations. Unlike most of the other gradations, Two-Point allows you to pick a starting and ending color for the gradation. The starting point for the gradation is the primary color in the Art Materials palette; the ending point is the secondary color.

Assume you want to provide a lighting effect by gradually blending a color from yellow to gray. Here are the steps using Two-Point gradation.

> **Note** *Before you create your gradation, create a new file, 4" by 7", with a resolution of 75 ppi.*

1. In order to see both the Art Materials :Colors palette and Art Materials :Grads palettes on screen at the same time, drag the Colors icon off the Art Materials palette.

2. In the Colors palette, first make sure that the primary painting color rectangle is activated. Then use the color ring and triangle to pick a bright yellow color.

3. Click on the secondary painting color rectangle to activate it. To create a gray shade, click on the left edge of the triangle, then click and drag up or down. By clicking on the left edge of the triangle, you pick a color with little saturation. No matter what the hue, a color with little saturation will be gray.

4. In the Grads palette look for the Two-Point Gradation icon. By default it is the first icon in the drawer front, the one with the overlapping rectangles. Since Painter switches the Grad icons as you work with grads, you may not see the Two-Point Gradation icon on the drawer front. If you don't see it , open the drawer and choose it from within the drawer. (Alternatively, you can choose it in the palette's pop-up menu.)

Changing the Gradation Type, Angle, and Order

Once you've picked the colors for the two-point gradient your next step is to pick the gradation *type*: linear, radial, circular, spiral, or angle. To choose a gradation type, you must first close the Grad drawer.

1. To close the Grad drawer, click on the drawer handle.

Once the drawer is closed, Painter displays the types of grads available, as shown in Figure 2.5. When you click on a type icon, Painter provides a preview in the square of the Grads palette.

2. Click on each of the Types icons to see a preview. The top left is linear, the top right is radial, the bottom left is circular, and the bottom right is spiral.

3. Assume you wish to create a linear gradation. Set the type of the gradation to Linear by clicking on the top left Types choice.

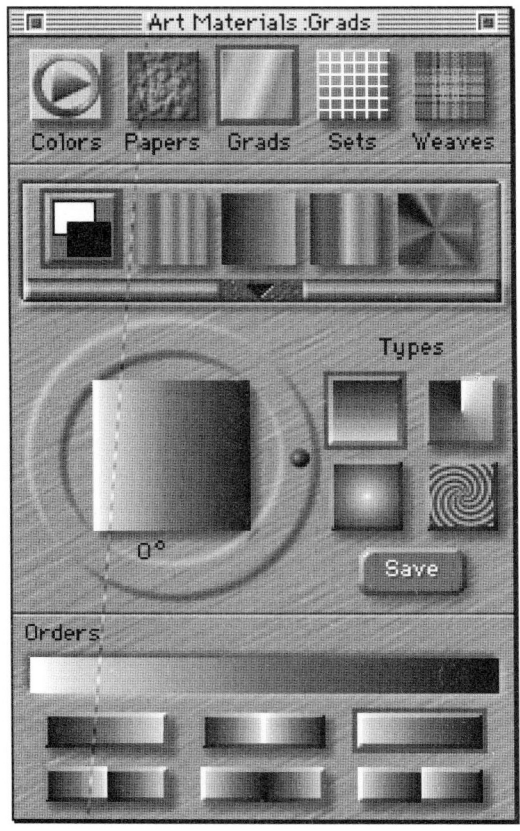

FIGURE 2.5: The Grads palette expanded with the drawer closed

You can now set the angle of the gradation by dragging on the tiny red circle on the ring surrounding the square gradation preview. As you drag, the readout indicates the angle in degrees.

4. Change the angle of the blend by dragging the red circle around the ring until the degree readout displays 45 degrees.

Tip *Click on the gradation preview square in the Grads palette to have Painter animate the preview of how the gradation will look at different angles. Click on the ring at the desired degree, and the animated preview will stop.*

5. Painter even allows you to choose the color order of your blend. To see the gradation's Orders options, the Art Materials :Grads palette must be expanded. If the palette isn't expanded, click on the palette's zoom box.

6. The best way to decipher how the Orders options will affect the gradient at the angle you've set is to watch the preview square change as you click on each of the icons below the Orders ribbon. As you read through the following explanation, click on each order icon to see the preview.

The first preview shows the gradation blending from left to right, mirrored left to right, and right to left. The second row creates a double gradation. The first icon in the second row creates both gradations blending left to right; the second icon creates a mirrored gradation blending left to right. The last icon in the second row creates the doubled gradation blending right to left.

7. Set the Orders icon to the first icon in the first row. This creates a blend from the primary to secondary color.

Tip *To produce a three-dimensional sphere effect, create a gradation in an oval selection with two similar colors using the Two-Point gradation and Circular Type option.*

Saving Gradations

After you've picked a gradation and changed the type, angle, and order, you can save the gradation on disk so it is easily accessible the next time you need it.

To save a gradation, click on the Save button that appears on the same screen as the gradation Types and Order icons. After you click the Save button, the Save Color Ramp dialog box appears. Enter a name for your gradation and click Save. Be sure to use a different name than one that is already used, or else that gradation will be replaced.

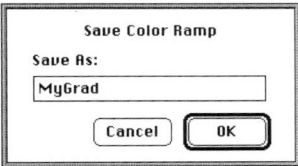

After you save, a thumbnail icon of your gradient appears at the top of the drawer palette. If you open the palette's pop-up menu, you'll find the name of your new gradation.

Applying Gradations

You can apply a gradation by using the Effects ➤ Fill command or by using the Paint Bucket. Each of these methods can fill a selection or the entire screen with a gradation. The Paint Bucket can also use a gradation to fill within the *borders* of a painted object.

> **Note** *When you use the Paint Bucket to fill an area that has already been painted, you can set a "lock-out color" to prevent the Paint Bucket from painting over this particular color. To set the lock-out color, first select the color using the Dropper tool, then double-click on the Paint Bucket. In the Lock-Out Color dialog box, click on the Set button, then click OK. If you later wish to turn off the Lock-Out color, double-click on the Paint Bucket, then deselect the check box next to the lock-out color in the dialog box.*

> **Tip** *If there is no selection on screen, you can drag the Paint Bucket to create a rectangular shape while simultaneously filling the shape with a gradation. In order to make this work, just make sure the Gradation and Image options are selected in the Controls :Paint Bucket palette.*

Try filling the entire screen by using the Paint Bucket tool. (Before using this tool, make sure that the Tools palette and the Controls palette are open on screen. If they aren't, open them from the Windows menu.) To use the Paint Bucket tool, simply click on it in the Tools palette. Once you click, notice that the entire Controls palette changes to display Paint Bucket options. The Controls :Paint Bucket palette allows you to fill using either a gradation or the current (primary) color. After ensuring that the Gradation and Image radio buttons are selected in the palette, move the Paint Bucket to your canvas and click. The entire canvas is filled with the gradation.

> **Note** *If you had selected an area of the canvas or created a selection, clicking with the Paint Bucket within the selection would have filled it with the gradation.*

Try executing the following steps to see the effects of different gradations in a selection.

1. Activate the Rectangular Selection tool.

2. Drag to create a rectangular selection in the middle of your canvas.

3. In the Art Materials :Grads palette, click on a gradient.

4. Activate the Paint Bucket tool, and make sure that the Gradation and Image radio buttons are selected in the Controls :Paint Bucket palette; then click within the selection on screen.

The new gradient will appear within the selection. Leave the selection on screen so you can test more gradients.

5. Click on any gradient in the Grads palette, then click in the middle of the selection.

If you'd like, keep sampling the other gradients in the drawer to see the different effects.

If you'd like to experiment some more, use the Effects ➤ Fill command to change opacities when applying a gradation. In the Fill dialog box, you can click and drag in a preview area to see how the gradation will affect different parts of your image. Before filling, click on the Gradation radio button in the dialog box, and lower the opacity by dragging the Opacity slider to the left. Try creating different effects by filling one gradation over another one with different opacities. Also, try blending a gradation with an image, by lowering the opacity of the gradation and then applying it over the image.

After you've completed your experiments with Painter's drawer of gradations options, you may want to add to the options in the drawer by creating your own custom gradations.

Creating Custom Gradations

Painter's custom gradation options allow you to create gradations from the colors in painted and digitized images. For example, you could create a gradation based upon the colors in a digital image of a bouquet of flowers.

To create a gradation based upon the colors in an image, use the Rectangular Selection tool to select the area of the image you want to use as the basis for your gradation. After the area is selected, choose Capture Gradation from the Tools ➤ Gradations submenu. Instantly, the Save Color Ramp dialog box appears. Enter a name in the Save As field, then click OK. Your new gradation now appears in the Art Materials :Grads palette, and the name you gave it appears in the palette's pop-up menu.

After the gradation appears, you can proceed to apply the gradation in the steps described in the previous section.

Gradations can also be used to replace the luminance (brightness values) of an image. By doing this, you can change a colored image to a grayed-out version of the image, or change the number of colors in an existing gradation. To achieve this effect, open an image on screen, select a gradation in the Art Materials :Grads palette, and, in the Tools menu, choose Gradations ➤ Express in Image. The colors in the image change to the color in the gradation. The luminance levels in the image are now *mapped* to the luminance levels in the gradation.

Using the Edit Gradation Command

Using the Edit Gradation command, you can control and precisely edit gradations to create extremely sophisticated color blends. To open the Edit Gradation dialog box choose Tools ➤ Gradations ➤ Edit Gradations.

In the dialog box, the colored ramp represents the current gradation. As you make adjustments in the dialog box, the ramp updates to reflect any editing changes. The gray markers on the far left and right below the gradation ramp represent the endpoint colors of the gradation. You can change an endpoint color by first clicking on the triangular marker to select it and then picking a new color in the Colors palette. You can add intermediate key colors to the ramp by clicking on the bottom of the gradation ramp bar. This creates another triangular marker below the bar. When one of these markers is selected, you can change colors using the Art Materials :Colors palette. If you wish to delete an intermediate key color, click on the appropriate triangular marker, then press the Delete key.

By default, Painter creates a blend using a linear transition between colors. If you deselect the Linear check box, you are then able to change the curve of the range for an endpoint or intermediate color by dragging the Color Spread slider. Dragging right adds more of the endpoint or intermediate key color; dragging left subtracts the color.

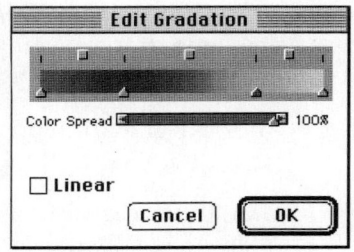

The tiny square box or boxes above the gradation indicate the midpoint between endpoint or intermediate colors. Each time you create a new triangular marker, a new rectangular midpoint box is created. When a midpoint box is selected, you can change the *colorspace* of the gradation using the Color pop-up menu. If you choose the RGB option, Painter creates the blend between the endpoint or intermediate colors based upon the RGB color space. In this three-dimensional color space, each RGB color can be plotted within a cube defined by each RGB color in the RGB color gamut.

When RGB is chosen, Painter picks the three RGB coordinates of one color and creates the blend through the colors that lead to the RGB coordinates of the other. If you choose Hue Clockwise, the blend is created using colors traveling clockwise around the Hue wheel. The Hue Counterclockwise choice creates the blend counterclockwise around the color wheel.

Once you've completed editing your gradation, click OK. This changes the current gradation in the Art Materials :Grads palette to the gradation you just created. You can now fill with this gradation and save it in the Art Materials :Color palette, if desired.

Creating and Loading Custom Gradation Libraries

Once you've saved custom gradations, you can create your own library of gradations. To create a library, choose Tools ➤ Movers. Then click on the Gradations Mover submenu. This opens the Gradation Mover dialog box.

To create a new library, click the New button in the Gradation Mover dialog box. Name your library in the dialog box that appears, then click Save. To move gradations into the library, click on the gradation name, then click the Copy button. To exit the dialog box, click Quit.

To load a gradation library, click on the Library button that appears in the Grads palette drawer. After you click on the Library button, the Open dialog box appears. Next open the Colors, Grads, Weaves folder (Windows users: the Supplies directory) to locate the Grads library you created. When you open the folder, you'll see another custom gradations library that was copied to your hard disk when Painter was installed. If you wish to reload the default grads, double-click on the Painter Settings file (the file is located in the same folder as Painter).

Now that you've learned how to create your own gradations, proceed to the next section to experiment with creating a gradation as the background for a cartoon scene.

Practice: Cartoon Character Using Gradations

In this section you'll create a cartoon image like that shown in Figure 2.6, by applying a gradation to the entire canvas and then creating a cartoon character (we call him Mister Pencil) using the Brushes palette.

1. Start by creating a new file 7 inches wide by 4 inches high. Set the image resolution to 75 ppi.

2. Your next step is to create a gradation. If the Art Materials :Grads palette is not open on screen, open it by choosing Art Materials from the Window menu. Next click on the Grads icon in the palette.

3. For an unusual color burst gradation effect, choose the Color Table gradation from the Grads pop-up menu.

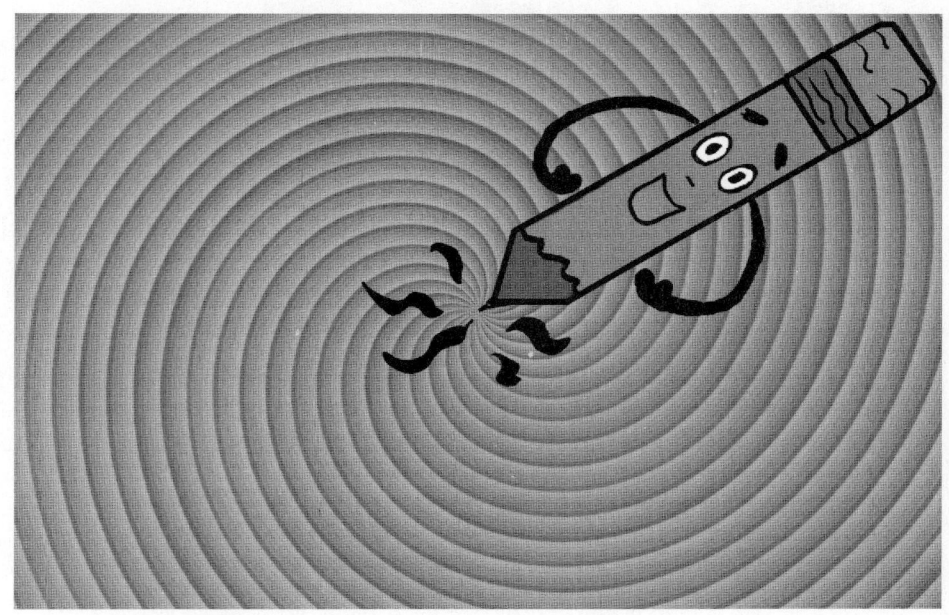

FIGURE 2.6: Cartoon character project

After you've picked a gradation pattern, your next step is to pick a gradation *type*.

4. To access the Type icon choices, close the palette drawer. Next click on the spiral icon (bottom right) in the Types group.

5. Fill the canvas with the gradation by choosing Fill from the Edit menu. In the Fill dialog box, click on Gradation and set the Opacity slider to 100%.

After you've applied the gradation, you can now create the cartoon character.

6. Choose a brush in the Brushes palette. If the Brushes palette is not open, open it by choosing Brushes from the Window menu. Click on the Pens pop-up menu in the Brushes palette, then choose Smooth Ink Pen from the variant pop-up menu. Set the Method pop-up menu to Cover and the Subcategory pop-up menu to Soft Cover.

7. Since the sketch of Mister Pencil consists of a triangle and three rectangles, as seen in Figure 2.7, change the Draw Style in the Controls :Brush palette from Freehand to Straight Lines by clicking on the Straight Lines radio button.

8. Use the Smooth Ink Pen variant to create the outline of the pencil character.

◆ In Figure 2.7 the pencil body and eraser were created with the Charcoal brush in the Brushes palette. After the sketch of Mr. Pencil is complete, change the primary color to orange, then paint the longest rectangle (the body of the pencil).

◆ Next choose Charcoal in the Brushes palette pop-up menu. Set the variant to Default. The Method pop-up menu should be set to Cover and the Method Subcategory pop-up menu set to Soft Cover.

◆ Fill the top rectangle (the eraser area) with pink and the other two shapes with gray.

9. For the finishing touches, use the Pens brush, Pen and Ink variant with the Method pop-up menu set to Cover and the Method Subcategory pop-up menu set to Soft Cover to add the facial features and arms.

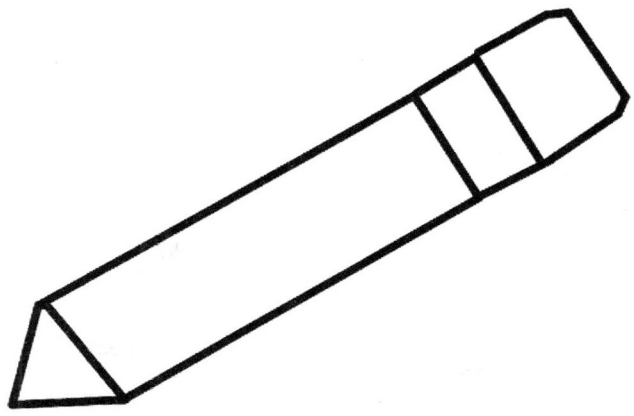

FIGURE 2.7: Basic shapes used to sketch Mister Pencil, the cartoon character

Working with Weaves

One of Painter's unusual mixed-media features is its ability to fill areas with weaves and change the colors of the weaves. These weaves can be used for background textures, unusual patterns, and even fashion designs.

To work with a weave you must first click on the Weaves icon at the top of the Art Materials palette. As soon as you click, the Art Materials palette changes to display the Weaves choices.

The steps for choosing and filling your canvas with weaves are virtually identical to the steps for picking and painting with a gradation.

Picking a Weave

The Weaves drawer front displays five different weave patterns. To see all the weaves available in the weave, click on the drawer handle to open the drawer. After the drawer opens, Painter displays its woven goods. Click on each weave to see its name appear in the palette's pop-up menu. The names *Satin Diamonds*, *Fancy Pattern*, and *Star Maze* provide a sense of the effects that the weaves produce.

Assume that you wish to apply the Buchanan weave. To select the weave, click on the icon that resembles a tartan kilt pattern. If you can't locate the weave visually, choose it by name in the palette pop-up menu. After the weave is selected, notice that it appears in the drawer front surrounded by a red

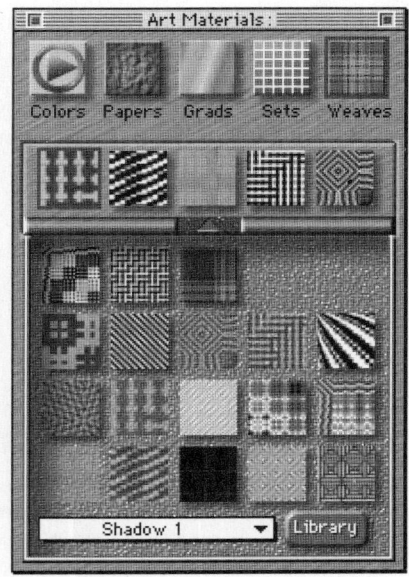

border. At this point, you could use the Paint Bucket or the Edit ➤ Fill command to apply the weave to your canvas, but before applying the weave, you may wish to change colors or the thickness of the weave.

Changing the Color of a Weave

The color of any of Painter's default weaves can be changed to fit in with any color scheme. Here's how to change the color of the Buchanan weave that you chose in the last section.

1. In order to access the weave's color options, close the Art Materials :Weaves drawer. To close the drawer, click on the drawer handle.

2. In order to change the color of a weave, open the Color Set palette of the selected weave. To open this palette, click on the Get Color button in the Weaves palette.

Next you need to pick the color you wish to add to the weave from the Art Materials :Colors palette.

3. In the Art Materials palette, click on the Colors icon to display the Colors palette. Using the color ring and triangle, pick a color that you wish to add to the weave.

4. To replace one weave color with another, press and hold the Option key (Windows users: Alt key), and, while still holding it down, click on the color in the weave's color set that you wish to replace. After you click, the primary color from the Colors palette replaces the color in the weaves color set.

5. To see a preview of how the color will look in the weave, click the Put Color button in the Art Materials :Weaves palette. The sample weave in the palette changes to reflect the color change.

6. Click the Save button to save your weave. In the dialog box that appears, enter a new name for the weave so that you don't replace the original.

Changing Weave Thickness and Scaling

When the Weaves palette is expanded and the drawer front is closed, you can access a set of sliders that allows you to change the thickness of the weave thread and the distance between the threads. If you don't see the sliders, click on the zoom box at the top right of the palette to expand the palette, and then click on the drawer handle to close the drawer.

The H Scale and V Scale sliders allow you to control the distance between the threads. The H Thick and V Thick sliders allow you to change the width of the threads. (The H and V stand for Horizontal and Vertical.)

To see the effects of enlarging the weave thickness, change both the H and V Thick slider to three. This will triple the horizontal and vertical thickness of the weave. Notice, once again, that Painter previews the weave change in the palette.

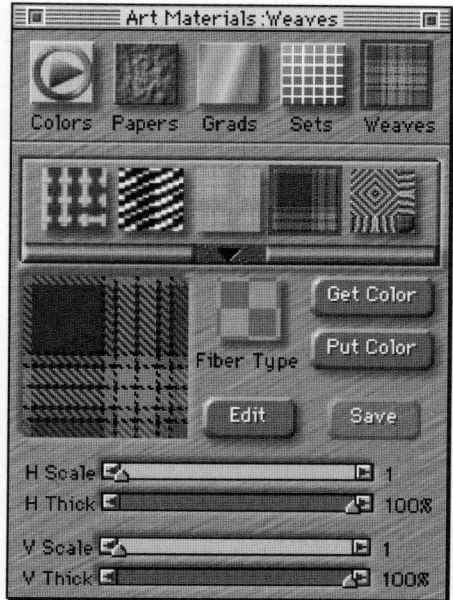

Note *If you wish to return to any weave that you edited back to its default settings, click on the Weaves palette's Library button in the palette drawer, then load the Painter Settings file.*

Note *You can edit the weaving of any pattern by clicking on the Edit button in the Weaves palette. This opens the Edit Weaving dialog box. Here you can edit the pattern by using a special "Weaving language" created by Fractal Design. This language is explained in Painter Tech Note number 4, which can be loaded from the Painter 3 Extras CD ROM.*

Saving Weaves and Creating a New Library

Once you've changed a weave's color, thickness, or scaling you can save the new weave so it can be used at another time. Once the weave is saved, it is automatically added to both the Weaves palette and the Weaves pop-up menu. To save the weave, click on the Save button in the Weaves palette. Enter a name in the Save Weaving dialog box that appears. The weave name can also be added to a library. The steps for creating a library of weaves are virtually the same as creating a library of gradations. To create the library, choose Tools ➤ Movers ➤ Weaving Mover. In the Weaving Mover dialog box, click the New button. Name the New library, then click the OK button. Your next step is to select a weave to add to the library. After doing this, click the Copy button. Move all of the weaves you wish into the library, then click Quit to exit the Weaving Mover dialog box.

Applying Weaves

You can apply weaves the same way you apply gradations: You can apply a weave by using the Effects ➤ Fill command or by using the Paint Bucket. If you wish to apply the weave to a selection on screen, first create a selection using the Rectangular or Oval Selection tools. If you wish to use the Paint Bucket, activate it in the Tools palette, then choose the Fill With Weaving and What To Fill Image options in the Controls:Paint Bucket palette. Then click within the selection with the Paint Bucket. To use the Fill command, choose Effects ➤ Fill. If you use the Effects ➤ Fill command, click on the Weaving radio button in the Fill dialog box that appears, and choose an opacity.

> **Tip** *With no selection onscreen and the Paint Bucket selected (with the Weaving and Image option selected in the Controls :Paint Bucket palette), you can drag to create a rectangular shape to apply a weave.*

Practice: Le Café Advertisement Using Weaves

In this section, you'll create an advertisement for a fictional restaurant called Le Café, as shown in Figure 2.8, by applying a weave to an entire canvas, then creating a coffee mug using the Brushes palette.

1. Start by creating a new file 5 inches by 5 inches with a resolution of 75 pixels per inch.

After the new canvas appears on screen, your next step is to apply a weave. Before you can apply a weave, you need to display the Weaves palette and open its drawer.

2. Choose the Shadow 1 weave from the Weaves pop-up menu.

Now you're ready to apply the weave.

FIGURE 2.8: Coffee mug on tweed

3. To apply the Weave, choose Fill from the Effects menu. After the Fill dialog box opens, click on the Weaving radio button, set the Opacity slider to 100%, then click OK to apply it.

After you've applied the weave, try creating the coffee mug using the selection tools and an Airbrush brush:

4. Create the top part of the mug as an oval selection using the Oval Selection tool. Once the selection is created, move it into position using the Path Adjuster tool (the arrow icon).

5. Change the primary color to brown, then fill the selection on screen with brown using the Effects ➤ Fill command. (When the Fill dialog box appears, choose the Current Color option and click OK, to fill the selection with the current primary color.)

6. With the selection still on screen, use the Airbrush with the variant pop-up menu set to Thin Stroke, the Method pop-up menu set to Cover, and the Method Subcategory pop-up menu set to Soft Cover. Then change the primary painting color to a light golden color to create a rim around the mug. As you paint with the Airbrush around the rim, the selection acts as a mask, preventing the color from spilling beyond it.

Tip *If you accidentally apply too much light golden color to the rim, you can quickly change the primary painting color back to brown using the Dropper tool. With the Airbrush activated, press the Command key (Windows users: Ctrl key) to change the Airbrush icon to the Dropper icon, and then click on the brown color. This changes the painting color to brown. To change the painting color back to the light golden color, press the same key again and click on the light golden color.*

Next you will deselect the oval selection, so that you can continue to create the outline for the mug.

7. To deselect, choose Edit ➤ Deselect or press Command+D (Windows users: Ctrl+D). Instantly the selection disappears.

8. Click on the Brush tool in the Tools palette to continue to use the Airbrush. Use the Airbrush to create the outline of the mug. Before you begin, change the primary painting color to a dark golden color and set the Draw Style in the Controls :Brushes palette to Straight Lines. Use the Airbrush to create an open rectangle:

◆ Start at the top left-hand corner of the rim of the mug and draw a straight vertical line,

◆ then draw a straight horizontal line,

◆ and finally another straight vertical line that ends at the top right-hand corner of the rim of the mug.

9. Use the Rectangular Selection tool to create a rectangle for the inside of the mug. Then create a two-point gradation using the light golden and dark golden colors. Set the primary painting rectangle to the light golden color and the secondary painting rectangle to the dark golden color. Before applying the gradation to the rectangular selection, make sure that Two-Point gradation is the selected icon in the Grads palette, the type is set to Linear, and the angle is set to 190 degrees. Use the Fill command to fill the selection. This will fill the selection with a gradation from light to dark.

Note *You'll learn more about how to use the Oval Selection tool and the Path Adjuster tool in Chapter 7, and the Rectangular Selection tool in Chapter 8.*

10. After you've filled the gradation, click away, using the Path Adjuster tool to deselect the selection. Use the Airbrush to paint the areas that don't have any color and to soften the edges of the gradation.

11. Use the Oval Selection tool again to create the curve that you can use as a guide for the handle of the mug. After the selection is created and is in the position you want, pick a painting color and use the Airbrush tool to paint the handle as seen in Figure 2.8. Refer back to steps 6, 7, and 8 to create a selection, move a selection, paint inside a selection, and deselect a selection.

12. Continue to use the Airbrush for the finishing touches, such as the steam coming out of the coffee mug and some shadow effects. You might want to use the Fat Stroke variant when creating the shadow effects, since its brush size is larger than the Thin Stroke variant.

Wrapping It Up

Now that you've learned the basics of picking and using colors, you're ready to explore the countless ways that color can be applied with painter's versatile brushes. In the next chapter, you'll learn what each of Painter's brushes can do and how they can be customized to create precisely the artistic effects you desire.

Using and Customizing Brushes

Using the correct brush makes a world of difference in every image you paint. Some brushes are better for sketching, while others are best suited for painting with water colors, applying washes, or adding detail. Some brushes paint with a soft stroke, some with hard strokes; some paint with close even bristles, others paint with bristles spread out like a rake.

Painter's vast array of brushes provides you with virtually limitless freedom. You can create a sketch, and then paint over it using watercolors, chalk, felt pens, or other brushes. You can paint over a digitized photograph to completely transform it into a painterly version of its former self. You can even make pieces of digital images flow out of a brush called an *Image Hose*.

In order to pick just the right brush to attain your artistic goals, you must familiarize yourself with the Brushes palette. In Chapters 1 and 2 you began your exploration of this abundant palette. In this chapter, you'll see how truly versatile the palette is, and how its brushes interact with other palettes, such as the Papers palette, the Brush Controls palette, and the Advanced Controls palette.

Exploring the Brushes in the Brushes Palette

The Brushes palette features 18 brushes, listed below in the order that they appear in the Brushes palette pop-up menu. Each brush paints in a different manner, simulating its real-life counterpart—if a real-life counterpart exists.

Pencils	Felt Pens	Cloners
Eraser	Crayons	Water Color
Water	Airbrush	Burn
Chalk	Liquid	Dodge
Charcoal	Brush	Masking
Pens	Artists	Image Hose

As you've seen from Chapters 1 and 2, Painter not only allows you to just pick a brush, it also provides numerous *variants* to vary how each brush paints; as well as a Method Category and Method Subcategory that controls how paint is applied.

The chapter is structured to help you understand exactly how paint flows from each brush, and what effects each of its variants, method categories, and subcategories produces. After you've learned about each brush, you'll learn how to customize brush components like size, spacing, and bristles to create your own variants.

But before you get started exploring the world of brush dabs, strokes, and bristles, you'll need a tool to help you quickly preview your brush strokes—the Brush Look Designer.

Using the Brush Look Designer

The Brush Look Designer is undoubtedly one of Painter's most helpful features. By providing a small window where you can test brush strokes, the Brush Look Designer helps you to quickly and easily understand exactly how all of Painter's various brush settings interact. As you read through this chapter you'll be able to use the Brush Look Designer to quickly try out sample strokes.

The following paragraphs will help you get started using the Brush Look Designer.

Before using the Brush Look Designer choose your painting color from the Art Materials :Colors palette (covered in Chapter 2).

Next, choose a brush in the Brushes palette.

Click on the Water Color brush icon or click on the Brushes pop-up menu and choose Water Color. If you'd like to use the Water Color brush but have no idea what the difference could be between the Simple Water, Diffuse Water, and Spatter Water variants, let alone the difference between Large Simple Water, Broad Water Brush, and Water Brush Stroke, you can preview the strokes with the Brush Look Designer.

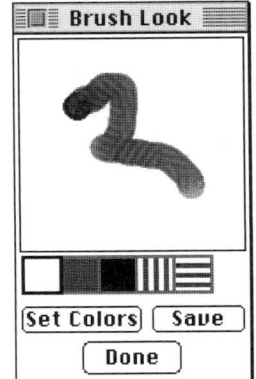

To open the Brush Look Designer, choose Brushes from the Tools menu. In the Brushes submenu, choose Brush Look Designer. This opens the Brush Look Designer dialog box. The stroke in the dialog box is a preview of the stroke of the brush selected in the Brushes palette. Click and drag in the preview area to create a new stroke. Immediately the stroke shows how the currently selected brush paints.

The color swatches below the Brush Look area are used for changing the background canvas color of the Brush Look Designer dialog box. The colors in the dialog box are based on the primary and secondary colors currently selected in the Art Materials :Colors palette. Click on a different color swatch to see the brush stroke over a different-colored background canvas.

> **Note** *In order to preview several of the variants presented in this chapter, you will may need to use either a colored or striped background, especially if you are using the Eraser, Water, or Liquid brushes. That's because there are brushes that don't always paint with a color; instead, they mix with your image's color.*

For best results when previewing a stroke with the Brush Look Designer,

◆ use a striped background when the Method Category is set for Drip.

◆ use a striped or colored background when the Method Category is set to Eraser.

If you wish to change the colors in the Brush Look Designer, pick new primary and secondary painting colors in the Art Materials :Colors palette. Changing the primary color also changes the brush stroke in the Brush Look Designer dialog box to the primary painting color. Then click on the Set Colors button in the Brush Look Designer dialog box. If at this point both the brush stroke and background colors are the same, you may wish to change the primary painting color one more time so that the brush stroke color is different from the background color.

> **Note** *You'll learn how to save brushes using the Brush Look Designer later in this chapter when the Advanced Brush palette is discussed.*

Now change the variant in the Brushes palette. Immediately the stroke in the Brush Look Designer is repainted to reflect the change in the Brushes palette. Switch to the Spatter Water variant and notice the change. Next change opacity in the Controls palette. Again the Brush Look Designer previews the change. To see a more drastic change, click on the Artists icon or choose Artists from the Brushes palette's pop-up menu. The Brush Look Designer responds by previewing the stroke.

Now that you have a quick means of previewing Painter's brush options, read through the following charts and preview each brush. Take your pick of the variants, Method Categories, and Method Subcategories.

The Brushes and Brush Variants

In the traditional art world, artists paint with different types of brushes, different types of pens, different types of airbrushes. Painter meets the demands for different brush tools by providing a set of variants for each brush. Since the variants are hidden in a pop-up menu, it's often quite time-consuming to choose exactly which variant suits the job at hand.

Use the charts that follow to quickly help you differentiate between variants so that you can efficiently pick the ones you need while painting.

Each chart begins with a brief description of the brush and then lists each variant for the brush. Along with each variant is a brief description of how it paints. As you read through the chapter, be sure to try out the variants that interest you, by painting a test stroke in the Brush Look Designer window.

> **Note** *When you choose a brush or brush variant, Painter automatically selects a default Method Category, specifically chosen to make the brush emulate traditional media. Choosing a different Method Category allows you to produce results that may be quite different, depending on the brush or variant, from those produced by the brush's default settings.*

Understanding Anti-Aliasing

In the Brush charts that appear in this chapter, you'll frequently see the words *anti-aliased*. As discussed in Chapter 1, anti-aliasing softens brush strokes by lightening the colors of the pixels that constitute the edge of a stroke. A semi–anti-aliased brush produces only slight smoothing. An aliased brush is a hard-edged brush with no anti-aliasing applied.

The Pencils Brush

The Pencils brush simulates drawing with a pencil. As you draw with the pencil each variant can be made to gradually darken to black. The pencil variants also can interact with paper grain. The most unusual variant is Thick & Thin Pencils. The illustration below shows the Thick & Thin Pencils variant with the Method Category set to Cover and the Method Subcategory set to Flat Cover.

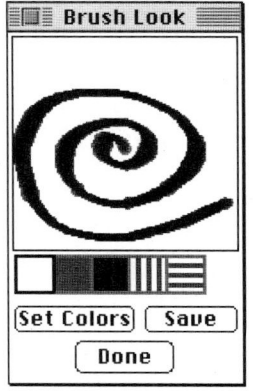

Note *This illustration and the others in this chapter were created using a stylus. If you are using a mouse instead of a stylus, your paint strokes may look somewhat different because many of Painter's brushes react to the pressure applied to a stylus. For instance, when pressure is applied to a stylus many paint strokes become more opaque and less paper grain is shown. If you don't have a stylus, remember that opacity and paper grain can be set in the Controls palette.*

Remember, if you're using a stylus you'll want to use the Brush Tracking dialog box (choose Brush Tracking from the Edit ➤ Preference submenu) to set the pressure and speed of how your stylus works in Painter.

Here are the variants for the Pencils brush.

Variant	Description
2B Pencil	Thin anti-aliased soft lead
500 lb Period	Thick, semi–anti-aliased lines
Colored Pencils	Semi–anti-aliased edges
Sharp Pencil	Hard lead, semi–anti-aliased lines
Single Pixel Scribbler	1-pixel-wide stroke. Add pressure to increase opacity.
Thick & Thin Pencils	Semi–anti-aliased; stroke varies from thick to thin, depending upon stroke direction

The Eraser Brush

The Eraser allows you to erase using the paper color as well as lighten or darken colors to produce highlights and shadows. To preview the different eraser variants when using the Brush Look Designer, use a colored or striped background. The following illustration shows the Flat Eraser variant with the Method Category set to Eraser and the Method Subcategory set to Soft Paper Color.

Here are the variants for the Eraser brush.

Variant	Description
Flat Eraser	Erases with paper color using hard edges
Fat Eraser	Erases with paper color using thick stroke. Fat, Medium, Small, and Ultra-fine Eraser erase with the paper color, using soft edges.
Medium Eraser	Erases with paper color, medium stroke
Small Eraser	Erases with paper color, small stroke
Ultrafine Eraser	Erases with paper color, hairline stroke
Fat Bleach	Thick stroke erasing to white. Fat, Medium, Small, Ultrafine, and Single-Pixel Bleach erase to white. How quickly it erases to white is controlled by the Opacity slider in the Controls palette. It uses soft edges.
Medium Bleach	Medium stroke erasing to white
Small Bleach	Small stroke erasing to white
Ultrafine Bleach	Hairline stroke erasing to white
Single Pixel Bleach	Single-pixel stroke erasing to white
Fat Darkener	Fat Stroke erasing to black. Fat, Medium, Small, and Ultrafine Darkener erase to black using soft edges. How quickly it erases to black is controlled by the Opacity slider in the Controls palette.
Medium Darkener	Medium stroke erasing to black
Small Darkener	Small stroke erasing to black
Ultrafine Darkener	Hairline stroke erasing to black

The Water Brush

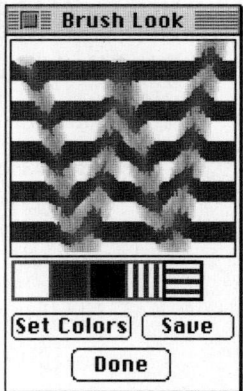

Water simulates diluting an image with water. Water does not paint with the primary color; instead, it smears pre-existing colors to make it look as though water was added to the brush stroke. To preview the different water variants when using the Brush Look Designer, use a striped background. The following illustration shows the Just Add Water variant with the Method Category set to Drip and the Method Subcategory set to Grainy Hard Drip.

Here are the variants for the Water brush.

Variant	Description
Big Frosty Water	Similar to the Frosty Water option, but creates larger strokes
Frosty Water	Adds water and smears colors together using a hard-edged bristle stroke
Grainy Water	Adds water with active paper texture
Just Add Water	Adds water and blends colors together using a smooth anti-aliased stroke
Single Pixel water	Adds water in one-pixel increments
Tiny Frosty Water	Works the same way the Frosty Water does, but instead uses a sharper stroke
Water Rake	Applies water using multibristles; can be adjusted in the Advanced Controls :Rake palette
Water Spray	Sprinkles water in one-pixel increments

The Chalk Brush

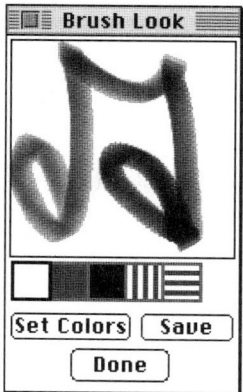

Chalk simulates the texture and look of pastels. When using a stylus, applying more pressure adds more opacity to the stroke. The following illustration shows the Oil Pastel variant with the Method Category set to Buildup and the Method Subcategory set to Soft Variable Buildup.

Here are the variants for the Chalk brush.

Variant	Description
Artist Pastel Chalk	Medium, semi–anti-aliased stroke
Large Chalk	A thick version of the Artist Pastel Chalk
Oil Pastel	Smears and paints at the same time, with a triangular chiseled edge
Sharp Chalk	A sharp version of the Artist Pastel Chalk
Square Chalk	Strokes with a rectangular chiseled edge

The Charcoal Brush

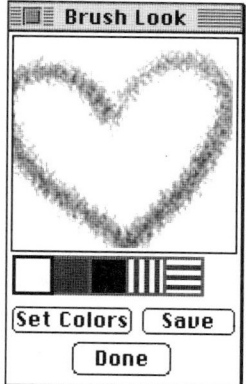

Charcoal simulates traditional charcoal, and thus is often used for sketching. When using the stylus, applying more pressure adds more opacity, and allows less paper grain to show through the charcoal stroke. Charcoal strokes can also interact with paper grain. The following illustration shows the Default variant with the Method Category set to Cover and the Method Subcategory set to Grainy Hard Cover.

Here are the variants for the Charcoal brush.

Variant	Description
Default	Semi–anti-aliased strokes
Gritty Charcoal	Semi–anti-aliased strokes, with strokes varying from thick to thin depending upon the direction of the stroke
Soft Charcoal	Soft anti-aliased strokes

The Pens Brush

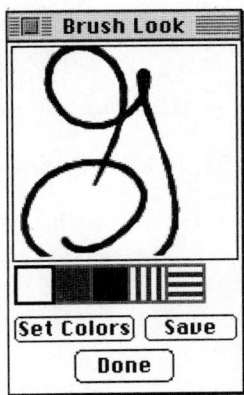

The Pens brush simulates drawing with a ballpoint or fountain pen. The following illustration shows the Pen and Ink variant with the Method Category set to Cover and the Method Subcategory set to Soft Cover.

Here are the variants for the Pens brush.

Variant	Description
Calligraphy	Simulates the strokes of a calligraphic pen
Fine Point	Simulates the strokes of a ballpoint pen
Flat Color	Creates thick strokes
Leaky Pen	Creates strokes resembling a leaky pen
Pen and Ink	Allows you to vary the width of your stroke by how fast you drag your stylus or mouse. Faster strokes produce thinner strokes. Slower strokes produce thicker strokes.

Variant	Description
Pixel Dust	Creates a dustlike stroke out of random sprays of pixels
Scratchboard Rake	This tool is similar to the Scratchboard tool (next on this list), except that it creates a multilined stroke. This option is good for creating crosshatching. Settings can be adjusted in the Advanced Controls :Rake palette.
Scratchboard Tool	If you paint with a light color on a black background it simulates a woodcut effect. Strokes change depending upon how hard you press the stylus. More pressure produces thicker strokes. Lighter pressure produces thinner strokes.
Single Pixel	Creates a single-pixel stroke
Smooth Ink Pen	Simulates the stroke of a fountain pen and inkwell

The Felt Pens Brush

The Felt Pens brush simulates a traditional felt pen. Overlaying felt pen strokes can gradually turn a color to black. When using a stylus, applying more pressure increases opacity. The following illustration shows the Felt Marker variant with the Method Category set to Buildup and the Method Subcategory set to Soft Variable Buildup.

Here are the variants for the Felt Pens brush.

Variant	Description
Dirty Marker	Change the width of this stroke by changing the angle of the stroke
Felt Marker	This stroke provides a softer shade than the Felt Pen. You can change the width of the stroke by changing the angle of the stroke.
Fine Tip Felt Pens	Draws narrow stroke. Pressure determines opacity.
Medium Tip Felt Pens	Similar to the Fine Tip Felt Pens but you can change the stroke by varying how fast you paint. Faster strokes produce thinner strokes. Slower strokes produce thicker strokes.
Single Pixel Marker	Creates single pixel strokes. Pressure determines opacity.

The Crayons Brush

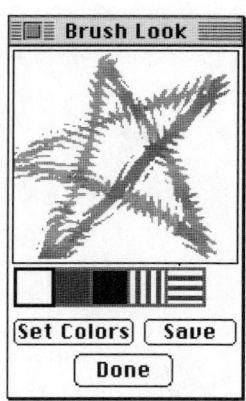

Crayons simulate traditional crayons, producing semi–anti-aliased strokes. Strokes get darker as you paint and interact with paper grain. Applying more pressure to a stylus increases opacity and decreases interaction with paper grain. The following illustration shows the Waxy Crayon variant with the Method Category set to Cover and the Method Subcategory set to Grainy Edge Flat Cover.

Here are the variants for the Crayons brush.

Variant	Description
Default	Simulates a crayon. Applying strokes on top of each other gradually builds up to darker colors. With stylus, pressure determines opacity and grain.

Variant	Description
Waxy Crayons	Smears painting color with underlying color. With stylus, pressure determines opacity and grain.

The Airbrush Brush

The Airbrush simulates a traditional airbrush by producing a delicate spray. The following illustration shows the Thin Stroke variant with the Method Category set to Cover and the Method Subcategory set to Soft Cover.

Here are the variants for the Airbrush brush.

Variant	Description
Fat Stroke	Large soft anti-aliased stroke
Feather Tip	Soft, anti-aliased strokes with varying widths
Single Pixel Air	Single-pixel spray
Spatter Airbrush	Paper-grain-sensitive with semi–anti-aliased stroke; adds random texture to stroke
Thin Stroke	Thin, soft, anti-aliased stroke

The Liquid Brush

Liquid brushes create a smearing effect, as shown in the following illustration, which uses the Distorto variant with the Method Category set to Drip and the Method Subcategory set to Drip. The Liquid brushes can also create an effect of paint being applied with a palette knife. Adjust the Opacity slider to vary the effect. If Opacity is set to 0%, Liquid brushes can create a floating, "liquidy" effect.

Here are the variants for the Liquid brush.

Variant	Description
Coarse Distorto	Moves paint but doesn't add color; semi–anti-aliased stroke
Coarse Smeary Bristles	Coarse semi–anti-aliased smear
Coarse Smeary Mover	Coarse version of Smeary mover (three options down on this list); doesn't add new paint
Distorto	Moves paint but doesn't add color. Drag mouse or stylus quickly to produce thin stroke; drag slowly to prduce thick stroke.
Smeary Bristles	Smears color into the canvas, paper-grain-sensitive
Smeary Mover	Smears existing rather than new paint
Thick Oil	Smears with thick paint
Tiny Smudge	One-pixel multibristle smudge
Total Oil Brush	More condensed Smears than those produced by Smeary Bristels

The Brush Brush

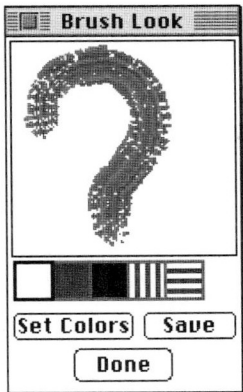

The Brush brush simulates painting with oils and acrylics. When using a stylus, most brushes increase opacity when more pressure is applied, and show less paper grain when more pressure is applied. The following illustration shows the Oil Paint variant with the Method Category set to Cover and the Method Subcategory set to Grainy Edge Flat Cover.

Here are the variants for the Brush brush.

Variant	Description
Big Loaded Oils	Wider version of Loaded Oils
Big Rough Out	Wider stroke than Rough Out option (see later in this list)
Big Wet Oils	Mixes with underlying colors
Brushy	Multibristle; absorbs colors it is dragged over; color depletes at stroke's end
Camel hair Brush	Soft, anti-aliased
Coarse Hairs	Small coarse hairs; size changes based on pressure
Cover Brush	Soft anti-aliased; does not interact with paper grain
Digital Sumi	Multiple single-bristle brush stroke
Fine Brush	Very fine-hair brush; size changes based on pressure
Graduated Brush	Semi–anti-aliased; interacts with paper grain; can paint with primary and secondary colors if more pressure is applied with stylus

Variant	Description
Hairy Brush	Semi–anti-aliased; paints hairy lines; shows paper grain
Huge Rough Out	Wider stroke than Big Rough Out (see above in this list)
Loaded Oils	Simulates stroke of a brush dipped in different colors
Oil Paint	Hard, aliased; interacts with paper grain
Penetration Brush	Hard, aliased; shows paper grain
Rough Out	For "roughing out ideas"; a dry brush that produces thinner lines the faster you drag a stylus; paper-grain-sensitive
Sable Chisel Tip Water	Fine; smears colors
Small Loaded Oils	Narrow version of Loaded Oil (see above in this list)
Smaller Wash Brush	Fine, with bristles close together; smears primary color with underlying colors
Ultrafine Wash Brush	Like Smaller Wash Brush (immediately above in this list), but wider

The Artists Brush

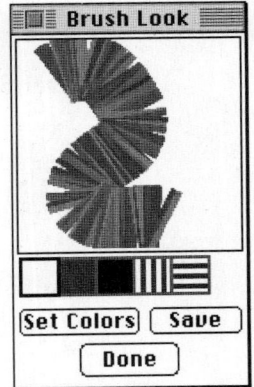

The Artists brush simulates the strokes of famous artists and piano keys. The following illustration shows the Piano Keys variant with the Method Category set to Cover and the Method Subcategory set to Grainy Hard Cover.

Here are the variants for the Artists brush.

Variant	Description
Auto Van Gogh	Works with the Effects :Esoterica palette to turn an entire image into a Van Gogh painting
Flemish Rub	Impressionistic smear of existing color; doesn't paint with primary color
Impressionist	Impressionist painting style
Piano Keys	Ribbonlike brush stroke
Seurat	Multicolored anti-aliased dots à la Seurat
Van Gogh	Multicolored anti-aliased à la Vincent Van Gogh

The Cloners Brush

Cloners allow you transform digital images into paintings and automatically clone (copy) one part of an image into another. These brushes are covered in Chapter 6.

Here are the variants for the Cloners brush.

Variant	Description
Chalk Cloner	Paints the clone with the same effect as the Artist Pastel Brush variant
Driving Rain Cloner	Creates a clone as if seen through a window with drops of rain
Felt Pen Cloner	Recreates the clone as if painting with a felt-tipped pen.
Hairy Cloner	Clones using brush strokes that show the brush lines of the brush, semi–anti-aliased brush strokes that can interact with paper grain

Variant	Description
Hard Oil Cloner	Clones with a hard-edged brush stroke that covers underlying brush strokes and can allow paper grain to show through the strokes
Impressionist Cloner	Provides an Impressionist effect by painting with short brush strokes in various colors taken from the source image
Melt Cloner	Clones by creating dripping brush strokes that can make an image appear as if it is melting
Oil Brush Cloner	Clones with anti-aliased brush strokes that cover underlying brush strokes
Pencil Sketch Cloner	Clones with a pencil-like brush
Soft Cloner	Clones with an airbrush type of stroke
Straight Cloner	Creates an exact duplicate of the original cloned image. Use this brush if you are working with another brush and wish to paint back the original image on screen.
Van Gogh Cloner	Clones with multicolored brush strokes using a Van Gogh style

The Water Color Brush

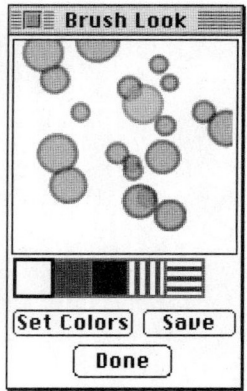

Water Color brush variants simulate painting with watercolors. When using Water Color brush variants, Painter automatically places you into a "wet" layer. This allows you to paint over and see an underlying image through your watercolors. While you paint, any editing affects only the Wet layer. When you've finished your painting, you can choose Dry from the Canvas menu, which "dries" the paint into one layer with the underlying image. For more information about using Water Color, see Chapter 6. The following illustration shows the Spatter Water variant with the Method Category set to Wet and the Method Subcategory set to Grainy Wet Abrasive.

Here are the variants for the Water Color brush.

Variant	Description
Broad Water Brush	Wide stroke, shows bristles
Diffuse Water	Brush edges diffuse the paint
Large Simple Water	Larger version of Simple Water (in this list)
Large Water	See-through watercolor stroke
Pure Water Brush	Adds water; not color
Simple Water	Watercolor stroke; no bristles
Spatter Brush	Randomly spatters
Water Brush Stroke	Bristle-brush stroke
Wet Eraser	Erases watercolor strokes in wet layer; stylus-sensitive, increasing pressure increases the speed of erasing

The Burn Brush

The Burn brush simulates the Burn darkroom technique, which is used to darken images. See Chapter 5 for more details on using the Burn brush.

The Dodge Brush

The Dodge brush simulates the Dodge darkroom technique, which is used to lighten image areas. See Chapter 5 for more details on using the Dodge brush.

The Masking Brush

The Masking brushes are used to create and edit masks; they are discussed in Chapter 7. Here are the variants for the Masking brush.

Variant	Description
Grainizer	Creates wide, very grainy, anti-aliased brush strokes
Big Masking Pen	Thick anti-aliased brush strokes
Masking Pen	Draws with anti-aliased lines; produces a smooth stroke
Masking Airbrush	Paints with diffused anti-aliased strokes
Masking Chalk	Creates semi–anti-aliased lines reflecting the currently selected paper texture
Single Pixel Masking	Adds or subtracts from mask in single pixel increments

The Image Hose

The Image Hose can create wondrous special effects. With this tool, you can command an endless supply of painted or digital images (or variants of the same image) to flow out of your brush. The images that come out of the Image Hose are based on the contents of a "nozzle" file. Painter comes with various nozzle files; you can also create your own from paintings and digitized images.

The illustration below shows the Clover nozzle with the variant set to Medium Random Linear, the Method Category set to Buildup, and the Method Subcategory set to Grainy Hard Buildup.

To load a nozzle, choose Load Nozzle from the Tools ➤ Image Hose submenu. (NOTE: If the Brush Look Designer is open on screen, you will need to close it first, before executing any menu command). When the Open dialog box appears, locate the Nozzle folder and open a nozzle file. The choices include shamrocks, coins, and splats. (You can also choose a nozzle file from the Nozzles folder on the Painter 3 Extra CD-ROM). Once the Nozzle file is loaded, you can preview the brush stroke with the Brush Look Designer. After you've previewed a Nozzle, click Done on the Brush Look dialog box.

Here are the variants for the Image Hose brush.

Variant	Description
3 Rank R-P-D	Randomness, pressure, and direction are controlled by sliders in the Advanced Brushes palettes.
Small Random Linear	This and the following Random Linear variants select elements from the nozzle file at random but spray the paint in a linear fashion.
Medium Random Linear	see above
Large Random Linear	see above
Small Random Spray	This and the following Random Spray variants spray nozzle file elements randomly. Placement of file elements on screen is random.
Medium Random Spray	see above
Large Random Spray	see above
Small Sequential Linear	This and the following Sequential Linear variants spray nozzle file elements linearly and do not place them randomly on the canvas. Elements of the nozzle file are placed in sequential order. Use the Brush Controls size and spacing palettes to control spacing.
Medium Sequential Linear	see above
Large Sequential Linear	see above

Variant	Description
Small Directional	This and the following Directional variants are controlled by direction settings built into the Nozzle file when it is created.
Medium Directional	see above
Large Directional	see above
Small Luminance Cloner	Paints in the clone according to brightness levels in the clone source. See Chapter 6 for more details.

Note *For more information on the Image Hose brush, see the Advanced Brush palette, Nozzles, section in this chapter. To learn how to create a nozzle out of a movie, see Chapter 11. For information on making a nozzle from a group of floaters, see Chapter 8. To see how to make a nozzle from a grid of images, see Chapter 9.*

The Method Category Pop-up Menu

After you choose a Brush variant, the next level in the Brush choice hierarchy to consider is the Method Category. The Method Category options generally control whether the paint darkens or mixes with previous strokes or whether it simply paints over without changing underlying color.

Each time you choose a Brush variant, the choices in the Method Category change to reflect options specific to the chosen variant. As mentioned earlier, Painter automatically selects a default Method Category when you choose a brush or brush variant. Often this Method Category is the best choice for achieving the optimum effect with the chosen brush. Here's a brief description of each Method Category.

◆ **Buildup**—builds up to black. Each time you paint over a previous stroke, the painting color grows darker.

◆ **Cover**—covers underlying pixels with the primary painting color. If your painting color is set at 100% opacity, painting over a color will not cause the color to darken, but will cover or hide the underlying color.

◆ **Eraser**—erases with the paper color or smears the underlying color.

◆ **Drip**—causes a smearing of the brush stroke.

◆ **Mask**—is used primarily for image editing. Choosing Mask allows you to create and edit masks in Painter's masking layer.

◆ **Cloning**—takes a source to duplicate and allows you to paint with it.

◆ **Wet**—allows you to create watercolor effects. This option works only with the *wet layer*, which is described in the Water Color brush section of this chapter.

The Method Subcategory Pop-up Menu

The Method Subcategory is a further refinement of the Method Category. For instance, assume you chose the Buildup Method category. You can use the Method Subcategory pop-up to specify whether or not you want paper grain to appear as the color builds up. The options in the Method Subcategory menu change depending upon the choice in the Method Category pop-up menu.

Here is a list of Method Subcategories for the first four Method Categories.

Buildup Method	Cover Method	Eraser Method	Drip Method
Soft Buildup	Flat Cover	Soft paper color	Drip
Grainy Soft Buildup	Soft Cover	Soft paint Remover	Hard Drip
Grainy Edge Flat Buildup	Grainy Soft Cover	Soft Paint Thickener	Grainy Drip
Grainy Hard Buildup	Grainy Edge FlatCover	Soft Mask Colorize	Grainy Hard Drip
Soft Variable Buildup	Grainy Hard Cover	Soft Grain Colorize	

Here is a list of Method Subcategories for the rest of the Method Categories.

Mask Method	Cloning Method	Wet Method
Flat Mask Cover	Hard Cover Cloning	Grainy Wet Abrasive
Soft Mask Cover	Soft Cover Cloning	Grainy Wet Buildup
Grainy Hard Mask Cover	Grainy Hard Cover Cloning	Soft Paint Thickener
Grainy Edge Flat Mask Cover	Grainy Soft Cover Cloning	Wet Remove Density
Grainy Soft Mask Cover	Drip	
Linoleum Scribe		

As the preceding lists indicate, you only need to understand a few terms to interpret the Method Subcategories. They are combinations of the following terms.

◆ **Soft**—Maintains the soft edges of the brush strokes. This is an anti-aliased brush stroke.

◆ **Flat**—Hard-edged strokes.

◆ **Hard**—Semi–anti-aliased.

◆ **Grainy**—Shows the paper grain (but hides underlying brush strokes).

◆ **Edge**—Thick, sticky appearance.

◆ **Variable**—First strokes are more transparent.

◆ **Soft Paint Remover**—Erases by whitening brush strokes. Available when Eraser brush or Dodge brush is selected.

◆ **Soft Paint Thickener**—Thickens color in image. Does not use the primary color set in the Art Materials colors palette.

◆ **Soft Mask Colorize**—Uses the primary and secondary colors to replace positive and negative areas of the mask you are painting over. See Chapter 7 for more details.

◆ **Grainy Wet Abrasive**—Works with Wet layer. Your strokes replace the underlying colors. The effect resembles actual watercolors. Paper grain is visible.

◆ **Soft Grain Colorize**—Paints with bleached primary color and shows paper grain.

◆ **Linoleum Scribe**—Removes masked area.

As you've seen in this section, paper grain plays a role in a brush's stroke. Once you begin choosing Method Subcategories that interact with paper grain, you can further customize your brush strokes by choosing and editing paper grain.

Working with Papers

If you wish to control the type of paper grain that appears in a brush's stroke, you need to take a brief stopover in the Art Materials :Papers palette. The Art Materials :Papers palette allows you to choose paper textures from a drawer full of choices or a library full of papers on disk.

To pick a paper, you must first click on the Papers icon at the front of the drawer in the Art Materials :Papers palette. As soon as you click on the Papers icon, the Art Materials :Papers palette is displayed.

Picking and Applying Papers

To pick a paper texture, either click on the Papers icon or select the paper texture by name in the pop-up menu in the palette's drawer.

If the Papers palette drawer isn't open, open it now by clicking on the drawer handle, so you can see all of the paper textures available. Once you've picked a paper texture, you can apply a paper texture to your canvas or onto the Brush Look Designer using a brush with a grainy Method Subcategory.

To see how a brush stroke changes when you use different papers, choose Brush Look Designer from the Tools ➤ Brushes submenu. As described earlier, the Brush Look Designer automatically previews brush strokes. In this case the preview reflects the paper grain. Complete the following steps to try out and experiment with the different paper grains. The example below uses the Chalk brush and the Grainy Hard Cover subcategory.

1. Choose Chalk from the Brushes palette

2. In the variant pop-up menu, choose Square Chalk. This provides a good reflection of the paper grain with a Grainy Method Subcategory.

3. Choose Cover as the Method Category.

4. Choose Grainy Hard Cover as the Method Subcategory.

5. Open the Drawer of the Papers palette, then click on a very obvious grain, such as Hatching. If you'd like, you can instead pick Hatching from the drawer's pop-up menu.

6. Now click and drag in the Brush Look Designer on a white background to create a stroke. Notice how the paper grain is visible in the stroke.

7. To see the different paper grains, click on each one in the drawer. As you click, the Brush Look Designer will repaint the original brush stroke. Each time it repaints you'll see the new paper grain in the stroke.

Editing and Applying Papers

The Art Materials :Papers palette also allows you edit a paper texture by inverting paper grain and changing its scale (grain size). To edit a paper texture in the Art Materials :Papers palette you need to expand the palette. Expand the palette by clicking on the zoom box.

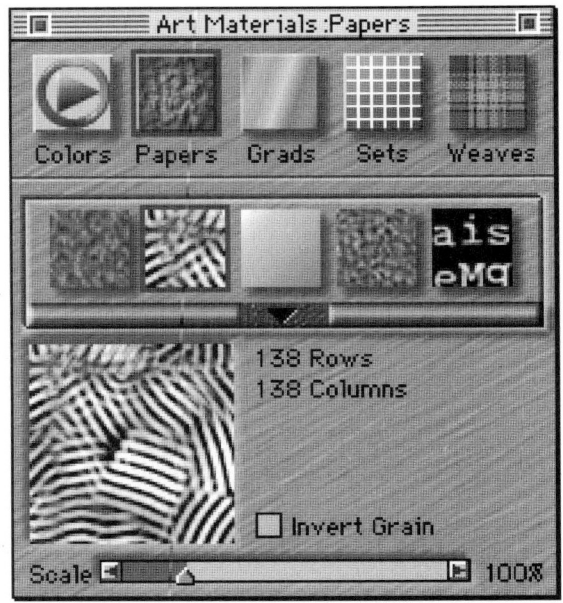

Changing the scale and inverting the paper grain are most obvious if you choose the Ciphertext paper.

1. Choose Ciphertext in the Papers pop-up menu (or choose the Ciphertext icon).

To change the Scale and invert the grain, you must close the drawer and have the expanded version of the palette.

2. Close the drawer by clicking on the drawer handle. Expand the palette by clicking on the zoom box.

3. To increase the size of the grain, drag the scale slider to the right.

As you drag, you'll see that the grain (which is text in this case) grows larger in the brush stroke.

Inverting creates a reversal of the grain. The colored part of your brush stroke is changed to your paper color.

4. Invert the grain by clicking on the Invert button.

As soon as you click, the color of the text in the stroke is reversed. If your text was white it is now black. The background stroke color changes to the paper color.

After you've experimented with applying a paper texture, you might want to adjust the textures or create your own textures.

Creating Custom Papers

You can create your own custom paper textures from scratch or you can capture a texture from an image and use it as the basis for your paper grain.

Using the Paper Texture Command

Here's how to create a paper texture using the Make Paper Texture command.

1. Choose Make Paper Texture from the Tools ➤ Textures submenu.

2. In the Repeating Texture dialog box, choose a pattern in the pop-up menu.

The two sliders allow you to control the angle and the space of the texture.

3. It's easy to see how these different options create a pattern if you choose an obvious shape such as diamond, set the spacing to 25, and the angle to 20. The diamond pattern and the change in angle will be obvious.

4. After you've created your pattern, enter a name in the Name field, and click OK to save it.

5. After you name it, the pattern appears in the Art Materials :Papers pop-up menu. Choose it from the pop-up menu and try painting with the new paper texture in the Brush Look Designer.

Capturing a Texture

Painter also allows you to create Patterns using an image as a basis for the paper texture. This means you can base a texture on a painting, a stock image, or a scanned/digitized image.

Here are the steps for creating a texture from a digitized image.

1. Open a digitized image. If you don't have an image of your own, use one of the stock photos included on the Painter CD ROM or load the Mission file from the Tutorial folder.

2. Once the image appears on screen, use the Rectangular Selection tool to select an area to be used as a paper texture.

3. To capture the texture, choose Capture Texture from the Tools ➤ Textures submenu.

4. When the Save Texture dialog box appears, drag the Crossfade slider to the right if you wish to blend texture edges. Then enter a name for your texture, and click OK.

Your texture now appears in the paper palette and can be used by any brush that interacts with paper grain.

Creating Custom Paper Libraries

You can create custom paper libraries from the paper textures you've made using the Paper Mover in the Tools ➤ Movers submenu. The steps for creating a custom library are essentially the same as those for creating a gradient or weave library. To create a custom library, choose Paper Mover from the Tools ➤ Mover submenu. Next click on the New button, and enter a name in the dialog box. After you click Save (Windows users: OK) select the name of the texture that you wish to copy into the library, then click the Copy button.

Anytime you want to use the library you created, you can open it by clicking on the Library button in the Papers palette. When you click the Library button the Open dialog box appears. At this point you can load any custom library you've created or any of the sample libraries that are installed with Painter.

Customizing Brushes with the Brush Controls Palette

When you choose brushes variants and categories in the Brushes palettes, you are choosing from preset pop-up menu options. Once you become very familiar with the Brush variants' categories and subcategories, you may wish to alter or fine-tune specific brush variants. The Brush Controls and Advance Controls palettes each provide options for customizing the selected brush in the Brushes palettes. As you'll soon see the possibilities are endless.

The Brush Controls palette provides further control of the brush stroke of the selected brush. This section explains each of the different subpalettes in the Brushes Controls palette.

The Brush Controls palette allows you to access five different sub-palettes: Size, Spacing, Bristles, Looks, and Nozzle. To begin exploring the different sub-palettes in the Brush Controls palette, open the Brush Controls palette now if it is not already open, by choosing Brush Controls from the Window menu.

> **Note** *The changes made in the Brush Controls palette are only temporary. Once you switch brushes, settings in the Brush Control palettes will switch to those of the currently selected brush. At the end of this chapter you will learn how to save palette changes by creating new brush variants.*

Using the Brush Controls :Size Palette

The first palette in the Brush Controls is Size. As you've no doubt guessed, this palette is primarily used to change the size or width of a brush stroke. Click on the Size icon to display the Size palette. This palette includes several Angle control sliders and Dab radio buttons. If you don't see these options, the palette needs to be expanded. To expand the palette, click on the palette's zoom box.

Notice that the Size palette has a preview window. This preview displays the size of the active brush. Click on a different brush or variant in the Brushes palette and notice that the preview changes to the default brush size for the current brush variant. You can change the preview from a soft brush to a hard brush and vice versa by clicking in the preview window. The soft brush preview displays a gray area around it. The hard brush does not. Try clicking in the preview to change the brush from soft to hard.

When changing the Brush Controls options it's important to remember that the options change the currently selected brush. While you have the palette open take a moment to click on the different brushes in the Brushes palette.

Notice that as you click on the different icons, the options in the Brush Controls :Size palette change to reflect the selected brush. Also, before proceeding to explore the palette options, notice the Build button in the palette. As you gradually depart from a brush's default settings, Painter often needs to "rebuild" the brush. If a brush needs to be rebuilt, the Build button will raise. If you forget to click on the Build button, an alert will appear warning you that the brush must be rebuilt before you can use it.

You can change the size of a brush by adjusting one of the three Size sliders in the Size palette.

◆ **The Size slider**—controls the width of the brush stroke. Drag the slider to the right and the brush size grows larger; drag it to the left and the size decreases.

◆ **The ±Size slider**—allows you to vary the difference between the thinnest possible and widest possible stroke. Drag the slider to the right to increase the difference; drag to the left to decrease the difference.

◆ **The Size Step slider**—allows you to specify how smooth or abrupt the transitions between the thick and thin widths of the stroke are. Drag the slider to the right to make stroke transitions appear more abrupt; drag the slider to the left to make transitions appear less abrupt.

To the right of the preview box are six brush tip profiles: Pointed, Medium, Linear, Dull, Watercolor, and 1-Pixel Edge. The icons themselves depict how the brush tips affect the brush strokes. In order for Painter to use the brush you create, you need to build it. Building allows Painter to run through the calculations to create the brush. To see a preview and use the brush, click on the Build button.

To truly see how these profiles paint and how the sliders affect a brush, watch the preview after you've built a brush, or use the Brush Look Designer to paint a stroke or two.

Below the size control sliders are the Angle controls.

◆ **The Squeeze slider**—squeezes the brush, making it more elliptical (oblong). Dragging the slider to the right makes the brush rounder, less elliptical.

◆ **The Angle slider**—changes the angle of an elliptical brush. Dragging the slider to the right rotates the brush clockwise, dragging left rotates it counter-clockwise.

◆ **The Ang Rng slider**—Ang Rng stands for angle range. Set the range to 90 and you can paint angles from 0 to 90 degrees. Set the angle to 180 and you can paint at every angle from 0 to 180 degrees.

◆ **The Ang Step slider**—produces an effect only if you set the Ang Rng slider immediately above it greater than 0 degrees. Setting this slider forces Painter to create a paint dab at regular intervals within the specified angle range. Assume that you set the Angle Range slider to 90 degrees. Setting the Ang Step slider to 10% forces Painter to place a dab every 10 degrees, up to and including 90 degrees. Dragging the slider to the right increases the Angle Step slider range, dragging to the left decreases the range.

Below the Angle sliders are a group of radio buttons that control the consistency of a paint dab. The character of Circular dabs is controlled by the Size palette. Bristle dabs are controlled by the Brush Controls Bristle palette. Captured dabs are created with the Tools Brushes Capture Brush palette. These palettes are described in later sections.

The 1-Pixel dab changes the size of a brush to one pixel. It's normally used after zooming in to edit images pixel by pixel.

Using the Brush Controls :Spacing Palette

All strokes are made up of series of brush dabs. The Brush Controls :Spacing palette allows you to adjust the spacing between paint dabs. Changing the spacing can be helpful when creating special effects with unusual shaped brushes. Adding spacing to a brush can also enhance the bristle effect of a brush.

To display the Brush Controls palette, click on the Spacing icon in the Brush Controls palette. To see all options in the Spacing palette, click on the zoom box to expand the palette.

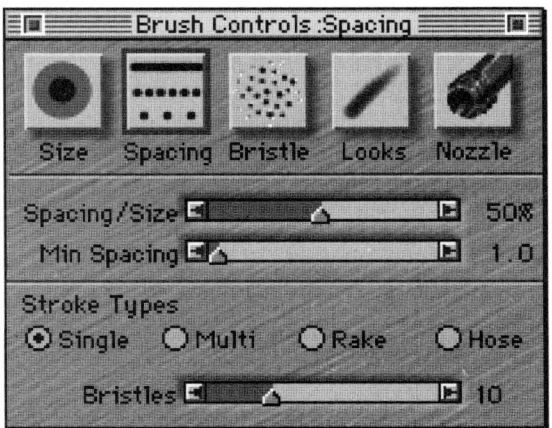

To add spacing to a brush, drag the Spacing slider to the right. To reduce spacing, drag the slider to the left.

The Min Spacing slider allows you to set the minimum distance in pixels. Dragging the slider to the right increases the distance, dragging to the left decreases the distance.

Beneath the Min Spacing slider are four radio buttons that control Stroke types. The stroke type allows you to spread brush strokes out. It can even cause different bristles to paint with different colors.

- ◆ **Single**—paints with one stroke.

- ◆ **Multi**—allows you to create strokes that are actually comprised of several brush strokes. The number of brush strokes is controlled by the Bristles slider, which appears at the bottom of the palette. To see the effect of painting with multicolors, pick a variant such as the Brush Cover brush (which paints with multicolors). When you paint, you'll notice a hint of the secondary color mixed with the primary color.

- ◆ **Rake**—another stroke comprised of several bristles, which can have more than one color. The Pen brush Scratchboard Rake is an example of a variant that creates a raked stroke.

- ◆ **Hose**—As mentioned earlier in this chapter, the Image Hose brush uses a Nozzle file. The Hose is a single stroke created from the currently selected Nozzle file. The Nozzle file can be selected from the Tools ➤ Image Hose submenu, or from the Brush Controls :Nozzle palette discussed later in this chapter.

Using the Brush Controls :Bristle Palette

The third option in the Brush Controls palette controls bristle brushes. (Remember that the Bristle dab type can be set in the Brush Controls :Size palette.)

Controlling bristles allows you to create truly realistic brush strokes, as if the strokes were created from real brush hairs rather than pixels. To display the Bristle palette, click on the Bristle icon in the Brush Controls palette. The Bristle palette allows you to change the bristles of a brush dab by adjusting four sliders.

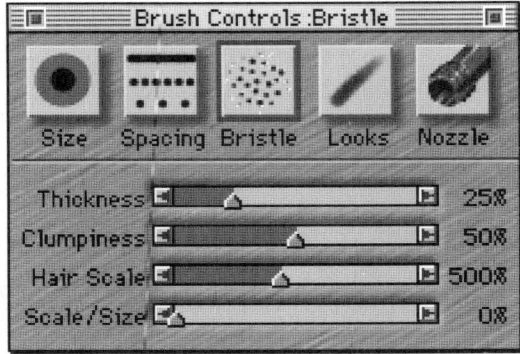

The following options are available in the Bristle palette. To see the effect of the sliders, try out the Brush's Camel Hair Brush variant.

◆ **Thickness**—controls the width of each individual brush bristle. Drag to the right to increase thickness; drag to the left to decrease thickness.

◆ **Clumpiness**—Dragging this slider to the right randomly varies the look of all of the bristles proportionally. If you increase clumpiness, bristle streaks will gradually turn solid.

◆ **Hair Scale**—controls the hair density of the bristles in the dab. The larger the percentage, the more visible the thickest bristles will appear.

◆ **Scale/Size**—This slider allows you to specify how much variation is allowed in the size of the brush's bristle set. If you set the slider to 0, no size change will occur. Setting the slider to 5 percent will produce a 5 percent variation in size. In order to use this slider the ±Size slider in the Brush Controls :Size palette must be set to at least 1.00.

Using the Brush Controls :Looks Palette

A very efficient way to store customized brushes is to paint a stroke in the Brush Look Designer, then click on the Save button.

The Brush Controls :Looks palettes contain a set of brushes saved from the Brush Look Designer. Click on the Looks icon to display the Looks palette. You can click on an icon in the drawer front to choose a look. If you open the drawer front you can choose from more icons and also use the Looks pop-up menu to pick a look. Every time you choose a look, you'll see a preview in the Brush Look dialog box.

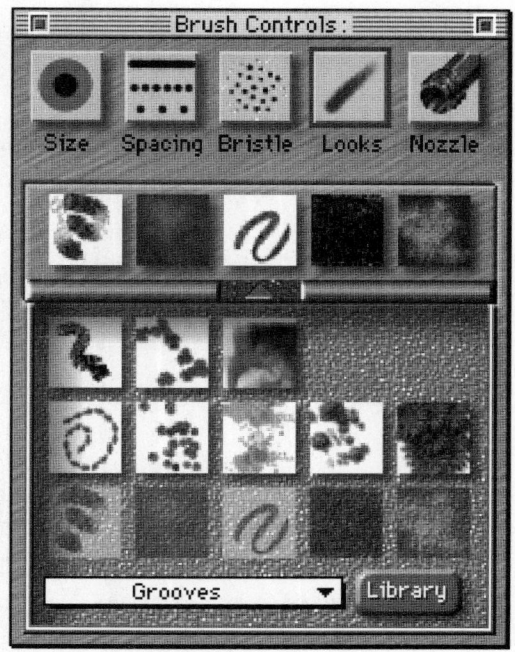

You can create and name different libraries using the Brush Look Mover in the Tools ➤ Mover submenu. Once you've created different libraries they can be opened by clicking on the Library button in the Looks palette.

Later in this chapter, you'll learn how to save your own brush variants, which will appear in the brush variant pop-up menu. If you don't want your saved customized brushes to appear in the Brushes palette, save them using the Brush Look Designer window. The brushes will be then be accessible in the Looks palette.

Using the Brush Controls :Nozzle Palette

The fourth palette in the Brush Controls palette is Nozzle. It's used to customize the images and designs that flow from the Image Hose brush. Click on the Nozzle icon to display the Nozzle palette. Click on the zoom box to expand the Nozzle palette and see all of its options.

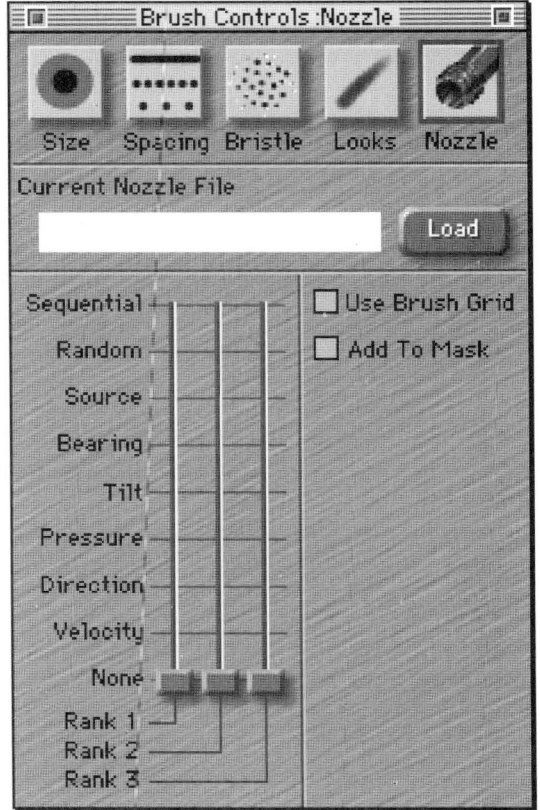

As discussed earlier, Painter allows you to paint not only with colors but with digitized images using the Image Hose brush. When you want to paint with an image hose, you must open a file called a Nozzle. The Brush Controls :Nozzles palette allows you to open and control how a Nozzles file paints. You'll learn how to create your own image hoses in Chapters 8 and 9.

Earlier in this chapter you learned that the Tools menu can be used to load a Nozzle file. You can also use the Brush Controls :Nozzle palette to load a Nozzle file. Complete the following steps to load the coin nozzle. After loading the nozzle file, you'll be able to paint money on screen.

Before loading the Nozzle file, select the Image House brush in the Brushes palette. To choose the Image Hose brush, click on the icon that looks like shamrocks flowing from a garden hose, or choose Image Hose from the Brushes palette pop-up menu.

1. Click on the Load button in the Brush Controls :Nozzle palette.

2. To see the list of nozzle files and begin the loading procedure, click the Load button in the palette. If the Nozzle folder doesn't appear in the Open dialog box, navigate to it with the mouse. Then open it. In the folder are the preset nozzle files that are installed with Painter. Double-click on the Coins Nozzle file to open it.

3. Now try clicking and dragging to paint with the coins nozzle file in the Brush Look Designer window, or in a new file. As you paint, a variety of coins will spill forth from the brush.

4. The amazing effect of painting with a nozzle file can be customized by using the sliders at the bottom of the palette. Try using the slider settings described below. If the sliders don't appear, click on the zoom box at the top right-hand corner of the palette. (Later you'll see that the Advanced Controls palette provides even more controls for changing the nozzle file.)

   ◆ **Sequential**—Images are painted in the order the images in the file are arranged.

   ◆ **Random**—Images are selected at random from the Nozzle file.

   ◆ **Source**—The luminance (or brightness values) of an image are replaced by associated luminance values in the nozzle file. For instance, if a luminance value of a nozzle file was 50%, it would only paint over image areas that have a luminosity of 50%.

   ◆ **Bearing**—Bearing is a stylus feature of Calcomp and Hitachi tablets. It is defined as the direction of the stylus in relation to the tablet. If your tablet and stylus support this feature, the image will be painted based upon the bearing of the stylus.

   ◆ **Tilt**—Tilt is a stylus feature of Calcomp and Hitachi tablets. Tilt means that the brush stroke will change according to the angle of the stylus to the tablet. If your tablet and stylus support this feature, the image will be painted based upon the tilt of the stylus.

   ◆ **Pressure**—This setting only works with a stylus. Images will flow on the screen based upon how much pressure you apply to the stylus. Apply more pressure, and more images will flow from the Image Hose brush.

◆ **Direction**—Images flow on screen depending upon the direction of the mouse or stylus stroke.

◆ **Velocity**—Images flow on screen depending upon the speed of the mouse or stylus stroke. The slower you stroke, the more images appear on screen.

◆ **None**—Only the last element in the nozzle file is painted.

◆ **Use Brush Grid**—This option limits the Nozzle painting to a grid area based upon the grid units defined in the Nozzle file. Essentially, this means that the painting on screen will look exactly like the array of images setup in the nozzle file. To learn how to set up a nozzle in a grid, see Chapter 9.

◆ **Add to Mask**—This allows you to create a mask as you paint with the Image Hose brush. You can use this option to paint multiple selections on screen in the shape of the Image Hose's nozzle file contents. See Chapter 7 for more information about using masks.

Rank Sliders in the Nozzle Palette

Each of the options described in the preceding section is found along a Rank slider in the Nozzle palette. The number of ranks is determined by how the actual nozzle file was created. For instance, in a nozzle with two ranks, Rank 1 might control the sizes of the objects in each row of the nozzle file, and Rank 2 might control which row in the nozzle file is selected. You could use the slider to assign Velocity to one rank and Direction to another. The more ranks created in the nozzle file, the more complex the Image Hose brush stroke can be. Most nozzle files that are included with Painter have only 1 rank.

You can find out how many ranks a nozzle file has by loading the nozzle file with the File ➤ Open command, then choosing File ➤ Get Info. The nozzle ranking can be recognized by its dimensions. For instance a one-rank nozzle file is recognized by one dimension—in the File Info dialog box for such a file you might see the following indication:

    3 items

A two-rank nozzle file can be recognized by two dimensions—in the File Info dialog box for such a file you might see the following indication:

`3 by 3 items`

A three-rank nozzle file can be recognized by three dimensions—in the File Info dialog box for such a file you might see the following line:

`2 by 3 by 4 items`

As you'll see, there are even more ways to control the effects of the Image Hose brush, as well as several other Painter brushes. These controls are found in the Advanced Controls palette.

Customizing Brushes with the Advanced Controls Palette

The Advanced Controls palette controls five different palettes: Rake, Well, Random, Sliders, and Water. As you read through this section and try out the different controls, experiment in the Brush Look Designer window. To begin exploring the different palettes in the Advanced Controls palette, open it now by choosing Advanced Controls from the Window menu.

Using the Advanced Controls :Rake Palette

The first Advanced Controls palette allows you to adjust brushes that use a rake stroke, such as the Scratchboard Rake Pen variant. To display the Rake palette, click on the Rake icon.

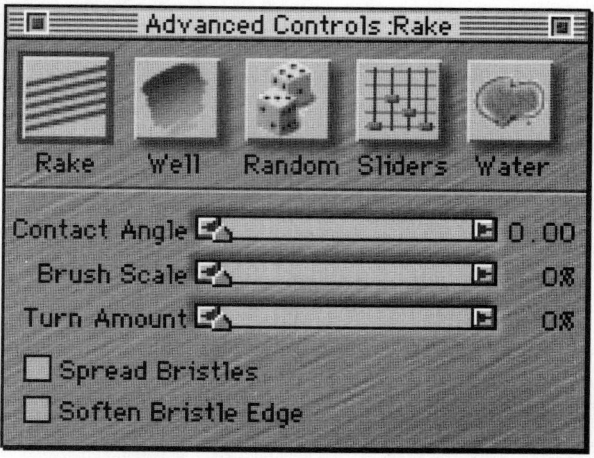

Tip *Remember, you can change a brush to a rake stroke by using the Brush Controls :Spacing palette.*

The Rake palette allows you to specify exactly how you would like the rake stroke to paint.

◆ **Contact angle slider**—Controls what parts of the brush touch the painting canvas. Dragging the slider to the left simulates a low angle. Dragging to the right simulates high contact (thus providing a wide stroke).

◆ **Brush Scale slider**—Sets the spacing between brush bristles. Drag to the right to increase spacing; to the left to decrease.

◆ **Turn Amount slider**—This slider helps simulate a bending bristle effect when a brush is turned. Brush edges move in and out more when the Turn Amount is increased.

◆ **Spread Bristles check box**—Associates the spacing between individual bristles according to pressure.

◆ **Soft Bristle Edge check box**—Causes the edges of the bristles to paint with more transparency.

Using the Advanced Controls :Well Palette

The Advanced Controls :Well palette allows you to control how paint flows from your brush. To display the Well palette, click on the Well icon in the Advanced Controls Palette.

The following options appear in the Advanced Controls :Well Palette.

◆ **Resaturation slider**—Each time you make a stroke, Painter dips the brush into its electronic paint well. This slider controls how much color is added before each stroke. Dragging the slider to the right makes the painting color last longer. Dragging to the left causes the paint to deplete faster.

◆ **Bleed slider**—Controls how painting colors mix together. Dragging the slider to the right causes more mixing, dragging to the left causes less mixing. The effects of this slider can be subtle. Try using the Brush's Loaded Oils variant to experiment with this slider.

◆ **Dryout slider**—This slider controls the distance in pixels until a brush runs out of paint. If you drag the slide to its far right position paint will not dry out at all. Dragging it to the left causes the paint to dry out more quickly.

Using the Advanced Controls :Random Palette

The Advanced Controls :Random palette allows you to add a sense of randomness to your Brush strokes. To display the Random options, click on the Random icon in the Advanced Controls palette.

Here are the options in the Advanced Controls :Random palette.

◆ **Dab Location: Placement**—adds a bit of splatter to your brush. This slider allows paint dabs to appear outside the path of your brush stroke. Drag the slider to the right to increases the amount of paint that can appear outside of the brush stroke's path.

◆ **Clone Location sliders**—control brushes that use a cloning source. (Cloning allows you to paint and copy an image while doing so. To learn more about cloning, see Chapter 6.)

  ◆ **Variability**—When Variability is increased, Painter grabs pixels from random areas in the clone source document to paint with.

  ◆ **How Often**—allows you to distort the original image. Drag this slider to the right and Painter will shift the pixels of the clone to other locations. Dragging it to the left produces a less distorted image because it does not displace the pixels as often.

◆ **Random Brush Stroke Grain check box**—makes the placement of the paper grain random. Brushes that spray and splatter can make use of the Random Stroke Grain.

◆ **Random Clone Source check box**—allows you to paint randomly from a clone source. The results can completely distort an image.

Using the Advanced Controls :Sliders Palette

The Advanced Controls :Sliders palette allows you to control how much the mouse or stylus affects a brush stroke. The controls in this palette can provide very unusual brush strokes. To access the palette, click on the Sliders icon in the Advanced Controls palette.

The following is a description of the Size slider options. The remainder of the sliders function virtually identically to the Size slider. For instance, the Grain slider allows you to control paper grain according to how you drag the mouse or stylus. The Colors slider changes colors according to how you drag the mouse or stylus.

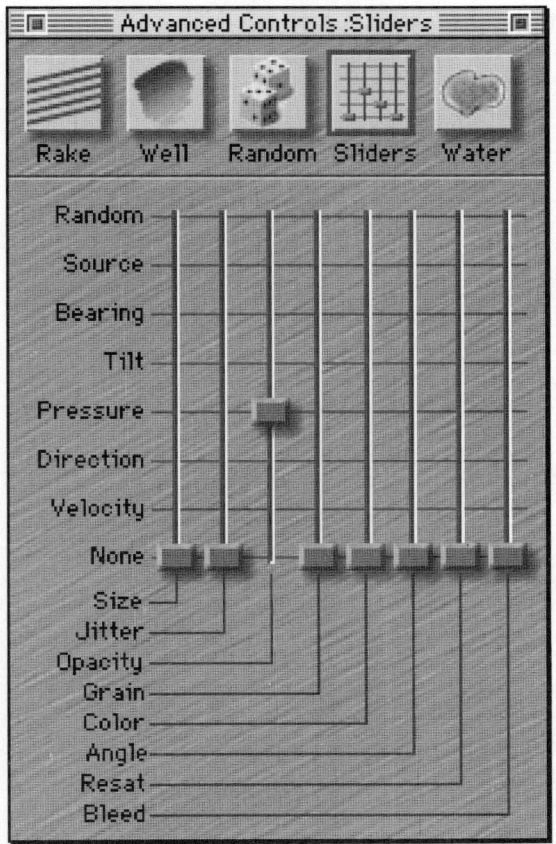

Note *The Size slider (the first slider below the settings in the palette) alters the width of the brush depending upon how the mouse or stylus is dragged. However, the settings for this slider will only affect width if the ±Size slider in the Brush Controls Size palette is set to 1 or greater.*

◆ **Random**—Brush width is determined randomly.

◆ **Source**—When working in a clone document, light and dark areas determine brush width. Light areas create a large width, dark areas a smaller width.

◆ **Bearing**—Bearing is a stylus feature of Calcomp and Hitachi tablets. It is defined as the direction of the stylus in relation to the tablet. If your tablet and stylus support this feature, the bearing of the stylus sets the width of the brush stroke.

◆ **Tilt**—Tilt is a stylus feature of Calcomp and Hitachi tablets. Tilt means that the brush stroke will change according to the angle of the stylus to the tablet. If your tablet and stylus support this feature, the tilt of the stylus sets the width of the brush stroke.

◆ **Pressure**—Hard pressure on a stylus produces wider brush strokes, lighter pressure creates narrower brush strokes.

◆ **Direction**—Dragging left or right makes strokes wider, down or left makes the strokes narrower.

◆ **Velocity**—Dragging the mouse or stylus quickly creates narrower brush strokes. Dragging slowly creates wider strokes.

◆ **None**—Brush width is unaffected by mouse or stylus.

Using the Advanced Controls :Water Palette

The Advanced Controls :Water palette allows you to customize the effect of painting with Painter's Water brush. In order to see the effect of changing options in this palette, click on the Water brush in the Brushes palette or choose Water from the pop-up menu.

◆ **Diffusion slider**—Drag this slider to the right to diffuse the water brush stroke into the paper grain. Drag to the left to decrease the diffusion. The diffusion occurs along the edge of the brush stroke.

Note *You can also diffuse an entire region painted with the Water brush, by first selecting an area, then pressing Shift+D on the keyboard. You can add more and more diffusion by pressing Shift+D repeatedly.*

Wet Fringe slider—The wet fringe slider simulates the effect of drying water colors. When watercolors dry, the color often drifts to the edges of the painted area. Dragging the slider to the right increases the amount of color deposits at the edges of brush strokes.

Now that you've see the countless ways that a brush can be customized, you may want to create your own brush variants, using the tools already presented. After you create a variant that you'd like to use again and again, you probably want to save it. The following section shows you how.

Saving Brush Variants

If you want to reuse the customized Brushes you create with the Brush Controls and Advanced Controls palette's, you must save them. Otherwise the brush changes are lost as soon as you switch to other variants.

Fortunately, creating a Brush variant in Painter is quite simple. After you change your settings in Painter's palettes, choose Save Variant in the Brushes ➤ Tools submenu. In the Save Variant dialog box, name your new variant, then click OK. The variant will then appear in the Variant pop-up menu whenever the currently selected brush is activated in the Brushes palette.

You can have up to 32 variants per brush.

> **Tip** *If you'd like to change an existing variant (instead of creating a new variant), choose Save Built Variant from the Brushes ➤ Tools submenu. If you later decide that you want the original variant reloaded, choose Restore Default Variant from the Brushes ➤ Tools submenu.*

Adding a Brush to the Brushes Palette

If you'd like to create a new brush and have it appear as an icon in the Brushes palette, you must first create an icon for it or import an image to use as an icon.

Once the image is on screen, select it with the Rectangular Selection tool. To name the new brush, choose Tools ➤ Brushes ➤ Save. In the New Brush dialog box, enter a new name, then click OK. The new brush and its icon appear in the Brushes palette. To paint with the brush, you need to create variants and save them as described above.

Creating a Brush Library

If you create many different brushes, you may want to create a new library for them. To create a new library, choose Brush Mover from the Tools ➤ Movers submenu. In the Brush Mover dialog box, click the New button. Name your library, then click Save. Next select the brush you want in your library, and click the Copy button. Repeat the same procedure for all brushes that you want copied to your library.

Capturing Brushes and Saving Them As Variants

You can create an image and capture parts of it to use as a brush or you can capture a digitized image and use it as a brush.

To capture a digitized image and use it as a brush, first open the image that you wish to use as a brush. If you don't have an image to use, open the Shells file in the Tutorial folder. When the file appears on screen, pick a brush from the Brushes palette. This will be the brush that you'll want to use to apply the digitized stroke.

Next use the Rectangular Selection tool to select a portion of the file. With the selection still activated choose Capture Brush from the Tools ➤ Brushes submenu. Activate the Brush Controls :Size palette and you will see a preview of the captured brush.

To apply this brush, choose a color and click in the Brush Look Designer (or in a new file): a stroke is created from your captured image. Click and drag to create a long continuous stroke of the image.

If you want to adjust the spacing, open the Brush Controls :Spacing palette. Drag both spacing sliders to the right, now click and drag. Notice that the spacing has changed, that images spread out as you paint.

If you want to use the captured brush again, you can save it as a variant following the steps described earlier.

● Hints for Creating Painter Art Work

Remember that art evokes a mood, and emotion. It can represent a moment in time or a fantastic image in your imagination.

The first step in creating a work of art is usually coming up with an idea, theme, or feeling that you want to portray. The next step is translating your artistic conception into a sketch. A sketch can help you put the pieces together, and make you become more aware of and familiar with the subject of your painting.

This is when you should begin to think about lighting, the colors you'll use, and the basic shapes that will create the subject and/or scene.

At this point, you may need to do some research to help you better conceptualize your subject matter. You may need to photograph your subject under different lighting conditions and positions. After you've taken photographs, you'll need to analyze them. You may finally determine that you need to use a live subject to help you truly convey your artistic goals. Creating a sketch or maybe a few sketches can help you plan your subject matter and lighting.

> **Tip** *When creating a sketch you may want to use the Rotate Page tool to rotate your canvas so that you can sketch at different angles.*

Once your planning is completed, you're ready to start choosing your brushes and paper grains.

Figure 3.1 shows the sketch for Figure 3.2. Figure 3.2 is the final painted version of the sketch. This figure was created by first placing a real vase on a table and arranging flowers in it. Next, lighting was changed to create a warm, inviting effect. From this live scene, a sketch was created in Painter. When the new file was created for the sketch, the paper color was changed from white to a light beige, since this was the desired background color for the image. Next a sketch was created using the charcoal and pencil brush. Later, oil pastels and water colors were used to paint over the sketch to create the final painting that can be seen in the color pages of this book.

FIGURE 3.1: A sketch created using pencil and charcoal

FIGURE 3.2: The final art work was created using chalk (oil pastel) and watercolor—turn to the color insert to see the image in color.

Figure 3.3 shows another example of how Painter's brushes can create a painting. The background was created with a variety of different brush variants and method categories. For instance, the Brush Oil Paint variant, Crayons, Chalk, and Pens were used to add colors to the background. Then, various Liquid brush variants, with the Method Category set to Drip, were used to blend the colors together. Water was also used to blend the colors together. Once the background was completed, the easel, hand, and landscape painting were created. The easel and hand were painted using different brushes. The landscape painting was originally a photograph

FIGURE 3.3: Image created using a variety of different brushes—turn to the color insert to see the image in color.

that was scanned, then altered and framed. The file was then saved in Photoshop format, and placed in Photoshop, where the other elements and effects were created. (The 3-D brush holder and sphere supporting the painter's palette were created in StrataVision.) To see a color version of this image, turn to the color pages.

Depending upon the subject of your painting, you may need to approach your work differently. Here are some issues to consider when working with different types of subjects:

◆ **Portraits**—When working with portraits, you might want to use a sketch to map out the facial features and expressions. Use the sketch to create accurate and convincing features and to flesh out the highlights in skin tones.

◆ **Nudes**—When working with nudes you should think about postures, lighting, skin tones, and mood. Think of how you want to portray your subject. As a god or goddess, or more as an ordinary person?

◆ **Still Lifes**—When working with still lifes, you might want to build a scene and then photograph it. You can then look at the photograph every so often instead of painting from memory. When planning the still life, pay close attention to lighting in order to add interest to the subject matter.

◆ **Landscapes**—When working with landscapes, you might want to begin by using washes to create the overall shapes, then gradually build the image up by adding tone and detail. What will be the focal points? Water, rivers, reflections, hills and mountains, the horizon, the sky, white clouds, trees and foliage, flowers? Also consider the weather—it will be a part of your image.

◆ **Wildlife**—When working with animals, start with basic shapes and gradually add details. Working from photos is a good idea because most animals aren't cooperative about posing for long periods of time. Try not to allow your painting to look static. Make it come alive by trying to capture motion.

◆ **Place and Atmosphere**—If your image consists of town scenes, you will have to spend time creating streets, buildings, cafés, markets, cars, and people. When creating exteriors and interiors you'll work with viewpoints, perspective, proportion, themes, textures, patterns, fabrics, depth, and space. Painter's Grid options can be very useful here.

Wrapping It Up

Apart from creating artwork with Painter's Brush tool, you may wish to combine your paintings with photographs to create collages. If you create collages, you may wish to scan the elements you place in them. The next chapter describes how to scan a photograph and how to choose the correct resolution for digitizing, resizing, and outputting images.

Digitizing and Manipulating Images

Although Painter is best known for its amazing ability to emulate brushes and other natural media, Painter is not for painting only. Painter shares many of the capabilities found in programs whose chief purpose is image editing, the enhancing and manipulating of *digitized images*. A digitized image can be a photograph that has been scanned by a scanner, a live image taken by a digital camera, or a frozen video frame "grabbed" by a video board. Fortunately, if you need to digitize images, you don't need to quit Painter to do it. As you'll learn in this chapter, you can digitize images directly from within Painter.

If you are going to be digitizing images, it's important that you understand the basic concepts of resolution and how it relates to image output. The goal of this chapter is to provide you with an overview of the digitization process, and to insure that you know how to digitize images correctly. The chapter concludes with a look at the types of image editing commands you're likely to need once you've digitized an image. You'll learn how to crop, rotate, flip, scale, and even distort images. These are skills that will come in handy even if you won't be integrating digital images into your artwork. (You'll learn how to enhance digital images in Chapter 5).

 # How Digital Images Are Created

Undoubtedly the most popular method for digitizing images is to use a *scanner*. Scanners analyze the colors in a photograph, slide, or chrome (a photographic transparency) and convert the image data into digital data. If you wish to digitize an image using a scanner, you should be aware that the color and clarity of the final scan often depend upon whether the digitizing device is a low-end, midrange, or high-end scanner. Scanners are usually categorized as flatbed scanners, slide scanners, and drum scanners. The most commonly used are flatbed scanners, because they are usually the most inexpensive. Using a flatbed scanner is somewhat similar to using a copy machine: you lift the lid and you place the image to be scanned on a glass plate. To scan the image, however, you don't press a Copy button on the scanner. Instead, as you'll learn later in this chapter, you need to use the program that is controlling the scanner. In this case, you use Painter's File ➤ Acquire command.

If you don't have a scanner but you find you have a need for images digitized on a scanner, you can contact a local prepress house or service bureau to do it for you. For a fee, you can have your images digitized and saved on a floppy disk or removable hard disk. Tell the service bureau to save the image in TIFF or EPS file format so that it can be opened by Painter. To learn more about different file formats, see Appendix A.

> **Warning** *Many high-end scanners can create CMYK (Cyan, Magenta, Yellow, Black) files, which are used to create color separations from which plates are created for output on a printing press. Painter does not allow you to edit CMYK files, so make sure that your scanned images are saved as RGB files, in either TIFF or EPS format.*

If you need to photograph your images before loading them into Painter, you may wish to use a digital camera such as Apple's QuickTake, or Kodak's DCS 420 digital camera. With a digital camera, there's no need to worry about running out of film or how long it takes to process the film—because there *is* no film. Images are instantaneously digitized and stored in the camera's memory. Later you can download them directly to the computer.

If you don't have a digital camera, but still want to digitize images of photographs you've taken, you may wish to consider using Kodak's Photo CD process. This process allows you to digitize negatives or slides directly onto a CD-ROM disk. To view the images, you need a CD-ROM player which generally costs anywhere from 200 to 700 dollars, depending upon the how fast the CD player can access and load images.

> **Note** *Painter will not open images saved in Kodak's Photo CD format. To open a Photo CD into Painter, you can purchase Kodak's Photo CD Acquire plug-in module. You can also load a Photo CD image into Painter using Apple's Photo Access System extension.*

You can also purchase stock images and background textures on CD from a variety of image sources. Here's a list of just a few: American Databankers Corp. (ADC), ArtBeats, Aztech New Media Corp., Classic PIO Partners, CMCD Inc., ColorBytes, Corel, D'Pix, Dana Publishing, Digital Stock Corp., Form + Function, FotoSets, Gazelle Technologies, Image Club, NEO Custom Painted Environments Inc., Periwinkle Software, PhotoDex, PhotoDisc, Pixar, Planet Art, Visual Software, and Xaos Photo CD Images.

If you'd like to digitize an image from a frame of videotape, you can use a video capture board. Radius and RasterOps manufacture video boards for both Macs and PCs. Intel and TrueVision are other well-known manufacturers of video boards for PCs.

No matter what process you use to obtain digital images, you need to determine the dimensions and resolution required for your artistic endeavors. In order to determine the resolution, you must first know how you will be outputting your image. Will the image be output on a printing press, to a slide or chrome, or viewed on computer screen in a multimedia production? If you don't properly calculate image resolution, your final image may look flat or display ragged gradations between colors.

Calculating Resolution

Before you digitize an image, you need to calculate its resolution. When you specify the resolution of an image you are digitizing, you're actually setting the image resolution of the Painter file it will open up into. The greater the resolution, usually the sharper the image, and usually the smoother the transitions between colors. If you digitize at too *low* a resolution, the image may look blurry when it is printed.

Since higher-resolution images are sharper, you may think it's preferable to digitize every image at the highest resolution possible. Unfortunately, images that are digitized at too *high* a resolution often appear flat. Also, the higher the resolution, the larger the file size. A 4-by-5-inch image created at 75 pixels per inch consumes 440 K of disk space. The same image size created at a resolution of 300 ppi consumes approximately 7 MB.

If you'll be outputting to video (or to a multimedia production viewed on a computer screen), image resolution need not be high. The top resolution for viewing a video image is 640 by 480 pixels. This translates to a resolution of 72 ppi. Creating files for video output at a resolution higher than 72 ppi does not increase quality, because most Macintosh monitors display images at approximately 72 pixels per inch. (Most PC monitors display at 96 ppi.)

If you will be outputting to a commercial printing press, you must calculate your image resolution based on the resolution of the printed output. Printing resolution is measured in lines per inch, often referred to as *screen frequency*.

Calculating Resolution for Commercial Printing

Before you can compute the resolution needed to create an image that will be output on a printing press, you must know the printing screen frequency. As mentioned earlier, screen frequency is measured in lines per inch (lpi).

Color images appearing in high-quality publications are often output at a screen frequency from 133 to 150 lpi. Images in newspapers are often output at about 80 lpi. To understand how lines per inch relates to image resolution, it's helpful to understand the entire digital production process. On its journey to a commercial printing press, a color digital image is first output on an imagesetter that produces four film negatives, one for each of the CMYK color components in the image. The printer uses these negatives to create four printing plates for each cyan, magenta, yellow, and black printing plate. The process of overlaying cyan, magenta, yellow, and black inks during the printing produces countless colors.

When the imagesetter outputs your digital image, it creates tiny pixels organized into cells of dots called *halftones*. Each line of dots is the equivalent to one *linescreen*, or one line per inch.

To output a high-quality digital image, the standard rule is to digitize at 1.5 to 2 times the screen frequency. This means that if you are outputting an image at a screen frequency of 150 lpi, you should digitize the image at 225 to 300 ppi.

If you will be scanning an image and increasing its size in Painter, you should increase the resolution. In the following section you'll learn how to compute resolution for images that you will be enlarging.

If you are unsure of the screen frequency that will be used to output your image, ask your printer.

> **Tip** *If your computer can't handle hi-res digitized image files, you may want to work with low-res images for position only (often referred to as FPO) in a sample layout. Once you've finalized the design, you can pay a service bureau or prepress house to replace the low-resolution images with high-resolution ones.*

> **Note** *When scanning black-and-white line art, prepress professionals recommend scanning images at your output resolution. For instance, if you are outputting on an imagesetter at 1250 dpi, you should scan at 1250 ppi. Such high resolutions are especially necessary because in line art there are no gradual tonal changes (which make the image look smoother), as there are in colored and grayscale images.*

Calculating Resolution for Images You Will Be Enlarging

If you need to scan a small image (such as a slide) and later increase its size in Painter, calculating the proper resolution requires a bit of math. When you increase the size of an image, Painter lowers the resolution by increasing the size of the pixels in the image. Painter needs to do this to compensate for the image enlargement. This means that you must also compensate, by calculating the proper scanning resolution.

Here's the formula to use, followed by a step-by-step explanation.

Take the product of:

    the longest dimension of final image in Painter

    times the screen frequency

    times the screen ratio (pixel-to-line screen)

And divide it by:

    the longest dimension of the scanned image

Here's how the formula works. Assume you digitize an image that is 2 inches by 4 inches and you wish to enlarge the image to 4 inches by 8 inches. Assume also that you will be outputting the image at a screen frequency of 150 lpi. Here's how you would calculate the scanning resolution.

1. Multiply the longest dimension of the intended *final* image (8 inches) times the screen frequency (150 lpi).

$$8 \text{ inches} \times 150 \text{ lines per inch} = 1200 \text{ lines}$$

2. As mentioned earlier, a commonly used screen frequency ratio is 2 pixels per every linescreen. So, your next step is to multiply by a factor of two.

$$1200 \text{ lines} \times 2 \text{ pixels per line} = 2400 \text{ pixels}$$

3. Next you must divide the product of the preceding calculation (2400 pixels) by the longest dimension of the *original* image.

$$2400 \text{ pixels} / 4 \text{ inches} = 600 \text{ pixels per inch}$$

The formula reveals that your 2"-by-4" image should be digitized at 600 ppi. When you resize your 2-by-4 image to 4-by-8, Painter automatically drops the resolution to 300 ppi because you've increased the image's dimensions. As discussed earlier, when you increase an image's dimensions, the pixels get larger; thus, there are fewer pixels per inch. You'll learn how to resize an image later in this chapter. In the next section, you'll find out how to digitize an image directly from Painter using the File ➤ Acquire command.

Digitizing an Image Using Painter's Acquire Command

Painter's Acquire command is the link between Painter and a scanner, digital camera, or video source. The Acquire command allows you to scan directly, load an image from a digital camera, or capture a frame from a videotape directly into Painter.

In order to use the Acquire command, you must first install either the scanner's, digital camera's, or video board's *plug-in* program on your computer's hard disk. A plug-in is a small program that Painter loads when you choose Acquire from the File menu.

RasterOps Video Capture   KODAK DCS 420   FotoLook PS 1.1   Kodak XLS 8600

You'll generally find plug-in software on the installation disks that are packaged with your digitizing device. Plug-in icons for a video-capture board, digital camera, and scanners are shown below.

After the plug-in is installed, you must guide Painter to the plug-in's location on your hard disk. To start the process, first select Preferences from Painter's Edit menu, then choose Plug-ins. A dialog box appears listing the files on your hard disk. Use the mouse to navigate to the folder that contains your plug-ins. Open the folder by double-clicking on it, or by clicking the Open button. Finally, double-click on the plug-in itself. In order to use the plug-in, quit Painter, then restart the program.

> **Tip** *Painter can load third-party plug-ins created for Adobe Photoshop. However, because Photoshop can read plug-ins that are in subfolders and Painter cannot, if you want Painter to read more than one plug-in, they all must be in the same folder. Also note that plug-ins created by Adobe for Photoshop 3.0 are proprietary and cannot be loaded into Painter.*

After your plug-in is installed on your hard disk and you've set the Edit ➤ Preferences command so that Painter can find your plug-in, once you restart Painter you're ready to digitize images using the Acquire command.

Capturing a Video Clip

Capturing a video clip is quite simple. First you must install a video board specifically engineered to capture video. Next, you need to hook up video output cables from your VCR, camcorder, or other video source to the video board. Put the videotape into your camcorder or VCR. After you've set up your cables and video source, choose Acquire from Painter's File menu, then click on the Plug-in name that appears. A dialog box showing your video board's software options appears. Figure 4.1 shows the dialog box for RasterOp's Video Capture software sold with RasterOp's MoviePak2 Pro Suite and its 24XLTV 24-bit video card. Notice that the resolution can be adjusted in the Size: pop-up menu. The 640 by 480 Resolution choice provides a full frame of video on a 14-inch monitor.

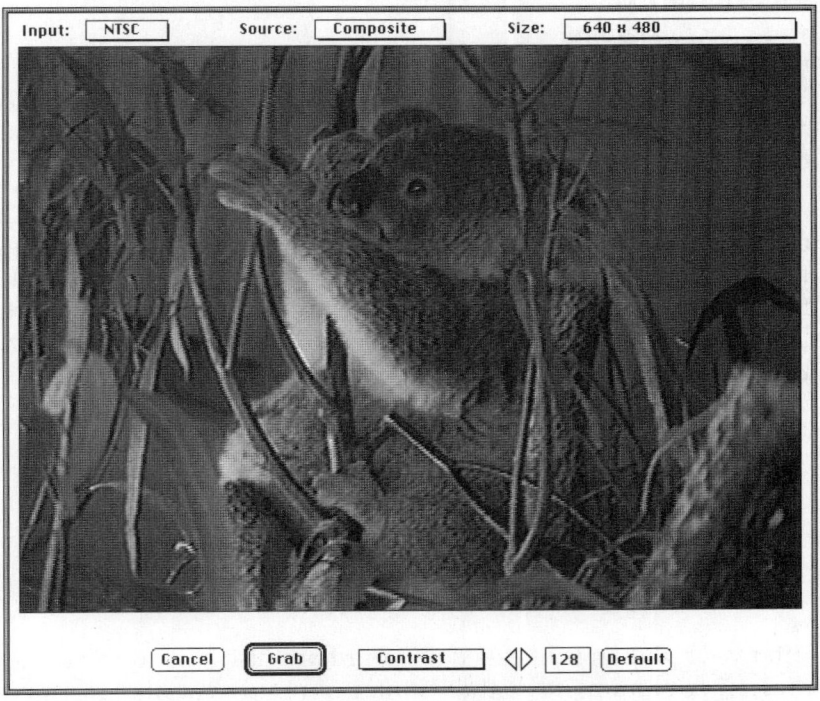

FIGURE 4.1: RasterOp's Video Capture software dialog box

Note *If you own an AV (audio-visual) Mac or a multimedia PC, a video capture board is already installed. Since these computers already include video capture software, you're usually required to use that software to grab a video image. To use the image in Painter, save the image in PICT or TIFF format from within the video capture program; you can then load the image directly into Painter.*

When the Video Capture dialog box opens on screen, you can start your tape and watch the video on your computer's monitor. When you see an image you want to capture, click the Grab button. The image is instantly placed into a new canvas in Painter. Once the image appears in Painter, you can edit it and save it. Later in this chapter you'll learn how to resize an image and increase the canvas size.

Acquiring an Image Using a Digital Camera

After you've shot photos with a digital camera, you need to connect the camera to your computer's serial or SCSI port in order to download the image. To download images from a Kodak digital camera, you start the process by choosing the Kodak plug-in from Painter's File ➤ Acquire submenu. Figure 4.2 shows the dialog box for Kodak's digital camera. In the dialog box, you see thumbnail shots of all of the images taken with the camera. In order to download an image, you select it, then click the Acquire button.

Scanning an Image

Before Painter can recognize your scanner, you must first turn the scanner on. After the scanner warms up, place the image you wish to scan into the scanner, then choose Acquire from Painter's File menu, and click on the Plug-in name that appears. A dialog box showing your scanner's scanning options appears. Figure 4.3 shows dialog boxes from two different scanners. The top image is the scanning dialog box for Agfa Fotolook Plus, which is provided with many of Agfa's desktop scanners. The bottom image shows the dialog box for the Kodak Professional RFS 2035 Plus Film scanner, which scans slides. This dialog box allows you to choose the slide film type and the scanning resolution (DPI), and to make color adjustments while you scan.

Digitizing and Manipulating Images

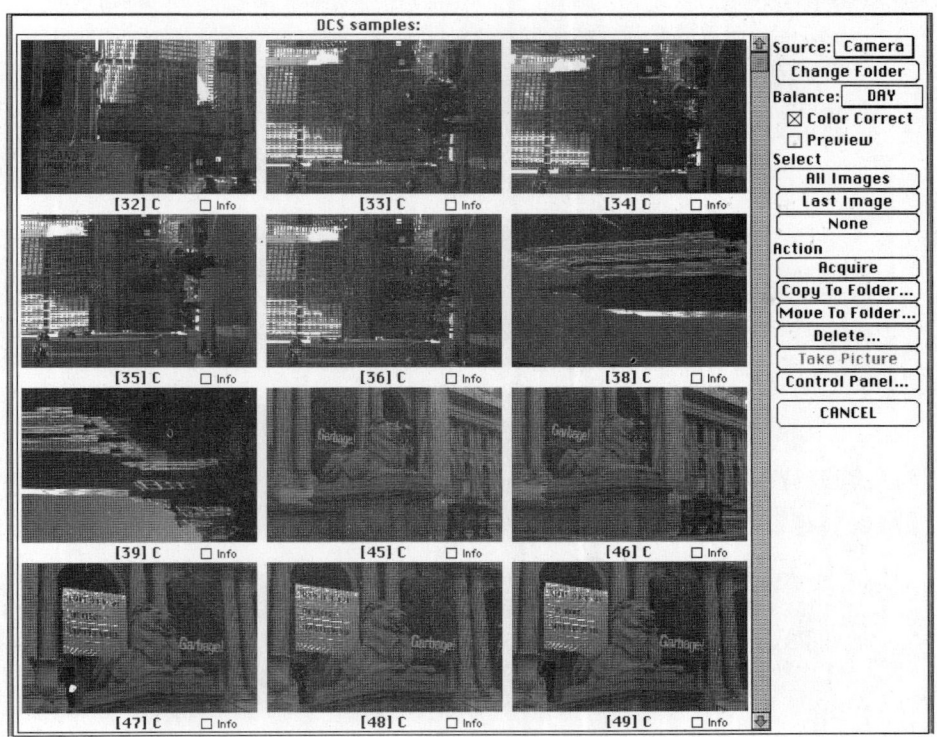

FIGURE 4.2: Kodak's digital camera software

Although each scanner provides different features, several options in the Agfa Fotolook Plus dialog box are common to most scanning software, and are worth reviewing. Before you begin to use your scanner, study the options provided by your scanner's software and consult your scanning manual to ensure you understand each choice. Knowing how to use all of your scanning software's features could make a crucial difference in the quality of your images. The following is a brief review of the options currently found in most scanning software.

◆ **Mode:** This option allows you to choose whether to scan in RGB color, grayscale, or black-and-white. (Black-and-white is often referred to as line art.) NOTE that although many high-end scanners allow you to create a CMYK color file directly from the scanner, Painter cannot edit CMYK images.

1

1

Artist: Adele Droblas Greenberg
Pears

2

Artist: Adele Droblas Greenberg
Bouquet

3

Artist: Adele Droblas Greenberg
Studio Magic

2

3

To learn how image 1 was created, see Chapter 6. To learn how images 2 and 3 were created, see Chapter 3.

4 Mario Henri Chakkour is a Natick, MA digital artist whose images often feature intriguing lighting and 3-D effects, usually with an added dash of humor. Mario is also the author of *Painting with Computers* and *The Joy of Pixels* video series.

Mario's Final Harvest image was created for Murad Publishing. Final Harvest, Dogville and Leaves of Bears are all from a collection: *Mario Henri Chakkour: A Portfolio of Digital Art.*

5 When Mario paints, he creates everything freehand and never uses filters. Although he doesn't create his own brushes, he often saves variants after changing brush sizes.

Mario usually starts by creating his images using a soft, small charcoal brush with a basic paper grain. Once a concept is finalized, he resizes his charcoal sketches. Then, he blocks colors over the soft charcoal, and blends them with water using the Just Add Water brush. He continues to use the water brushes until obtaining just the right amount of hues and tones. Mario's next steps are to patiently use the Masking brushes to aid in refining one image area at a time.

6 The sunburst effect in Final Harvest was created by first painting with an airbrush variant, then applying water. As Mario puts it, the effect is simple, yet lyrical. To create the organic metal in Final Harvest, he used the Airbrush with a flat stroke and the Liquid brush Total Oil variant (set very thinly)—with a little help from the Liquid brush Distorto variant. To create the neon effect in Dogville, he used the Pens brush Flat Ink variant over the Airbrush.

4

4
Artist: Mario Henri Chakkour
Final Harvest

5
Artist: Mario Henri Chakkour
Dogville

6
Artist: Mario Henri Chakkour
Leaves of Bears

5

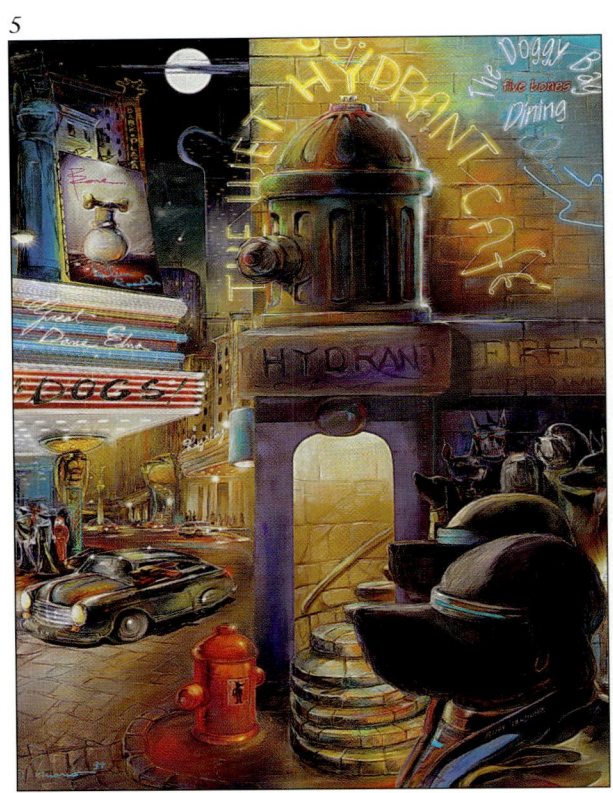

6

7 This image was created for an art gallery show by New York artist, writer and multimedia director Rodney Allan Greenblat. Rodney created the flowers and bunny in Macromedia Freehand. He loaded the images into Painter, and painted them using Pencil, Charcoal and Watercolor brushes. In Painter, he created a pattern tile out of the flowers. He loaded the flower tile into Adobe Photoshop and used the Offset filter to see if the tiled edges matched. Then he used the flower tile as a texture map for the image seen on the far right side, which he rendered in Byte by Byte's Sculpt 3-D.

8 Anne's Dream is a scene from *Dazzeloids* (published by Voyage), a clever and whimsical CD-ROM storybook created by artist/writer Rodney Greenblat.

To create Anne's Dream and many of the other Dazzeloids scenes, Rodney first sketched out black-and-white images on paper and then scanned them. Next he traced the scanned images using the Pen tool in Macromedia Freehand. After the images were sketched, he saved them as EPS files and loaded them into Painter. To color the black-and-white sketches, Rodney used the Paint Bucket tool. Afterwards, he used the Pencil and Charcoal brushes to fine-tune the images and enhance details. Once he was happy with a scene, Rodney saved it in PICT format and imported it into Macromedia Director where the final animation was created.

9 Mark, an Oakland, CA cartoon comic artist began this image by creating a line art drawing. He then scanned the line art drawing at a low resolution. He colored it using the Paint Bucket's Cartoon Cell fill option. Next, he used different custom brushes, masks and paper textures to add detail and texture. Mark applied Adobe Gallery Effects' Watercolor filter to the overall image and a Kai's Power Tools gradient to the background. Mark likes to place different elements in floaters—that way he can use the Masking brushes to reveal and hide different parts of the images in the floaters.

10 Chuck, a St. George, UT multimedia artist and illustrator created this image entirely in Painter with a Wacom stylus and tablet. The image was created for the *Manhole* CD-ROM game published by Cyan Inc.

Chuck initially created the sketch of this image using the Pen brush Scratchboard Tool variant. Then he added detail and texture to the image using the Water Color brush, Airbrush and Chalk brush with pastel variants. Finally, he added the final line work with the Scratchboard Tool variant. The image took about 2 hours to create.

7

7

Artist: Rodney Greenblat
Bunny Garden

8

Artist: Rodney Greenblat
Anne's Dream

9

Artist: Mark Badger
Mr. Bad meets the Hero's

10

Artist: Chuck Carter
Rabbit on Vine

8

9

© Scott Lobdell & Mark Badger

10

11 James, a Santa Rosa, CA artist created this image for *The Confessions of a Night Owl*, a storybook that he is writing.

James started by creating a pencil sketch of the rat image. After the sketch was completed, he scanned it and painted it using custom brushes in Painter. When painting, he used real rats, that his son's 8' Burmese Python used to eat, as a reference. The Python is in the story.

James added texture to the ground area of the image by painting with custom brushes and Painter's paper textures. James created the texture on the rat very much the way he used to do it when working with traditional oils. He starts by adding loose colors. Then he slowly blends them together with a soft blending brush until he achieves the desired effect.

12 This image is featured on the cover of the book *Ronald Dragon*, a medieval tale about a lonely dragon who eats knights and longs for a companion princess whom he eventually finds in this story.

James started with a rough sketch which he sent to the client (Michael Bremer, the author of the book) for approval. After Michael approved the image, James turned the sketch into a low-resolution color rough. Once James received final approval, he completed the illustration using custom brushes and Painter's paper textures.

James loves to use the textured brushes to apply texture directly to an image. To enhance the texture James often inverts the paper texture and primary painting color, depending upon whether he is applying the texture to a highlight or shadow area.

13 This intriguing image was created for Vanstar Corporation's computer catalog. After James and Art Director Charles Drucker conceived the image, James began to assemble the elements. The product shots were scanned and then silhouetted in HiRes QFX and Photoshop. They were resized and saved so they could later be imported into Painter.

In Painter, James filled the paths and gave each one a feathered edge. He created custom brushes to produce a soft effect when painting the grass and background. The man in the image is James himself. He took the picture with his Polaroid camera while standing in front of a wheelbarrow. He scanned the image, loaded it into Painter, then painted over it with various brushes. The textures in the jeans and shirt were applied with Painter's soft grain brushes and paper textures—as were the textures in the pumpkins, corn husks and gourds. The sky was softened using an Adobe Gallery Effects Glow filter. The wagon was rendered in Crystal Topas 3-D, which provided James with the fastest method of attaining accurate wheel shapes and shading. The computers, screens and hardware boxes were assembled in QFX and Adobe Photoshop.

11

11

Artist: James Dowlen
Roman's Rat

12

Artist: James Dowlen
Ronald Dragon

13

Artist: James Dowlen
Harvest

12

13

14 Stacy, a Newark, DE artist started this undersea image by first creating the background using several rectangular selections and gradation fills—pink to light blue for one, and then light blue to a darker blue and so on. The seaweed was created using the Image Hose brush. After the seaweed was sprayed on, he used the Masking brushes and stroked a few of them and adjusted colors.

The three small fishes were created with Masking brushes and filled with gradations. The two small fishes at the bottom left are the same fish but scaled and rotated. After rotating the fish, he adjusted its colors. The dolphin was sketched with a pencil first and then airbrushed in. Stacy also used the Water brush Just Add Water variant and the Eraser brush for texture. The bubbles were created using Kai's Power Tools. All of the fish were turned into floaters and placed on the background, then Stacy moved them several times until he found the best position.

15 Corinne, a San Francisco, CA artist and instructor at Foothill College in Los Altos Hills, CA, created this image for the packaging of the Painter 3 can. Corinne began this image by creating a pencil sketch and then scanning it. After the image was scanned, she increased the brightness and contrast. She then generated a mask using Painter's Mask command with the Image Luminance option. This created a mask which enabled Corinne to safely work within the pencil lines or color the pencil lines themselves. With the mask set so that she could color the pencil lines, Corinne colored them with a rust color using a large Charcoal brush. Later, she used a fat Airbrush to paint broad strokes of color in the fish. Then she used the Color Overlay command to apply a flat color on top. Next, she selected each fish and added lighting using the Apply Lighting command.

To create the textured patterns on the fish, she scanned Origami paper in grayscale, increased the brightness and contrast in Photoshop, and captured the texture in Painter using the Capture Texture command. This placed the texture as a paper in the Papers palette. She stroked the textures over the fish using a soft Charcoal brush. To create the bordered rice paper she used the Color Overlay command's Paper Grain (with a rice paper texture) and Dye Concentration options.

16 Stacy began this image by creating a black background. He then painted in the blue-green algae using the Image Hose brush. Next he used the Distort command to swirl it around, then he sprinkled in some color with the Pens Pixel Dust brush variant. He also used Masking brushes, gradation fills, and the Apply Surface Texture command's Image Luminance and Paper Grain options. The lips and eyes were created with Kai's Power Tools.

17 This image was created with the Image Hose brush, with a nozzle created from floaters. To learn how to create a nozzle file using floaters, see Chapter 8.

14

14

Artist: *Stacy A. Hopkins*
    Flipper

15

Artist: *Corinne Okada*
    Boys' Day Kite

16

Artist: *Stacy A. Hopkins*
    Flying Goldfish

17

Artist: *Adele Droblas Greenberg & Seth Greenberg*
    Flower Hose

15

16

17

18 George, a San Francisco artist, created this intriguing image with Painter's Image Hose brush using a nozzle file he constructed out of 3-D objects. The 3-D objects were all modeled in Strata StudioPro with most textures created in Painter. Each 3-D object was rendered with an alpha channel, then opened in Adobe Photoshop. In Photoshop, a drop shadow was applied to each object by offsetting and feathering the selections around the objects six pixels down and to the right. Then all the images were arranged in a grid three columns wide and ten rows deep. Each cell was 360 by 300 pixels.

George then opened the file in Painter, and saved it as a RIFF file. He began with a 640 by 480 pixel canvas (since this was to be a multimedia background), selected the Image Hose brush and then loaded his 3-D nozzle file. In the Nozzle Definition dialog box, he specified that each unit in the nozzle file was 360 by 300 pixels, and that there were 30 total elements. After closing the dialog box, he started painting with his stunning "digital junk."

19 Ben, Art Director of *Info World* magazine, created this image for an article about network management.

He started by creating a sketch using traditional pencil and paper. He then scanned the sketch into Photoshop and saved the black-and-white image as a 72-ppi PICT file. He brought the scan into Adobe Illustrator where he used the Pen tool to outline the sketch with a 2-point brown stroke. He saved the Illustrator file in EPS format. He then rasterized the EPS file in Adobe Photoshop at the size and resolution (240-ppi) it would be reproduced. Once the file was rasterized it was saved as a TIFF file and opened in Fractal Design Painter.

In Painter, Ben used the Paint Bucket tool to pour flat color in between the lines. He used the Dodge, Burn, and Airbrush to achieve light and dark values in the flat colors. He used the Apply Surface Texture command with the Wheat String paper from the More Wild Texture library. He applied the Motion command to the ground. The crowd was created by scanning a photograph of people at a convention, blurring it, then pasting it into the final image.

20 Triska, a San Diego, CA artist, created this image for a Spanish version of the Little Red Hen, a children's story, published by Josten's Learning Corp. She began creating this image traditionally by creating an ink sketch. The sketch was scanned and then painted in Painter using Water Color brush variants. As she painted, she used the Printable Colors Only option. First she colored the border. She used the Simple Water brush and Spatter Water brush to achieve the bubble effect. Then she painted the figures. She used the Pure Water variant to blend the colors together, and added texture using the Spatter Water brush.

18

18

Artist: George Krauter
Digital Junk

19

Artist: Ben Barbante
Lion Tamer

20

Artist: Triska Seeger
La Gallinita Roja

19

20

21 This ecological image appears on sweatshirts and T-shirts sold in college bookstores around the country. It was created by artist Johannes Giardoni, owner of Product Code 31, a New York company that specializes in creating unique artistic designs on clothing. Johannes created the outline of the image with Painter's Soft Pencil brush. He then used the Mask command's Image Luminance option to make a selection out of the black-and-white electronic sketch. Next, he filled the selection with black to add more body to the image outlines.

Since Save the Earth was to be silkscreened, Johannes worked with only three colors, painting the continents and oceans using the Water Color brush. He then turned each colored section into a floater and overlapped the colors to produce a multicolored "gel" effect. Later he copied the floaters and image outlines into a new file and saved it in TIFF format.

Johannes needed to separate the three colors into different plates for silk screening, so he exported the TIFF file to Freehand where he enlarged each image, and printed separations on individual sheets of acetate. These were later used to expose screens for Product Code 31's silkscreen press. On a T-shirt the image looks exactly the same as it does on the computer.

22 Dennis is a Tiburon, CA artist and owner of digital ARTs™, a digital art studio producing both fine and commercial art. Rainy Season is a non-photographic painting created from a variety of Image Hose nozzles files and brushes that Dennis will be publishing on CD-ROM. The collection includes nozzle files for numerous trees such as Eucalyptus and Acacia. Also included in the collection are a variety of flowers, vines and grasses.

After painting with the Image Hose brush using different nozzle files, Dennis adjusted the hue, saturation and value of various image elements. He also used a variety of textured Airbrushes to create the atmospheric effects. The twigs in the image were created using Masking brushes and the Airbrush.

23 Dennis is an Ivyland, PA artist and Creative Director at K.I. Lipton in Doylestown, Pa. He was inspired to create this beautiful image by the beautiful patterns of brightly colored foliage and strong sunlight on the island of Barbados. The hazy highlights and rich deep shadows were perfect for a loose watercolor approach. He began by penciling a variety of shapes into the image, then blocked in colors with larger Chalk brush pastel strokes. He then applied the Adobe Gallery Effects Watercolor filter on top of the image. To complete the image, he used the Water Color brush.

21

21

Artist: Johannes Giardoni
Save the Earth

22

Artist: Dennis Berkla
Rainy Season

23

Artist: Dennis Orlando
Caribbean Watercolor

22

23

24 Kent, a Redwood City, CA artist and Associate Professor at Foothill College in Los Altos Hills, CA, began creating this image by scanning a piece of bread and grains. Once the bread was scanned he used Painter to posterize the bread. In a separate Painter document he painted a keyhole, fork and hats using the Crayon brush, and then posterized them.

He created a floater of the bread and grain to composite the image. Finally, he imported a path of text from Adobe Illustrator.

Kent says that the message behind this image is: "We live in an age where people are influenced and manipulated...often in ways that are dishonest and unhealthy. From pushing chemically altered foods to promoting hate by intolerance, leadership positions often act selfishly promoting their own manufactured sense of good. The real problem is that people keep asking for bread and are not asking for good soil to plant seeds."

25 Mina Melinda, a San Francisco artist, began this piece by sketching on a piece of paper in an attempt to resolve ideas and design possibilities. She believes the impetus for the piece came from observing chefs at work in restaurants with counters.

When Mina Melinda was happy with the sketch, she scanned it and saved it as a TIFF file. In Painter, she started by selecting the Printable Colors Only option in the Art Materials :Colors palette in order to retain color integrity as much as possible for the printed piece. Then she painted over the scanned image using only two or three brushes and textures to maintain a cohesive style. She used two of the Chalk brush variants; the Sharp Chalk and the Oil Pastel, both with the Grainy Soft Cover Method Subcategory. She primarily used the Watercolor 2 paper texture from the More Paper Textures library. Around the edges she also used a paper texture. She created masks for all the elements in the foreground, so that she could make color modifications in the background.

Mina Melinda says; "I like technique that appears artless, innocent; the way I imagine a stroke of genius would be...spontaneous!"

26 Kent started this image by creating sketches on traditional paper using litho crayons and white gesso. During the image development, he photocopied the sketches. He scanned a grayscale version and only used the Colored Pencils variant with the Method Category set to Cover and the Method Subcategory set to Flat Cover. He also used the Paint Bucket to paint over the image to give it the appearance of a screen print. He altered brush sizes and painting color, using a custom color palette.

Kent says that the message behind Scripts is: "As individuals we have many hats and halos to wear. Our choices, our decisions and our actions are often divided by honorable intentions and dominant self-interest. The potential for good is in our hands but often the consciousness of one hand does not respect the motivation of the other hand."

24

© Kent Manske 1994

25

26

© Kent Manske 1993

Painter Tips

We hope that you enjoy the color inserts of this book and that you find the images inspiring.

When choosing images for the color inserts, we tried to include an assortment that exhibited a wide range of styles and techniques. As you've seen, some of the artists started by sketching images directly into Painter. Some sketched images on paper, then scanned their images into the computer, and later painted them in Painter. Others started with photographs, then turned the images into paintings by painting over them or by using Painter's cloning features. Several of the artists created their own nozzle files, then used Painter's Image Hose brush to paint their canvases with the digital images from the nozzle files. Some used Adobe Illustrator, Adobe Photoshop and Macromedia Freehand as starting points.

To enhance their images, a few of the artists turned to special effects filters such as Kai's Power Tools, Xaos Tools Paint Alchemy, or Adobe Gallery Effects. Others imported and/or exported their Painter images into other programs such as Adobe Photoshop, Macromedia Director, and 3-D modeling and rendering programs such as Strata StudioPro, Crystal Topas and Ray Dream Designer.

No matter how the images were created, each artist started with a vision and a concept of his or her project before beginning. If you start with a concept, it will provide you with the direction needed to focus on only the specific Painter brushes and commands that you'll need to attain your artistic vision. Without a vision or goal, you run the risk of wasting time, and getting sidetracked among the countless options Painter provides. On the other hand, if you have plenty of time on your hands, you'll find that Painter allows for endless experimentation and avenues of expression.

After you've completed the conceptualizing stages of your work, you need to ensure that you're familiar with the basics of using Painter. Without a fundamental knowledge of Painter, you may find it difficult to complete your project. As you read through this book, and work on your own projects, you'll undoubtedly become more proficient at Painter. You'll be amazed at the masterpieces you'll soon be creating.

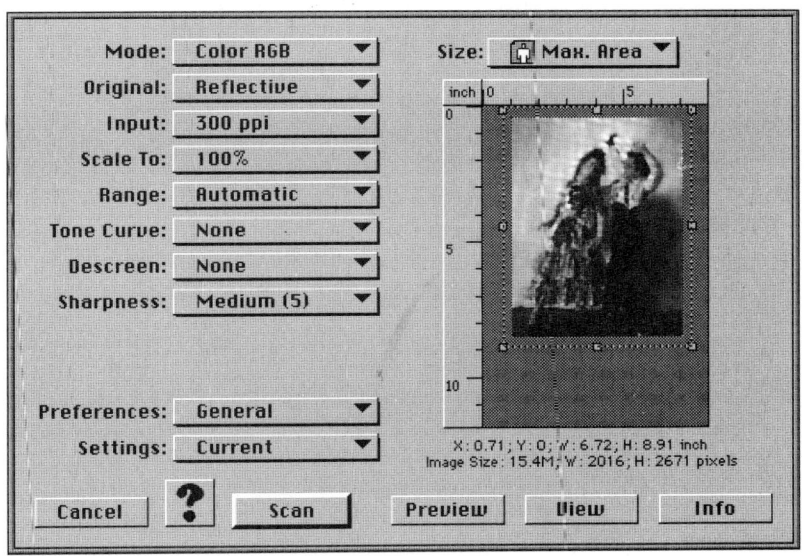

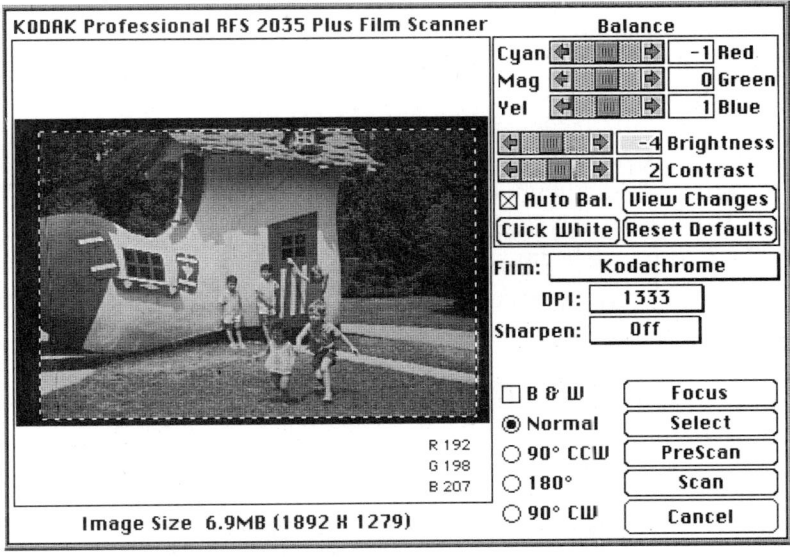

FIGURE 4.3: Top: Agfa's Fotolook Plus scanning software dialog box. Bottom: Kodak's RFS 2035 Plus Film Scanner dialog box.

◆ **Original:** Many midrange scanners allow a transparency attachment so that slides and chromes can be scanned. The Original pop-up menu allows you to choose whether to scan reflective art (drawings and photos) or transparencies (slides and chromes).

◆ **Input/Resolution:** Scanning resolution is sometimes called input resolution. Many scanners provide resolution settings ranging from below 72 ppi to over 1000 ppi. The Fotolook software also allows you to change this pop-up menu so that you can choose resolution according to printing output resolution. (Remember, printing output resolution is measured in lines per inch, rather than pixels per inch.)

◆ **Scale To:** Many scanners allow you to scale an image by choosing a percentage by which to enlarge or reduce the image. (You can also scale an image in Painter. Painter's Scale command is covered later in this chapter.)

◆ **Other options:** The Fotolook dialog box allows you to set the tonal range being scanned from the image's darkest point to its lightest point. It also allows you to choose whether the image will be sharpened, or "descreened." Descreening allows you to eliminate moiré patterns that can occur when a printed image is scanned.

◆ **Preview and Crop:** Most scanning software allows you to specify the image area that you need to use in Painter. Often a preview of the scan appears in this area. The right side of the Agfa Fotolook Plus dialog box shows this preview area. Clicking the Preview button produces a preview. By clicking and dragging in the preview box, you specify exactly what part of the image you want digitized into Painter. Specifying the image area before scanning keeps the file size of an image as low as possible.

◆ **Scan button:** To scan the cropped area, press the Scan button. In a few moments the image will appear in Painter, in an untitled canvas.

Note *After you digitize an image you'll probably need to adjust the brightness or contrast, the highlights, the midtones or shadows, or the color in an image. See Chapter 5 for more information.*

Once an image is properly digitized into Painter, you may need to crop it. We'll discuss techniques for doing that next.

Cropping with the Paste ➤ Into New Image Command

When you digitize an image, it's often a good idea to acquire a bit more of the image than you really need. This helps insure that you don't inadvertently miss any image areas. Once you've digitized your image, you may want to crop or cut extraneous image areas.

Painter does not feature a cropping tool. If you want to crop an image, you'll need to use the Edit ➤ Paste ➤ Into New Image command. When you execute this command, Painter automatically creates a new file containing only the selected and copied image.

If you want to try out the Edit ➤ Paste ➤ Into New Image command, you first need to select the image area that you wish to include in your new image. To do this activate the Rectangular Selection tool. Next click and drag to select only the image area that you wish to include in your final image. From the Edit menu, choose Copy. To automatically place the selected area in a new file, choose Paste from the Edit menu, then choose Into New Image. Painter automatically opens a new file, and pastes the image portion you need into it. The image is pasted at the same resolution as your original.

> **Tip** *If you had chosen Paste Normal instead of Paste Into Image, the selection would have been pasted into the middle of whatever image you had on Painter's screen.*

If you are copying an image or portion of an image from one file into another, always make sure that both files have the same resolution. If you paste a high-resolution file into a low-resolution file, the high-resolution image will enlarge. It enlarges because there are more pixels in every square inch of a high-resolution file than a low-resolution file.

> **Note** *If after you digitized your image it came out crooked, either redigitize it or proceed to the section on rotating (a few pages further on) and follow the instructions there to rotate the image. Then return to the "Resizing an Image" section (immediately following this note).*

Resizing an Image

After digitizing an image, you may need to enlarge it or reduce it. The process of resizing an image is the same no matter whether it was created from scratch or whether it was digitized by a scanner, a digital camera, or a video board.

If you would like to practice resizing an image, load any digitized image.

To resize the image, choose Resize from the Canvas menu. When the Resize dialog box appears, notice that the Constrain File Size check box is selected. This means that changing image dimensions does not affect the size of the file, and that Painter will not add or subtract pixels when the image is resized.

```
                    Resize Image

 Current Size:   20MB
        Width:   6.62      Inches
       Height:   8.777     Inches
   Resolution:   300.0     Pixels per Inch

    New Size:    20MB
        Width:  [7.467  ]  [ inches ▼ ]
       Height:  [9.9    ]  [ inches ▼ ]
   Resolution:  [266.0  ]  [ pixels per inch ▼ ]

              ☒ Constrain File Size

              [ Cancel ]   [   OK   ]
```

Try changing the width of your image. As soon as you adjust the width, the height changes proportionally. This ensures that the image is not distorted.

You may have also noticed that as soon as you changed the width, the resolution changed. If you increase the image's dimensions with the Constrain File Size check box selected, the image's resolution drops. Why? Painter decreases the number of pixels per inch in the image in order to compensate for the increase in width and height. If the width and height increase, fewer pixels are needed to make one square inch of an image. This inverse relationship between dimension and resolution explains why the scanning formula previously discussed is needed to calculate the resolution for images that you will enlarge. The top part of Table 4.1 summarizes the relationship between an image's resolution and its dimensions with the Constrain File Size check box selected. Notice that when the image's dimensions decrease, its resolution increases (and vice versa).

TABLE 4.1: Results of increasing or decreasing dimensions and resolution

With Constrain File Size SELECTED:

	Effects of Increasing	**Effects of Decreasing**
Dimensions	If you Increase dimensions,	If you Decrease dimensions,
	… resolution is *decreased*	… resolution is *increased*
	… and file size is *unchanged*	… and file size is *unchanged*
Resolution	If you Increase resolution,	If you Decrease resolution,
	… dimensions are *decreased*	… dimensions are *increased*
	… and file size is *unchanged*	… and file size is *unchanged*

With Constrain File Size DESELECTED:

	Effects of Increasing	**Effects of Decreasing**
Dimensions	If you Increase dimensions,	If you Decrease dimensions,
	… resolution is *unchanged*	… resolution is *unchanged*
	… and file size is *increased*	… and file size is *decreased*
Resolution	If you Increase resolution,	If you Decrease resolution,
	… dimensions are *unchanged*	… dimensions are *unchanged*
	… and file size is *increased*	… and file size is *decreased*

If you resize an image and its resolution drops too low or rises too high, you can still change the resolution by breaking the linking relationships between image resolution, dimensions, and file size. To do this, you turn the Constrain File Size check box off. If you do this, however, you must pay a price, because Painter must add or subtract pixels from your image. This process of adding or subtracting pixels is called *resampling*. Whenever Painter resamples, the file size changes, and the image quality can be adversely affected.

When Painter adds pixels, image quality may suffer because Painter must compute a new color for each pixel it adds. This process is called *interpolation*. The bottom part of Table 4.1 summarizes the effects of changing an image's dimensions or resolution when the Constrain File Size check box is deselected.

With your image still on screen, try this experiment. Turn off the Constrain File Size check box. Enlarge the dimensions of your image, but keep the resolution at 75. Click OK. Your image will enlarge. Look carefully at it. You'll see that image quality has deteriorated because Painter had to add pixels.

> **Warning** *Do not decrease the dimensions of an image with the Constrain File Size check box deselected and then increase the dimensions. When you decrease the size of the image, Painter must subtract pixels from the image. When you increase image size, Painter cannot replace the new image with the pixels that were removed. Your best bet is always to keep a backup of any image that you need to resample. That way, you can always return to the original.*

After reducing or enlarging your image, you may wish to enlarge your canvas without enlarging the dimensions of the image within it, so that you can work in a border area around the digitized image. That's the topic of the next section.

● Changing Canvas Size

Once you're ready to begin working with any digitized image, you may wish to expand the canvas area. Painter allows you to increase the canvas size without enlarging the image in it. When the canvas size is increased, Painter adds a border around your image which appears in the current paper color. If you want to change the paper color of your image, first change the primary painting color in the Art Materials palette, then choose Canvas ➤ Paper Color.

If you'd like to try increasing the canvas size of an image, load any image on screen. To increase the canvas size of your image, choose Canvas ➤ Canvas Size. In the Canvas Size dialog box, you can choose to add space to the top, bottom, left, or right side(s) of your canvas. Values must be entered in pixels. Thus, if you wanted to add a 1-inch work area around a 75-ppi image, you would enter 75 pixels in each entry field. If your image is 300 ppi, enter 300 in each entry field. In the Flamenco project shown at the end of this chapter (in Figure 4.5), 100 pixels were added to each field. After you've entered values in the appropriate fields, click OK.

```
┌──────────────────────────────────────────┐
│▒▒▒▒▒▒▒▒▒▒▒▒ Canvas Size ▒▒▒▒▒▒▒▒▒▒▒▒▒│
├──────────────────────────────────────────┤
│ Current Size:                            │
│     Width:  1986  pixels                 │
│     Height: 2633  pixels                 │
│                                          │
│ Increase Size:                           │
│     Add: │100│  pixels to top            │
│     Add: │100│  pixels to left           │
│     Add: │100│  pixels to bottom         │
│     Add: │100│  pixels to right          │
│                                          │
│              [ Cancel ]   (   OK   )     │
└──────────────────────────────────────────┘
```

When you change the canvas size of an image, Painter does not automatically resize the window. You have to click on the zoom box to zoom out and see the canvas extension border around your image, or choose Zoom To Fit Screen from the Window menu.

Changing Orientation

After an image is digitized, or after an image is loaded on screen, you may wish to make orientation adjustments so that you can rotate or flip an image. Painter's Effects ➤ Orientation submenu allows you to rotate, flip, scale, or distort an image in order to create special effects. The following sections describe each option in the Orientation submenu. As you read through the following descriptions, try out the commands with an image on screen. All orientation commands affect any active selection on screen. If no area is selected, the entire image is affected.

Rotate

Painter's Rotate command allows you to tilt an image on an axis. Rotation can be useful if you've scanned an image crookedly and need to make minor adjustments. To rotate an image or selected area within an image, choose Effects ➤ Orientation ➤ Rotate.

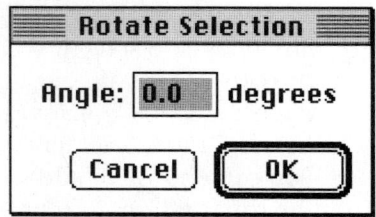

The Rotate Selection dialog box allows you to specify the rotation degree by entering a value. After you enter a value, dotted lines appear on screen indicating how the image will be oriented once it's rotated. You can also rotate the image in a more intuitive fashion, by clicking and dragging with the mouse. To rotate the image with the mouse, click on any of the handles (dots on the corner of the image) and drag until you've attained the desired rotation angle.

Once you are satisfied with the rotation angle, click OK.

Scale

The Scale command allows you to stretch or shrink an image. To scale an image, first select the area that you wish to scale. Choose Effects ➤ Orientation ➤ Scale.

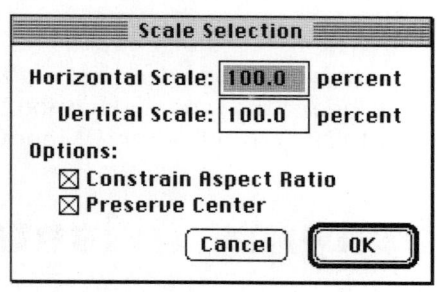

The Scale Selection dialog box allows you to adjust the percentage by which you wish to enlarge or reduce the image. If the Constrain Aspect Ratio check box is selected, changing width or height changes the other dimension proportionally. If you do not enter a percentage, you can click and drag with the mouse to scale your image. To use the mouse (or stylus) you must drag any of the handles that appear on the wireframe box that appears over your image. If you leave the Preserve Center check box on, dragging on one handle will cause all other handles to pull inward or outward the same distance from the center of the box. If you turn off the Preserve Center check box, scaling will not take place equidistantly from the center of the check box.

Distort

The Distort command allows you to bend and twist an image to create special effects. If you wish to distort only part of an image, select the area you wish to distort. To access the command, choose Effects ➤ Orientation ➤ Distort.

The Distort dialog box allows you to distort an image by clicking and dragging the mouse. In the preview area, drag any image handle in any direction. The top image in Figure 4.4 shows the selected text and the placement of the distort handles before the command was applied. The bottom image shows the effect of the distortion to the text. In the bottom image the text was filled with the weave, Our Shadow Weave.

The Distort dialog box also allows you to control the quality of the final image. If you select Better (Slower), it will take longer than normal to process the image, but the quality of the final image will be improved.

To see how Distort works with type, first create a new file 5 inches by 5 inches, then activate the Text Selection tool in the Tools palette. After you select the Text Selection tool, the Controls :Text Selection palette allows you to select a type face and set *tracking* (the spacing between letters). Select a sans serif font (such as Helvetica or Arial) in the Controls :Text Selection palette's Font pop-up menu, then set the size to 50. After setting the type face and size, click in the middle of your image, then type the word **DISTORT**.

Activate the Distort command by choosing Effects ➤ Orientation ➤ Distort. Click and drag on the handles that appear. Drag the handles on the left up and the handles on the right down, as shown in the top image in Figure 4.4. To execute the Distort command, click OK in the Distort dialog box. After the distortion appears on screen, fill the text with either the current primary color, a gradation or weave. First make your selection from the Art Materials palette, then choose Effects ➤ Fill. In the Fill dialog box, choose the option you want, then click OK. When the text is filled, deselect the text by choosing Deselect from the Edit menu.

Flip

Painter's Flip commands enable you to flip an image that was scanned upside-down or that is facing the wrong way. In the Effects ➤ Orientation submenu, you'll find both Flip Vertical and Flip Horizontal.

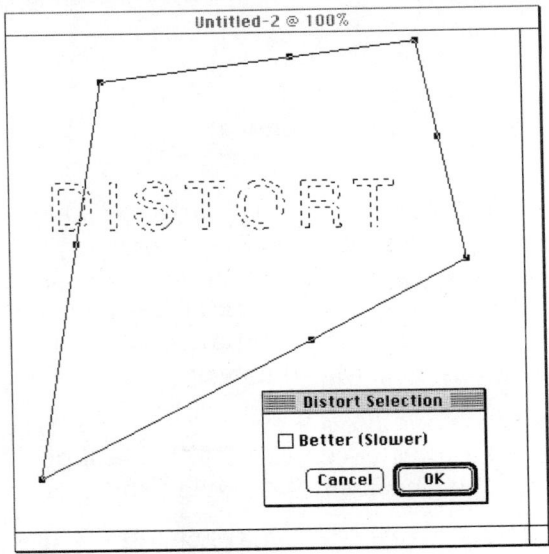

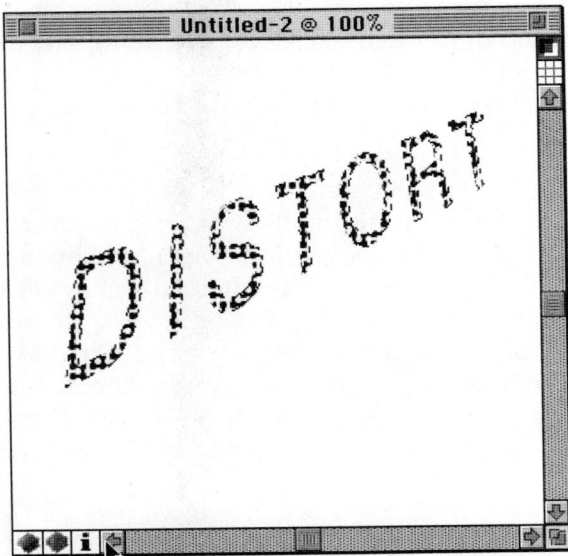

FIGURE 4.4: Top: Shows Distort image handles after they were adjusted. Bottom: Displays the text after it was distorted and filled with a weaved.

Note *Now that you've been introduced to some of the basic commands used to enhance and manipulate digital images, try your hand at an art project to practice your skills.*

Practice: Creating a Small Poster

In this section you'll create a small poster, similar to Figure 4.5, that you could use as one side of an event announcement or flyer. As you complete the project, you'll copy one image and paste it into another; then you'll scale the copy and move it into position.

FIGURE 4.5: The Flamenco project

Digitizing and Manipulating Images

1. If you have a scanner, start by choosing two photographs or slides. One image should be the main image, the other will be the image that you'll use repetitively in the border.

   Note *If you don't have a scanner or images to use, you can work with the Sailboat and Shells tutorial images. Use the sailboats as your main image, and select a shell to use in the border.*

2. Once you've picked the images, scan them in at the desired resolution. Remember, if you're only creating practice images or if you are creating images that will only be seen on your computer monitor, you should scan at 72 ppi. If you'll be outputting to a commercial printing press, you should use a resolution that is twice the screen frequency that will be used to output the image. If you are enlarging the image, you should calculate resolution using the formula provided earlier in this chapter.

   Tip *Many professional artists who work with digitized images begin their images by creating low-resolution versions of their work. Since low-resolution images consume less memory than high-resolution images, working in "low res" allows them to experiment with different artistic concepts in less time than it might take at higher resolutions. Once they determine the colors and the content, they recreate the image at a higher resolution.*

3. After you've decided which images you're going to use and have digitized them, you are ready to begin creating the poster. If your main image is not on screen, open it now. (If you are following this exercise using tutorial files, load the Sailboat image from the Painter Tutorial folder as your background image.)

   With the background image on screen, your next step is to enlarge the canvas size so that you can add the image you will be using as a border and some text.

4. When you increase the canvas size, the extra canvas area will be whatever the paper color is set to. Change the paper color to one of the colors in the background image. Do this by activating the Dropper tool and positioning the mouse pointer over any color in the

background image, then click. As soon as you click, the primary painting color in the Art Materials :Colors palette changes to match the color that you clicked on. To make the Canvas border area change to the primary painting color, choose Canvas ➤ Set Paper Color.

5. After you've set the paper color you are ready to extend the canvas area. Do this by choosing Canvas ➤ Canvas Size. In the Canvas Size dialog box, type **100** in the Top, Left, Bottom, and Right fields to add 100 pixels all around your image. Click OK to activate the changes. Instantly, your canvas size increases. The canvas color around your image will be the new paper color. You may need to increase the size of your document window to see the increase in canvas size.

6. Now you're ready to begin the procedure for adding images to your canvas border. If the image you wish to use for your border isn't on screen, open it now. (If you are following this exercise by using Painter's Tutorial images, load the Shells file.) After the file loads, use the Rectangular Selection tool to select the portion of the image that you wish to use as your border.

7. Once the image is selected, choose Edit ➤ Copy, so that you can paste it into the main image on screen. After you've copied the image, you can close the file you copied the border image from.

Remember, if you use two images with different resolutions, when you paste one into the other the size of the pasted image will change. For example; if you paste a high-resolution image into a low-resolution image, the high-res image's dimension will enlarge after it is pasted into a lower resolution file (because there are more pixels per inch in the high-resolution image).

Next paste the border image into the main image.

8. With the main image activated, choose Edit ➤ Paste ➤ Normal. When the border image appears, activate either the Rectangular Selection tool or the Floating Selection tool and drag the selection to the top left-hand corner of your image.

Digitizing and Manipulating Images

Note When you paste an image using the Paste ➤ Normal command, Painter turns the image into a floater, which occupies a layer above the underlying pixels. Floaters can be moved and edited without affecting the underlying pixels. To see a listing of the objects that are floating, you can open up the Objects palette. In the Objects palette, click on the F. List icon. In the Objects :Floater List palette a list of all the floaters on screen is displayed. If you deselect a floater, you can easily reselect it by clicking on it with the Floating Selection tool (the pointing hand in the Tools palette). For more information on floaters, see Chapter 8.

In our example the border image was too large to fit in the 100-pixel-wide canvas edge. The Scale command was used to resize the selection so it fit into the border area.

9. To resize the image, choose Effects ➤ Orientation ➤ Scale. When the Scale Selection dialog box appears, leave the Constrain Aspect Ratio option selected, but deselect the Preserve Center option. Click on the bottom right-hand corner of your selection, and drag up and left to make the image smaller, as shown in Figure 4.6. After you've resized your image to fit into the border area, click OK to activate the changes. If you need to move the selection into position, use the Floating Selection tool. Don't deselect.

Next you'll copy and paste the image that you scaled so that copies of the image can be used as a border.

10. To copy the image from step nine, first make sure the image is still selected. If it isn't, click on it with the Floating Selection tool. Then choose Copy from the Edit menu. Next press Command+V (Windows users: Ctrl+V) to paste a copy of the image. When the image appears, use the Floating Selection tool to move it into position. Continue to paste and drag images until the left border is complete.

Next copy the image to the upper right corner of your canvas. If you'd like, flip the image so that it is facing the other way. (To flip the image, choose Effects ➤ Orientation ➤ Flip Horizontal.) When you're satisfied with the position of the image, copy it and continue pasting again and again until the right side of the border is filled.

Your last step is to add text.

11. Select the Text Selection tool from the Tools palette. Then choose a Font, Point Size, and Tracking (tracking is the spacing between letters)

FIGURE 4.6:   A rose image being scaled to fit into the border

from the Controls :Text Selection palette. After you've made your selections, move the Text Selection tool to the bottom area of the
empty canvas, click, and begin typing. In Figure 4.5 the space
bar was pressed after every letter so that there was more space between them.

12. After you've typed the letters, you may want to move the text. To do
so, first activate the Path Adjuster tool or the Floating Selection tool.
Then, with either of these two tools selected, you can use the arrow
keys on your keyboard to position the text in the desired location.

13. Once the text is in place, add a color from your image to it. To do
this, first activate the Dropper tool, then position the tool over one
of the colors in the border and click (this changes the primary painting color). The primary painting color is now the color you clicked
on. Now choose Effects ➤ Fill. In the Fill dialog box, make sure that
the Current Color option is selected, then click OK. The text selection is filled with the primary painting color.

14. When the text at the bottom of the poster is completed, copy it and paste it at the of top of the image so that it looks similar to Figure 4.5. You may want to use Painter's grid to vertically align both the top and bottom text. See Chapter 1 to review working with a grid.

If you'd like, continue to embellish the poster. Otherwise, use the File ➤ Save As command to save your work.

Note *If you want to save your file so that you can reactivate its floating selections, make sure that you save it in Painter's native file format, RIFF. See Chapter 8 for more information about using floaters.*

● **Wrapping It Up**

Now that you've learned the fundamentals of manipulating digitized images, proceed to the next chapter to learn how to enhance your digitized image. In Chapter 5, you'll learn how to change the brightness and contrast, adjust colors, sharpen and blur, and add lighting effects.

Enhancing Images

In traditional painting, if you paint an image too dark or too light, or discover you dislike the colors you used, you can often paint over whatever you don't like. With Painter, changing colors or making dark areas bright can be accomplished by executing a few simple menu commands. This chapter covers the commands you need to know to adjust colors, tonal range, and lighting in an image. It also covers several Focus Control commands that allow you to sharpen images to make them crisper, or blur the edges to soften them. Using Painter's tonal, focal, and lighting adjustments, you'll be able to correct and enhance not only the images you paint, but digitized images as well.

Changing Tonal Control

Painter's Tonal Control commands allow you to tune up your images, by adjusting the brightness and contrast as well as by targeting specific colors to be changed.

> **Note** *When using the Tonal Control commands, Painter allows you to adjust either the entire image or a selected area in an image. To select an area, you can use the Rectangular Selection tool, Oval Selection tool, or Magic Wand. For a complete discussion of selecting techniques, see Chapter 7.*

One of the easiest ways to improve an image is to adjust its brightness and contrast.

Adjusting Brightness and Contrast

After creating or digitizing an image, you may wish to brighten or darken it or adjust its contrast.

Adjusting brightness and contrast in Painter is quite easy. As you'll see in this section, it's simply a matter of clicking and dragging the mouse in the Brightness/Contrast dialog box. If you'd like to experiment with Painter's Brightness and Contrast controls, first load an image that you wish to correct. If you don't have a file to use, you can load any image to practice on. If you wish to adjust brightness and contrast in a specific area in your image, select it first. After the file is loaded, assume that you would like to adjust its brightness to make the image darker. To access Painter's Brightness/Contrast controls, choose Brightness/Contrast from the Effects ➤ Tonal Control submenu.

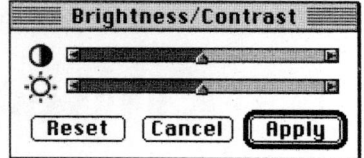

Notice that the Brightness/Contrast dialog box features two sliders. The top slider controls Contrast, the bottom slider controls Brightness. To make the image on screen darker, click and drag the lower darkness slider to the left. As you drag to the left, the image darkens. As you drag to the right, the image lightens.

Next try adjusting contrast. When you adjust contrast in an image you increase or decrease the difference between the darkest and lightest image areas. Increasing contrast can often sharpen details in an image. To increase the contrast, click and drag the top slider to the right. As you drag, the difference between the darkest and lightest tones in the image grows. To decrease contrast, click and drag to the left.

If you'd like to experiment more with the Brightness/Contrast command, try painting a few blue brush strokes in a new file, then paint a few bright yellow strokes. Remember that yellow and blue are color complements—colors which are on opposite ends of the color wheel (see Chapter 3 if you need to review working with color). Then try changing the contrast of the yellow and blue colors on screen. The yellow and blue will grow more intense when you increase contrast, because the difference between the light and dark tones increases. When you decrease contrast, the hues gradually begin to resemble each other.

When you wish to apply the changes, click the Apply button. To reset the image to its original tones, click the Reset button.

To gain even more control over tonal adjustments of your image, proceed to the next section to learn about the Equalize command.

Equalizing an Image

The Equalize command redistributes an image's brightness values over the entire available range, often increasing contrast and enhancing detail. Equalize is often used to improve the quality of digitized images that are too flat, too light, or too dark.

The best way to understand how Equalize works is to put the command to work at correcting an image that needs tonal adjustment. Try loading an image that is very light or very dark. If you don't have an image to use, load the Rose image from the Tutorial folder.

> **Tip** In order to avoid changing the tutorial file, use the File ➤ Save As command to rename the Rose file as Rose2.

After saving the file with a new name, execute the Equalize command by choosing Equalize from the Effects ➤ Tonal Control submenu. If you are equalizing a large file, you may see a screen prompt notifying you that Painter is "collecting histogram data." You'll learn more about histograms later in this section.

As soon as the Equalize dialog box appears, Painter immediately previews the effects of equalizing the image. When Painter equalizes the image it stretches the image's tonal values over a broader range of brightness values. This often results in increased image contrast, as shown in Figure 5.1.

FIGURE 5.1: Image of the Parthenon in Greece (top) before applying Equalize, (bottom) after applying Equalize

In the Equalize dialog box, you'll see a chart which resembles an oddly shaped mountain. This chart, called a *histogram*, plots the tonal range of the image. When you first open the dialog box, the histogram shows the image's tonal range before it was equalized. The horizontal axis plots the tonal range

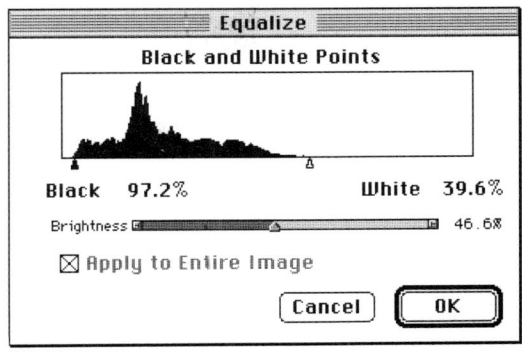

from dark to light: from 100% black to 0% white. The vertical axis plots the number of pixels at each tonal percentage.

Darker image areas, often called *shadow areas*, are plotted on the left side of the histogram. The bright areas are plotted on the right side. These are called *highlights*. The midrange pixels, or *midtones*, are plotted in the middle of the histogram. If a graph bulges in the middle, the image has more midtone pixels. If the image has more highlights, the graph rises on the right side. If the image is predominantly dark, the graph will rise on the left side of the histogram.

To see how the Equalize command can redistribute the tonal range of an image, click OK. After you click OK, the tonal range of the image is changed to match the preview you saw when the Equalize dialog box was

opened. To see the histogram of the equalized image, choose the Equalize command again from the Effects ➤ Tonal Control submenu. When the histogram appears, you'll see that it now stretches over a greater tonal range.

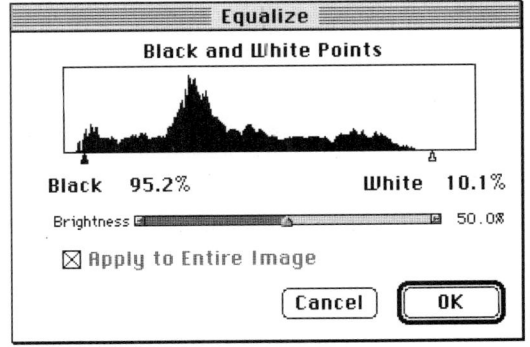

The Equalize command works by automatically setting a white point (a highlight value) and a black point (a shadow value). After picking white and black points, Painter stretches the tonal range between the two points. This often improves the quality of an image.

Occasionally, Painter's automatic setting of the black and white points creates image areas that are too light or too dark. If this is the case, you can set the white and black points manually, by clicking and dragging the sliders under the histogram. The white triangle on the right of the histogram sets the white point, the dark triangle on the left of the histogram sets the black point of the image.

When you click and drag to set the white point, Painter takes all values lighter than the white point's percentage and makes them white. In other words, it grabs pixels in the image that fall beyond the white point marker and turns them white. When you drag the black triangle, Painter changes values darker than the black point marker to black.

Apart from stretching the tonal range between the lightest and darkest portions of an image, the Equalize dialog box allows you to change the midtones of an image as well. Midtones are adjusted by clicking and dragging the Brightness slider. When you drag the Brightness slider you do not affect the lightest and darkest portions of the image, only the midtone areas of the image. As you drag the slider, Painter previews the change in your image. If you click and drag the slider to the left, the midtones lighten. If you drag to the right the midtones darken.

> **Tip** *To equalize an entire image even if a selection exists on screen, select the Apply to Entire Image check box.*

If you'd like to experiment with the white-point and black-point sliders, try clicking and dragging on each to see the effect. After setting the white and black points, fine-tune the image further by adjusting the brightness slider. If you wish, click OK to apply the changes.

Now that you've learned how the Equalize command changes the tonal range, proceed to the next section to learn how to adjust the colors in an image.

Adjusting Colors

Painter's Adjust Colors command allows you to adjust the hue, saturation, and value in an entire image or in a selection. Using this command, you can intensify the colors in a dull image, shift the hue, or increase or decrease a color's brightness.

To see the Adjust Colors dialog box in action, first load an image on screen. If you wish to adjust only a specific area of an image, select it first.

To adjust the colors in the image or selection, choose Adjust Colors from the Effects ➤ Tonal Control submenu.

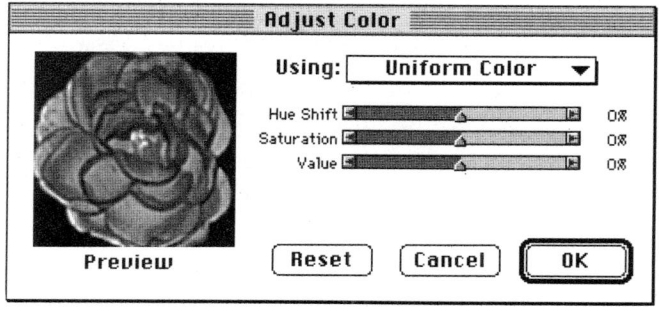

When the Adjust Colors dialog box opens, notice that a portion of your image appears in a preview box. The preview allows you to predict how color adjustments will affect your image before you apply the command. By clicking and dragging in the preview box with the mouse, you can move the preview image so the area that you're most interested in is center stage.

The sliders in the dialog box allow you to shift the hue, saturation, and value of the image or a selected area on screen. (For an explanation of Hue, Saturation and Value, see Chapter 2.) Adjust the Hue Shift slider to the right and the colors in the image shift as if you were moving around the color wheel in a clockwise direction. Drag the slider to the left and the colors shift as if you were moving counter-clockwise on the color wheel. Both the Hue Shift and the Saturation sliders can be adjusted from −50% to +50%.

The Using: pop-up menu allows you to choose the "source" of the color to change. If you choose Uniform Color, the color of the image or selection changes according to the slider values. If you choose Paper Grain, the paper grain currently selected in the Art Materials :Papers palette is applied according to the slider values. If you choose Mask, Painter adjusts colors within a mask according to the grayscale values of the mask. For instance, if you created a mask with a masking brush with the primary color set to a light gray, the Adjust Colors command will provide different results than if you had created the mask with a dark shade of gray. Image masks can be created with masking brushes and the Edit ➤ Masks command. You'll learn more about masks in Chapter 7.

If you choose Image Luminance in the Using: pop-up menu, the image's luminance values are used to determine the color change. An image's

Enhancing Images

luminance values are its brightness values. As mentioned earlier, you can view a graph of an image's brightness values by opening the Equalize dialog box. If you choose Original Luminance, the image's clone source's luminance is used as the basis of the color adjustment in the clone image. You'll learn how to create clones in Chapter 6.

To see the effects of the Adjust Color command, try setting the Using: pop-up menu to Uniform Color, then watch the preview change as you experiment with the Hue Shift, Saturation, and Lightness sliders. To apply the effects to your image, click OK.

Making Selective Color Adjustments

Painter's Adjust Selected Colors command is very much like a magical search-and-replace command for color. It allows you to select a color range and to replace the color in the selected area with a new color. For instance, you can take an image of a red rose in a blue vase and change only the color of the rose to yellow or blue.

If you'd like to try out the Adjust Selected Colors command, first open an image that you wish to make color adjustments to. If you don't have an image, load the Rose file from the Painter Tutorial folder.

To open the Adjust Selected Colors dialog box, choose Adjust Selected Colors from the Effects ➤ Tonal Control submenu. The Adjust Selected Colors dialog box is somewhat similar to the Adjust Colors dialog box. The dialog box includes a preview area, which allows you to predict how the changes will affect your image. You can click and drag in the preview area to move the part of the image that you want to change into view.

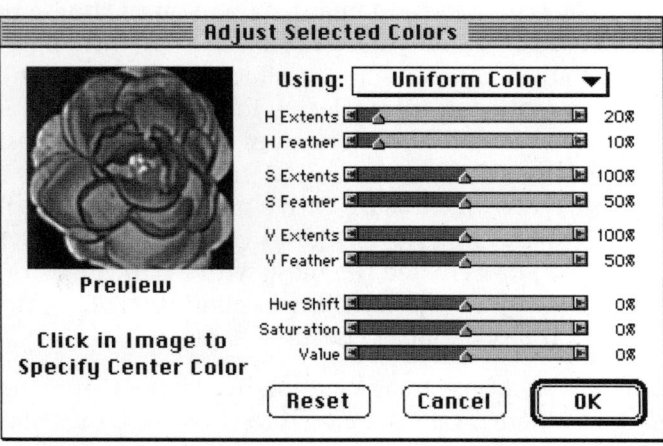

Before you adjust colors in your image, you must indicate to Painter the color you wish to change. You do this by clicking in your image. When you click, Painter samples the color you selected. After you click, use the sliders to adjust how much of the image area and how much hue, saturation, and value that you wish to change.

To change hue, saturation, and value, you click and drag on the Hue Shift, Saturation, and Value sliders, as you did with the Adjust colors command (this time they're at the bottom of the dialog box). To control the color range of the change, you click and drag on the H, S, and V Extents sliders. When you drag the Extents slider, Painter computes a range of contiguous pixels from the sampled color that can be changed. For instance, the further you drag the H slider to the right, the greater the hue range that will be changed to the color selected by the Hue, Saturation, and Value sliders at the bottom of the dialog box. Thus, if you click on a pink rose with the H Extents slider set to 10%, Painter adjusts hues in areas similar in hue to the pink rose. If you click and drag the slider to 75%, Painter changes not only the pink rose, but the green stem as well.

When you drag the Feather sliders to the right, Painter extends the edges of the image area that is changed.

The Using: pop-up menu in the Adjust Selected Color dialog box allows you to select a source for the color adjustment. The choices are the same as those for the Adjust Colors command described earlier in this chapter. The choices are Uniform Color, Paper Grain, Image Luminance, Mask, and Original Luminance.

To see how the Adjust Selected Colors command works, try moving the mouse pointer over a color in your image that you wish to change (make sure you click in your image, not in the color preview box). To use the HSV values from your image for the color adjustment, make sure that Uniform Color is selected in the Using: pop-up menu.

Next, click on the bottom Hue Shift slider and drag it to the right, to about the 20% mark on the slider. This tells Painter to make a hue shift 20 percent along the color wheel away from the sampled color—the color that you clicked on.

To set the color range of contiguous pixels from the sampled color that you want Painter to change, click and drag on the H Extents slider. As you drag to the right, you increase the area that Painter applies the change to.

Enhancing Images

To soften the edges of the color transitions, drag the H Feather slider to the right. Next adjust the Value and Saturation sliders to fine-tune the color adjustment.

If you'd like to experiment more with the Adjust Selected Colors command, try sampling different image areas, then adjusting the Hue, Saturation, and Value.

Using Dye Concentration

Painter's Dye Concentration command allows you to adjust a color's intensity. It can be very helpful if you wish to adjust an image that is under or overexposed. Apart from adjusting color intensity, Dye Concentration also allows you to add more texture to your image.

To try out the Dye Concentration command, load an image. If you wish to adjust only a portion of the image, select it first. If you don't select an image area, Dye Concentration change is applied to your entire image. Now, choose Effects ➤ Surface Control ➤ Dye Concentration.

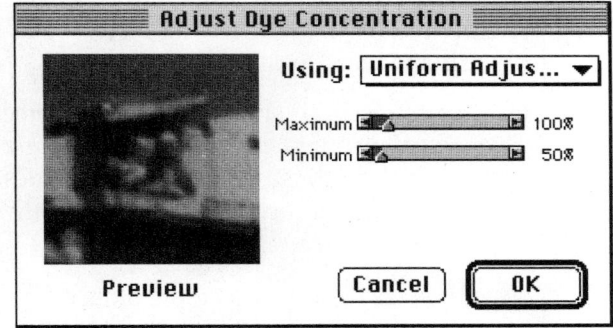

In the dialog box, the Using: pop-up menu determines how the Dye Concentration command is applied. Here's a list of the choices:

- ◆ **Uniform Adjustment**—Color is adjusted, but no texture is added.
- ◆ **Paper Grain**—Texture is based on the selected paper grain in the Art Materials :Papers palette. You may change paper grains with the Dye Concentration dialog box open on screen.
- ◆ **Image Luminance**—Painter uses the image's brightness values as a basis for adding texture.

◆ **Original Luminance**—The brightness values of a clone source are used to add texture to a cloned image. (Cloning is covered in Chapter 6.)

◆ **Mask**—Texture is added along the edges of a selection.

The Maximum and Minimum sliders allow you to control the intensity of the effect. When the Uniform Adjustment is chosen, only the Maximum slider affects the image. Dragging the slider to values above 100% increases color density, usually darkening them; dragging it below 100% decreases color density, usually lightening them. When any of the other options in the Using: pop-up menu are chosen, the Maximum and Minimum sliders control the high and low points of the texture. Dragging the Maximum slider to the right raises the highest points of the texture. Dragging the Minimum slider to the right raises the lowest points of the texture. Thus, dragging the Maximum slider as far right as it will go (800%) and the Minimum slider to the far left (0%) creates the most dramatic effect.

To see the effects on your image, pick an option in the Using: pop-up menu, adjust the sliders, then click OK.

> **Note** *A color's density determines how much light is absorbed or reflected by it. Darker colors have more density than lighter colors.*

Using the Dodge and Burn Brushes

If you need to fine-tune tonal adjustments in an image, Painter's Dodge and Burn brushes could very well be the best tools for the job. The Dodge brush lightens, the Burn brush darkens. These brushes can be extremely helpful when you wish to touch up underexposed and overexposed image areas. The brushes are based upon traditional darkroom techniques of the same names.

To use the Dodge brush, first activate the Brush tool in the Tools palette, then choose Dodge in the Brushes palette. Leave the Method Category and Method Subcategories set to their default settings. Click and drag over image areas that are too dark. Increasing the Opacity setting in the Controls palette intensifies the lightening effect.

To darken image areas, select the Burn brush and leave the Method Category and Method Subcategories at their default settings. Click and drag over your image to darken areas. To intensify the darkening effect, increase the Opacity setting in the Controls palette.

> **Note** *If you wish to change the size of the Dodge or Burn brush stroke, use the Size slider in the Brush Controls :Size palette.*

Posterize

The Posterize command allows you to reduce the number of color levels in an image. Posterizing is often used to create special effects, or when only a small number of colors must be printed. For instance, Posterize can be used if you wish to create spot colors. For more information about creating spot colors in Painter, see Chapter 2.

To experiment with the Posterize command, open an image. If you don't have an image to load, try using the Shells tutorial file. Before posterizing the image, use the Save As command to save it under a new name. To posterize the image, choose Posterize from the Effects ➤ Tonal Control submenu. In the Posterize dialog box, type **3**. This will reduce the number of color levels to three.

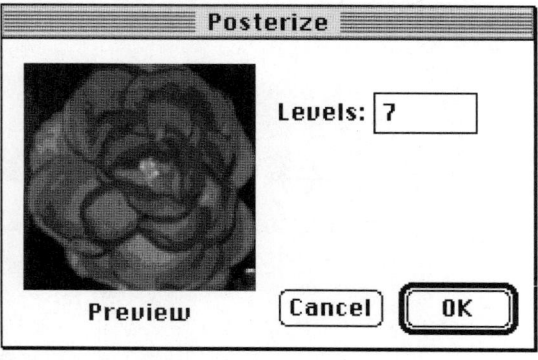

If you want to specify exactly which colors are to be used with the Posterize command, you can posterize by choosing the Posterize Using Color Set command from the Effects ➤ Tonal Control submenu. This will posterize an image using the current color set. To review how to create a Color Set, see Chapter 2.

Creating a Negative of Your Image

Painter's Negative command allows you to create a negative of your image. When you create a negative, image areas that are black turn white, and colored image areas are transformed to their complements on the color wheel.

If you wish to create a negative of only part of your image, select the image area first. If you don't select an image area, Negative will create a negative of your entire image.

To execute the command, choose Negative from the Effects ➤ Tonal Control menu. Immediately, Painter transforms the image into a negative of its former self. In Figure 5.2, text was created with the Text Selection tool and filled with blue. Next, half of the text was selected with Rectangular Selection tool. The Negative command was applied to the selected area. The selected blue text turned yellow (blue's complement), and the selected white area turned black.

FIGURE 5.2: Inverted text

Adjust Focus

The Adjust Focus commands allow you to sharpen and soften images. Sharpening images helps enhance details and image contours, and is particularly useful when you need to correct images digitized by scanners and digital cameras. Painter's Soften command can be used to blur hard edges or jagged edges that might occur in digitized images. Blurring can also be used to lessen the effect of distracting image elements as well as to remove blemishes and wrinkles.

Sharpening an Image

Painter's Sharpen command sharpens by increasing the contrast around image edges and image contours. If you're working with scanned images, you'll be amazed at how Painter's sharpening powers can transform a soft blurry image into one with crystal-clear edges.

To sharpen an image, first select the area that you wish to sharpen. If you do not select an area, Painter will sharpen the entire image. To start the sharpening process and open the Sharpen dialog box, choose Sharpen from the Effects ➤ Focus submenu.

The Sharpen dialog includes a preview area and three sliders. If the image area that you wish to sharpen does not appear in the preview box, click and drag in the box until it comes into view.

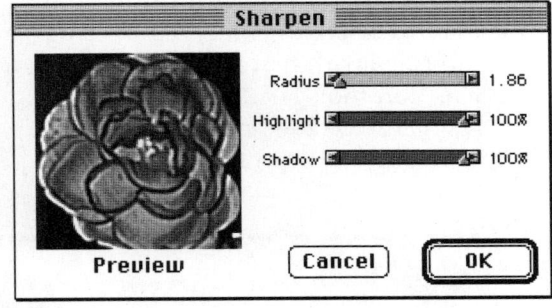

In the Sharpen dialog box, the Radius slider controls the width of the image edge along which the sharpening will take effect. The farther you drag the Radius slider to the right, the greater the width of the edges that are sharpened. The Highlight slider controls how bright the highlight or brightest areas of the image will be. Dragging the slider to the right increases brightness. The Shadow slider controls how dark the darkest image areas will be. Dragging the Shadow slider to the right darkens shadows, dragging to the left lightens them. In general, bright highlights and dark shadows create more contrast in an image, and thus can enhance the sharpening effect.

Softening an Image

The Soften command blurs or softens images. Use the Soften command when edges and color transitions in an image are too harsh. Use the Blur command to create special effects. You could blur image areas to create a sense of motion, or blur areas to create shadow effects.

If you wish to blur a specific image area, you must select it first; otherwise Painter softens the entire file. To execute the Soften command, choose Soften from the Effects ➤ Focus submenu. The Radius slider allows you to specify the range for the softening effect. Drag the slider to the right to increase the distance along which the blurring will take effect.

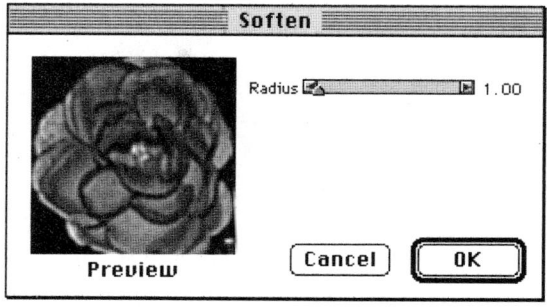

As you've seen in the previous sections, Painter's tonal and focal adjustment commands provide quick and efficient techniques for correcting images. Painter allows you to take image enhancement a sophisticated step further by allowing you to apply different lighting effects.

Apply Lighting to an Image

Lighting can evoke a mood, change the focus of attention, and create intriguing background effects. Painter's Apply Lighting command allows you to quickly change lighting and experiment with multiple effects. It's certainly much less work than moving real spotlights and fill lights around in a studio, or testing different combinations of paint to simulate light. Figure 5.3 shows the Apply Lighting dialog box used to create the light effect seen in Figure 5.4.

To learn how you can change the lighting in an image with the Apply Lighting command, first load an image on screen. If you don't have a file to use, load the Trees file from Painter's Tutorial folder. (If you're using the Trees file, use the File ➤ Save As command to rename it so that you don't overwrite the Trees file.) After your image is loaded, choose Apply Lighting from the Effects ➤ Surface Control submenu.

> **Note** *Unless you have a PowerMac, if your computer does not have a coprocessor or FPU chip, you cannot use the Apply Lighting command.*

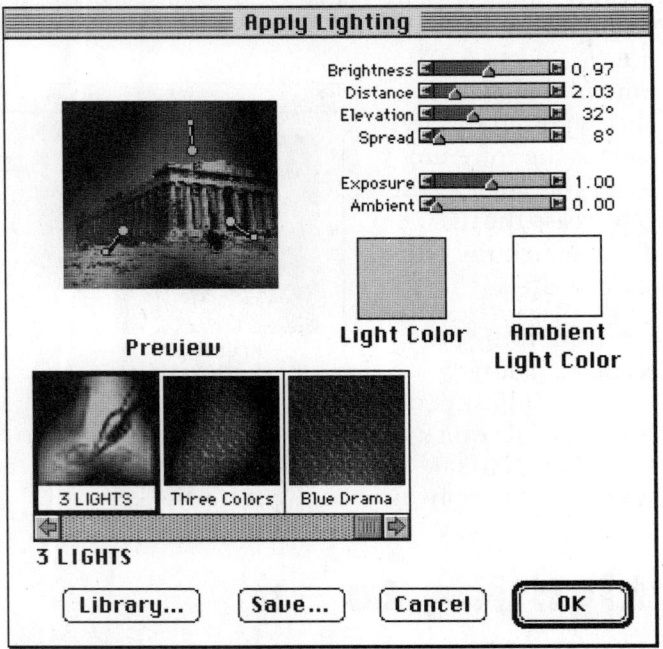

FIGURE 5.3: The Apply Lighting dialog box settings for creating the effects seen in Figure 5.4

Before you begin to apply different lighting effects, you should familiarize yourself with the different features available in the Apply Lighting dialog box. First, notice the familiar preview window. As you adjust lighting options, Painter previews the effects in the window and marks the placement of the electronic lights with tiny light icons.

The lower left corner of the dialog box features a scrolling palette of preset lighting effect variants. The selected lighting variant is framed with black and its name appears below the scroll bars. To see the other variants, click on the right arrow in the scroll bar. To pick one of the variants, simply click in the variant box. The preview box changes to display the effect on your image.

Above and to the right of the variants are two swatch boxes that allow you to change the Light Color and Ambient light color. The Light color is the color of the light you point at your image. The Ambient color is the

FIGURE 5.4:   The Parthenon in Greece, after using the Apply Lighting command setting shown in Figure 5.3

light emanating from the image. When you click on either swatch, the Apple Color Picker or Windows Color dialog box appears, which allows you to choose a color for the light.

Once you've picked a variant from the library or changed light colors, you can alter the effects of the light.

The easiest way to adjust a light is to click and drag on the light icon in the preview box. The light icon appears as two connected circles, one large and one small. The large circle indicates where the light is in your image. The small circle indicates the direction that the light is shining.

You can click and drag on the large circle to reposition the light, and you can click and drag on the smaller circle to change the direction of the light.

If you wish to create more lights, simply click anywhere in the preview box. After you click, a new light will appear. If you wish to delete a light, click on the light icon to select it, then press the Delete key. After you create a light, click on a light to select. You can edit its effects by dragging on the sliders. Here is a brief description of each slider:

◆ **Brightness**—Clicking and dragging to the right brightens the light. Clicking and dragging to the left dims it.

◆ **Distance**—Clicking and dragging to the right simulates moving the light further from the light source. Dragging to the left moves the light closer to the light source.

◆ **Elevation**—Controls the angle of the light.

◆ **Spread**—Controls the width of the light beam. The greater the spread, the greater the width of the light beam.

◆ **Exposure**—This slider simulates an exposure setting in photography. Drag the slider to the right to increase exposure, drag to the left to decrease exposure.

◆ **Ambient**—Controls the light emitted from the image, as opposed to the light being directed at it from the lights in the Preview box. Dragging the slider to the right creates a soft ambient effect, dragging left creates a harsher effect.

Now that you've been introduced to the different options in the Apply Lighting dialog box, try out a few lighting effects. First, click on the Plain light from the lighting palette choices, then drag the light so it illuminates a dark portion of your image. Next, try out the Drama light by choosing it from the scrollable preset lighting effects, then change the Ambient lighting color to orange or red. After you've seen the effects of changing Ambient light, try adjusting the different sliders to see how each affects your image.

After you've found just the right lighting effect, you can save your lighting setup by clicking on the Save button. When the Save dialog box appears, enter a name for your lighting variant. After you save, the variant appears in the scrollable lighting presets in the dialog box.

If you'd like, you can create a library of lighting variants or add a variant to a pre-existing lighting library. To create a lighting library, choose Lighting Mover from the Tools ➤ Movers submenu. In the Lighting Movers dialog box, click New. In the Save dialog box, enter a name, then click Save. Next, select a lighting variant name from the list, and click on the Copy button to move the variant into your library.

If you wish to copy your variant to a different library, first close the new library that you created, then click on the Open button to open the other library. When you have completed adding to your lighting library, choose Quit.

Wrapping It Up

Now that you know how to make adjustments to a digitized image, you are ready to proceed to more advanced topics. The next chapter introduces you to using Painter's powerful cloning tools. The cloning tools can help you transform a digital image into a painting, blend images together, and seamlessly clone away image flaws.

Cloning and Using
Tracing Paper

One of Painter's most powerful features is its ability to seamlessly clone one image into another. Cloning can also be used to blend images together, to create vignettes out of images, and to create painterly effects in digitized photographs. Cloning can also be used as a means of retouching an image. For instance, you can remove unattractive telephone wires from an otherwise charming street scene by cloning over them with surrounding elements, such as trees and sky.

In this chapter you'll learn how to retouch images using Painter's cloning commands. You'll also explore the Use Clone Color option in the Art Materials :Colors palettes, which allows you to turn digital images into paintings. You'll also have a chance to clone one image into another using the Cloner brushes in the Brushes palette. At the end of the chapter, you'll learn how to use Painter's Tracing Paper option, which allows you to paint over an image as if you were using tracing paper. When you use Tracing Paper, you can actually see the underlying image while you trace on top of it in a new document.

You'll start by examining how the Auto Clone command can be used to create a painting out of a digitized photograph.

Cloning a Picture Using the Auto Clone Command

The Auto Clone command takes a clone (a copy of an image) and automatically applies a Painter brush stroke to it. Using Auto Clone, you can quickly transform a digital photograph into a digitized painting, as shown in Figure 6.1.

Complete the following steps to learn how to use the Auto Clone command. In this exercise you'll use the Auto Clone command with the Art Materials palette's Use Clone Colors option.

1. Start by loading a photograph that you want to transform into a painting. If you don't have an image to use, load the Sailboat image in the Tutorial folder.

    Tip *After your image appears on screen, you may want to use the Effects ➤ Tonal Control ➤ Brightness/Contrast command or Effects ➤ Tonal Control ➤ Equalize to add contrast to your image. To review how the Equalize command works, see Chapter 5.*

    Your next step is to create an exact duplicate of the image on screen, using the File ➤ Clone command.

2. To create a clone, choose Clone from the File menu. Immediately a duplicate of your image appears. This duplicate uses your original document on screen as its *clone source*. You'll apply the Auto Clone command to the clone on screen, not to the original document; this insures that you won't affect the original file, only the duplicate.

    When you apply Auto Clone, the options set in the Brushes palette paint your image according to the palette settings. If you are auto cloning a digitized photograph, Auto Clone magically transforms it into a painting.

3. If you'd like to create a colored-pencil effect, choose the Pencils option in the Brushes palette. Then, set the variant pop-up menu to Colored Pencils. Set the Method Category to Cover and the Method Subcategory to Flat Cover. If you'd like a more painterly effect, try choosing the Artists brush with the Seurat brush variant.

FIGURE 6.1: A photograph (a) before applying the Auto Clone command, (b) after applying the Auto Clone command and the Seurat brush

4. Before you apply the Auto Clone command, select the Use Clone Color check box in the expanded Art Materials :Colors palette. This makes Painter paint with the colors from the clone source, rather than from the primary color designated in the Colors palette.

Now you're ready to apply the Auto Clone command.

5. Choose Auto Clone from the Effects ➤ Esoterica submenu. In a few moments, your image gradually transforms itself into a painting. When you are happy with the effects of the command, click the mouse or stylus on the image to stop auto cloning.

If you'd like to explore more auto cloning options, immediately choose Undo from the Edit menu. Then try using the Auto Clone command with other brush settings. You can also try using new brush variants created from different settings in the Brush Controls and Advanced Controls palette. (Remember to select the Use Clone Color option.) For a more dramatic effect, you can change the opacity and grain in the Controls palette. To vary color, adjust the Color Variability sliders in the Art Materials :Colors palette.

When you're done experimenting, close the clone file and save it, if desired. Leave the original document on screen, and proceed to the next section to learn how to use the Auto Van Gogh command.

Cloning Using Auto Van Gogh

The Auto Van Gogh command transforms an image to make it look as though Van Gogh painted it. Figure 6.2 shows the effects of applying the Auto Van Gogh command to the first image in Figure 6.1. To use the Auto Van Gogh command, first load the image that you wish to alter, or use the clone source image on screen from the previous exercise. To create a cloned image to apply the Auto Van Gogh command to, choose Clone from the File menu.

Before executing the Auto Van Gogh command, you should choose the Auto Van Gogh brush variant in the Brushes palette. To access this variant, first select the Artists brush in the Brushes palette. (The Brushes palette drawer must be open in order to access the Brushes pop-up menu.)

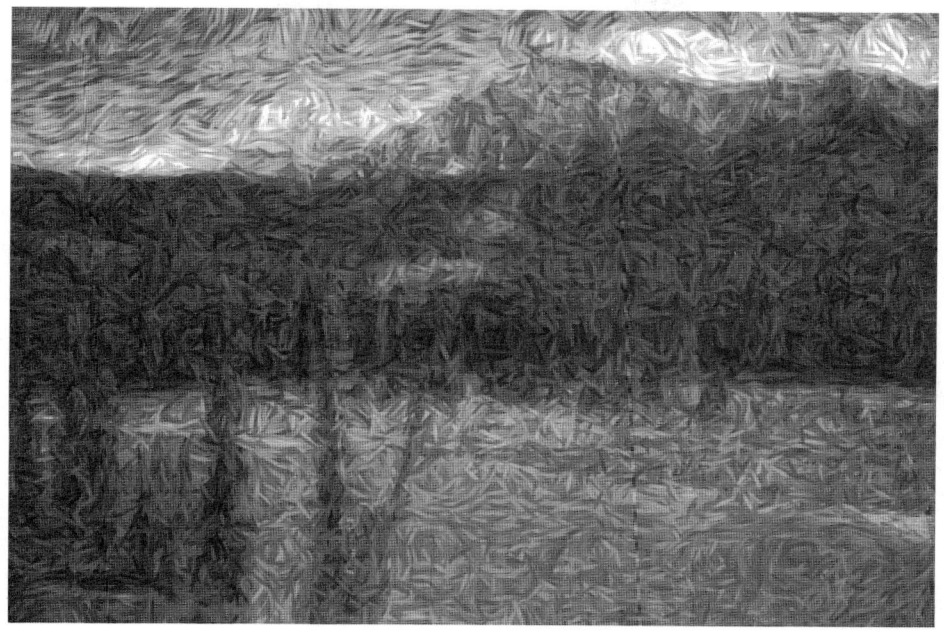

FIGURE 6.2:   Image after applying the Auto Van Gogh command to Figure 6.1a

Then choose Auto Van Gogh from the Brush variant pop-up menu. Leave the Method Category and Method Subcategory pop-up menus at their default settings. To produce an intense effect, increase the Color Variability sliders in the Art Materials :Colors palette.

> **Note** *If you are working with a high resolution file, you may want to increase the brush size in the Brush Controls :Size palette in order to create thicker brush strokes.*

If you'd like, you can also adjust the Opacity and Grain sliders in the Controls :Brush palette.

In order to create the Van Gogh effect with colors from the clone image, make sure the Use Clone Color check box in the Art Materials :Colors palette is selected.

Once you've chosen the Auto Van Gogh brush variant, and set the Use Clone colors check box, choose Auto Van Gogh from the Effects ➤ Esoterica submenu. You'll have to wait a few moments for the effects to take place because Painter must make two passes over the image. Gradually you'll see the thick, stylized Van Gogh strokes transforming your image.

If you don't like the effect, choose Undo from the Edit menu and reapply the Auto Van Gogh command after you've changed settings in the Brush Controls palette and Color Variability sliders in the Art Materials :Colors palette.

Manually Cloning with the Use Clone Color Option

Both Auto Clone and Auto Van Gogh provide quick methods of applying painterly effects to an image. If you'd like more control over the painterly effects, you can paint manually with the Use Clone Color option set in the Art Materials :Colors palette.

In this section you'll start by choosing the Use Clone Color option to paint over a digitized photograph to provide it with a painterly effect. You'll also paint over an image using tracing paper.

Painting Over a Digitized Photograph with the Use Clone Color Option

You can paint using the Use Clone Color option in the Art Materials palette to make a digitized photograph look more painterly. When you activate Use Clone Color, Painter allows any brush to work as a cloning brush. The painterly effect is created in the cloned image based upon sampled pixels in the clone source.

If you'd like to try out your hand at painting with the Use Clone Color option, open any image. If you don't have an image to use, open the Sailboat file from Painter's tutorial folder.

Your first step is to create a clone of the image on screen by choosing Clone from the File menu. Next, you need to pick a brush, variant, Method Category, Method Subcategory, Opacity, and Grain. For an unusual impressionistic effect, choose the Flemish Rub variant. To access this variant, first choose the Artists option in the Brushes palette pop-up menu. Then choose Flemish Rub from the Variant pop-up menu. Leave the other pop-up menus at their default settings. Next, select the Use Clone Color check box in the Art Materials :Colors palette.

In the cloned image, begin painting. As you paint, the colors of the image will begin to smear. To alter the painterly effect, try changing the opacity and grain in the Controls palette.

If you would like to try more cloning experiments, you can return the clone to its original state with the Effects ➤ Fill command. After choosing Effects ➤ Fill, select the Clone Source in the Fill dialog box, then click OK. Alternatively, you can activate the Rectangular Selection tool to select the entire image, then fill the selection with the clone using the Paint Bucket. Before clicking in the selection with the Paint Bucket, pick the Image and Clone Source options in the Controls :Paint Bucket palette.

Painting on a Blank Canvas Using the Use Clone Color Option

Another technique for manually creating painterly effects from a clone source with Painter's Use Clone Color option and Clone command is to completely delete the clone image, then paint over the blank screen with the Use Cloned Colors set in the Art Materials :Colors palette. As you paint, a painterly version of the cloned image appears.

To try out this technique, first clone an image, then delete the entire image after first selecting it. Try using these different variants at different opacities and grain settings: Colored Pencils (Pencil brush), Artist Pastel (Chalk brush), and Thin Stroke (Airbrush brush). Remember that you need to set the Use Color Clone option every time you choose a different brush. This option does not stay activated. After you've tried a brush you can delete the new image by double-clicking on the Rectangular Selection tool and pressing Delete on your keyboard.

In the next section you'll learn how to paint over tracing paper with the Use Clone Color option activated.

Using Tracing Paper

Painter's Tracing Paper option allows you to paint over a clone of a sketch or a digitized photograph.

Figure 6.3 shows an image before and after using the Water Color brush and the Tracing Paper option.

Here's how to use Painter's Tracing Paper option. In this exercise, you'll also learn how Painter's Wet Layer works with Water Color brushes.

1. Open an image you want to trace over, either a photograph or a sketch. When the image is on screen, choose Clone from the File menu. This creates a clone on screen.

Your next step is to delete the clone. By first deleting the clone, you can create a new painted version from scratch.

2. To delete the clone on screen, select the entire canvas by double-clicking on the Rectangular Selection tool, then pressing Delete on the keyboard. The document on screen will be filled with the current paper color.

3. Now click on the Tracing Paper icon at the top right-hand corner of the canvas window. Immediately, a ghost or grayed-out version of the image appears, which you can trace over.

4. Now you're ready to trace over the image with any brush variant you desire. In Figure 6.3b, the Pens brush's Pen & Ink variant with the Art Materials :Colors palette's Use Clone Color option was used to outline the pears. Try tracing over your clone with the Pen & Ink Variant, or with any other variant in the Brushes palette. Be sure to select the Use Clone Color option before you begin.

Tip *To obtain the desired effect when tracing you may need to resize the brush stroke and change its opacity.*

5. After the image is outlined you may wish to color it in using a different brush. In Figure 6.3b, the Water Color brush was used to fill the pears. If you wish to duplicate this effect, set the brush pop-up menu to Water Color, the variant to Water Brush Stroke, the Method Category to Wet, and the Method Subcategory to Grainy Wet Abrasive. Next select Use Clone Color in the Art Materials palette.

FIGURE 6.3: A digitized photograph of pears (a) before using the Tracing Paper option, (b) after using the Tracing Paper option, the Use Clone Color option, and the Pens and Water Color brushes. Turn to the color insert to see the final image in color.

Working in the Wet Layer with the Water Color Brush

When you paint using a Water Color brush variant with the Method Category set to Wet, Painter automatically puts you into *Wet Paint* mode. When you work in Wet Paint mode, you paint in a wet layer above Painter's canvas. You enter this layer automatically anytime the Method Category is set to Wet. If you choose a Method Category other than Wet, you automatically drop from the Wet Layer to the background canvas layer. The paint in the wet layer, however, remains wet until you "dry" it.

As you paint in the wet layer, you can remove water color from unwanted areas by setting the Method Subcategory to Wet Remove Density. (In Figure 6.3, the areas beyond the outline of the pears were removed using this technique.) In order to remove water color from your image with Wet Remove Density, you must remain in the Wet Paint mode. If you want to save your work in Wet mode, you must use Painter's default file format, RIFF. If you don't, the image will dry and you will not be able to remove water paint with Wet Remove Density.

If you choose Dry from the Canvas menu, the wet paint in the wet layer immediately dries. Once it dries, you will not be able to remove paint with Wet Remove Density. So, you might not want to dry your image until you're finished painting.

> **Note** *To control how water color diffuses with paper grain, and to adjust color along the edges of water color brush strokes, use the Diffusion and Wet Fringe sliders in the Advanced Controls :Water Palette. For more information about using the Advanced Controls palette, see Chapter 3.*

When you work in Wet Paint mode it's important to realize that Painter's selection tools and selection commands do not affect the wet layer. Thus, if you make a selection and press Delete, only the dry paint on the background canvas is affected, not the paint in the wet layer. If you wish to use selection tools with elements created in the wet layer, you must first choose Canvas ➤ Dry to dry the paint in the wet layer.

Working with the Cloners

The Cloners brush variants are specifically designed to provide different brush effects when cloning. For instance, the Pencil sketch variant paints your clone with a sketchy pencil effect. The Melt Cloner produces the effect of applying paint with a palette knife. When you paint with Cloners, you can paint over a blank clone or a cloned image, but you don't need to select the Use Clone Color option in the Art Materials palette. Cloning with the Cloners also creates a more precise clone than when cloning with the Use Clone Color option selected. Later in this chapter, you'll use Cloners to retouch an image and to merge two images together.

Before using the Cloners, you might wish to read through the following descriptions of the Cloner brush variants. This will give you an idea of the effects the Cloners produce.

◆ **Chalk Cloner**—Paints the clone with the same effect as the Artist Pastel Brush variant

◆ **Driving Rain Cloner**—Creates a clone as if seen through a window with drops of rain

◆ **Felt Pen Cloner**—Recreates the clone as if painting with a felt-tipped pen

◆ **Hairy Cloner**—Clones using brush strokes that show the brush lines of the brush, semi–anti-aliased brush strokes that can interact with paper grain

◆ **Hard Oil Cloner**—Clones with a hard-edged brush stroke that covers underlying brush strokes and can allow paper grain to show through the strokes

◆ **Impressionist Cloner**—Provides an Impressionistic effect by painting with short brush strokes in various colors taken from the source image

◆ **Melt Cloner**—Clones by creating dripping brush strokes that can make an image appear as if it is melting

◆ **Oil Brush Cloner**—Clones with anti-aliased brush strokes that cover underlying brush strokes

◆ **Pencil Sketch Cloner**—Clones with a pencil-like brush

◆ **Soft Cloner**—Clones with an airbrush type of stroke

◆ **Straight Cloner**—Creates an exact duplicate of the original cloned image. Use this brush if you are working with another brush and wish to paint back the original image on screen.

◆ **Van Gogh Cloner**—Clones with multicolored brush strokes using a Van Gogh style

Note *When using any Cloner brush variant, Painter automatically sets the Method Subcategory to Cloning. If you change the Method Subcategory, a Cloner will not clone.*

Varying the Effect of Cloner Brushes

As you paint with Cloner brushes you may wish to vary their effect by adjusting the controls in the Advanced Controls :Random palette.

In this palette, you can adjust the Clone Location Variability slider. If you drag this slider to the right, Painter randomly picks up image areas in the clone source and applies them to the destination image. For a completely random effect, select the Random Clone Source check box in the palette.

If you change the Clone Location Variability slider, you may also wish to adjust the Clone Location How Often slider. This slider controls how often Painter picks up random pieces from the Clone source. Dragging this slider to the left distorts the image more; dragging to the right produces the opposite effect.

Using the Cloning Method Subcategories

When working with Cloners, the following Method Subcategories are available.

- ◆ **Hard Cover Cloning**—Cloning covers the underlying image areas with hard brush strokes.

- ◆ **Soft Cover Cloning**—Cloning covers the underlying image areas with soft brush strokes.

- ◆ **Grainy Hard Cover Cloning**—Cloning covers the underlying image areas with hard strokes that reveal paper grain.

- ◆ **Grainy Soft Cover Cloning**—Cloning covers the underlying image areas with soft strokes that reveal paper grain.

- ◆ **Drip Cloning**—Clones in paint drips. Useful for creating special effects and adding painterly effects to digitized photographs.

Now that you've reviewed the features of Painter's Cloners, proceed to the next section to use a Cloners brush.

Using Cloning to Retouch and Edit an Image

Cloning can help you clean up imperfections in an image. For instance, assume you wish to use a digitized photograph of a mountain as a background for a painting, but unfortunately, the scene was marred by a few campers pitching a tent in the distance. Using Painter's Cloning Method Category and the Control key (Windows users: Shift key) you could simply hide the people by cloning foliage from the image over the people. Using similar cloning techniques, you can also restore old images that have faded or have been damaged, as shown in Figure 6.4.

To learn how to use the Cloning Method Category and the Control key (Windows users: Shift key) to enhance an image, open any digital image that you wish to retouch. If you don't have an image to use, you can load the Shells file from the Painter Tutorial folder. If you use the Shells file,

FIGURE 6.4: Damaged photograph (a) before cloning, (b) after using cloning

make sure that you use the Save As command to rename and duplicate the file to ensure that you don't inadvertently overwrite it.

Before you begin to clone, you must pick a Cloners brush variant. Start by choosing Cloners in the Brushes palette pop-up menu. Notice that the Method Category automatically switches to Cloning. In order to clone, you must leave the Method Category set to Cloning. To create a soft effect, use the Soft Cloner brush variant.

Your next step is to pick a Method Subcategory, which can control how softly your brush paints or whether it interacts with paper grain. Pick the Method Subcategory most appropriate for your image. If you are using a painted image that interacts with paper grain, you'll probably want to pick either Grainy Soft Cover Cloning or Grainy Hard Cover Cloning. If you are cloning in a digitized photograph, you'll probably want to choose Hard or Soft Cover cloning.

Once you've picked a brush, the Method Category, and the Method Subcategory, you're ready to clone.

> **Tip** *When cloning different areas, you may need to change brush size in the Brush Controls :Size palette or change opacity in the Controls :Brush palette.*

To begin cloning within the same document, you first need to sample the source area for cloning. To do this, move the mouse pointer over the image area that you wish to clone. Next, press and hold the Control key down (Windows users: Shift key). The mouse pointer changes to a cross hair. While still holding the Control key down (Windows users: the Shift key), click the mouse. Only after clicking should you release the key. Then move the mouse pointer over the area where you want your clone to appear.

To begin the cloning process, click and drag without releasing the mouse button. As you drag, the clone begins to appear over the area you are dragging over. Notice that the cross-hair pointer reappears, moving equidistantly to your mouse strokes. The cloning source is always in the region underlying the cross-hair pointer, which never varies in distance from the target area being cloned. If you keep clicking and dragging, Painter keeps cloning. Once you release the mouse button the cloning stops.

Tip *If you want to clone more precisely within a specific area, you may wish to create a mask and clone within the masked area. See Chapter 7 to learn how to create and use masks.*

As mentioned earlier, cloning can be used to retouch unattractive areas of images. It can be used to remove scratches and stains from digitized images and to soften the transition between images that you've copied and pasted together in one document. In the next few paragraphs, you'll see how cloning can be used to blend image areas from one file directly into another.

Blending Two Images Together

Using Cloners, you can blend two completely different images together. As you can see in Figure 6.5, the mountain scene shown earlier in this chapter has been combined with an image of a young boy, making it appear that the boy is in the mountain setting. To create the blended image, the boy's image was cloned into the mountain image. The trick behind cloning two images together is to first open two different images on screen, then set one of them to be the clone source by using the File ➤ Clone Source command. Once you have an image and a clone source on screen, you can clone the clone source into the other image with a Cloners brush variant. Alternatively, you can use a non-Cloners brush with the Method Category set to Cloning, or you can paint in one image with the Use Clone Color option selected in the Art Materials palette.

To begin, first open two images that you want to blend together. If you don't have images you might want to use, open the Trees and Sailboat tutorial images.

Once you have two images open on screen, you need to decide which image will be cloned into the other. The image that gets cloned is your clone source. To create the clone source, first activate the image that will not be the clone source. This is the image that will be your final, or target, image. The target image will be the image that your clone source appears in. If you are using the Trees and Sailboat tutorial images, activate the Trees file. To set up the second image as the clone source, choose Clone Source from the File menu. A pop-up menu appears, allowing you to choose any open document as your clone source. Choose the file that you want to clone

FIGURE 6.5: Cloning a boy into the scenery

into the active document on screen, your target file. If you are using tutorial files, choose the Sailboat file.

> **Tip** *Here's a shortcut for automatically creating a clone source and loading a document to clone into. If you have one file open on screen, you can automatically load a file to clone into by pressing Option (Windows users: Ctrl) and choosing Clone from the File menu. In the Open dialog box that appears, choose the file that you wish to clone the active document into.*

With the target file active, pick a Cloner brush and begin cloning. You may want to start cloning with the Cloners' Soft Cloner variant in order to smoothly blend one image with the other. As you clone, you'll see the clone source image gradually appear in your target image.

If your image appears in the wrong place when you begin cloning, immediately choose Edit ➤ Undo or File ➤ Revert. You can use the Canvas Size command to add canvas area to the clone source image. This will shift the position of the clone when it appears in the target image. For example, if you want the clone image to be further to the right and higher up in the target image, use the Canvas Size command in the clone source image to add canvas area to the left and to the bottom. After you've applied the Canvas Size command to the clone source, you need to activate the target file before you resume cloning.

If you clone too much of the source image into the target image, you can clone more of the target image back over the clone image by using the keyboard+mouse technique of Control-clicking (Windows users: Shift-clicking), described earlier in this chapter.

If you'd like to keep experimenting, try changing brush opacity and grain. To save your work, make sure you choose the Save As command so that you don't overwrite your original target file.

● Wrapping It Up

In this chapter you learned how to create unusual painterly effects and to blend one image into another. In the next chapter, you'll learn how to create more digital magic using selections and masks.

Working with Paths, Selections, and Masks

In Painter, as in many Mac and Windows painting programs, selections are used to isolate image areas so you can fill them with color, edit them, move them, or copy them. In these programs, selections appear as a blinking *marquee*, often referred to as "marching ants." Unfortunately, in most painting software, when you deselect, the parade of marching ants stops in its tracks—the selection disappears, and is gone for good. In Painter, however, selections have a life of their own. They don't disappear; instead, they can be deactivated, reactivated, resized, and easily moved around on screen, almost as if they were separate objects.

Another extremely important feature of selections is that they can be used as *masks*. A mask allows you to protect image areas so that you can paint and apply effects to only the non-protected areas. If the concept of a mask sounds confusing, assume you need to paint a windowsill. To prevent the paint from spreading beyond the sill onto the walls, you could apply masking tape around the edges of the sill. When you paint, the masking tape around your work area keeps your wet brush from affecting the taped area.

If you've never used an electronic mask before, this chapter will open up a new world of painting control for you. Brush effects that you might have thought too difficult or too intricate to try will now be at your command.

Your introduction to masks will start with a look at how masks and selections interact. You'll begin by taking a look at how the Objects :Path List palette allows you to keep track, rename, activate, and deactivate selections. You'll learn how to use the mask drawing and visibility icons in the palette, which allow you to use selections as masks. Once you understand the concept of how masks are used, you'll learn how to use Painter's Masking brushes. With a Masking brush you can edit a mask or create a mask from scratch using a brush stroke. The chapter concludes with a look at how to use Painter's powerful Edit ➤ Mask command to create fascinating effects which blend one image with another.

● Understanding Selections in Painter

In Painter, one of the most common ways to create a selection is to use the Oval Selection, Text Selection, Outline Selection, or Rectangular Selection tool.

When you create a selection with any of these tools, you can fill it using the Edit ➤ Fill command. You can also copy the selected area with Edit ➤ Copy or cut the area with the Edit ➤ Cut command. What you may not realize, though, is that while you work, Painter automatically saves every selection you make, except those created with the Rectangular Selection tool.

Selections created with the Rectangular Selection tool can be stored in the Objects :Floater List palette. Selections created by the Outline Selection, Oval Selection, and Text Selection tool are listed in the Object :Path List palette. Selections created by the Edit ➤ Magic Wand command and the Edit ➤ Mask menu commands also appear here. These selections are listed in the Objects :Path List palette because each selection is created from a *path*. As you'll see later, a path is a type of wire-frame outline that appears on screen and can be moved, adjusted, and transformed into a blinking selection marquee. All selections that appear in the Path List and Paths palette can also be used as masks that protect image areas.

Note *Selections created with the Rectangular Selection tool are listed in the Objects :Floater List palette, not in the Path List or Paths palette. Masks created within floaters are generally used to hide or reveal image areas in the floater. When a mask in a floater is used to hide a portion of a floater, it reveals the corresponding part of the underlying background canvas. Using floaters and masks created in floaters is covered in Chapter 8.*

Creating a Painting Using Masks

As mentioned earlier, a mask allows you to protect image areas so that you can paint or create effects in the non-protected areas while protected areas remain unchanged.

This section introduces you to how to use masks, and how masks interact with selections created using Painter's selection tools.

In the following sections you'll use masks to create a simple scene composed of a moon and stars. Instead of painting these objects freehand, as some artists would, you'll make them by first creating masks using the Oval selection tool. Once you've created a mask, you'll paint within the masked area or fill the mask to create an object.

Working with the Oval Selection Tool and the Objects :Path List Palette

The Objects :Path List palette keeps track of all selections created by the Oval Selection, Text Selection, and Outline Selection tools.

Selections listed in the Path List palette can be activated or deactivated. Selections can also be viewed in their deactivated state as wire frames. Selections that can be viewed as both a wire frame and blinking selection are referred to as paths. Don't worry if all of this seems a bit confusing now; as you work through this chapter, you'll learn the difference between the types of selections and how they can be activated and deactivated.

In the following exercise you'll explore the Objects :Path List palette by creating selections with the Oval Selection tool, the easiest to use of Painter's selection tools.

Note *In Chapter 2, you used the Oval Selection tool to isolate different image areas and fill them with colors.*

As you work through the exercise you'll see how to use the Objects :Path List palette to activate and deactivate selections. You'll also learn how to turn your selections into masks and view them within a mask overlay.

You'll start the exercise by creating a circular selection.

Before you begin the exercise, create a new canvas to work in, 7 inches by 5 inches at 75 ppi. Set the canvas color to white.

1. With the new, blank canvas on screen, activate the Oval Selection tool and then create a circular selection.

Creating selections with the Oval Selection tool is easy and straightforward. With the tool selected, click and drag over an area you want to select, or over the area where you want to create an oval selection.

2. To open the Objects palette, choose Objects from the Window menu. The Objects palette can show you a list of all selections. To see the list, click on the P. List icon. When the Path List palette is displayed, you'll see that Painter designates the path selection on screen as a path. The first selection is called Path 1. Each subsequent path selection is named Path 2, Path 3, etc.

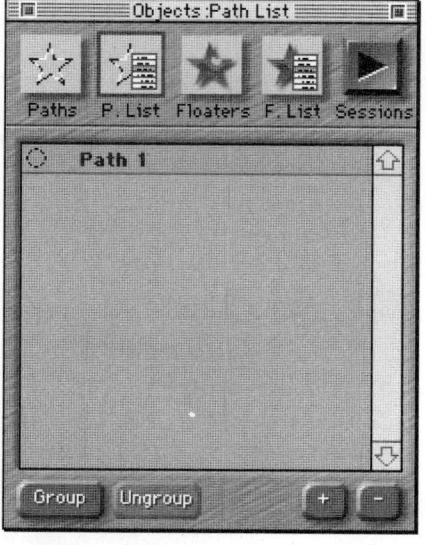

One handy feature provided by the Path List palette is an option for renaming the selections. Naming the selection will help you keep your masking work organized and make it easier to manage multiple selections on screen.

3. To rename the path, double-click on the word *Path 1* in the Objects :Path List palette. When the Path Attributes dialog box appears, type the word **Oval Path** in the Name field. Before closing the dialog box, notice that it also allows you to move a selection by entering pixel coordinates in the Position fields. At the bottom of the dialog box is a re-view of the different paths that Painter can create. Don't worry about these now; you'll learn about them as you work through this chapter. After reviewing the dialog box options, click OK.

> **Path Attributes**
>
> Name: Oval Path
>
> Position: Top: 38.017
> Left: 40.000
>
> Cancel   OK
>
> Path Types
>
> Path 1 — Selection (rendered into the mask).
> Path 2 — Inactive (not rendered into the mask).
> Curve 3 — Bézier Curve.
> Group 4 — Closed Group of paths.
> Mask Group 5 — Open Group (of representative paths).
> Mask 6 — A representative path (computed from the mask).

Note *To move a rectangular selection, choose Tools ➤ Selections ➤ Edit Rectangular Selection. In the Edit Rectangular Selection dialog box you can resize or move the selection by entering pixel coordinates.*

Now that you've named your selection, notice the tiny circle with the dotted-line frame, next to the path name in the Path List palette. The tiny circle indicates whether the selection is active or not.

When a selection is activated it appears as a marquee (blinking lines). Activated selections can be filled or stroked, or can be used as masks. When a selection is activated, the tiny circle next to the path name in the Path List palette resembles the dotted lines of a selection marquee. If the selection is deactivated, the tiny circle icon next to the path name is grayed out. When a selection is deactivated, it appears on screen as an outline, or wire frame. When the selection is deactivated, you can not fill it, stroke it, or use it as a mask.

1. To deactivate the selection on screen, first select the Path Adjuster tool (arrow icon) in the Tools palette, then click on the tiny circle icon to the left of the path name *Oval Path* in the Path List palette. After you click on the circle icon, the path selection on screen changes to resemble a wire frame. The edges of the circle icon in the Path list palette become gray and solid.

2. To make the selection marquee reappear on screen, click again on the circle icon in the Path List palette. After you click, the blinking marquee reappears on screen. Only when the marquee appears on screen can you fill or stroke the selection.

Tip *You can quickly transform a selected wire-frame path into a blinking marquee or turn a blinking marquee into a wire-frame path by pressing the Enter key when the Path Adjuster tool is selected.*

Note *If you click on the dotted circle icon next to the path name in the Objects :Path List palette without the Path Adjuster tool activated, the path selection on screen will disappear. Click again on the icon to make the selection reappear.*

As mentioned earlier, one of the most powerful traits of Painter's selections is that they can be resized and moved with the Path Adjuster tool, without affecting the canvas. When you wish to edit a selection created with the Oval Selection, Text Selection, or Outline Selection tool, you must use the Path Adjuster tool (arrow icon). Before proceeding, make sure the Path Adjuster tool is selected in the Tools palette, and the oval selection you created earlier is on screen. Moving a selection with the Path Adjuster tool is easy. Simply click inside the selection and drag it to the desired location.

3. The oval selection is going to be transformed into a moon. Click in the middle of it and drag it to the top left corner of your canvas so that you have room to create stars and clouds later in this chapter.

Warning *If you fill a path selection and then resize it with the Outline Selection tool, only the outline path will be resized, not the filled object. If you wish to resize the image area within a path selection, use the Effects ➤ Orientation ➤ Scale command. For more information about the Effects ➤ Orientation commands, see Chapter 4. In order to move a filled selection, it must be turned into a floater. Floaters are covered in Chapter 8.*

4. To give yourself a bit more room, you may wish to decrease the size of the oval selection. To do so, position the Path Adjuster tool on one of the handles around the path selection, then click and drag. The handles are the tiny boxes surrounding the selection, as shown in Figure 7.1. If you move one of the corner handles, the path selection is resized without distorting the image. If you move either the

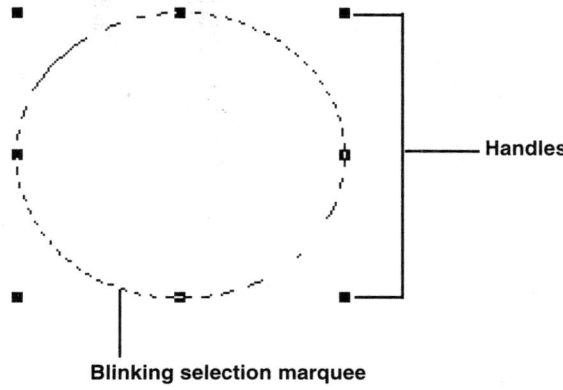

Handles

Blinking selection marquee

FIGURE 7.1: Click and drag the path selection's handles to resize the oval

right or left handle, the path selection's width is resized. If you move either the top or bottom handle, the path selection's height is resized.

Note *The Controls :Path Adjuster palette displays a selection's dimensions and position in pixels when the Path Adjuster tool is activated. To see the measurements as you resize the path selection, open the Controls :Path Adjuster palette.*

Now that you've edited the oval selection, you're ready to investigate its masking properties. Keep the oval selection on screen and proceed to the next section to learn how to use masks to paint inside and outside a selection.

Painting inside and outside a Mask

Selections created by the Oval Selection, Text Selection, and Outline Selection tools can function as masks. This means you can use a selection as a type of stencil in your image. When you use the selection as a mask you can protect the areas outside the selection from being edited. You can also change mask attributes to protect the areas *inside* the selection from being edited.

The Path List palette's masking buttons allow you to control the masking properties of selections. These buttons appear at the bottom of the Path List palette (as shown in Figure 7.2) and the Controls :Path Adjuster palette. A pencil icon and an eye icon identify two rows of masking buttons. To see the masking buttons, the Path List palette must be expanded. If you don't see the masking buttons at the bottom of the palette, expand the palette by clicking on the zoom box in the upper right corner.

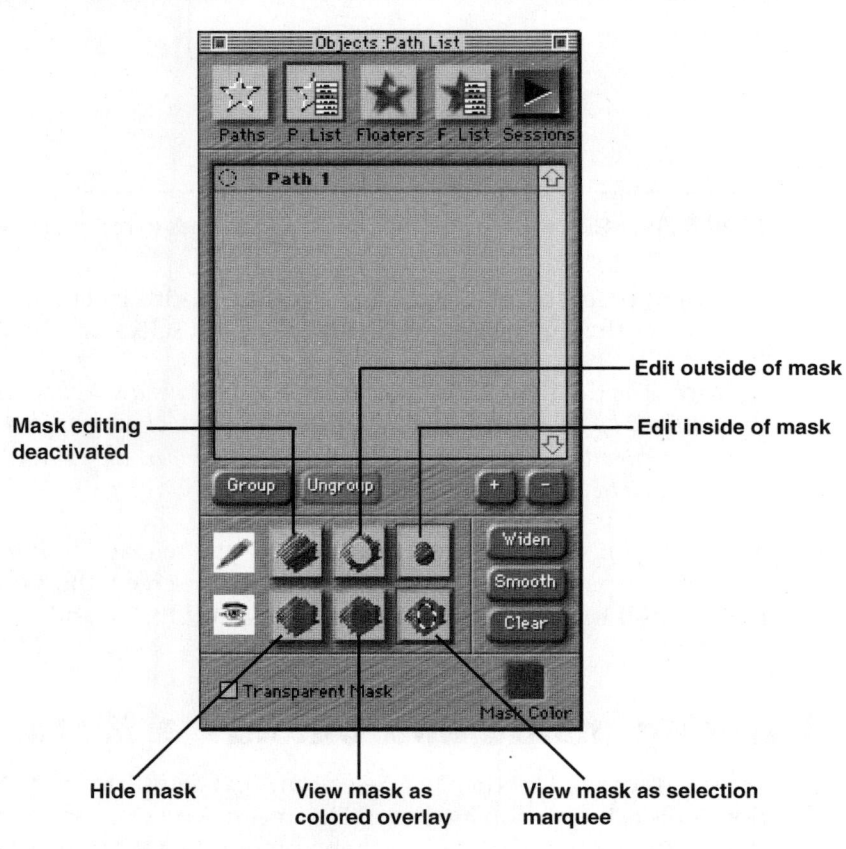

FIGURE 7.2: The masking buttons

The masking buttons control whether you can edit within or outside a selection; also whether a colored overlay or a blinking marquee represents the mask. The colored overlay makes the mask (the protected area of your image) more obvious. The default color for the overlay is red, which resembles a traditional mask called a rubylith (created from red film). Painter's masking buttons allow you to make your selection appear as a cutout in the overlay. Or, if you prefer, you can use the masking buttons to make the colored overlay appear over the selected area.

The two rows of masking icons are headed up by a pencil icon and an eye icon. The pencil icon that appears at the bottom left of the Path List palette is called the *drawing icon*. The row of buttons adjacent to the pencil controls what part of the selection (mask) can be edited. Below the pencil icon is an eye, the *visibility icon*. The row of buttons to the right of the eye icon control how the mask appears on screen.

Here's a brief explanation of how each button affects the mask. After you have read through the descriptions, you'll have a chance to see the mask properties of a selection in action.

The first drawing button turns off masking, and allows you to paint over any area on screen regardless of whether a selection exists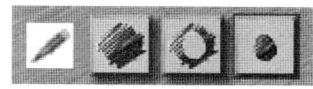
or not. The second drawing button protects the area within a selection so that changes can only be made outside of it. The third button protects areas outside of a selection so changes can be made only inside it.

The first visibility button hides the mask so it can not be seen on screen. The second visibility button creates a red overlay which covers
the protected area of the mask (the area that cannot be edited). The third button makes the blinking selection marquee appear on screen as the outline of the mask.

> **Note** *You can change the Drawing and Visibility mask controls by clicking on the icons at the bottom left corner of the canvas window. The icons function exactly as they do in the Controls :Path Adjuster palette and the Path List palette.*

If you are unfamiliar with the concept of a mask, perhaps the easiest way to understand it is to see the mask overlay in action. Before you can see the mask overlay, though, you must make sure that the selection marquee of the path selection you have on screen is activated. If it isn't, activate it now by clicking on the circle icon next to the path name in the Path List palette.

1. To see the mask overlay (see example in Figure 7.3), click on the second visibility icon in the Objects :Path List palette. If the third drawing button is not selected, select it now. As mentioned earlier, this drawing button ensures that editing changes take place only within the oval selection. As soon as you change visibility buttons the colored mask overlay appears on screen over the protected area. If you wish, you can change the color of the mask overlay by clicking on the colored Mask Color swatch at the bottom right of the Path List palette.

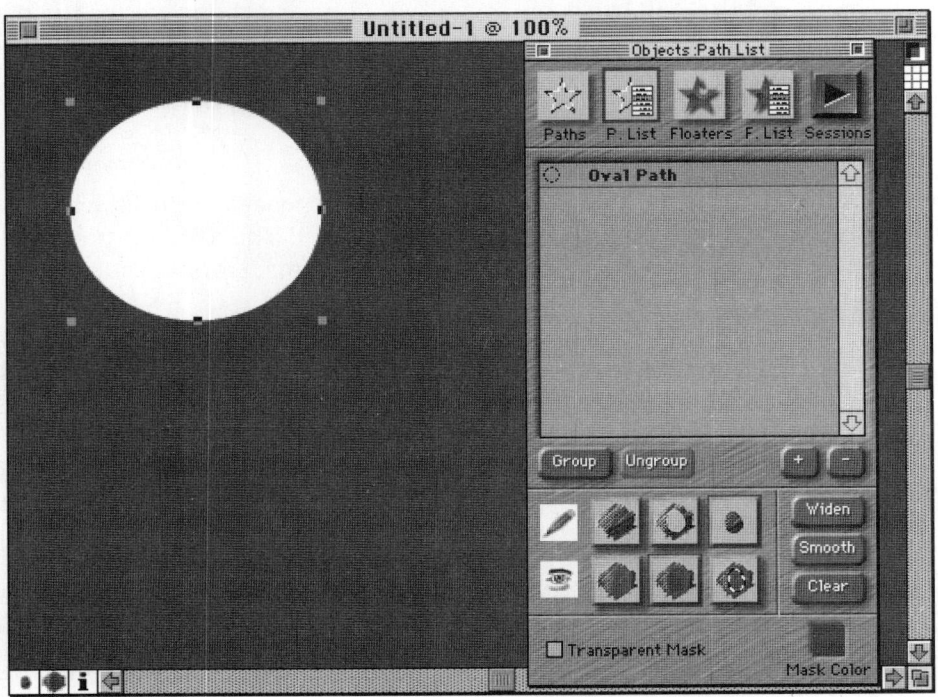

FIGURE 7.3: The areas outside of the oval are protected by a mask.

Note *When you create a mask in Painter, you are actually creating it in a layer called the mask layer. The mask layer will be discussed in more detail when you learn about Masking brushes later in this chapter.*

2. Now activate any brush (perhaps the Big Loaded Oils brush), and paint with a good moon color (perhaps a yellow/orange) over the overlay and cutout portion of the overlay. In order to paint, make sure the Brush tool is selected in the Tools palette. If you are using the Big Loaded Oils brush you can vary the colors by moving the Color Variability sliders in the Art Materials palette.

As you paint, you can only paint within the oval because the mask is protecting the other image areas.

3. If you don't wish to see the red overlay on screen, but still wish to edit within the oval selection, switch visibility icons so that the last visibility icon in the Path List palette is selected (or choose the last visibility icon from the document window mask icons). The selection now returns to the screen and the colored overlay disappears. As you paint, try painting over both the selected and nonselected areas. Notice that only the area inside the selection is affected. If you try to paint outside the selected area nothing happens. This is because the oval selection functions as a mask.

Tip *You can hide the edges of a selection marquee but still utilize it as a mask, by selecting the first visibility icon and the second or third drawing icon.*

Now assume you wish to paint outside the oval selection, but not splash paint into the interior of the oval.

4. To reset the masking mode so that the unprotected area comprises everything *but* the oval selection, select the middle drawing button in the Path List palette. Keep the last visibility button in the eye column selected.

5. Now set the primary painting color to a blue sky color, and start painting. Notice that no matter how hard you try, only the outside of the oval is colored, not the interior. To see the mask overlay click on the second visibility button.

Tip *For an interesting effect, use the Liquid Distorto brush variant to smear the oil paint in the sky area.*

6. To return the selection marquee back to the screen and hide the red mask overlay, click on the third visibility button.

Warning If both the third visibility button and the first drawing button are selected, the selection marquee will not function as a mask. By clicking on the first drawing button you deactivate the mask, even though the selection (or red overlay) can still be seen on screen.

Now that you've been introduced to the concept of how a mask works, proceed to the next section to see how you can edit the mask by subtracting one selection from another.

Note To delete a path selection from the screen and remove it from the list in the Path List palette, click on its name in the palette, then click the Clear button.

Before you proceed to the next section, save your file in Painter's file format (RIFF) and name the file **Moon**.

Working with the Objects :Path List Palette

In the previous section you learned how to use the Objects :Path List palette to rename, show, and hide a path and path selection. In this section you'll use the Objects :Path List palette to bring one path in front of another one, and edit a mask by subtracting a selection from another. If you don't have an oval selection on screen from the previous section, create one now.

To get started, you'll need to create another circular selection. By subtracting the new circular selection from the previous one on screen, you'll turn the first circular selection from a moon shape into a crescent. Instead of creating a circle path from scratch, use a keyboard shortcut to duplicate the oval selection that's already on screen.

1. To copy the oval selection on screen, first activate the Path Adjuster tool. Next, press and hold the Option key (Windows users: Alt) and, while still holding it down, click and drag in the middle of the oval selection on screen. As you drag, a duplicate of the oval appears.

2. Now take a look at the Objects :Path List palette. Another path listing is created beneath the Oval Path. To change the name of the second Oval Path, double-click on this path to rename it. When the Path Attributes dialog box appears type **Negative Oval Path** in the Name field. Then click OK to change the name of the path. This path is called Negative Oval Path because you will subtract this from the Oval Path selection.

3. Before subtracting one selection from another, you need to position the negative oval path over the oval path, as shown in Figure 7.4. To do this, click and drag to move the Negative Oval Path selection so it is to the right of the oval and overlaps it as shown below.

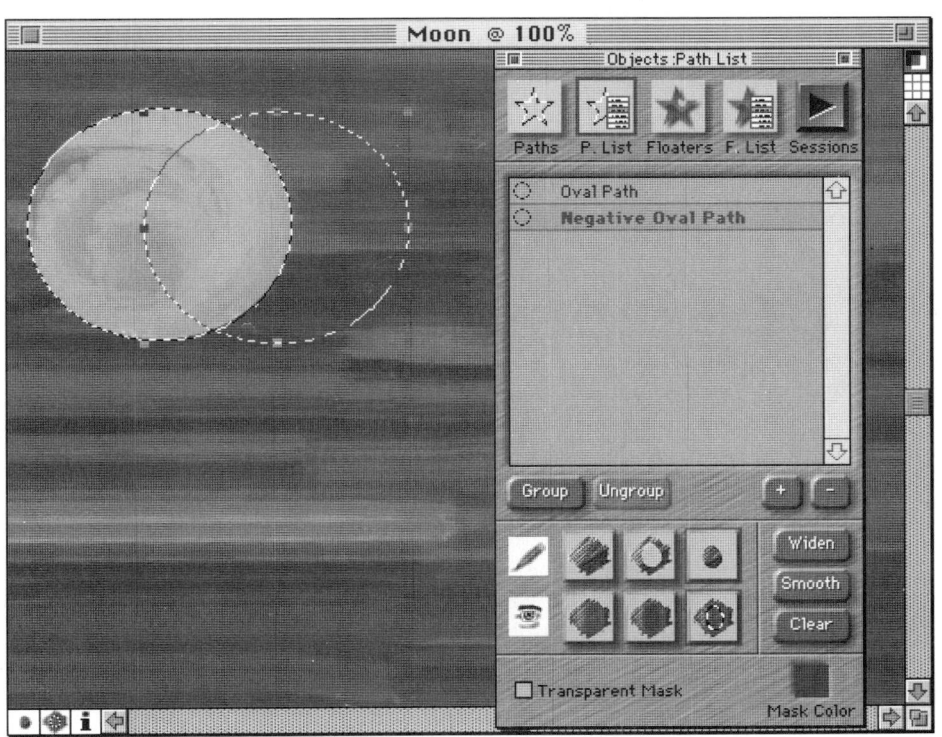

FIGURE 7.4: The negative oval overlaps the original oval to produce a crescent.

Before continuing to the next step, make sure that Negative Oval Path is still selected in the Path List palette. The activated selection is the one with a gray shade over its name. If the Negative Oval Path is not shaded with gray, click on it now to select it.

4. To subtract the selection, click on the minus-sign button (–) in the Objects :Path List palette (you can also use the Controls :Path Adjuster palette). This turns the path into a negative path, cutting one selection out of another. Painter indicates this by turning the words *Negative Oval Path* red in the Path List palette.

5. You still need to make one more alteration before you can create the crescent moon object. You need to place the negative selection in front of the oval. You might think that the second selection you created is in front of the first because it was created after the oval. In actuality, the stacking order of the selections is indicated by their order in the Path List palette. The path at the top of the list is the frontmost path selection and the one underneath is behind. To reverse the order of the paths, click on the words *Negative Oval Path* and drag it above the words *Oval Path*. Release the mouse, and the order of the two paths has changed.

6. Before you can see the effects of subtracting one selection from another, both selections must be activated. If the oval and negative path are not activated, click on the circle icon next to the names of the paths in the Path List palette so that the blinking selection marquee appears on screen.

7. Now you're ready to see how subtracting the selection creates a crescent selection. The easiest way to see this is to first apply the mask overlay. To do this, click on the second visibility button and make sure that the third drawing button is selected.

Notice that the area where the two ovals overlap is covered with the mask overlay, as shown in Figure 7.5. Painter allows you to make the mask overlay transparent, so you can see your image through the colored overlay.

8. Activate the Transparent Mask option in the Path List palette to see your image through an overlay at 50 percent.

9. To paint outside of the crescent moon and not affect the inside, make sure that the second drawing button is selected, and click on the third visibility button. Continue to use the same blue sky

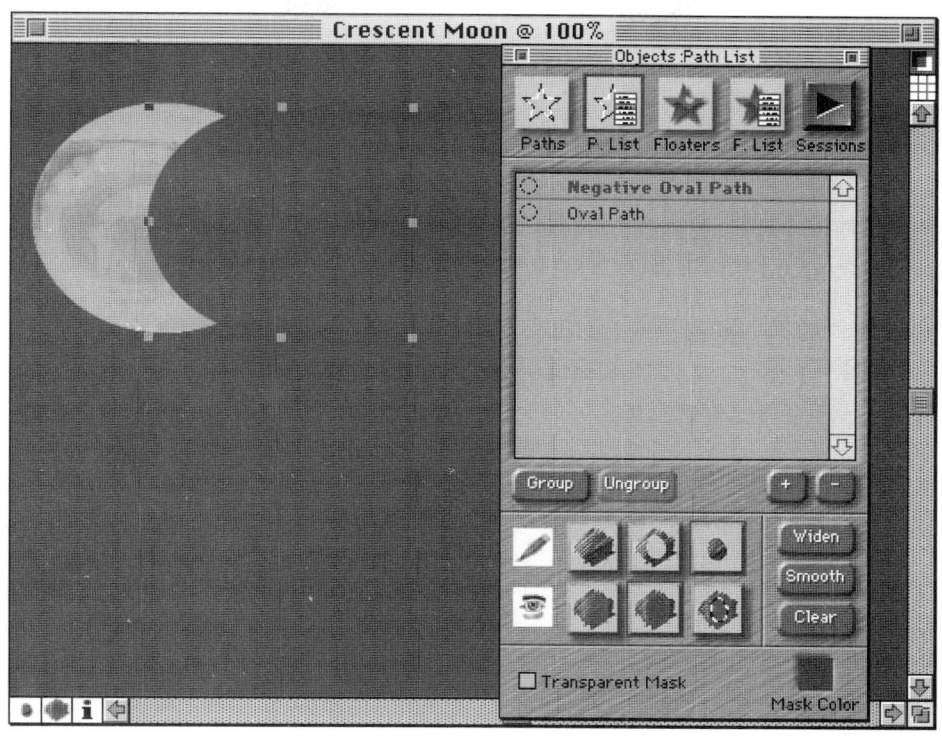

FIGURE 7.5: Mask overlay, Negative, and Oval path used to create crescent shape

primary color and brush as you did in the previous section, and begin painting. Notice that the inside of the crescent moon is not affected.

Tip *To combine different path selections into one selection or to turn a negative path selection into a normal path selection, click the positive (+) button in the Path List palette. For instance, you can convert three overlapping circular selections into one snowman-shaped selection by using the + button.*

If you are working with many paths that you want to activate and deactivate with the click of one button, you can place them into a group. To group paths, first press the **Shift** key, then click on the names of the paths that you wish to include in your group. Next click the Group button. To ungroup, click on the Ungroup button.

Note *The only option you haven't used in the Path List palette is the Smooth button. This button allows you to smooth sharp edges of a path.*

In the next section you'll add stars to the canvas on screen. But before you proceed, use the File ➤ Save As command to create another version of your file so that your original moon file stays intact. Name the new file **Crescent Moon** (Windows users: **CrscMoon**).

Note *You can also use the previously described techniques to select objects in any painting.*

Working with the Objects :Paths Palette

The Paths palette stores selections so that they can be reused. In this section you'll use the Objects :Paths palette to create stars. The Paths palette features twelve built-in path shapes. As you'll learn later, you can add to its storehouse of paths.

To open the Objects :Paths palette, click on the Paths icon in the Objects palette. Then click on the drawer handle to open the drawer and see all the selections available.

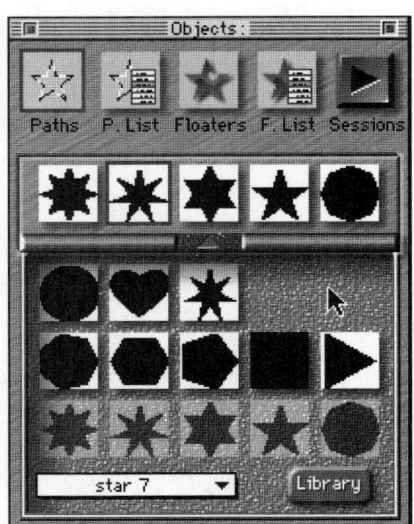

1. When the Paths palette is displayed, click on any star icon or choose a path in the pop-up menu. After you've made a choice, click and drag the star onto your canvas. Instantly a star is born in your canvas. Also notice that the star path now exists in the Objects :Path List palette.

    If you'd like, you can use the Path Adjuster tool to move or resize the star.

2. To resize the star, click and drag on any corner handle. Hold the Shift key to scale proportionally. To move the star, click and drag in the interior of the path.

3. After you've resized the star, you may want to save it so it can be reused easily. You can save the star shape you created by using the Path Adjuster tool to drag the path into the open drawer of the Paths palette. After you release the mouse, the Save Path dialog box appears.

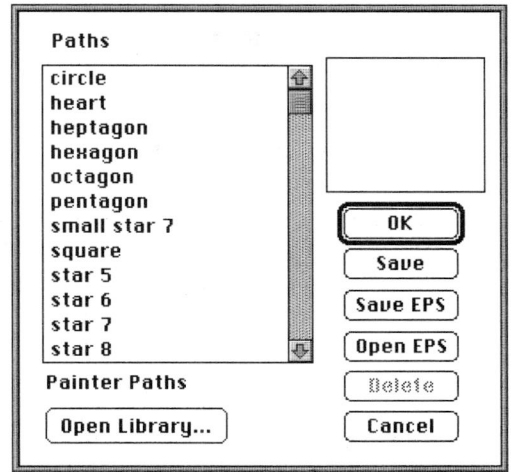

4. When the Save Path dialog box appears, enter a new name. Click OK to save the path. Now that you've saved the star that you resized, you can drag out several more stars from the palette. Note that the name of the new star you created also appears in the Objects :Paths palette pop-up menu.

Note *To save a path selection as an EPS file, choose Tools ➤ Selections ➤ Save Selection As EPS. This choice allows you to export the path into programs such as Adobe Illustrator and Adobe Photoshop. You can also import paths from Illustrator, Photoshop, and Freehand by choosing Tools ➤ Selections ➤ Open EPS As Selection.*

5. You can use the Effects ➤ Fill command to fill the star. You can also *stroke* the star by using the Stroke Selection command in the Tools ➤ Selections submenu. When you stroke a selection, Painter paints the selection with the active brush from the Brushes palette and with the active primary painting color. (Therefore, it is a good idea to pick a Brush variant before you apply the Stroke Selection command. You may also wish to adjust the brush size from the Brush Controls :Size palette, because the brush size is what determines the width of the stroke.)

Once you've created a selection on screen, you can also soften the edges of the selection to give it a glowing effect.

If you wish, save your work; then proceed to the next section.

Using the Feather Option to Create a Glowing Star Effect

To create a star with a glow affect you need to *feather* it first, then fill it. Feathering allows you to soften the edges of a selection. You can feather a selection using the Feather slider in the Controls palette when the Path Adjuster, Oval Selection, or Floating Selection tool is activated. You can also feather a selection by using the Edit ➤ Mask ➤ Feather Mask command. Figure 7.6 shows a glow effect on the border of a star. This effect is produced by subtracting a smaller star's selection from a larger star selection to create a border, then feathering the border selection.

FIGURE 7.6: Star with glow effect on its border

1. To create this effect, either use the file from the previous exercise or create a new 7-by-5-inch 75 ppi file on screen.

2. Start by dragging a star from the Objects :Paths palette to your canvas. Either use Star 7 or the star you saved in the previous section.

Next, you'll use the Widen button in the Path List palette to create a new larger star selection. When you click the Widen button, Painter creates a new path on screen that is wider than the selected path.

3. Before you press the Widen button, activate the Path Adjuster tool and make sure that the star on screen is selected. To select the star, either click on the star itself or click on its name in the Path List palette. (If the Path List palette is not

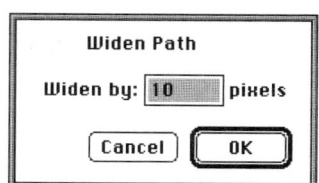

open, click on the P. List icon in the Objects palette). If the Path List palette isn't expanded, you won't see the Widen button. To expand the Path List palette, click on the zoom box in the top right-hand corner of the palette. Now, click on the Widen button in the Path List palette. If the star is not activated in the Path List palette, the Widen button can't be accessed. When the Widen Path dialog box appears, type 10 and click OK.

4. Instantly another star is created. Notice that the star is larger and that Painter assigns the new star the same name as the old star in the Path List palette. To avoid confusion, change the name of the larger star to **Feathered Star**. To rename the larger star, double-click on its name in the Path List palette, and enter the new name.

5. To feather the edges of the larger star, first select it with the Path Adjuster, if it is not already selected. Open the Controls :Path Adjuster palette, and drag the Feather slider to the right, between 3 and 15.

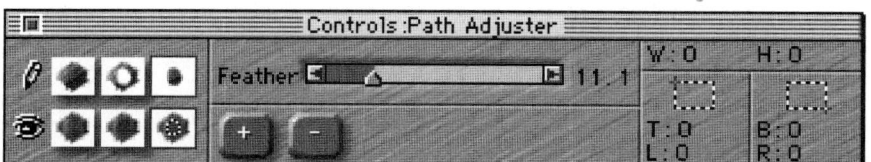

Note *The effect of the feathering depends upon the size of the object and the resolution of your file.*

6. So that only the border of the larger star is feathered, you must subtract the smaller star from the larger star. To do this, first activate the smaller star by either selecting the smaller star on screen with the Path Adjuster tool or by clicking on the name of the star in the Path List with the Path Adjuster tool. Now press the minus-sign button in the Path List palette. Notice that in the Path List palette, the name of the smaller star turns red. This means that the smaller star will be cut out of the larger one so that only the border of the larger star will be affected when you fill it.

7. In order to see the smaller star in the mask overlay and to fill only the border of the larger star, you need to place the smaller star in front of the larger star. To do this, click on the name of the smaller star in the Path List palette and drag it on top of the larger star (feathered star).

8. To properly view the mask overlay and create the desired effect, you must activate the selection marquees of both stars. With the Path Adjuster tool, click on the circle marquee in front of the name of each star in the Path List palette.

9. After the stars' selection marquees are displayed, you can use the visibility and drawing buttons in either the Controls :Path Adjuster palette or the Path List palette to display the mask overlay. Click on the second visibility icon to see the mask overlay. Keep the third drawing button selected. Notice that the edges of the larger star have a soft white glow and that the edges of the smaller star are hard and crisp, as shown in Figure 7.7.

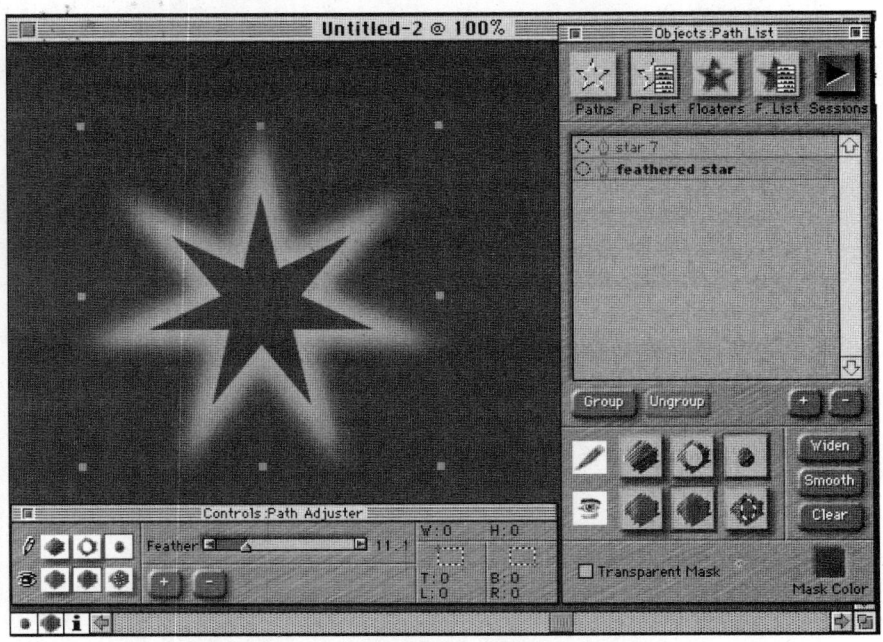

FIGURE 7.7: The glowing star seen through the mask overlay

10. After you've viewed the mask overlay, click on the third visibility button to bring the selection marquee back and hide the mask overlay.

11. To fill the feathered selection, pick a bright yellow primary painting color from the Art Materials :Colors palette. Then choose Fill from the Effects menu. In the Fill dialog box, choose the Current Color option and click OK. When the selection is filled, a soft glow appears only around the edges of the larger star. To deselect and see the star without the selection marquee, activate the Rectangular Selection tool and click away, or choose Deselect from the Edit menu.

12. If you wish to fill the inside of the smaller star with another color, you need to first make sure that the larger star is deactivated and the smaller star is selected. With the smaller star activated, change it from a negative path to a positive path by clicking on the plus-sign (+) button in the Path List palette (you can't fill a negative path). Now you can fill it with the primary color, a gradient, or a weave.

Later in this chapter, you'll use the feather option again—this time to create a vignette.

Image Editing with Masks

You can use masks, created with the Oval Selection, Text Selection, and Outline Selection tools to help edit images.

In the following sections, you'll see how masks can be used to create a photomontage and *vignette*. In a vignette, the image edges gradually fade out into the canvas. To create the photomontage, you'll use Painter's Outline Selection tool, Magic Wand command, and Masking brushes. To create the vignette, you'll use Painter's Feather option.

Creating a Vignette Using Painter's Feathering Option

You have probably seen an old photograph with a vignette effect, as shown in Figure 7.8. Vignettes can make an image look more interesting.

FIGURE 7.8: Old photograph before and after vignette effect

In Painter you can create a vignette effect by feathering a selection, then copying it into a new file. Complete the following steps to create a vignette effect.

1. Open an image. If you don't have an image to use, use one of the Painter tutorial images.

2. Once you have an image on screen, select the area you want to be included in the vignette. If you've selected an area using the Oval Selection tool or the Outline Selection tool, you can edit the selection and fine-tune it with the Path Adjuster tool.

   After you've selected an area, you need to feather it. With the Oval Selection tool or the Outline Selection tool activated, you can feather the selection using the Feather slider in the Controls palette.

3. To feather the selection, click and drag the Feather slider in the Controls palette to the right. The larger the feather, the bigger the fade out. If you are using a high-resolution file, you will need to make the feather larger than you would in a low-resolution file.

4. If you wish to see the feathered edges, you can apply the mask overlay to your image. To see the mask overlay, the selection marquee must be activated on screen, and the third drawing and second visibility buttons must be selected. In the Path List palette, select the Transparent Mask option. To turn the mask overlay off and bring back the selection marquee, keep the third drawing button selected and select the third visibility button.

5. After you've selected and feathered an area, you need to copy it to create a vignette effect. Choose Copy from the Edit menu.

6. Next you need to paste it into a new document that is at least as large as the size of the image on screen. To see how big your image is on screen, click on the **i** icon at the bottom left-hand corner of the canvas. Create a new document with the required dimensions and resolution. (Make the Paper Color the color that you want your vignette to fade into). When the new document appears on screen, choose Normal from the Edit ➤ Paste submenu. The image appears on screen with a soft cloudy effect around its edges.

In the next section, you'll learn how to create a variety of different shaped selections with the Outline Selection tool. All selections created with this tool can be feathered and also function as masks.

Working with the Outline Selection Tool

In order to take full control of Painter's masking capabilities, you'll need to be able to create selections of any shape and size. Painter's Outline Selection tool is your pathway to intricate selections or silhouettes. This tool, which appears as a pen in the Tools palette, allows you to create freehand, straight, and curved outline selections. The camel shown here was selected with the Outline Selection tool's Bézier Curves option. The camel was then copied and pasted into the bridge shown in Figure 7.9.

FIGURE 7.9: Photograph of bridge to be used in the photomontage

The koala image seen here was selected using Painter's Magic Wand command and Masking brushes. Like the camel, the koala was also then copied and pasted into the bridge of Figure 7.9 to produce the final image (Figure 7.10). The text in the final image was edited by adjusting the Bézier Curves option and using Masking brushes. You'll learn how to do this later in this chapter.

After you learn how to use the Outline Selection tool, you'll learn how to select using the Magic Wand and Color Mask commands, and Masking brushes.

The Outline Selection tool works somewhat like the Pen tools in Adobe Illustrator, Macromedia Freehand, and CorelDRAW. In these programs, the pen path is often used for filling and stroking. In Painter, however, the

FIGURE 7.10: Photomontage of camel, koala, and text on the bridge

path must be converted to a blinking closed selection marquee before it can be filled, stroked, or used as a mask.

Painter's Outline Selection tool's power is divided into three options: Straight Lines, Freehand, and Bézier Curves. The Straight Line and Freehand options are quite easy to use. The Bézier Curves option, used to create precise curves, is a bit more complicated. The following sections introduce you to each of the Outline Selection tool's options.

Creating Freehand Selections

Painter's Freehand selection mode allows you to click and drag to create freehand selections of any shape. For instance, you could use it to add clouds to the moon and stars image you created earlier in this chapter. To practice using the Freehand option, open the moon and stars image, or create a new 7-by-5-inch file to practice in. Activate the Outline Selection tool. In the Controls :Outline Selection palette, click on the Freehand radio button.

To create the cloudlike shape, simply click and drag to make an oval-like shape.

After you release the mouse, a blinking marquee in the figure appears on screen. If you didn't end the selection where you began it, Painter will close the selection for you.

One of the great features of working with the Outline Selection tool (except the Bézier Curves option) is that it can be used to easily edit selections (except those created with the Rectangular Selection tool). Try adding to the selection on screen by pressing Command (Windows users: Ctrl). On screen, a tiny plus sign will appear next to the mouse cursor. After you see the plus sign, click and drag over a selection edge. The new selection is added to the old one. To subtract from a selection, press Command+Option (Windows users: Ctrl+Alt). This causes a tiny minus sign to appear on screen. Next, click and drag over a selection edge. The selection is reduced in the area that you clicked and dragged over. If you wish to move or resize the selection, you must first switch to the Path Adjuster tool. Next, click on the selection, then click and drag on any handle to resize it.

> **Note** *If you wish to use the Bézier Curves option to edit a selection created with the Freehand option, first convert it to a curve by choosing Tools ➤ Selection ➤ Convert To Curve. See the Bézier Curves section for more details.*

At this point you could fill the path using the Effects ➤ Fill command, stroke it by using the Selection ➤ Stroke command, or use the selection as a mask and then paint inside of it with a brush. To create a cloud effect, you might wish to drag the feather slider in the Controls Palette to 30, then fill the selection with a color other than the background color, by using the Effects ➤ Fill command.

After you've created a freehand selection, it appears in the Objects :Path List palette, listed as a path. As with selections created with the Oval Selection tool, you can rename the path by double-clicking on it. You can also click on the circle icon to deactivate the selection. Before proceeding to the next section, close the file on screen; save it, if you wish.

Creating Straight Line Selections

The Outline Selection tool's Straight Line option creates closed straight line selections. It works by connecting mouse clicks. Use this option to select or create polygons, triangles, and diamond shapes.

Here's how you would use the Straight Line option to create a kite shape:

First create a new file to practice in. To help create a perfect kite, use Painter's grid. To place the grid on screen, click on the grid icon at the top right corner of your canvas. Then, activate the Outline Selection tool, if it isn't already selected. Next move the mouse cursor to the point that you wish to start creating your kite, then click.

Now move the mouse down and to the right, where you wish the right edge of the kite to appear. Click the mouse. Immediately Painter connects the two endpoints. Now move the mouse down to where you wish the bottom edge of the kite to appear, then click. After Painter connects the two endpoints, continue clicking to create the kite.

Finish the kite by returning to your starting point. Once you click on your starting point, Painter creates the blinking marquee.

After you've created a kite shape, you no longer need the grid. Turn off the grid by clicking on the grid icon.

To stroke the kite (outline it with color) with the currently selected brush, color, and feathering options, choose Tools ➤ Selection ➤ Stroke Selection.

If you'd like, add a design to the kite. To add a tail to your kite, first deselect the selection by choosing Deselect from the Edit menu or by pressing Command+D (Windows users, Ctrl+D). Now use any of the brushes to paint a design on the face of the kite, and to add a tail. When you've finished the kite, save your work, if desired.

> **Note** *If you wish to create straight-lined selections at 45 or 90-degree angles, hold the Shift key down as you click the mouse with the Straight Line option activated.*

Creating Bézier Curve Paths

The Outline Selection tool's Bézier Curves option allows you to create smooth and intricate curves. Although this tool can be used for creating shapes and filling them, it's primarily used for outlining or silhouetting objects or image areas that already exist.

The Bézier curve is named after the French mathematician Pierre Bézier, who demonstrated how a curve could be created and manipulated using four control points. As you'll soon see, by adjusting the points, you can control the shape and size of the curve.

Becoming proficient at using the Bézier Curve option takes practice. To master it, you'll need to start slowly by creating simple selections. Be patient; gradually you'll get the hang of it.

When using the Outline Selection's Bézier Curve option, you don't draw curves by clicking and drawing as you do in freehand mode. When using the Bézier Curves option you create curves by connecting mouse clicks and dragging the mouse. Figure 7.11 shows an outline path created by the Bézier Curve tool. Notice that the path includes square dots, called *anchor points*, and lines with dots at endpoints. These lines are called *direction lines*. By clicking and dragging on the anchor points, the size of each curve can be adjusted. By clicking and dragging on the direction lines, the shape and direction of the curve can be adjusted. To create this complex selection, the direction of the path had to be changed at various times. As you'll learn later, you can use the Option (Windows users: Alt) key to change the direction of a direction line and eventually change the direction of a curve.

FIGURE 7.11: The Bézier Curve option was used to draw an outline path around this camel image used earlier in the photomontage

If you're familiar with the Pen tool in drawing programs like Adobe Illustrator, Macromedia Freehand, and CorelDRAW, you'll find Painter's pen tool fairly easy to use. However, unlike drawing programs, Painter requires you to close the path in order to use it. This means that the starting and ending point must be the same. Only if the path is closed can you turn the path into a selection and use it as a mask.

Bézier Curve Exercises If you're new to Bézier curves, you should try out the following exercises, which demonstrate the fundamentals of creating curves and changing smooth curve points to corner points. Once you can create and edit curves, you'll be able to outline selections to use as masks or to use when copying and pasting. In the next exercise you'll learn how to create curves using the Outline Selection tool's Bézier Curves option. You'll use curves to create an oval shape. Then you'll transform the oval shape into a heart by converting curve points into corner points.

Before you begin drawing an oval, create a new 7-by-5-inch document, and make sure that the Outline Selection tool is activated. Next click on the Bézier Curve option in the Controls Path :Outline Selection palette. The mouse pointer changes to a small ×.

> **Note** *You may wish to activate Painter's grid to aid you in creating the oval.*

In order to create an oval you'll create four anchor points, similar to the way you created the kite shape earlier in the chapter. When you created the kite shape, you moved from one position to another and clicked to create straight lines. To create the oval you are going to click and drag to create curves rather than straight lines, as seen in Figure 7.12.

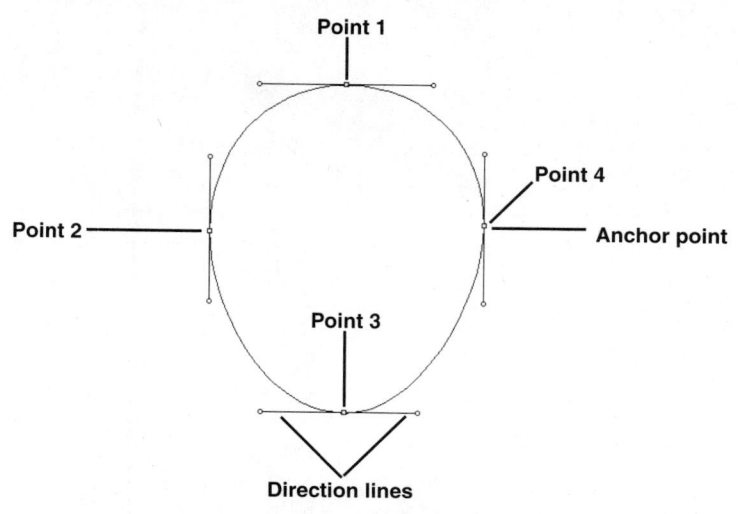

FIGURE 7.12: Shape created with Bézier Curves.

1. First, move the mouse to the top, middle portion of your canvas. Since the
first curve you draw will slope down-
ward, start by clicking and dragging
horizontally to the left about an inch or
so. This creates a direction line. After
you've made a point and set the direction line, move the mouse pointer di-
agonally down about 2 inches. Next, click and drag downwards for
about half an inch and click the mouse. Release the mouse to create
your first curve, as shown here.

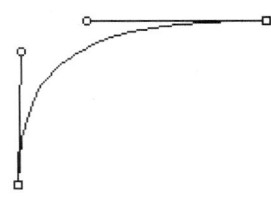

Note *You must click and drag to create a curve. If you click but do not drag,
the Bézier Curve option creates a straight line.*

2. Next move the mouse pointer another 2 inches or so diagonally
down to the right, so that the mouse pointer is directly below the
first point, as shown back in Figure 7.12. Click and drag to the right
about half an inch. As you drag, you'll see the curve take shape. Release the mouse.

3. Now create a third curve by first moving the mouse pointer another
2 inches or so diagonally to the right and up, so that it is directly
across from the second point. Then click and drag up about half an
inch to create your third curve.

As you can see, by clicking and dragging you can create smooth
curves that seamlessly change from one to another.

4. To close the oval shape, click and drag on the first point. Now that
you've drawn your first curves, you may wish to edit the curves. If
you wish to make a curve larger or smaller, simply click on an anchor point and drag in any direction. If you want to change the size
or slope of the curve, click and drag on any of the direction lines.
When you have finished experimenting, the oval should like similar
to Figure 7.12.

Before proceeding to convert the oval shape into a heart, take a look
at the Path List palette. Notice that the Bézier curve is listed in the
palette. As with paths created with the Oval Selection tool, you can
rename your curve by double-clicking on the curve name in the Path
List palette. As mentioned earlier, you can also change a path into a
selection, as long as it is a closed path.

To convert the oval into a heart, as shown in Figure 7.13, you need to convert the top and bottom smooth-curve points into corner points.

5. To change the top curve to a corner point, press Control (Windows users: Shift) while you drag the top right direction line's endpoint diagonally up. Next press Control (Windows users: Shift) again while dragging the top left direction line's endpoint diagonally up.

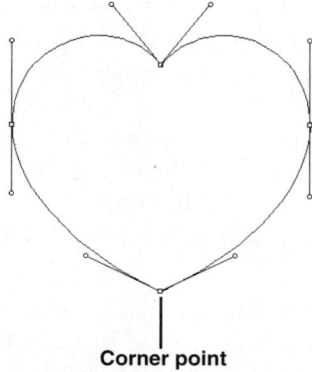

Corner point

FIGURE 7.13: Converting smooth curve points to corner points transforms the oval shape into a heart shape.

6. To change the bottom curve into a corner point, press Control (Windows users: Shift) while dragging the bottom right direction line's endpoint diagonally up. Keep the Control (Windows users: Shift) key pressed as you drag the bottom left direction line's endpoint diagonally up. For your heart to take shape, you may need to make some adjustments.

If you want to fill with a color, gradient, or weave, you must first change the heart path into a marquee selection by clicking on the circle icon next to the path name in the Path List palette.

Save if you wish, then close your file. In the next section you'll learn how to create a heart by creating two scalloped curves, curves that arc in the same direction.

Using Scalloped Curves to Create a Heart In the previous section, you changed a smooth curve into a corner point after you created the oval. You can also convert a curve point into a corner point by pressing the Option (Windows users: Alt) key to change the direction of a direction line. This creates a sharp corner point between curves rather than the smooth transitional points created in the previous exercise. The following exercise provides practice for this technique. In it, you'll recreate the heart, but this time you'll make the corner points as you produce the shape shown in Figure 7.14.

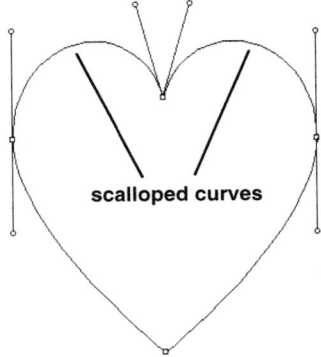

scalloped curves

FIGURE 7.14: Heart shape created from two scalloped curves

Start by creating a new canvas, 7 by 5 inches. Then activate the Outline Selection tool's Bézier Curves option.

1. Move the mouse point to the top left edge of the canvas, a few inches away from the top edge. Since the first curve will slope upwards, click and drag upwards about an inch.

2. Move the mouse to the right about two inches. Click and drag downwards about an inch. This creates the first up-sloping curve, as shown here.

3. To make the next curve slope up, you need to make the second direction line point up. In order to do this, press and hold down the Option key (Windows users: Alt key) and click the mouse diagonally up. A direction line appears, pointing upwards.

4. To create the second curve, move the mouse pointer to the right about two inches, horizontally across from the second point. Click and drag up about 1 inch. The next curve appears, sloping in an upward direction. You've just created two curves, both sloping up. You can use the Path Adjuster tool to move the direction lines or points to perfect your curves.

   When you have finished editing the two curves, reactivate the Outline Selection tool's Bézier Curves option so that you can finish drawing the heart.

5. To finish the heart shape you need to click once to create the point of the heart, as seen in Figure 7.14, and then click and drag on your starting point to close the heart shape.

6. After you've closed the heart shape and made any necessary adjustments, you can turn it into a selection and fill it.

If you wish, save your work, then close the file. In the next section you'll learn how to convert a text selection into a curved path.

Converting a Text Selection into a Curve Path

The Text Selection tool, like the Oval Selection tool, allows you to create selections and paths that can be edited.

You can convert a selection created by the Text Selection tool into a curve path that has direction lines and anchor points. By dragging these anchor points and direction lines, you can create special effects, such as the extended bars on the letters shown in Figure 7.15.

In this section you'll use the Text Selection tool to create text that will be converted to a path.

Before you begin, create a new 4-by-4-inch canvas, with a resolution of 75 ppi.

FIGURE 7.15: Type altered using Bézier Curve option

1. Activate the Text Selection tool.

2. In the Controls :Text Selection palette choose a font and point size. In Figure 7.15 the font is Helvetica Bold set to 100 points.

3. After you've picked a font and size, move the Text Selection tool to the middle of the left edge of the canvas and type the word **Type**. If you'd like, you can use the Path Adjuster tool (arrow icon) to move or enlarge the text on screen or to *kern* the letters (move the letters closer or further apart from each other). Your screen should look somewhat like Figure 7.16.

4. Open the Path List palette if it isn't already opened. Notice that the letters *T*, *y*, *p*, and *e* are listed as paths and that the circle icon next to each letter in the palette is activated.

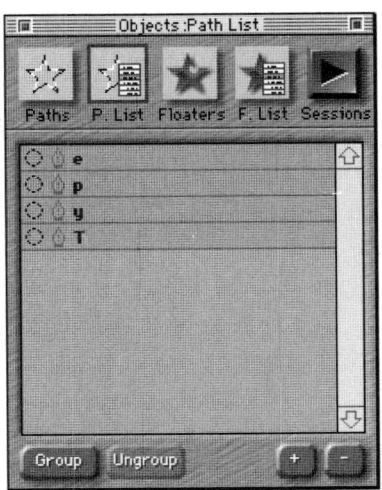

You can convert the path selection to a curve by either choosing Convert To Curve from the Tools ➤ Selections submenu or by activating the Pen icon next to each letter in the Path List palette.

5. Choose Convert To Curve from the Tools ➤ Selections submenu. Instantly the selection marquee on screen turns to Bézier curves, and the Outline Selection tool becomes the active tool in the Tools palette.

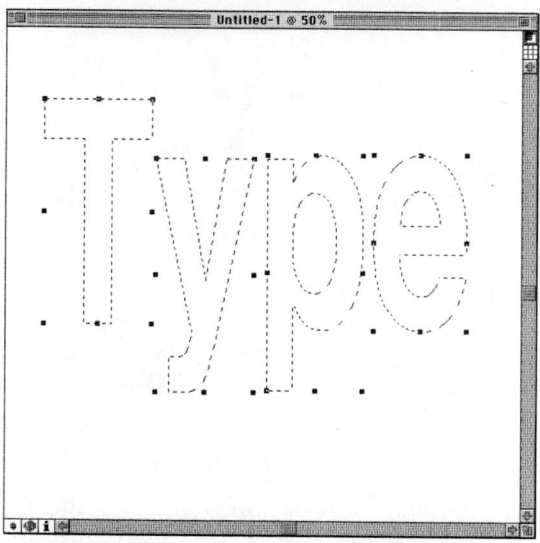

FIGURE 7.16: The word "Type" in 100-point Helvetica Bold, ready to be modified

The text selection is now converted to a curve path. Notice that the Path List palette reflects this by displaying the pen icon next to the letters. Also, notice that the circle icons next to the letters are dimmed. You can now manipulate and/or distort the text.

6. Try altering the text by clicking and dragging on any one of the anchor points or direction lines (as shown in Figure 7.17, for example).

After you've altered the text path, you need to turn it back into a selection in order to fill or stroke it with a color.

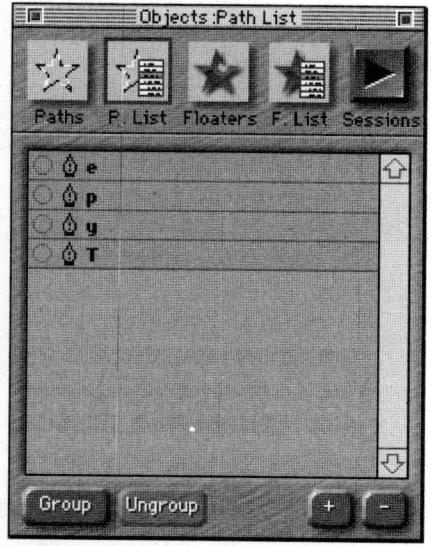

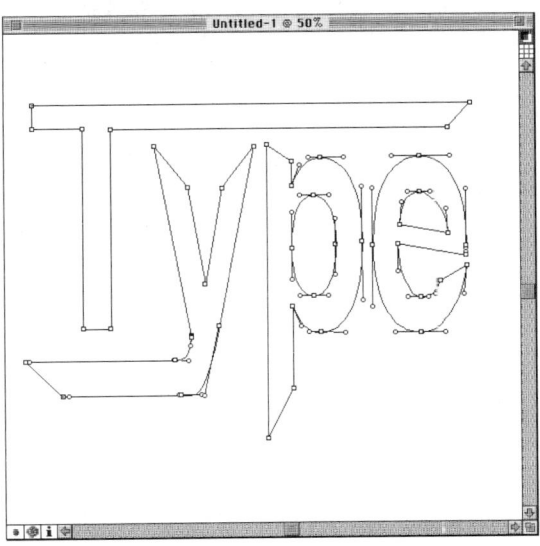

FIGURE 7.17: Type with various anchor points moved from their original positions

7. To convert the Bézier curves to a selection, either click on the oval icon next to each letter in the Path List palette or choose Convert To Selection from the Tools ➤ Selections submenu. If you choose the Convert To Selection command, you must first use the Path Adjuster tool to click and drag over the letters to select them and display the selection handles.

Tip *After the text is converted into a selection, you can also edit it using Painter's Masking brushes. You'll learn how to use the Masking brushes later in this chapter.*

8. Before you fill the selection, choose a weave from the Weaves palette. Then choose Effects ➤ Fill. In the Fill dialog box, choose the Weave option, then click OK. In Figure 7.15 the text was filled with a weave.

Tip *Since text is created as a selection, you can experiment with text effects in a low-resolution file, then increase the file's resolution by using the Canvas ➤ Resize command (with the Constrain File Size check box deselected, and the measurement unit in inches). When you increase the resolution with the Constrain File Size check box deselected, Painter resamples (see Chapter 4). Thus, you may wish to delete any painted text you created in the file by double-clicking on the Rectangular Selection tool, and then pressing Delete. Now you can refill the text in the high-resolution file.*

Warning *If you press Delete with the Path Adjuster tool selected and the path selection activated, you will delete the path selection.*

Save your file, if you wish; then proceed to the next section to learn how to select using the Magic Wand command.

Understanding and Using Painter's Mask Layer

When you create a mask in Painter, you are actually working in a layer, called the mask layer. As you've worked through this chapter, you've seen how selections can be converted into masks. When you create a mask with the Oval Selection tool, Text Selection tool or Outline Selection tool, it's as if you are slicing a shape out of or cutting a stencil in this mask layer. But there's more to Painter's mask layer than simple stencils. When you work in Painter's mask layer, you can actually make the mask reflect the feathering in a selection and you can use the mask to help create effects that blend selected image areas with other images.

In order for the mask to handle blending effects and feathering, Painter can assign different areas of the mask grayscale values from black to white. (The mask values can be from 0 to 256, which is why the mask is sometimes called an 8 bit mask). When you work with Painter's Magic Wand command, Edit ➤ Mask, and Masking brushes you create masks with different values. For instance, as you'll see later in this chapter, if you paint using a Masking brush with black, you create a different effect than when painting with gray. By turning these masks into selections, then filling them or copying and pasting, you'll be able to create beautiful and unusual effects.

Working with the Magic Wand and the Mask Color Commands

Creating intricate selections by hand can often be quite time consuming and complicated. Painter's Edit ➤ Magic Wand and Edit ➤ Mask Color commands allow you to select image areas by color similarity. Often it provides a quick alternative to creating selections one path segment at a time with the Outline Selection tool's options.

1. To see how the Magic Wand works its magic, open any image on screen.

2. Once the image opens, choose Magic Wand from the Edit menu. The Magic Wand dialog appears.

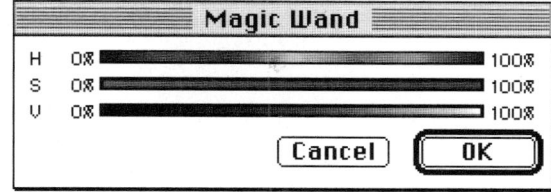

The Magic Wand dialog box features a slider for each HSV color component. When the Magic Wand selects, it selects a range of contiguous pixels based on the HSV values that you click and drag over.

3. To create a selection, first move the pointer over your image. Notice that the mouse pointer changes to a Wand icon. Next, click and drag the Magic Wand over the color area that you wish to select. The selection will appear as a mask in the mask overlay color. The H, S, and V sliders now reflect the color range selected, as shown in Figure 7.18.

To extend the selection, press Shift, then click and drag the wand over adjacent color areas. As an alternative to Shift and then clicking and dragging, you can also extend the selection by adjusting the H, S, and V sliders.

4. Once you're satisfied with the mask area that is selected, click OK. When the dialog box closes, the mask area is surrounded by a blinking selection marquee. If the blinking selection marquee is red, it is a negative selection, which means it is a hole within the selection.

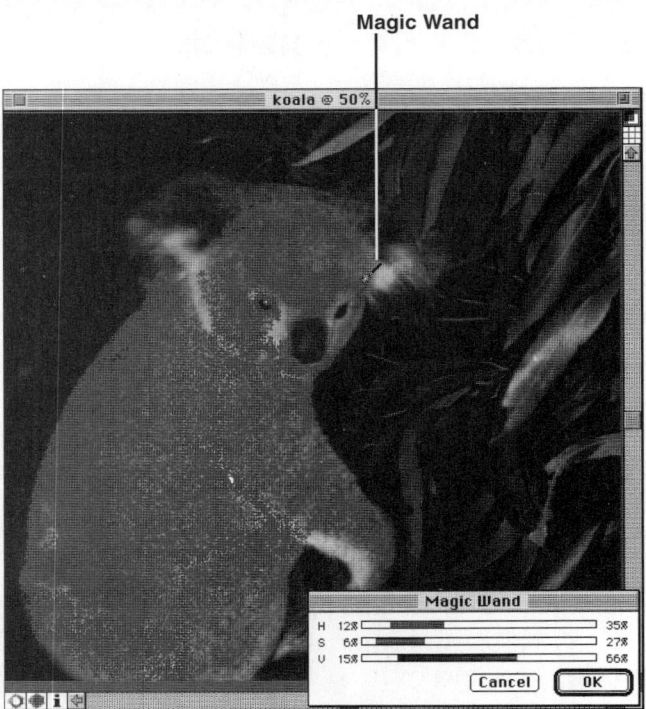

FIGURE 7.18: Magic Wand used to select according to similarity of colors in an image.

Now, take a look at the Path List palette. Notice that Painter creates a Mask Group—a group of selections. By clicking on the Mask group in the Paths palette, you can access any selection within the group. This means that you can deactivate or reactivate any part of the selection.

Tip *If you'd like the Magic Wand to select contiguous and noncontiguous areas based on color, first select the entire image area with the Rectangular Selection tool, then choose Edit ➤ Magic Wand.*

Like the Magic Wand, the Color Mask command also selects according to an image's color. Unlike the Magic Wand, however, Color Mask selects noncontiguous areas. The colors are selected based upon settings in the

Color Mask dialog box's H, S, and V sliders. The command allows you to add a feather to the selection by clicking and dragging on its H, S, and V Feather sliders.

To use the Color Mask command, choose Edit ➤ Color Mask. Start by dragging the H, S, and V color sliders to choose a color range that you want to have selected. If desired, click and drag

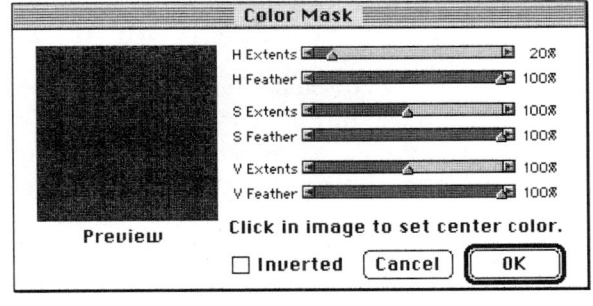

on the Feather sliders to soften the edges of the selection. As you work, you can see the selection being built in the Preview box.

Many times the Magic Wand or the Color Mask command will not select the entire object that you need to select. In these instances, your best bet is to turn to the Masking brushes for help. Masking brushes can be used to easily edit a mask.

If you'd like to try fine-tuning the selection on screen with a Masking brush, don't deselect it. Proceed to the next section to learn how to edit a mask using Masking brushes.

> ***Tip*** *To quickly deselect a mask on screen, choose Edit ➤ Mask ➤ Clear Mask.*

Working with Masking Brushes

Painter's Masking brushes can be used to either edit a pre-existing mask or create a mask from scratch. When you paint with a Masking brush, you alter the mask according to a brush stroke. If you're adept at using a brush, you'll probably prefer making your alterations using a Masking brush instead of the Outline Selection tool.

Before you learn about each of the Masking brushes, make sure you have the selection you created in the previous section on screen. If you don't have a selection on screen, open an image and use the Oval Selection tool to select a portion of it. If you don't have a file to use, load the Shells file from the Tutorial folder, and select a shell.

To see the mask overlay on screen, select the red mask visibility icon (the second icon) in the Objects :Path List palette. To set the overlay so you can paint away the red overlay with black, choose the third drawing icon.

Before you begin, make sure that the Objects :Path List palette is open. To see the image through a translucent overlay, select the Transparent Mask option in the Path List palette. Next, you need to set your painting color in the Art Materials palette. Painting with black dissolves the mask overlay (thus increasing the selection). Painting with white adds to the mask over-lay (decreasing the selection). Painting with gray produces a masking ef-fect similar to a feathered selection.

Remember, working with Masking brushes is different from working with other types of brushes. When you work with the third drawing button and third visibility button selected, painting with a brush other than a Masking brush only affects areas *within* a selection. If you are painting with the third drawing button selected with the mask overlay on screen (second visibility button), you can only paint in areas not covered by the overlay.

Before you start to paint, make sure that you have the third drawing but-ton selected. (If you have the second drawing icon selected instead, paint-ing with black adds to the overlay and painting with white dissolves the overlay. Painting with gray still produces the effect of a feathered selec-tion. When you work with the second drawing button and third visibility button selected, painting with a brush other than a Masking brush only af-fects areas *outside* of a selection. If you paint with the second drawing but-ton selected and the mask overlay on screen—second visibility button— you can only affect areas not covered by the overlay.)

> **Note** *Painter's Fill command always fills within a selection regardless of which drawing button is selected. However, when you fill with the mask over-lay on screen (second visibility button), the Fill command only fills areas not covered by the mask overlay.*

Now you're ready to choose a Masking brush from the Brushes palette. If the Brushes palette isn't open, open it now. Open the palette drawer and choose Masking from the pop-up menu. Notice that the icon at the top of the drawer switches to the Masking brush icon. To create a soft-edge effect, choose the Masking Airbrush variant. Notice that the Method Category automatically changes to Masking, and that the Method Subcategory changes to Soft Mask Cover.

If the Opacity setting in the Controls Brushes palette is less than 90%, raise it to 90% so you can better see the effects of the Masking brush. Next, set the primary painting color to black.

Now gradually begin painting over the edges of the mask with the Masking Airbrush. As you paint, the mask gradually disappears, as seen in Figure 7.19.

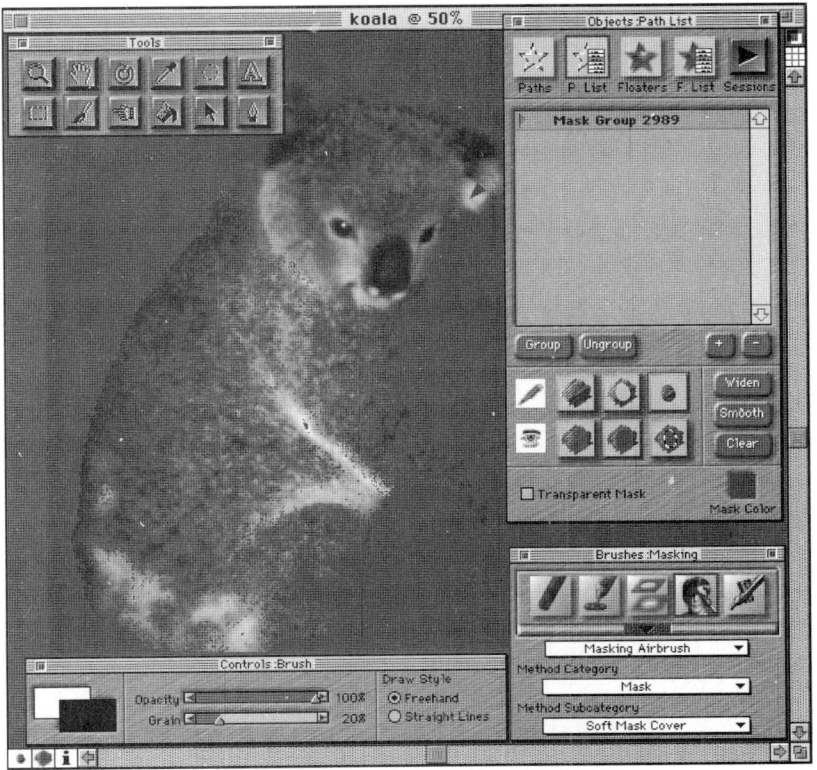

FIGURE 7.19: The Masking Airbrush used to wipe away the mask overlay and extend the selection

Tip *Remember, you can change the size of a brush's stroke by opening the Brush Controls :Size palette and adjusting the size slider.*

If you remove too much of the mask, you can paint back masked areas by changing the Method Subcategory to Linoleum Scribe, or by changing the painting color to white.

After you've completed your mask, turn your mask into a marquee selection by clicking on the third visibility button in the Path List palette (leave the third drawing button selected). Notice that the Path List palette designates a selection created with a Masking brush as a Mask Group. Now you can paint within the selected area or copy the selected area and paste it into another file.

Now that you've seen how a Masking brush works, try experimenting with other mask variants and subcategories. Here's a description of the mask variants.

♦ **Grainizer**—Creates wide, very grainy anti-aliased brush strokes. The grain in the mask is the paper texture that is currently set.

♦ **Big Masking Pen**—Very large anti-aliased brush strokes.

♦ **Masking Pen**—Draws with anti-aliased lines. If you are using a stylus, more pressure widens the stroke.

♦ **Masking Airbrush**—Paints with a diffused anti-aliased stroke.

♦ **Masking Chalk**—Creates semi–anti-aliased lines reflecting the currently selected paper texture.

♦ **Single Pixel**—Adds or subtracts from mask in single-pixel increments. Zoom in to use this brush to fine-tune intricate areas.

Note *You can turn any brush into a Masking brush by changing the Method Category in the Brushes palette to Mask. Also, note that the second visibility icon must be selected to paint with a masking brush.*

Once you choose a Masking brush, and set the Method Category pop-up menu to Mask, you must then choose a Method Subcategory. Be aware that a Method Subcategory can change the effects of a soft-edge variant to hard and vice versa. The Masking Method Subcategories are as follows.

♦ **Flat Mask Cover**—Produces hard-edged brush strokes that cover underlying strokes.

◆ **Soft Mask Cover**—Produces soft-edged brush strokes that hide underlying strokes.

◆ **Grainy Hard Cover**—Produces semi–anti-aliased brush strokes that show the paper grain and hide underlying strokes.

◆ **Grainy Edge Flat Mask Cover**—Aliased, thick brush strokes producing the effect of sticky paint that shows paper grain and hides underlying brush strokes.

◆ **Linoleum Scribe**—When you're painting with black, this option adds or removes the mask overlay, depending upon which mask drawing icon is selected.

Now that you've reviewed Painter's wide choice of Masking brushes, feel free to experiment with the different brushes. After you've finished experimenting, proceed to the next section to learn how to create unusual effects using Painter's Auto Mask command.

Note If you wish to load your image with its mask into Photoshop, first activate the selection mask, then save your file in Photoshop 2.0 or 3.0 format with the Save Mask Layer option selected. Then run Photoshop and open the file. The Painter mask will appear in the Photoshop Channels palette as an Alpha Channel.

Using Auto Mask

Painter's Auto Mask command allows you to automatically create a mask out of different image areas. As you'll see in this section, the command can be used to create a mask based upon the brightness values in an image, or the brightness values in a clone file or an image's paper grain. If you experiment with this command, you can create a variety of interesting effects. An example is shown in Figures 7.20 and 7.21.

To see how the Auto Mask command can blend two images together to create special effects, first load an image on screen. Then choose Edit ➤ Mask, and in the Mask submenu, choose Auto Mask.

The Auto Mask dialog box allows you to create a mask over your entire image, based upon the following choices in the Using pop-up menu.

FIGURE 7.20: An image created by blending two images using Auto Mask

◆ **Paper Grain**—The mask is created from the texture of the currently selected paper grain set in the Art Materials :Papers palette.

◆ **3D Brush strokes**—Creates a mask based on the difference in the color values between a source image and its clone.

◆ **Original Mask**—Creates a mask in a cloned document based on the luminance values in the source document. Use this to blend a source and clone together.

◆ **Image Luminance**—Creates a mask based on the brightness values of the image. Basically this command translates image brightness values to gray values (from 0 to 256) in the mask layer. You can use this after scanning in a black-and-white sketch, to have Painter create a mask of your sketch. Then you paint within the mask borders. You can also use this option to create interesting blending effects between two images.

FIGURE 7.21: The images that were blended to create Figure 7.20

Note *You can use the Paint Bucket tool to fill the mask layer with the luminance values of a color, weave, gradient, or clone. To use this feature, select the second mask visibility and second or third mask drawing icons. Then choose the Mask option in the Controls palette with the Paint Bucket tool selected. The Controls :Paint Bucket palette also includes a Cartoon Cel option. If you choose this option, Painter fills a mask that was created based on luminance values. If you are filling a selection created by the Image Mask's Luminance option using the Paint Bucket's Cartoon Cel feature, you can control how anti-aliased selection areas will be filled by adjusting the Mask Threshold slider in the Lockout Color dialog box. To access the Lockout Color dialog box, double-click on the Paint Bucket tool.*

To blend one image with another, the Image Luminance option is your best bet, because the brightness values of one image pasted into another can create an interesting ghosting effect. Choose Image Luminance from the Using menu, then click OK to have Painter create the luminance mask. If you don't see the mask on screen, click on the third mask visibility button in the Path List palette. Next choose Edit ➤ Copy, then open up another image. After the image loads, choose Edit ➤ Paste ➤ Normal. The luminance values of one image will drop over the image. The result will be a blend between the two images.

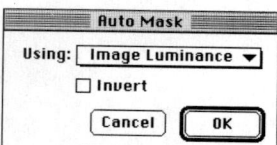

Note *You can use the Edit ➤ Mask ➤ Invert command to reverse a mask selection. After you execute this command, everything except the mask will be selected on screen. To feather a mask on screen, you can choose the Edit ➤ Mask ➤ Feather command. To clear a mask from the screen (but not delete it), you can choose Edit ➤ Mask ➤ Clear.*

Wrapping It Up

Now that you've learned the basics of using masks, you have the power to create any type of selection. Of course, becoming an expert at creating masks takes practice—and some trial and error. But if you keep working at them, you're certain to improve your selecting skills.

In the next chapter, you'll learn about another type of Painter selection, called a floater. Floaters place your selections in a layer above the underlying pixels, and you can also create masks in floaters.

Working with Floaters

Floaters open up a whole new world of painting and image-editing possibilities. Floaters allow you to freely move objects around on screen, and to blend them into their surroundings. With floaters you can easily experiment with multiple design possibilities without the need of selecting and reselecting.

In many respects a floater is like a rectangular layer that floats above the background canvas. You can layer one floater over an image and superimpose one floater over another. If you don't like the effect, you can move the floater or delete it without changing the underlying pixels.

This chapter provides you with an in-depth look at floater fundamentals. You'll learn how to create floaters, move them around on screen, and layer one floater on top of another. Once you master the basic concepts of using floaters, you'll learn how to create special effects such as drop shadows, raised type, and image fadeouts. You'll also explore the artistic possibilities provided by the Floater Mask visibility icons. Using the visibility icons and Painter's Masking brushes, you'll explore how to create fascinating blends between a floater and a background image. At the end of the chapter, you'll learn how to create an Image Hose nozzle from a group of floaters.

What Is a Floater?

A floater is a selection that floats above the background pixels as if it were in its own electronic layer. Perhaps the easiest way to understand the concept of floaters is to think of them as rectangular sheets of acetate containing painted or digital images. At any time you can move the sheets around the screen and apply effects to them, individually or as a group. As you'll learn later in this chapter though, floaters provide more artistic possibilities than acetate sheets. Using Painter's controls, you can control the transparency of a floater. You can create beautiful superimposition effects between a floater and its background, or you can make it appear as if part of the floater is completely transparent while other parts are completely opaque.

With all the artistic power packed into floaters, you might think that they are difficult to create and work with. On the contrary, as you'll see throughout this chapter, floaters are extremely easy to create and quite easy to use.

How to Create a Floater

Floaters are created out of selections. At times, Painter actually creates them for you automatically. For instance, if you select an area, then copy and paste or cut and paste, the pasted selection is automatically turned into a floater.

Painter will also allow you to turn any selection into a floater by hand. To turn a selection into a floater, you need only click inside it with the Rectangular Selection tool or click inside it with the Floating Selection tool.

Using Floaters

In the following sections you'll learn how to use floaters by manipulating basic shapes. You'll turn a rectangular selection and text selection into floaters, then you'll move one floater on top of another and edit the two independently of each other. As you work with floaters, you'll keep track of them in the Floater List palette.

The Objects :Floater List Palette

The Objects :Floater List palette is your command center for managing floaters. All floaters that are created appear in the Floater List palette. In order for you to see what floaters are in use and which of them are activated, you will need to keep the Floater List palette open on screen.

To view the Objects :Floater List palette, open the Objects palette by choosing Objects from the Window menu. To access the Objects: Floater List palette, click on the F. List icon at the top of the palette.

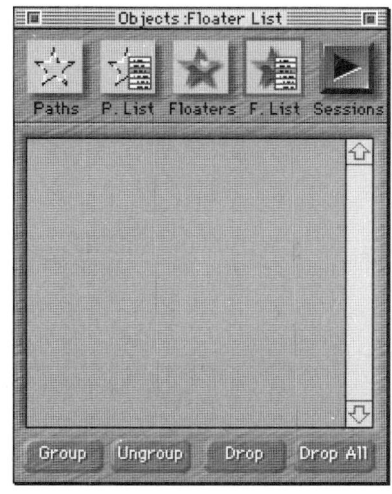

With the Floater List palette open on screen, you'll be able to rename floaters, reorder and group them, trim them (trim the blank space around them) or expand them, drop them onto the background pixels, and set their masking properties.

To see all the features of the Floater List palette, you need to expand the palette. Click on the zoom box in the top right-hand corner of the palette. When the palette is expanded, the Group, Ungroup, Drop, Drop All, Trim, Expand, Collapse, Restore, and Mask Visibility buttons are displayed. As you read through this chapter you'll learn how to use all the features of the Floater List palette.

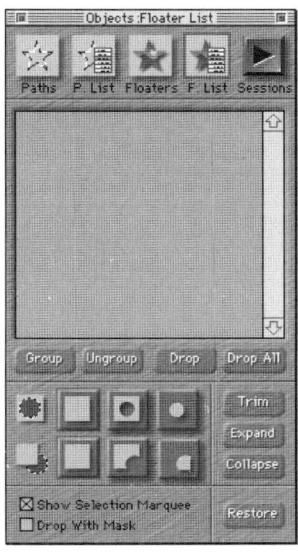

Converting a Selection into a Floater

In this section, you'll convert a selection into a floater, then you'll be able to begin to experiment with all of the features that floaters provide.

Start by creating a new file 7" × 5" with the resolution set to 75 ppi. Leave the paper color set to white.

Next, activate the Rectangular Selection tool and create a rectangle. Fill the rectangle with a gradient by choosing Effects ➤ Fill, then click on the Gradient option before clicking OK.

To turn the rectangular selection into a floater, click inside it with the Rectangular Selection tool (you can also click in it with the Floater Selection tool). When you click you'll see a pointing hand icon appear momentarily. After you click, the word *Floater 1* appears in the Floater List palette. (If this is not the first floater you created in a Painter session, it will not be Floater 1.)

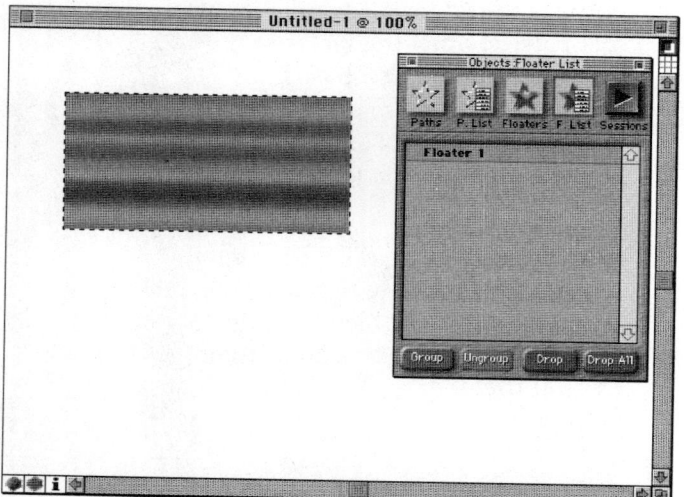

Now that the colored rectangular selection is a floater, you can manipulate it as if it were in a separate layer above the background pixels. First activate the Floating Selection tool, then click and drag on the floater to move it.

The floater appears to move across the screen without affecting the background pixels. In reality, the floater does alter your background pixels the first time you move it. You just won't see it if your paper color and background canvas are the same color. If you had filled the background with a different color, then dragged the rectangular floater across the screen, Painter would have ripped a rectangular hole out of the background canvas, and filled the hole with the paper color. The next section describes this problem in detail and provides a solution. Keep the current file on screen, because you will be using it later to learn more about floaters.

Floater Problems and Solutions

One of the problems when you a create a floater is that it can sometimes cut a hole out of your canvas the first time you move the floater. This can happen when your background color is different from your paper color. It's important to know how to get a floater to float when your canvas color is not the same color as your paper color.

To understand the problem, you might want to try this short exercise: Create a new file. Fill the new file with a color, grada-tion, or weave. Next create a rectangular se-lection using the Rec-tangular Selection tool. Turn the selec-tion into a floater by clicking inside the se-lection with the Rec-tangular Selection or

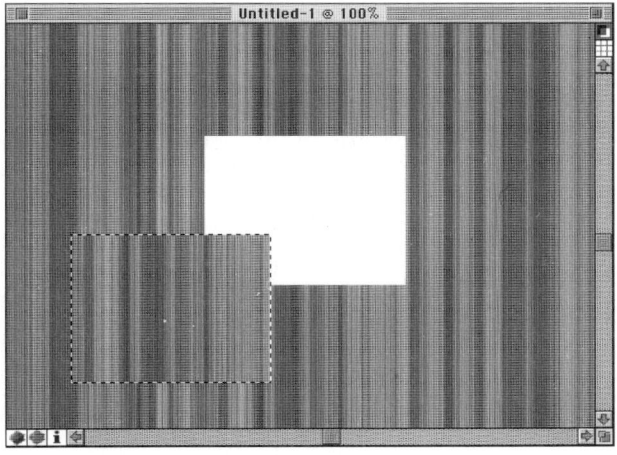

Floating Selection tool. Now click and drag in the floater. As you move the floater, notice that Painter rips a rectangular hole out of the background canvas and fills the hole with the paper color.

Now that you've seen how a floater rips a hole in the canvas, here's the solution: close the file you just created, create a new file, and fill the entire canvas with a color (other than the paper color), gradation, or weave. Now create a rectangular selection using the Rectangular Selection tool. Before

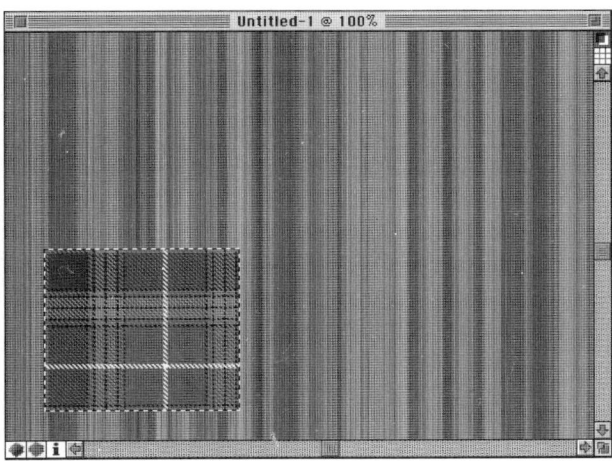

you fill the selection, press and hold the Option key (Windows users: Alt key) while you click inside the selection with the Rectangular Selection tool. This creates a floater, and copies the background color onto the pixels underlying the floater. Now fill the floater with a color that is different from the canvas color. As you move the floater, notice that you don't rip a hole out of the canvas.

Next time you use this technique, remember that it is very important that you fill the rectangular selection with a color, gradient, or weave *after* you press the Option key (Window user: Alt key) and not before. If you had filled the rectangular selection before you made it a floater, you would be altering the canvas area within the selection with the fill color. If you then pressed Option or Alt and clicked and dragged to move the floater, you'd have a patch on screen with the fill color left behind.

If you would like to see an example, close the file you just used and create a new file. Fill this canvas with a color other than the paper color, or fill it with a gradation or weave. Make a rectangular selection using the Rectangular Selection tool and fill the selection with a color other than the paper color. Now, press and hold the Option key or Alt key while you click and drag in the selection with the Rectangular Selection tool or Floating Selection tool. After you move the floater, a colored rectangular area is left behind. Not only do you have a colored rectangular floater but you also have painted the canvas with a colored rectangle.

The moral of this story is: When converting selections to floaters, if they are over a colored background that is not the same color as your paper color, you need to press and hold the Option key (Windows users: Alt key) and click inside a selection with either the Rectangular Selection or Floating Selection before you fill or paint inside it.

If you created a new file for this example, close it now.

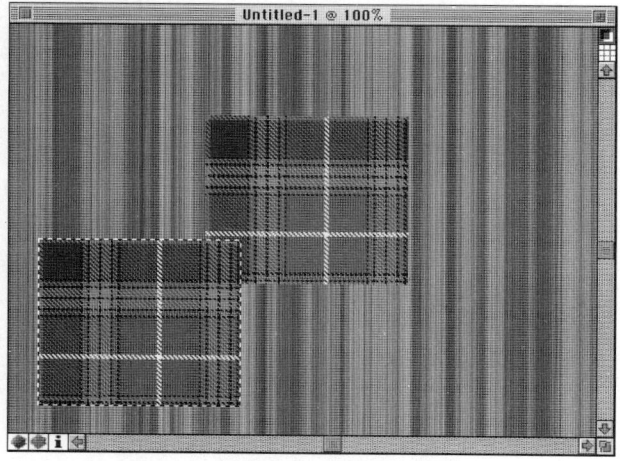

Activating and Reactivating a Floater

When you use floaters, it's important to remember that you can deselect them and reselect them as if they were separate objects on screen.

If you don't have a file with a rectangular floater filled with a color, gradient, or weave, create one now. Try deselecting the floater on screen by clicking away from it with the Floating Selection tool or Rectangular Selection tool activated, or click below the name of the floater in the Floater List palette. After you click, the selection marquee disappears—you might interpret this to mean that the floater has dropped down and attached itself to the background pixels. But in reality, the floater is still floating; you just need to reactivate it. To reactivate the floater, click on Floater 1 in the Floater List palette. Alternatively, you can click on the floater itself with the Floating Selection tool. Immediately, the selection marquee returns to the floater on screen, and you can now click on the floater and move it around on screen.

To see how floaters interact with each other, create another floater. This time, use the Text Selection tool (the icon with the letter *A*) to create some text a few inches away from the floater on screen. Type the word **FLOATER**. When the text selection is on screen, you can use the Path Adjuster tool (the arrow) to resize it and move it. Try resizing the text with the Path Adjuster tool to make it larger.

Next use the Floating Selection tool to click inside the text selection to turn it into a floater. When you click inside the text, make sure you click on an area that is not overlapping the rectangular floater. Otherwise, the text selection will not turn into a floater; instead, you will be activating the rectangular floater.

After you click inside the text selection, a new floater is created; it appears in the Floater List palette. With the floater still selected on screen, use the Effects ➤ Fill command to fill the text selection with a different color than the one used to fill the rectangular floater. Now move the text selection so that it overlaps the rectangular floater.

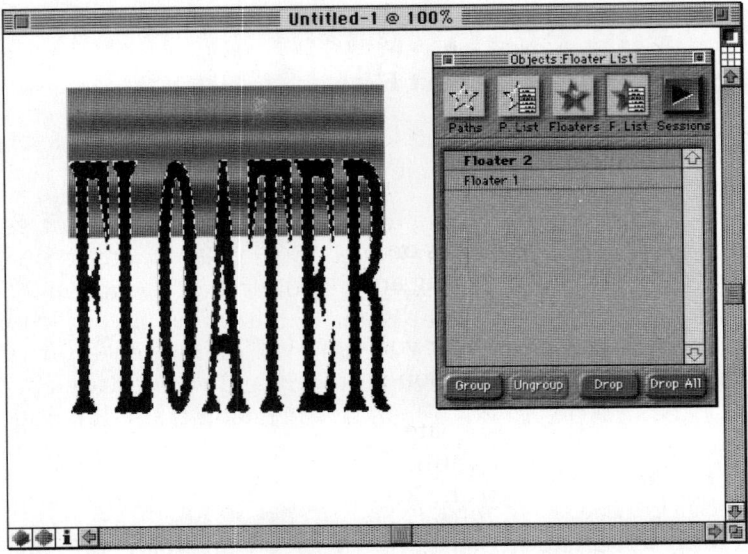

Renaming a Floater

Naming floaters allows you to keep all floating selections organized on screen.

To rename the rectangular floater, click on Floater 1 in the Floater List palette, then press Enter on your keyboard. When the Floater Attributes dialog box appears, type **Rectangular Floater** in the Name field. Notice that the Position fields in this dialog box allow you to reposition a floater by changing the Top and Left values. The positions correspond to pixel coordinates on screen. Thus, if you wanted to move the floater five pixels from the top corner of your image and ten pixels from the left of your image, you would type 5 into the Top field and 10 into the Left field. Click OK to rename the floater.

To rename the text floater, click on the name of the floater in the Floater List palette and then press Enter on your keyboard. When the Floater Attributes dialog box appears, type **Text Floater** in the Name field and click OK to rename the floater.

Reordering Floaters

When you have two or more floaters on screen, you can reorder them, bringing one to the front and sending another behind. You can do this in one of two ways. You can either drag the name of a floater above or under another in the Floater List palette, or you can use the Front and Back buttons in the Controls: Floating Selection palette.

In order to bring the rectangular floater in front of the text, you first need to select it, either by using the Floating Selection tool to click inside the rectangle or by clicking on the name Rectangular Floater in the Floater List palette. Now you can either click on the Front button or drag the name Rectangular Floater in the Floater List palette above the name Text Floater.

After you've sent the rectangle behind the floater, bring the text back in front again by clicking on the Front button, or dragging it to the front in the Floater List palette.

Note To lift a floater up to the front of overlapping floaters, click on the right arrow icons in the Controls :Floating Selection palette. To send a floater to the back of overlapping floaters, click on the left arrow icons in the palette.

Grouping Floaters

If you work with several floaters on screen at the same time, you may find it helpful to be able to move the floaters together on screen. To move more than one floater at a time you must group them.

Here's how to group the two floaters on screen: Click on one floater in the Floater List palette, then press and hold the Shift key while you select the other floater in the Floater List palette. After both floaters are selected in the Floater List palette, click on the Group button. Instantly the floaters are grouped. Notice that the word *Group* now appears in the Floater List palette, and that below the group are the names of the floaters in the group. Notice also the small triangle in front of the word *Group*. When the triangle points down, Painter shows you the names of all floaters in the group.

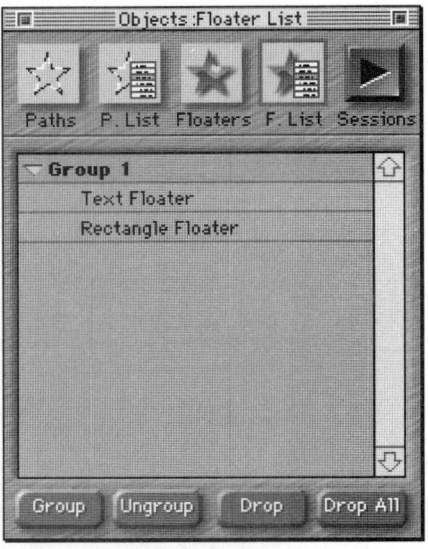

In order to move the floater group as a unit, the group must be closed. To close the group and hide the floaters, click on the triangle next to the word *Group*. Make sure that the word *Group* in the Floater list palette is selected. When it is, a selection marquee will appear around both floaters on screen. Use the Floating Selection tool to click inside the selection marquee and drag to move the two floaters together.

Note You can rename, attach notes to, and reposition a group by double-clicking on the name of a closed group in the Floater List palette, or selecting the Group in the Floater List palette and then pressing Enter on your keyboard. When the Floater Attributes dialog box appears, enter a new name, type some notes in the Notes field, or type a new position. To activate the changes, click OK.

Even though the two floaters are in a group, they can still be moved and edited independently of each other. For instance, assume that you wanted to change the color of the text floater. First open the group by clicking on the triangle next to the group name. Next, select the text floater. On screen, you'll see that only the text floater has been selected. Now you can fill only this floater, even though it's part of a floater group. You can also move this floater independently of the rectangular floater.

Now try ungrouping the floaters by first clicking on the name of the group in the Floater List palette and then clicking on the Ungroup button.

> ***Tip*** *If you wish to remove a floater from a group, you can drag it away from the group in the Floater List palette. If you wish to add a floater to a group, you can drag it inside the group in the Floater List palette.*

Dropping and Deleting Floaters

If you don't need your floater to float any more, clicking the Drop button in the Floater List palette drops the selected floater onto the background pixels. Once dropped, it becomes part of the background canvas, and you will not be able to refloat it. If you wish to drop a floater, first select the floater in the Floater List palette, then click on the Drop button. If you wish to drop all floaters, click on the Drop All button. Later in this chapter you'll learn how to drop a floater that contains a mask with the Drop With Mask option.

If you ever wish to delete a floater, first make sure that the floater is selected, then press Delete on your keyboard or choose Edit ➤ Clear. Try this out now by deleting the rectangular floater from the screen.

> ***Warning*** *After you delete a floater, you cannot retrieve it by choosing Edit ➤ Undo.*

Painting inside and outside Floaters

Since floaters remain in a separate layer above the background canvas, you can paint in a floater without fear of changing the background canvas. Conversely, you can safely paint the background without affecting the floater. This can be very handy when you want to apply paint to different image areas on screen.

To see how you can paint in one floating layer independently of the background, you should have the word *FLOATER* selected on screen. *Text Floater* in the Floater List palette should also be selected. If you don't have this floater on screen, use the text tool to create some text, then click inside it with the Floating Selection tool to turn it into a floater.

Now try painting over the letters. Pick a brush such as the Brush's Big Loaded Oils variant. Now try painting over the text. Notice that as you paint, only the letters are affected; the paint does not drip down to the background canvas.

Since the floater is in a separate layer from the background canvas, you can also fill the background of the canvas with a color and not affect the floater. To do this, you must first deselect the floater. To deselect, click away from the floater selection with the Floating Selection tool. When the floater is deselected, you can fill the canvas area behind it. Try filling the background canvas with a gradation. Open the Grads palette and pick a gradation. (We used Gold 1.) Then choose the Effects ➤ Fill command. In the Fill dialog box, pick the Gradation option and choose OK. The background, not the text, is filled with the gradation.

At this point, you may wish to save your work. If you wish to save your floater with your file, you must save the file in the RIFF file format or Photoshop 3.0. If you don't save your file in either RIFF or Photoshop 3.0 format, Painter merges the floaters with the canvas layer.

Working with the Floaters Palette

The Floaters palette allows you to save floaters and reuse them at a future date. You can also use one of the preexisting floaters that Fractal Design has created. To open the Objects :Floaters palette, click on the Floaters icon in the Objects palette.

To save a floater that you've created on screen, simply drag it with the Floating Selection tool to the open Floaters palette drawer or drawer front. This opens the Save dialog box. If you wish to leave the floater on screen and save it, press Option (Windows users: Alt) before you click and drag the floater to the palette.

In the Save dialog box enter a name for your floater, then click OK.

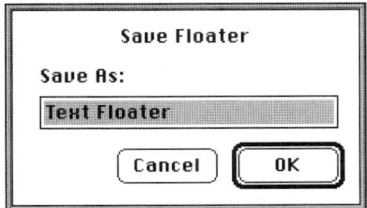

A thumbnail of the floater now appears in the drawer front. When you want to reuse your floater, or if you want to use any of the preset floaters in the palette, click on its icon above the drawer or in the drawer and drag the floater onto the canvas. If the floater you wish to use does not appear at the top of the drawer, you can choose the floater by name by clicking in the pop-up menu in the drawer. After you choose the floater in the pop-up menu, it will appear on the drawer front.

> **Note** *The unusual floaters that are provided in the Floater List palette may give you the mistaken impression that floaters can be objects of any shape. In reality, all floaters are rectangular. The "shape" of many floaters you see in Painter's preset floaters list is produced by creating a mask in the floater. You'll learn more about using masks in floaters later in this chapter.*

Using a Floater Library

If you wish to open a library of floaters, click on the Library button in the drawer. After navigating to the floater library file name on your hard disk, click the Open button. To manipulate floaters in the floater library or libraries, choose Tools ➤ Movers ➤ Floater Movers. The floater library dialog box functions like all library dialog boxes. To review using a library dialog box, see Chapters 2 and 3.

Creating Special Effects with Floaters

Now that you have a basic idea of what floaters are and how to create them, you can use floaters to create special effects. Floaters can be used to create drop shadows, text effects, and blending effects and fade outs.

Applying a Drop Shadow to a Floater

Drop shadows can add a professional three-dimensional touch to images. Creating a drop shadow from scratch with just the right amount of light and dark areas could prove exceedingly time-consuming. Fortunately, if you are using floaters, Painter can create an automatic drop shadow.

Once you create a floater, you can apply the Effects ➤ Objects ➤ Create Drop Shadow command to instantly apply a drop shadow to a floater.

Before you apply a drop shadow to your text from the previous section, you should have the word *FLOATER* on screen and in float mode from the previous exercise. (If you don't, type the word FLOATER and then float it by clicking inside the text selection with the Floating Selection tool.)

With your text selected and in float mode, choose Create Drop Shadow from the Effects ➤ Objects submenu.

```
╔═══════════════════ Drop Shadow ═══════════════════╗
║  H-Offset: [5   ]  pixels    Radius: [10.00] pixels ║
║  Y-Offset: [7   ]  pixels    Angle:  [114.5]  °     ║
║  Opacity:  [62  ]  %         Thinness:[44  ]  %     ║
║  ☐ Collapse to one layer      ( Cancel )  [ OK ]   ║
╚════════════════════════════════════════════════════╝
```

In the Drop Shadow dialog box you can control exactly how you want the drop shadow to appear by specifying values that control the drop shadow's position and size.

◆ **X-Offset**—Allows you to set how many pixels to the left or right you want the shadow to appear. Typing a positive number offsets the shadow to the right, negative numbers offset the shadow to the left.

◆ **Y-Offset**—Allows you to specify how many pixels above or below your floater you want the shadow to appear. Positive numbers put the shadow below the floater, negative numbers place the shadow above the floater.

◆ **Opacity**—Allows you to vary the opacity of the shadow. Low opacities make the shadow more transparent.

◆ **Radius**—Controls how long the shadow is. A larger radius produces a larger shadow.

◆ **Angle**—Controls the actual shadow angle. For instance, a 90° setting makes the drop shadow appear pretty much straight up and down.

◆ **Thinness**—Controls how fast the shadow fades out. The larger the number the slower the fade-out.

When you create a drop shadow, Painter creates a drop shadow layer, which is grouped to the original floater.

In the dialog box, the Collapse To One Layer option allows you to create the shadow in the same floater layer as the floater. For this exercise, don't pick this option—because you won't be able to make any alterations to the shadow floater independently of the text floater.

After you've adjusted the dialog box settings, click OK to create your drop shadow.

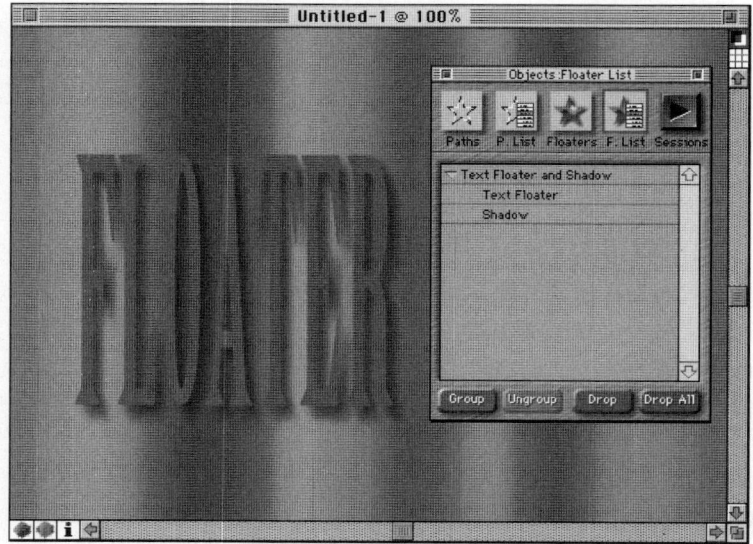

Tip *You can change the color of a drop shadow by selecting the shadow floater in the floater group and then filling it with the color of your choice.*

Note *If you'd like to apply a drop shadow to several floaters, you can group the floaters and then apply the drop shadow.*

Creating a Raised Text Effect

In this section you'll create a raised text effect, as shown in Figure 8.1. Start by opening a digitized image or a background texture. If you don't have an image to use, you can use one of the Painter tutorial files or create a new file, and then apply either a gradient or weave to the entire canvas.

1. Once you have an image on screen, activate the Text Selection tool.

2. Before you begin typing, pick a font from the Font pop-up menu in the Controls :Text Selection palette and move the Point Size slider between 50 and 200.

3. Now type some text on screen. In Figure 8.1 the words **CARVED IN STONE** were typed.

FIGURE 8.1: A Raised Text effect superimposed on a digitized image

4. When the text appears on screen, use the Path Adjuster tool to move the text into the middle of the canvas. Then increase or decrease the size of the text selection to the size desired.

5. When the text selection is in the desired position, turn the text selection into a floater by activating the Floating Selection tool and clicking inside the text selection marquee. If you think you might be moving the floater later, Option (Window users: Alt) click on the selection instead so you won't rip a hole in the canvas.

6. Open the Objects: Floater List palette. In the palette, you'll see that a floater is created. Double-click on the name of the floater in the Floater List palette. When the Path Attributes palette appears, name the floater **Text**. Click OK to activate the changes.

7. To apply a drop shadow to the text selection, choose Create Drop Shadow from the Effects ➤ Objects submenu. Click OK to create a drop shadow of your text on screen.

8. In a few moments a gray drop shadow for the text is created. When the drop shadow is created, notice that a floater group exists in the Floater List palette. Click on the triangle to expand the group. The original text floater and the shadow floater can be found within this group. Click on the text floater, then feather it by clicking and dragging on the Feather slider in the Controls :Floating Selection palette or by using the Edit ➤ Mask ➤ Feather Mask command. Feather the text somewhere between 3 and 25 pixels.

If you wish to darken the shadow, activate the shadow floater by clicking on it in the Floater List palette. Then move the Opacity slider in the Controls :Floating Selection palette to the right.

If you wish to brighten the text, select the text floater in the Floater List palette, then use the Brightness/Contrast or Equalize command found in the Effects ➤ Tonal submenu. In the image shown in Figure 8.1 we increased the brightness and reduced the contrast. To offset the shadow more, we moved the activated shadow floater by pressing the arrow keys on the keyboard.

To create more of a raised effect, duplicate the text floater by pressing and holding the Option key (Windows users: Alt key) and clicking and dragging on the text floater with the Floating Selection tool. Once the floater is duplicated, name it **Highlight**. Now use the arrow keys on your keyboard to move the highlight floater up and to the left so that it offsets the text floater. After it's offset, fill the floater with white. Next, move the highlight floater behind the text floater. Click and drag the highlight floater below the text floater in the Floater List palette. If you wish, continue to adjust the individual floaters. As you work, you might want to hide the selection marquee around the activated floater. To do this, deselect the Show Selection Marquee check box in the Floater List palette. Even though you don't see the marquee, the floater is still selected. (Remember to reselect the check box when you've completed this exercise.)

Working with the Composite Methods

When you move a floater on top of an image or another floater, you can use the options in the Controls :Floater palette to create composite effects. You can change the opacity of a floater, feather it, or use a special composite effects pop-up menu to create an unusual blending effect as shown in Figure 8.2. To create the effect, the images in Figures 8.3a and 8.3b were composited together using the Magic Combine composite method from the Controls :Floating Selection palette.

To experiment with the composite effects, drag a preset floater out of the Floater palette, then drag another floater on top of the first floater. In the Controls :Floating Selection palette, start by clicking and dragging on the Opacity slider. By dragging the Opacity slider to the left, you make the top layer more and more transparent. This is perhaps the easiest way to superimpose one floater over another.

Using the Feather slider in the Controls :Floater palette, you can also soften the edges of a floater. (Feathering is visible on text floaters, circular floaters, and floaters created from paths.) This can be handy when creating collages where you wish floaters to softly blend in with their surroundings.

> **Tip** *To expand the edges of a floater in order to add feathering, click the Expand button in the Floater List palette. You can then enter the amount in pixels that you wish to expand the floater's rectangular bounding box by. If you need to trim the floater's bounding box, click on the Trim button in the same palette.*

FIGURE 8.2: Composite created with the Magic Combine option in the Composite Effects pop-up menu.

FIGURE 8.3a: Background used to create composite.

The Controls :Floating Selection palette also includes preset composite effects. These composite options, found in the Composite methods pop-up menu, analyze every pixel in the floater and the pixels it floats over, then apply different effects based upon the floaters and the underlying pixel values.

To try out each effect, you need an activated floater floating over a background image or floating over another floater. Try out each option in the Composite Method pop-up menu as you read its description.

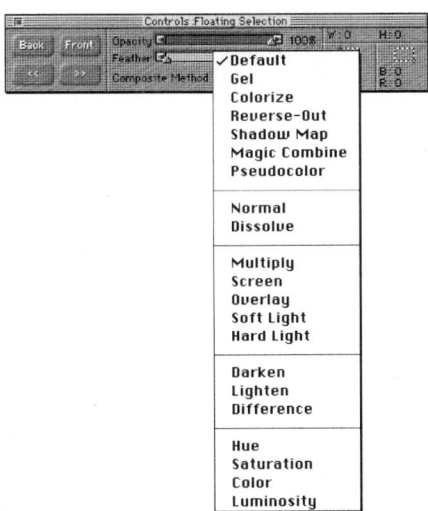

FIGURE 8.3b: Floater used to create composite.

- ◆ **Default**—Hides image areas behind the floater.

- ◆ **Gel**—Simulates placing a film gel in front of a light. The effect adds a tint of the floater's color to the underlying image.

- ◆ **Colorize**—Replaces the hue and saturation of the underlying pixels with that of the floater. Since Colorize does not change the underlying brightness values, the underlying image contours remain. To use this feature to colorize a grayscale image, open the scanned image, place a colored floater over the image, then choose Colorize in the Composite Method pop-up menu.

- ◆ **Reverse Out**—Changes the underlying pixel colors to the reverse or complement of the floater's colors. Thus, if the floater were white, the background would change to black. If the floater were yellow, the background would change to blue.

- ◆ **Shadow Map**—Darkens an underlying image allowing you to create shadow effects from the top floater.

◆ **Magic Combine**—Combines the floater with the underlying image, based upon the luminance values of the two images. If an image area of the floater is lighter than the underlying image, it appears in the underlying image. A common use of Magic Combine is to make a floater appear in underlying black type.

◆ **Pseudocolor**—Translates the overlying floater's luminance values into color. Use this to create unusual color effects or to transform a grayscale floater into color.

The following composite methods correspond to layer modes in Adobe Photoshop. If you load a Photoshop image that uses a layer mode into Painter, Painter's composite methods will provide either a perfect or close match to the Photoshop effect. If you don't use Photoshop, you'll find that the following composite methods open up new possibilities for blending floaters.

If you'd like to experiment with these composite methods, create two floaters. (Remember, to create a floater you can copy and paste, or click within a selection with the Floating Selection tool or the Rectangular Selection tool activated.) Each floater should have an image, gradation, or weave in it. Next, drag one floater on top of the other, then try out the composite methods. As you work, remember to keep the Floating Selection tool activated, so you can access the Composite Methods in the Controls palette.

◆ **Normal**—Operates like the Default mode. Pixels beneath the floater are hidden by the floater's colors when Opacity is set to 100%.

◆ **Dissolve**—Causes colors from the floater to break up randomly. The result is a mixture of the floater's colors and the colors from the underlying pixels. The result is often a speckled blend between the floater's pixels and the underlying pixels. Use the Opacity slider to control the effect.

◆ **Multiply**—Multiplies color values, usually darkening them. It produces the same effects as if two positive transparencies were laid over each other and viewed on a light table. Black areas of the floater will be unchanged. White areas of the floater are replaced with the dark areas of the underlying pixels.

◆ **Screen**—Bleaches or whitens. It produces the opposite effect of Multiply, simulating the effect of laying one negative over another.

◆ **Overlay**—Multiplies dark images and screens light images. When applying this method, the highlights and shadows of the underlying image areas are preserved.

◆ **Soft Light**—Produces the effect of directing a soft spotlight at your image. Colors in the floater that are lighter than underlying pixels are generally lightened; floater pixels darker than the underlying pixels are generally darkened.

◆ **Hard Light**—Produces the effect of directing a harsh spotlight at your image. Colors in the floater that are lighter than the underlying pixels are generally lightened; floater pixels darker than the underlying pixels are generally darkened.

◆ **Darken**—Compares the floater's colors with underlying pixel colors and emphasizes darker image areas. In more technical terms, Darken compares the floater's and underlying pixel's RGB values and takes the lower one (the lower the RGB value, the darker the color). When using this mode, the colors in the composite image may be different from the floater's and the underlying image areas. For instance, if a floater's pixel has RGB values of Red 25, Green 50, Blue 75 and the pixel beneath it has RGB values of Red 150, Green 100, Blue 50; the resulting RGB values would be Red 25, Green 50, Blue 50.

◆ **Lighten**—Produces the opposite effect of Darken. This mode compares the floater's and underlying pixel's RGB values and takes the higher one (the greater the RGB value, the lighter the color). As with Darken, Lighten may result in a color change. For instance, if you were creating a composite image of a Red 25, Green 50, Blue 75 pixel with a Red 150, Green 100, Blue 50 pixel, the resulting pixel would be Red 150, Green 100, Blue 75.

◆ **Difference**—Subtracts the floater's color values from underlying pixel values. Thus, if you were creating a composite image of a Red 25, Green 50, Blue 75 pixel with a Red 150, Green 100, Blue 50 pixel, the resulting pixel would be Red 125, Green 50, Blue 25. When using this mode, black areas in the underlying image are replaced in the composite by the floater's colors. White underlying areas are replaced in the composite by the complement of the corresponding colors in the floater.

◆ **Hue**—Replaces the hue of underlying pixels with that of the floater's pixels. The saturation and luminosity of the underlying pixels remain the same. Thus, the composite image is a combination of the floater's hues and the saturation and luminosity of the underlying pixels. Since white and black have no hue, they are ignored by the Hue composite method.

◆ **Saturation**—Replaces the saturation of underlying pixels with that of the floater's pixels. The hue and luminosity of the underlying pixels remain unchanged. Thus, the composite is a combination of the floater's saturation and the hue and luminosity of the underlying pixels.

◆ **Color**—Replaces the hue and saturation of the underlying pixels with that of the floater. The underlying luminosity values remain unchanged. You can use this method to colorize an underlying gray image.

◆ **Luminosity**—Replaces the luminosity values of the underlying image with that of the floater. The underlying hue and saturation values remain unchanged. Thus, the composite is a combination of the floater's luminosity and the hue and saturation of the underlying pixels.

Working with Floaters and Masks

Painter floaters provide amazing layering options when you begin to combine floaters and masks. Painter allows for two types of masks: a background mask and a floater mask.

The background mask is essentially a mask layer that affects the background canvas. As discussed in Chapter 7, masks can be created with the selection tools, the Edit Mask command, and Painter's Masking brushes. Using the same tools, you can create a mask in a floater. When you create a mask in a floater, you can specify which portions of the floater are visible and which portions of the underlying image are visible in relation to the floater's own mask. For instance, with the Outline Selection tool, you could create a triangular mask in a rectangular floater. When you move the floater over an object, you can make the rectangular floater appear as if only a triangle, or you could make the floater appear as a rectangle with a transparent triangular hole in it. Through the triangular hole you would see the underlying image. To control how a floater with a mask appears, you use the first row of visibility icons in the Floater List palette. These buttons are called the Floater Mask visibility buttons. To control the appearance of a floater that covers an image with a background mask, you use the second row of visibility icons in the Floater List palette. These buttons are called the Image Mask visibility buttons.

Using the Floater and Image Mask Visibility Icons

Using Painter's Image and Floater Mask visibility icons, you can control what portion of a floater is visible above the background pixels. Using the visibility icons in conjunction with the Masking brushes allows you to create unusual blends between a floater and a background image.

For instance, Figure 8.4 shows an image created by compositing a floater of a clock with a background image of an Alaskan glacier (both shown in Figure 8.5). To create the floater, we clicked the Floating Selection tool in a

FIGURE 8.4: Composite created with the Floater Mask visibility buttons

rectangular selection of the clock. Then the Outline Selection tool's Straight Line option was used to mask out the actual image area of the clock. Next the clock was pasted over the glacier image. By using the Floater Mask visibility buttons the area within the floater's mask was made visible over the iceberg. By painting with gray over the clock with Painter's Masking brushes, the blend between the two images was created.

FIGURE 8.5: Top: Floater used to create composite. Bottom: Background used to create composite.

Using the Floater Mask Visibility Buttons

The Mask visibility buttons at the bottom of the Floater List palette control how a floater interacts with masks. The first row of the floater visibility buttons control how a mask within a floater affects the floater's appearance. These control what portion of a floater and what portion of its mask are visible.

In order to experiment with the Floater Mask visibility buttons, you need to create a mask in a floater. To do this, open up any image. Next, create a selection using the Oval Selection tool or the Outline Selection tool. After you've created the selection, copy and paste it into another file that has an image in it. The selection is pasted into the file as a mask within a floater. Now you can experiment with the Floater Mask visibility buttons. Try out each button by clicking on it as you read each description. After you click on each button, try painting with black, white, and gray using a Masking brush. When you paint with a Masking brush you can make a floater dissolve, or reveal different parts of the floater.

> **Tip** *As you work, you can hide the blinking selection marquee that outlines a floater or a mask by clicking in the Hide Selection check box in the Floater List palette.*

◆ **Masking Disabled**—The entire floater is visible. The floater's mask is ignored. When this icon is set, painting with a Masking brush in the floater has no effect.

◆ **Masked Inside**—The mask cuts a hole in the floater. The inside of the mask appears to be transparent, allowing the underlying floater or background to be seen through the floater's mask.

If you are using Masking brushes you can reveal more of the underlying layer by painting with black. Painting with white hides the background layer and shows more of the floater.

◆ **Masked Outside**—This allows the floater area within the mask to appear over the background image. The floater area outside the mask is invisible.

Using the Masking brushes has the opposite effect of painting with the Masked Inside button set. If you are using Masking brushes, you can reveal more of the underlying layer by painting with white. Painting with black hides the background layer and shows more of the floater.

If you wish to see how the Masking brushes can change an image, choose a Masking brush from the Brushes palette. Try painting a gray shade over the floater. As you paint with gray, the floater will become more transparent.

> **Note** *If you activate the Drop With Mask option in the Floater List palette before you press the Drop button, you drop the floater and keep the floater's mask. After you drop the floater, its mask can be accessed in the Path List palette. To review how to use the Path List palette and Path Adjuster tool, see Chapter 7.*

Using the Image Mask Visibility Buttons

The icons in the second row of the Floater List palette are called Image Mask visibility buttons. These control how a floater interacts with an image's background mask. Using these buttons you can make a floater appear within the area covered by the background mask or outside of the background mask.

Figure 8.6 shows an image of the clock from Figure 8.5 blended together with a highway (Figure 8.7). To create the effect, a mask was created in the clock by using the Edit ➤ Mask ➤ Auto Mask command. In the Mask dialog box, Luminance was chosen in the Using pop-up menu. This created a mask of the brightness levels in the clock. Next, the highway image was pasted over the clock image. The third image masking icon was then selected. This made the highway image appear through the mask area in the clock image. In the final image, the Masking brushes were used to bring out the white lines in the image.

To see the power of the Image Mask visibility buttons, you need to create a mask in a background image, then drag or paste a floater on top of it.

FIGURE 8.6: Composite created with the Edit ➤ Mask ➤ Auto Mask command

FIGURE 8.7: The highway image that was pasted over the clock mask in Figure 8.6

To set up a floater to try out the Image Mask visibility buttons, load an image on screen. If you don't have an image to load, use the Mission file from Painter's tutorial folder. Create a mask by using one of the Masking brushes to paint over the file. Before you paint, click on the third Mask Drawing icon and the second Mask Visibility icon in the lower left-hand corner of the screen (or in the Objects :Path List palette).

Before continuing, switch visibility icons to the third Mask Visibility to view your mask as a selection. Now that you have a background mask created, copy and paste an image or selection over the mask. If you don't have an image to paste, select an area from the Trees file in Painter's tutorial folder. Then paste it over your background image and its mask. Once the file is pasted, it is automatically turned into a floater. Now click on each Image Mask button to experiment and to see the effects. As you work, try deselecting the floater, then painting with black, white, or gray in the background image with a Masking brush.

◆ **Masking Disabled**—The floater is entirely visible, and is not changed by the mask in the background canvas.

◆ **Masked Inside**—Only the floater image areas that are outside of the background mask are visible. If you paint the background mask using a Masking brush, painting with white hides background areas, and reveals more of the floater when the floater is activated. Painting with black shows more of the background and hides more of the floater.

◆ **Masked Outside**—The floater appears within the background mask. If you paint in the background mask using a Masking brush, painting with black hides more of the background, and reveals more of the floater. Painting with white shows more of the background and hides more of the floater.

Creating a Nozzle from a Floater Group

One of Painter's most fantastic features is its ability to spray digital images across a screen using its Image Hose brush. As discussed in Chapter 3, Image Hose brushes use nozzle files to create their startling effects. Using floaters you can easily create your own nozzle file, as shown in Figure 8.8. Once you create the nozzle file, you can paint the screen with the floaters from your nozzle file, as shown in Figure 8.9.

FIGURE 8.8: A nozzle file to be used with an Image Hose brush

FIGURE 8.9: A painting made with an Image Hose using the nozzle file from Figure 8.8

Here are the steps for creating a nozzle file out of floaters.

1. Create a new file for your nozzle. The file should be large enough to hold the floaters you will place in it. Set the resolution to 75 ppi. (If you wish, you can also create the file at a higher resolution.)

2. Place several floaters on screen in a grid arrangement of columns and rows. If you don't have any floaters to use, drag some floaters from the Objects: Floater palette. Arrange the floaters in rows and columns. If you are using your own floaters, you might wish to use the Outline Selection tool to mask out or silhouette your floaters. Otherwise each floater will appear as a rectangular block when it is painted with the Image Hose brush.

Tip *When creating a nozzle out of a group of floaters, click the Trim command to trim away excess bounding area around the floater. When you click Trim, Painter makes the rectangular floater surrounding the floater as small as possible.*

3. If you wish to spray the floaters on screen sequentially, order your floaters from top to bottom in the Floater List palette.

4. Next, create a floater group by holding down the Shift key then clicking on each floater in the list. Once all of the floaters are selected, click the Group button. Close the group by clicking on the down arrow next to the name *Group 1* in the Floater List palette.

5. To create the Nozzle, choose Tools ➤ Image Hose ➤ Make Nozzle From Group. A new untitled document appears. Save the file in RIFF format. This is the nozzle file that you must load when you want to paint the screen with the floaters.

6. When you wish to use your nozzle file, load it by choosing Tools ➤ Image Hose ➤ Load Nozzle. In the Open dialog box, select the name of your nozzle file, and open it. Alternatively, you can load a nozzle file by clicking on the Load button in the Brushes Controls :Nozzle palette. In the Brushes palette, set the brush to Image Hose, then pick a brush variant. Then paint the screen. Your floaters will spray across the canvas. If you wish to experiment more with Nozzle controls, open up the Brush Controls :Nozzle palette and adjust the Rank 1 slider settings. To learn more about creating nozzle files, see Chapters 9 and 11.

● Creating Fadeouts with a Floater Mask

You can use floaters and masks to make your image fade to its paper color to create the effect shown in Figure 8.10. To create this effect, start by loading an image on screen. If you don't have an image, use one of the tutorial images. If you want to fade the image to a specific color, change the paper color by first changing the primary painting color to that color, then choose Canvas ➤ Set Paper Color.

With an image on screen, double-click on the Rectangular Selection tool to select the entire canvas. Then use either the Rectangular Selection tool or the Floating Selection tool to click in the selected area to create a floater. Keep the floater selected.

Your next step is to fill the floater's mask layer with a white and black Two-Point gradation. Start by making the primary painting color white and the secondary painting color black. Next, choose the Two-Point gradation from the Art Materials :Grads palette. To make a horizontal fadeout, set the degrees to 70 or 90. To make a vertical fadeout set the degrees to 0 or 180.

Now use the Paint Bucket to fill the mask layer with the gradation. Click on the Paint Bucket tool in the Tools palette. In the Controls :Paint Bucket palette, set the What To Fill option to Mask and the Fill With option to Gradation. Now click in the image. To see the fade, make sure either the second or third Floater Mask visibility button (in the first row) in the Floater List palette is selected. Instantly the fadeout to your paper color appears. Switch between the second and third Floater Mask visibility buttons to reverse the effect.

If you want to make certain areas in the fadeout more opaque or more translucent than others, experiment with the Masking brushes.

● Wrapping It Up

As you've seen from the many examples in the chapter, floaters provide numerous possibilities for editing images and juxtaposing them. When you start working on your own projects with floaters, remember to try out different effects with Painter's Masking brushes and Auto Mask command. You're sure to find that the image editing possibilities are endless.

FIGURE 8.10: Top: Image before fade-out. Bottom: Image after fade-out

Creating Special Effects

Painter is capable of creating many fantastic and stunningly beautiful special effects. As you've seen in earlier chapters, you can convert a photograph into a Van Gogh or Seurat painting, posterize and convert images into negatives, apply lighting effects, create raised text, distort images, and clone or merge images together using various composite methods.

Now you're ready to delve deeper into the world of special effects—particularly into the world of unusual effects. In this chapter you'll learn everything from creating simple three-dimensional textured effects to bending and twisting an image almost beyond recognition. As you work through this chapter, you'll learn how to warp and emboss images; create glass distortions, marbling, and blobs; apply texture to images; and fade images.

You'll also take a tour of third-party special effects plug-ins—programs that extend Painter's special effects capabilities. You'll also discover how stand-alone special effects programs and 3-D programs can be used with Painter. So, if you're interested in the wild and unusual, read on.

● Painter's Effects Menu

Painter's Effects menu is your gateway to special effects. The special effects covered in this chapter are found in three Effects submenus: Surface Control, Esoterica, and Focus. Although each submenu provides different effects, the similarities among them are helpful to understand.

Each of Painter's Effects commands can be applied to an entire image or to a portion of an image. If you wish to apply the effect to only a portion of an image, you must select the portion first. To select, you can use any of Painter's selecting tools, including the Oval Selection, Rectangular Selection, and Text Selection tools, or the Magic Wand. You can also apply special effects to selections created with Painter's Masking brushes, and you can apply effects to floaters. (When a floater is selected, the effect is applied to the floater; the underlying background image is not affected. When a floater is not selected, only the underlying background image is affected.)

Each time you apply any of the commands in the Effects submenus, Painter opens up a dialog box allowing you to control exactly how the command will affect your image. Since the execution of some of the commands can be quite time-consuming, Painter often allows you to preview the effects in a preview box. In most Effects dialog boxes, you can click and drag in a preview area to see how executing the effect will change different parts of your image—before you click OK. As you work through this chapter, be sure to take advantage of the preview box. It could save you from wasting time waiting for effects that you might eventually end up discarding.

Painter's Effects menu also provides a convenient way of repeating the effects you use the most. As you work, the menu updates itself so that the names of the last two effects you applied appear at the top of the Effects menu. The last two effects are also assigned keyboard shortcuts: Command+slash (Windows users: Ctrl+slash) re-executes the last effect you applied, and Command+semicolon (Windows users: Ctrl+semicolon) re-executes the second-to-last effect that you applied. Now that you know a few shortcuts for using the Effects menu, you're ready to start applying special effects.

Working with the Surface Control Commands

The Surface Control commands allow you to change the surface texture and color of images. The Surface Control commands include: Apply Lighting, Apply Screen, Apply Surface Texture, Color Overlay, Dye Concentration, and Image Warp. In Chapter 4 you learned how to use the Apply Lighting command. In Chapter 5 you learned how to use the Dye Concentration command. In the following sections you'll learn how to use the Apply Screen, Apply Surface Texture, Color Overlay, and Image Warp commands.

Using the Apply Screen Command

The Apply Screen command allows you to create unusual flat and textured effects from three colors. The result can be like that created from a mezzotint (a black-and-white image created entirely from dots) that has been colored. Figure 9.2 shows the effects of the Apply Screen command when applied to Figure 9.1. Figure 9.3 shows the settings used in the Apply Screen to achieve the effect in Figure 9.2.

FIGURE 9.1: Photograph of a trolley to be used to demonstrate some simple effects

Creating Special Effects

FIGURE 9.2: Image after using the Apply Screen command

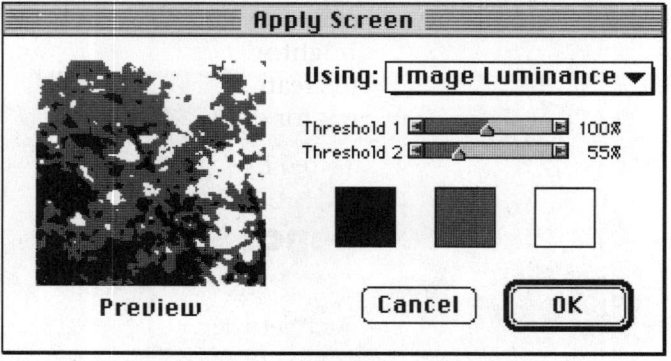

FIGURE 9.3: The settings used in the Apply Screen command

To achieve the effect seen in Figure 9.2, load a digitized image, then choose the Apply Screen command from the Effects ➤ Surface Control submenu. In the Apply Screen dialog box, you pick each color you wish to use in your image by clicking on a swatch. After you click on the swatch, the Macintosh Color Picker (Windows users: Windows Color dialog box) appears where you can choose colors by clicking the mouse or entering values. Once you close the Color Picker dialog box, you can control the intensity of the colors by using the Threshold sliders. The first Threshold slider controls the intensity of the last and middle swatch colors in the image. Dragging this slider to the left increases the amount of the right color swatch in your image; dragging to the right increases the amount of color in the middle color swatch. The second Threshold slider controls how much of the middle and left swatch colors appear in your image. Dragging this slider to the left increases the amount of the middle color swatch; dragging to the right increases the amount of color in the left color swatch.

The choices in the Using pop-up menu combine with the colors and the Threshold slider effect to produce the final effect. The Using menu includes the following choices:

◆ **Paper Grain**—Applies the currently selected paper grain. If the Art Materials palette is open, you can change paper grains while the Apply Screen dialog box is open.

◆ **Image Luminance**—A flat colored effect is created based upon the brightness levels of the image.

◆ **Original Luminance**—A flat colored effect is created in the cloned document based upon the brightness levels of the source document image. Use this command to create unusual blends between a source image and its clone. The steps for doing this are described below.

◆ **Mask**—The mask area is affected by Apply Screen.

Using Original Luminance with Apply Screen

To create an unusual blending effect between one image and another using three colors, open any image. Next open another image and choose File ➤ Clone Source. Set the inactive document (the first one you opened) as the Clone Source. Now execute the Apply Screen command. In the Using pop-up menu, choose Original Luminance. Click on the color swatches to choose your colors, and use the sliders to control the intensity of the colors. As you experiment, notice that the preview box shows a high-contrast version of the clone image and active image on screen mixed together.

Note *If you find the concept of luminance confusing, it's often helpful to imagine a grayscale version of your image, and view the different luminance levels as different gray levels.*

Using the Apply Surface Texture Command

The Apply Surface Texture command allows you to add paper grain and/or embossing to an image, along with an added touch of lighting. Figure 9.4 shows a stock image of a surfer (Image courtesy of Digital Stock Corp.) before the Apply Surface Texture command was applied. Figure 9.5 shows an image of a surfer after using the Apply Surface Texture command to create an embossed effect. Figure 9.6 shows the settings used in the Apply Surface Texture to achieve the embossed effect.

To use Apply Surface Texture, first load an image, then choose Effects ➤ Surface Control ➤ Apply Surface Texture. Notice that the dialog box not only provides an image preview but a lighting effect preview box. Click

FIGURE 9.4: Photo CD image of the surfer before using the Apply Surface Texture command. (Image courtesy of Digital Stock Corp.)

FIGURE 9.5:   Embossed image of surfer created using the Apply Surface command

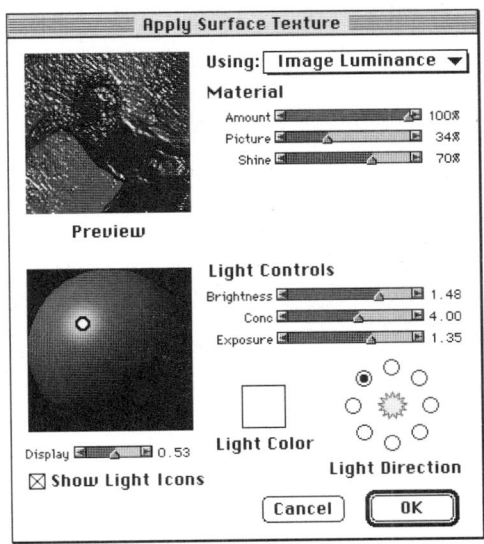

FIGURE 9.6:   The settings used to create the embossed effect.

on any of the Light Direction circle icons to change the light direction, then click on the Light Color swatch to change the Light Color. The Using pop-up menu allows you to pick the source for applying the texture:

◆ **Paper Grain**—Texture is applied using the paper grain currently selected in the Art Materials :Papers palette.

◆ **3D Brush Strokes**—Creates a three-dimensional effect by subtracting the source from the cloned image. This option will not be available unless a clone and clone source are on screen. The effect can make the clone source look as if it is embossed in the clone.

◆ **Mask**—Texture is applied around mask edges.

◆ **Image Luminance**—Texture is applied based upon the image's brightness values.

◆ **Original Luminance**—Texture is applied in a cloned image based upon the clone source's brightness values.

The Material sliders and Light Controls sliders allow you to control the degree of the 3-D surface effect. The Amount slider controls the intensity of the surface texture effect. Dragging to the right accentuates the effect. The Picture slider works like a lighting diffusion slider on a matte surface. Dragging to the right creates a more diffused effect. The Shine slider controls the strength of *specular highlights*. A specular highlight is an area that is pure white, like a reflection or glare. Dragging to the right accentuates specular highlights.

The Brightness slider controls the overall intensity of the light. The Conc (Concentration) slider controls how concentrated or spread out the light is over the surface texture. Dragging to the right makes the light more concentrated toward a point in your image, dragging to the left makes it less concentrated. The Exposure slider adjusts the overall brightness and darkness of the light.

The Display slider only affects the image in the lighting preview box. Dragging to the right brightens the display to make it show more of the effect of the lighting adjustments.

To apply an embossed effect to an image, open it and then choose the Apply Surface Texture command from the Effects ➤ Surface Control submenu. Set the Using pop-up menu to Image Luminance. Drag the

Amount slider to 100% to create a more intense effect. Use the Picture and Shine sliders to fine-tune the effect.

Use the Light Controls to adjust the lighting brightness, concentration, and exposure. You can also change the lighting of the color by clicking in the Light Color swatch. To adjust the direction of the emboss effect, click on one of the Lighting Direction circle icons. Click OK to apply the effects.

You can also use the Apply Surface Texture command to create an embossed effect from shapes you create with paths, as seen in Figure 9.7.

1. To create an embossed effect from a path, first create a new file.

2. Fill the canvas with a light color. After you choose a color from the Art Materials :Colors palette, choose Fill from the Effects menu. In the Fill dialog box make sure that the Current color option is selected, then click OK.

FIGURE 9.7: Embossed shapes created using the Apply Surface Texture command

3. Now you can either use the Outline Selection, Oval Selection, or Text Selection tool to create a shape, or drag one of the paths from the Paths palette onto the canvas. In Figure 9.7 the Heart and Star 5 paths from the Paths palette were used. (To review how to create paths, see Chapter 7.)

4. After you have a path shape on screen, you can use the Path Adjuster tool to either move or resize the path.

5. Next, use the Path List palette to select the shapes on screen. In the Objects :Path List palette the circle icon in front of each path name should be selected, so that the path is selected. If the selection marquee is not displayed on screen, select it with the Path Adjuster tool.

6. Before you execute the Apply Surface Texture command, click on the third Drawing button and first Visibility button at the bottom of the Path List palette. You won't see these buttons if the palette is not expanded. To expand the palette, click on the zoom box in the top right hand corner of the palette. By clicking the first Visibility button, you ensure that the effect is applied to the entire image, not just a selection in the image.

7. Choose the Apply Surface Texture command from the Effects ➤ Surface Control submenu.

In the Apply Surface Texture dialog box, set the Using pop-up menu to Mask. To enhance the embossed effect, set the Amount slider to 100%. Use the other sliders and the Lighting Direction icons to enhance the effect.

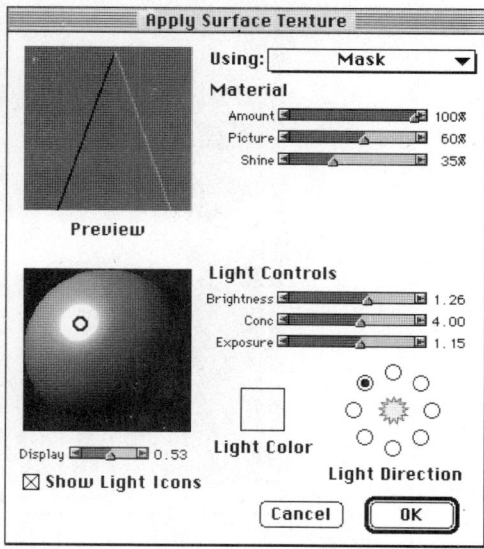

8. After you've embossed your shape, you can reapply the Apply Surface Texture command to add a texture to your image. Before you choose the command, make sure the Art Materials :Papers palette is open. In the Apply Surface Texture dialog box, set the Using pop-up menu to Paper Grain. The paper grain of the active paper in the Papers palette is displayed in the Apply Surface Texture dialog box's preview area. If you want to use another pa-

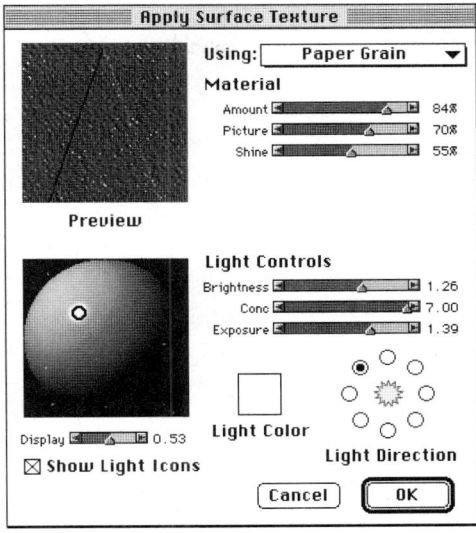

per, click on a different paper in the Papers palette. The preview is automatically updated. Experiment with different papers and settings in the dialog box. When you are happy with the preview, click OK to apply the effect to your image.

Using the Color Overlay Command

The Color Overlay command allows you to add a colored tint to your image and add texture, if desired.

Figure 9.8 shows Painter's Coppery gradation. Figure 9.9 is the Coppery gradation after applying the Color Overlay command. Figure 9.10 shows the settings used in the Color Overlay dialog box. Texture was added to the image by using the Paper Grain option, and cyan was applied to the image.

To use the Color Overlay command, either load an image or create a new file and apply a gradation to it (so that you have a colored image on screen). At this point, make sure that the Art Materials palette is on screen so that you can experiment with different colors and paper textures once the Color Overlay dialog box is opened. Before opening the dialog box, pick a primary painting color. This is the color Painter applies to your image when the Color Overlay command is executed.

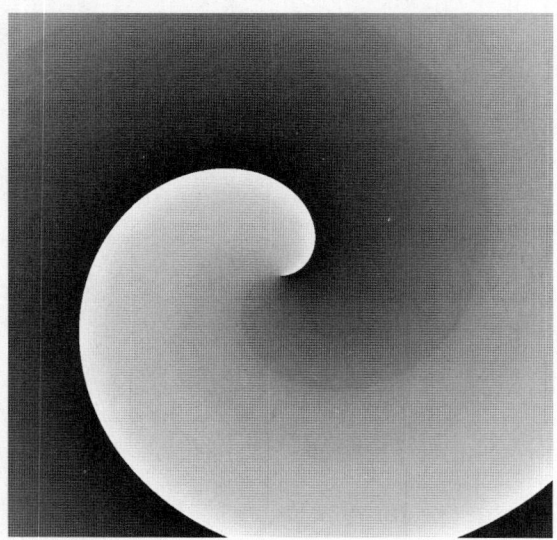

FIGURE 9.8:   Painter's Coppery gradation

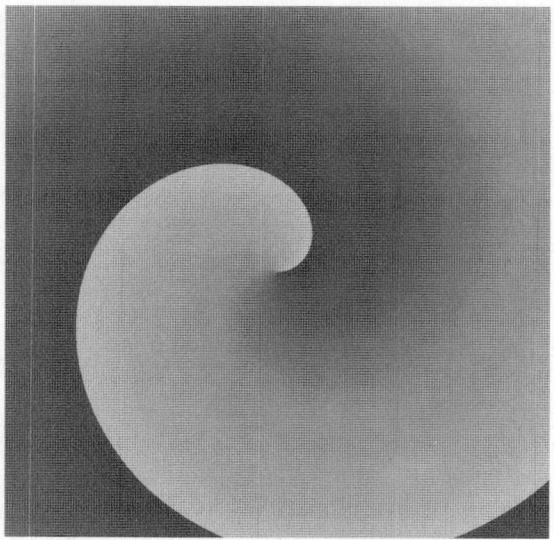

FIGURE 9.9:   The gradation after applying the Color Overlay command

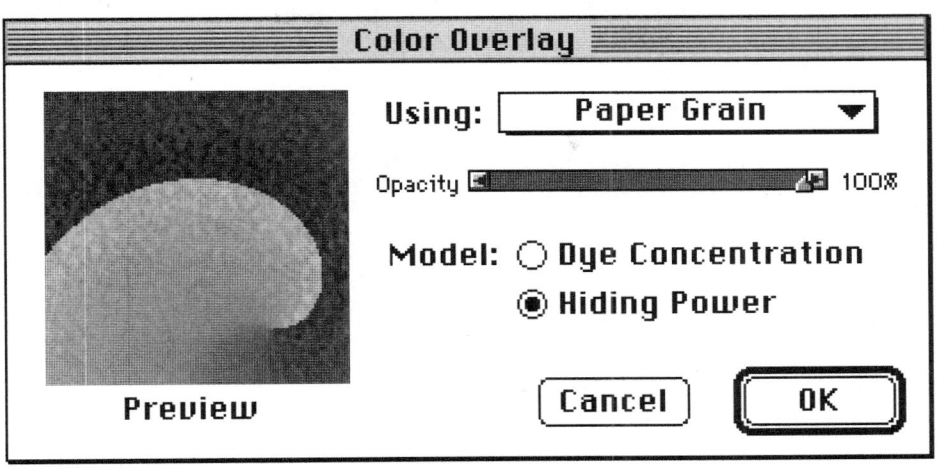

FIGURE 9.10: The settings used in the Color Overlay dialog box

Now, choose Color Overlay from the Effects ➤ Surface Control submenu. In the Color Overlay dialog box, you can add texture to your image by selecting several options on the Using pop-up menu. The choices are very similar to those in the Surface Control dialog box.

◆ **Uniform Color**—Adds a tint to your image. When applied, you can see the background image through the tint. To see more of the underlying image, lower the opacity, using the Opacity slider.

◆ **Paper Grain**—Adds texture based upon the paper texture selected in the Art Materials :Papers palette—accessible while the dialog box is open. The current primary painting color is also overlaid over the paper grain. If you don't like the preview of the currently selected paper grain, you can choose another paper grain from the Art Materials palette.

◆ **Image Luminance**—The color overlay is applied based on the brightness levels in the image.

◆ **Original Luminance**—A colored overlay is applied to a clone based upon the brightness levels of the clone source image. Use this to combine the source and clone images together.

◆ **Mask**—Texture is added around the border of a mask.

After you've chosen a Using option, pick a Model. In most instances, Dye Concentration creates a darker effect than Hiding Power. When Hiding Power is chosen, dragging the Opacity slider to the right can completely hide your image with the primary painting color.

To fine-tune the effect, use the Opacity slider, which changes the translucency of the effect. You can also switch to another primary painting color in the Art Materials: Colors palette. Click OK to apply the effects to your image.

Expressing Texture in an Image

The Express Texture command allows you to transform a colored image into a textured grayscale version of the image.

If you wish to add texture to a specific area on screen, select it first before choosing Surface Control ➤ Express Texture from the Effects menu. If you don't select an area, the Express Texture command affects the entire image on screen.

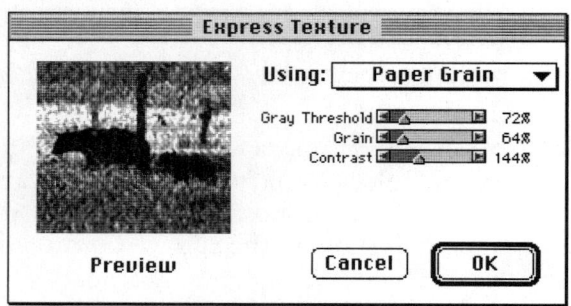

In the dialog box, a preview area allows you to view the results of the Express Texture command before you click OK. If you wish to view another part of your image, click and drag in the preview area until the desired image area comes into view.

In the dialog box, the Using pop-up menu allows you to pick a source for the texture. Here is a description of the Using choices.

◆ **Paper Grain**—The currently selected Paper Grain in the Art Materials palette is used as a basis for the texture.

◆ **Mask**—The value of the mask is used as the source. For instance, if you use a Masking brush to create a mask, the effects will change depending upon the shade of gray used to create the mask.

◆ **Image Luminance**—The image's brightness values are used as the source.

◆ **Original Luminance**—The luminance of the clone source is used to create the effect in a clone.

To fine-tune the effect of the Express Texture command, Painter provides three sliders. As you use the sliders, pay close attention to how they affect the preview. This will further your understanding of how each slider changes the texture.

◆ **Gray Threshold**—Allows you to specify the gray shade that Painter uses as the point at which to change image areas from light to dark. Use the Gray Threshold to intensify the effect of the texture.

◆ **Grain**—Allows you to control how much paper grain appears in the texture. Dragging to the right adds more grain, dragging to the left reduces grain.

◆ **Contrast**—Adds more contrast to the texture, accentuating the difference between light and dark areas. Dragging right adds contrast, dragging left reduces contrast.

Using the Image Warp Command

The Image Warp command turns your image into putty, allowing you to distort an image in a variety of different ways. Figure 9.11 shows the image before distortion (image courtesy of ColorBytes, photography by Eric Wunrow). Compare it to Figure 9.12, which shows how the Image Warp can distort an image. If you're experimenting with text effects, Image Warp has a lot to offer. Figure 9.13 shows the effects of warping a text image.

> **Note** *If you're not using a Power PC, your computer must have an FPU (floating point unit), sometimes called a coprocessor, for the Image Warp command to work.*

To use Image Warp, open an image that you wish to distort, then choose Effects ➤ Surface Control ➤ Image Warp. To warp your image, click and drag in the preview area of the dialog box—not in your image—over the image area that you wish to warp. As you drag, a circle appears showing the area that will be affected by the warp. Once you release the mouse, Painter warps the image area. If you wish to make the warping area larger, drag the Size slider to the right; to make it smaller, drag it to the left.

FIGURE 9.11: Image of a door and window before distortion. (Image courtesy of ColorBytes, photography by Eric Wunrow)

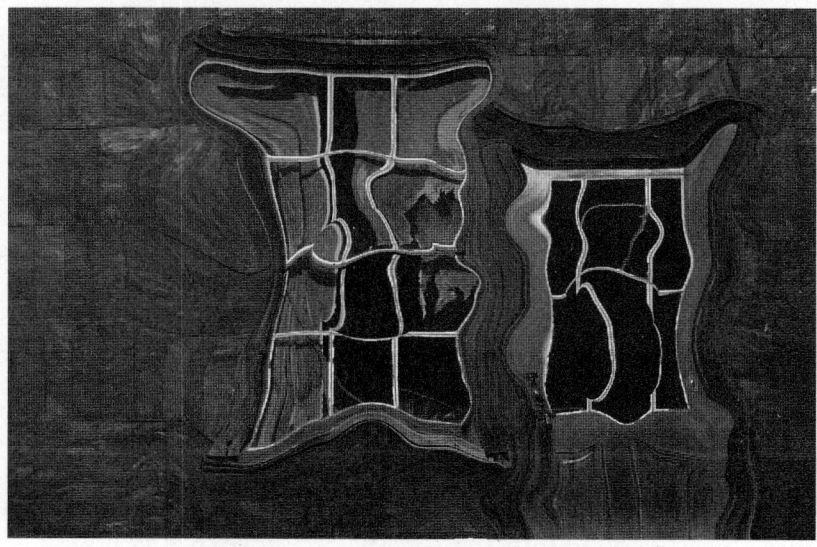

FIGURE 9.12: Image of a door and window after distortion

FIGURE 9.13: Warped text over image of the Maine coast

To alter the warping effect, Painter provides three radio buttons. When Linear is selected, it's as if you're pulling a hill shape out of your image. Choose Cubic to create a wave in a flat surface. Choose Sphere to create a lens-shaped distortion.

Once you're satisfied with the effect, click OK.

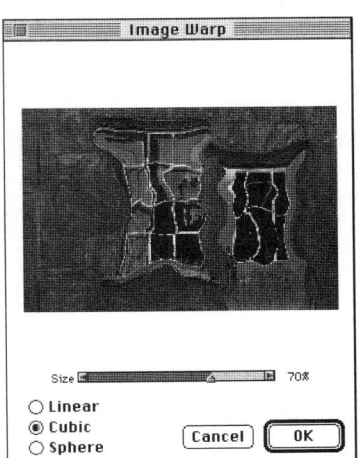

Using Image Warp to Distort Text

To use Image Warp to distort text without affecting the background, as seen in Figure 9.13, you need to convert the text into a floater before you move it or warp it. To create the effect, start by opening an image that you wish to place text over. If you don't have an image, use one from Painter's Tutorial folder.

1. Once you have an image on screen, add some text using the Text Selection tool. If you wish to move the text, or adjust the text on screen, use the Path Adjuster tool.

2. To turn the text into a floater, activate the Floating Selection tool, then press and hold the Option key (Windows users: Alt key) while you click inside the text selection. Instantly, the text selection turns into a floater. Pressing the Option key (Windows users: Alt key) insures that you won't rip a hole out of your background if you move the floater. For more information about floaters, see Chapter 8.

3. Fill the floater you just created with the current color, gradient, or weave.

4. Choose Image Warp from the Effects ➤ Surface Control submenu to warp your text. Even if the preview box doesn't show that only your text is warped, click OK. The text will be warped, but not your background image.

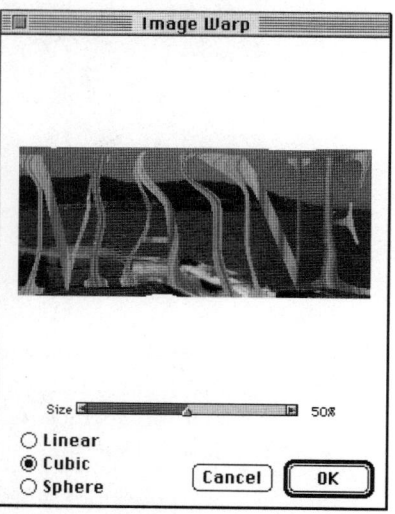

Working with the Focus Commands

The Focus commands allow you to change your image as if viewing it through a lens. There are four Focus commands: Glass Distortion, Motion Blur, Sharpen, and Soften. In Chapter 4 you learned how to use the Sharpen and Soften commands to correct digitized images. The following sections cover how to use the Glass Distortion and Motion Blur commands.

Using the Glass Distortion Command

The Glass Distortion command allows you to add a glass texture effect to an image. This command can also be used to apply texture to your image. Figures 9.14 and 9.15 show a photograph of La Boca in Buenos Aires, Argentina before and after applying the Glass Distortion command. Figure 9.16 shows the final version of the image after painting tango dancers, using different brushes on the background. The tango dancers were painted in a separate file and selected with the Outline Selection tool. Afterwards, they were copied and pasted into the background file where they appeared in a floater. Since the dancers were in a floater, they could be moved and resized without affecting the background. Next the Apply Surface Texture command was used to add texture to the dancer. The last step was to adjust lighting using the Effects ➤ Surface Control ➤ Apply Lighting command. Turn to the color insert to see this image in color.

FIGURE 9.14: Image of La Boca in Buenos Aires, Argentina

FIGURE 9.15: Image after applying the Glass Distortion command

FIGURE 9.16: Image after painting tango dancers and using the Apply Lighting command. (To see this image in color, turn to the color insert.)

To use the Glass Distortion command, load an image or create a new file and fill it with a gradation. Next, choose Glass Distortion from the Effects ➤ Focus command.

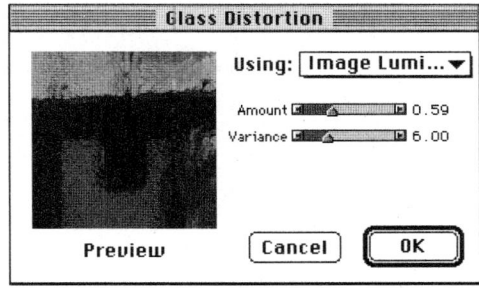

Next, select a choice from the Using pop-up menu. Here are some basic descriptions of the choices.

◆ **Paper Grain**—Adds texture based on the paper texture selected in the Art Materials :Papers palette.

◆ **3D Brush Strokes**—Adds texture by taking the difference between the source image and its clone.

◆ **Mask**—Adds texture around the border of a mask.

◆ **Original Luminance**—Adds texture in a cloned image based on the brightness values of the clone source.

◆ **Image Luminance**—Adds texture based on the brightness levels in the image.

Once you've specified a choice in the Using pop-up menu, use the Amount and Variance sliders to fine-tune the effect. The Amount slider controls the intensity of the glass distortion. Drag this slider to the right to increase the effect; drag left to diminish the effect. The Variance slider controls the distortion. The further right you drag this slider the more your image will begin to break up. When you are happy with the effect, click OK to activate the changes.

Using the Motion Blur Command

The Motion Blur command allows you to add motion to a static image. The effect simulates the blur that would appear when a camera is moved while taking a picture. Figure 9.17 shows a stock image of a pair of dice before applying Motion Blur (image courtesy of CMCD, Inc.). Figure 9.18 shows the same image in motion after applying Motion Blur.

FIGURE 9.17: Photo CD image of dice before applying Motion Blur. (Image courtesy of CMCD, Inc.)

FIGURE 9.18: Image of dice after applying Motion Blur

1

Artist: Adele Droblas Greenberg
Sculpture

2

Artist: Adele Droblas Greenberg
Tango in La Boca

3

Artist: Adele Droblas Greenberg
Friday

To learn how these images were created, see Chapter 9

4 John is currently the resident artist of Fractal Design's Entertainment Technology Center in Burbank, CA. His credits include rotoscoping for the movie of Robert Heinlein's The Puppet Masters.

John created this magical image in three parts; the wizard's body and head, the crystal ball and left hand, and the reflection of the right and left hand. All of these pieces were painted as separate objects in separate documents. John first created a rough sketch using Painter's 2B Pencil, then used a soft cover Airbrush to add color, along with the Water brush Frosty Water variant (with a soft cover) to blend the colors together.

After each portion was finished it was then masked and turned into a floater. Next, John created a new document and filled it with a gradient. Then he placed all of the floaters into the new document. He then lit the individual pieces.

5 This hair-raising image was created as a promotion for a snowboard company. John started the image with a large rough sketch of the reflection in the glasses as the entire canvas. He then increased the canvas size and added more detail to it. He zoomed back and used a soft cover Airbrush to lay in the color. He then blended the color using the Frosty Water brush variant with a soft cover method. Next he applied the Glass Distortion command using the paper texture option. Then he applied lighting on top of the Glass Distortion. He used the Liquid brush Smeary Bristles variant to create the smeared snowflakes on the lenses.

After the reflections in the glasses were completed, John painted the rest of the snowboarder using the soft cover Airbrush and Spatter Airbrush (using a paper texture) in conjunction with the Frosty Water brush variant.

6 John started this image by creating a sketch on paper. He then scanned the sketch. With the sketch on screen he began to add color to the face using the Spatter Airbrush with the Surface2 paper texture (from the More Paper Textures Library). John added details using a thin stroke Airbrush. He then used the Liquid brush Frosty Water variant to blend the colors together.

After the face was completed, John painted the hat using the Spatter Airbrush, Thin Airbrush and Frosty Water. He also painted using paper textures. After all image areas were painted, John masked each object and applied lighting effects.

4

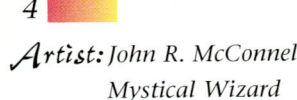

4

Artist: John R. McConnell
Mystical Wizard

5

Artist: John R. McConnell
Screaming Snowboarder

6

Artist: John R. McConnell
The Mad Hatter

5

6

7 Mark is a senior designer at Rucker Design Group of Mountain View, CA, which specializes in software packaging and illustration.

Mark began creating this image by scanning photographs that he took of people sleeping on walls. After scanning the images, Mark used Painter's Charcoal brush to sketch the figures and the Total Oil Brush to add detail. Mark used the Apply Surface Texture command with the Image Luminance option to add luminance and texture.

To create the walls, Mark used Painter's Charcoal brush with the Grainy Soft Cover Cloning method to clone a section that he liked. He used the Grainy Soft Cover Cloning method so that it wouldn't look like the section was being repeated. Mark then opened the image in Photoshop, where he created feathered masks for each figure. The figures were composited together using Photoshop.

8 This image is one in a series of ads for Acer Computers. In order to create this image, Mark began searching for an antique train. When he found the train he was looking for, he photographed it and then scanned it into Photoshop.

With the image on screen, he used Photoshop's Pen tool to outline the train, converted the path into a selection and saved the selection to an alpha channel. Mark then brought the train image and mask into Painter. In Painter, he used various brushes and textures to create a painterly background.

9 This image is a promotional piece for Ray Dream, Inc. The texture on the 3-D vase was created in Painter using various brushes and variants, including Charcoal and Oil. When painting, he also used paper textures, and the Apply Surface Texture command with the Image Luminance option. The snake image was created in Adobe Illustrator and imported into Painter as a path.

The texture for the floor pattern was created by first importing a path from Illustrator into Painter. Then the color was added using the Charcoal brush and paper texture.

Mark then used Ray Dream Designer to create the 3-D vase and wrap the texture on the vase as well as map the texture to the floor. For the finishing touches, Mark applied lights and rendered the image.

7

Artist: Mark Jenkins, Rucker Design Group

Timeless Sleep

8

Artist: Mark Jenkins, Rucker Design Group

Acer Toy Train

9

Artist: Mark Jenkins, Rucker Design Group

Aztec Vase

10 Pat, a Truckee, CA artist who teaches Graphic Design and Computer Design at Sierra Nevada College, created this image without utilizing any scanned photos. He started by using Adobe Illustrator to block out the illustration. He then imported the image into Painter. In Painter he added colors using a Wacom stylus and tablet with Painter's Chalk brush and Just Add Water. He created the trees and ocean using Painter's Airbrush and Movers. The highlights in the water were created using the Airbrush and Chalk brush. To create the textures for the quasi-sand dunes around the car, Pat used Kai's Power Tools. He then shaded the texture and added a few extra pixels for a sandy look. Pat also used KPT to create the base texture for the water and clouds.

11 Dorothy, a Marshfield Hills, MA artist and professor of computer graphics at the Massachusetts College of Art, began this intriguing image by opening an early wood engraving and image of a Renaissance woman into Painter. The wood engraving was colorized using the Color Overlay command with the Hiding Power and Paper Grain option selected. Then the black lines were lightened using the Dye Concentration command with the Image Luminance option selected.

Using the wood engraving as the clone source, Dorothy cloned parts of it into the portrait of the Renaissance woman using the Soft Cloner brush.

Dorothy then opened a third image of a young woman, from artist/photographer Jan Doucette's Wood Nymph series. She then filled the entire image with a gentle gold sweep using the metallic presets in KPT's Gradient Designer. Next, Dorothy copied and pasted the young woman into the main image using the Normal Composite Method at 75% Opacity. She then intensified the head and part of the body back using the Soft Cloner brush. Finally, she used Water Only to smooth irregularities and soften edges, and intensify the shadow areas with the Artists Pastel brush.

12 Dorothy started by loading an image of a face from artist/photographer Jan Doucette's Wood Nymph series. Next she cloned it and filled the clone with a gentle gold sweep from the metallic presets in Kai's Power Tools Gradient Designer. Using Painter's Surface Control command, she applied a surface texture using the Original Luminance option. She then cloned the face and bits of the flowers back into the embossed gold surface. She saved the merged image and cloned it.

Dorothy then opened a photograph of a dove and pasted it into the clone of the merged image using the Default Composite Method at a 75% Opacity. She cloned the merged image to strengthen some of the details in the embossed gold surface, then used chalk to soften the feathers of the dove, using Just Add Water to smooth the transitions.

Finally, she created the border by selecting a narrow rectangle and adjusting the Brightness and Contrast, and executed Apply Surface Texture based on Original Luminance.

10

10

Artist: Pat Watson
Coast

11

Artist: Dorothy Simpson Krause
Angel on my Shoulder

12

Artist: Dorothy Simpson Krause
Dove

11

12

13 John is VP of Creative Design at Fractal Design. John started the image using a photograph of a Paris morning scene that reminded him of an Edward Hopper painting. John began by removing cars from the photograph by cloning them away. First he masked out an area, then used the Pixel Dust brush to clone with a concrete texture from the photograph. Next he created shadows using the Outline Selection tool's Bézier Curves option to make outlines which he feathered and filled with black.

To create the people, John imported the image into Fractal Design Poser. In Poser, John added the adult and child, positioned them and set the lighting.

To produce the shadow for the characters, he created separate files to use as silhouettes that would be placed into Painter as floaters. He saved the image in Poser with the figures rendered into the background, then loaded them into Painter. Using the Poser image as a clone source, John painted clothing over the figures. He did this with the tracing paper option set so that he could see through to the original image as he worked. To add an Impressionist touch to the image, he activated the Impressionist brush. In the Advance Controls :Sliders palette, he set the Angle slider to Source, which caused the luminance values of the source image to control the angle of individual brush strokes in the clone. This added to the hand-painted look. He then used the Auto Clone command to apply the brush to the image. John's last step was to use the Apply Surface Texture command to add an impasto surface to the painting.

14 Jeremy is a Palo Alto, CA artist who teaches at the Academy of Art College in San Francisco, CA. When creating the image, Jeremy wanted to capture Picasso's vibrant zest for life. He didn't use any scans or trace any images to create the portrait. All of the work was created by painting freehand with a Wacom stylus and tablet.

Jeremy primarily used pastel brushes and a customized air brush with a Grainy Method Subcategory. He began by creating a Picasso-like dream image and a bullfight image. He cloned the dream into the bullfight image and began painting it over to create the portrait. To produce the effect of Picasso's face emerging from the background, Jeremy played back a session using the Liquid brush Distorto variant. As a final touch, he cloned in some cubism using Xaos Tools' Paint Alchemy's Cubism filter.

15 Chelsea, a Hollister, CA artist, was commissioned by Fractal Design to create this image which is included in Fractal Design's paint can poster. John Derry gave her a black-and-white video grab of a paint can and asked her to create a surreal effect with a Salvador Dali and René Magritte style.

Chelsea started by using the Charcoal brush to sketch the image. She then added color using the Oil Paint, Coarse Hairs and Loaded Oils brush variants. After she finished painting the image, she added lighting and texture using the Apply Surface Texture command.

13

13

Artist: John Derry
Paris Morning

14

Artist: Jeremy Sutton
Picasso

15

Artist: Chelsea Sammel
Rene meets Sal

14

15

16 JW is a Texas artist/photographer who created this image as one in a series of advertisements for Pepsi. JW started with an 8x10 transparency of an athlete, and images of a Doritos bag and a Mountain Dew bottle that he scanned. In Adobe Photoshop he converted the color photo to black-and-white (Bitmap Mode) and then back to color to achieve a dithered effect. He then increased the resolution to make the pixels stand out. Next, he brought the image into Painter and colored it using masks to help fine-tune his work.

Finally, he added thin Airbrush strokes around the image.

17 This image of Jimi Hendrix appeared in Car Stereo Review magazine in an article on remastering Jimi Hendrix's music. To create an updated version of Jimi Hendrix, JW used Kai's Power Tools to create a fractal in the background and twisted the neck of the guitar using Valis Metaflo.

Before colorizing Jimi in Painter, JW created masks for the highlight and shadow areas. In general he added cooler colors in the shadow areas and warmer colors in the highlight areas.

18 Pat started this image by scanning a black-and-white photograph of a ski racer. Once the image was loaded into Painter, Pat cloned it and began to redraw it in color using the Chalk brush. After coloring the image, Pat used the Just Add Water variant to smooth the color and blend the edges.

To add a sense of movement, Pat used the Liquid brush with the Smeary Mover, Coarse Smeary Movers and Distorto variants to push pixels to attain the desired effect—trying to balance distortion against a realistic depiction.

Finally, he used the Airbrush tool to retouch areas, and then smeared them again and again in order to make these areas match their surroundings.

16

© 1994 J. W. Burkey

16

Artist: JW Burkey
Pepsi Ad

17

Artist: JW Burkey
Jimi

18

Artist: Pat Watson
Skier

17

18

19 Nick is a San Francisco, CA artist/photographer whose work has appeared in many national publications. This unusual image first appeared in an advertisement insert in *Info World* magazine. Nick started the image by first creating a pencil sketch. He then scanned the sketch and cloned it. He deleted the image and filled the canvas with black and then activated the Tracing Paper option. Using a customized brush, he removed black and created the final image.

20 Mark is a San Francisco, CA cartoon comic artist. This image was created for a Batman miniseries called *Jazz* published by DC Comics. Mark created the image in separate parts: the jazz figure, Batman and the buildings. Mark scanned two sketches: one of Batman and another of the jazz figure. He then used masks and customized brushes to add depth and color to the images. He also used Kai's Power Tools and Adobe Gallery Effects' Watercolor filter to add more texture to the image.

Next, he composited the images together in Painter using floaters and masks. Once it was composited, the floaters were dropped and Mark blended the images together using a custom Oil Pastel brush using a Drip method.

21 This lively image appeared in *Step-By-Step* magazine to illustrate an article Nick wrote about Painter. Nick started out with a loose pencil sketch of three jazz musicians. He scanned the figures individually so that he could work more efficiently in three small files rather than one large file. Working on each figure individually, Nick cloned and applied the Tracing Paper option. Next, with a Wacom stylus and tablet, he applied the undertones with broad brush strokes. To give the broad strokes of the undertones texture, Nick used a rough paper texture. After the undertones were created, Nick outlined the musicians and applied Water Color brush strokes. Once he was happy with the results, he imported the musicians into one file where the final touch-up work was completed. The file was eventually loaded into Photoshop where it was converted to a CMYK file for print output.

19

19

Artist: Nick Fain
  Playing with the Big League

20

Artist: Mark Badger
  Batman: Jazz

21

Artist: Nick Fain
  Trio

20

21

22 JW created this romantic image for a Valentine's Day party invitation. He started by creating the sky with Painter's Airbrush. The foreground texture was created from blobs of paint mixed together. To add perspective and depth to the ground, JW used the Distort command. The edges were created by feathering a selection and filling them with white.

JW bought an old heart sticker and scanned it. In Painter, he created masks and added depth to the heart by using the Airbrush to add yellow to the light areas, and black to the dark areas. He also used the Airbrush to add a shadow under the heart so that it wouldn't look like it was floating in the air.

JW photographed a man and woman in his studio. He later scanned the photo, and resized it before placing the couple in the final image. As a final touch he created the shadow of the people by making a selection, feathering and filling it with black.

23 Gary is an artist and Assistant Professor of Art at Bloomsburg University in Bloomsburg, PA. The idea for the image started when Gary began photographing mannequins with a Canon RC 570 still-video camera. He began earnestly to work on the image when Fractal Design asked him to submit a piece of artwork.

Gary began the image by experimenting on watercolor paper with colored and tempura inks. Once he obtained the marbled and painterly quality he desired, he scanned the image at 500 dpi. This allowed him to choose small details of the ink study which he resized and scaled to 11 by 17 inches. He then used the Dodge brush to lighten different sections and bring out details. His next step was to clone in two mannequin heads. Once the two top mannequins were in place, Gary enhanced them using the Dodge and Burn brushes. The kiwi was created by carefully scanning a real kiwi in his scanner. After solarizing the image in Photoshop, he loaded it into Painter. Next the white mannequin was cloned into place. The stalk of wheat was scanned and touched up by hand with the Colored Pencil and Eraser Single Pixel Bleach variant.

24 Adam is an artist who was born and raised in Russia. He now resides in Palo Alto, CA. Nevertheless, he has kept his own Russian style.

To create this image, Adam used various brushes in the Brushes palette. As he worked he broke down each figure into smaller parts using the Outline Selection tool's Freehand, Straight Line and Bézier Curve options. He then converted the curves into selections. He also used the Apply Surface Texture command to apply different paper textures to the image. To add luminescence to the image, he applied different types of lighting using the Apply Lighting command. To create the female breasts, he used preset selections from the Paths palette, scaled them and applied a weave using the Paint Bucket. Later, he turned them into floaters, adjusted opacity and used the Shadow Map Composite Method to composite the image with the background canvas.

22

© 1991 J. W. Burkey

22
Artist: JW Burkey
Valentine

23
Artist: Gary Clark
Dictates of Conscious

24
Artist: Adam Sadigursky
Big City Love

23

24

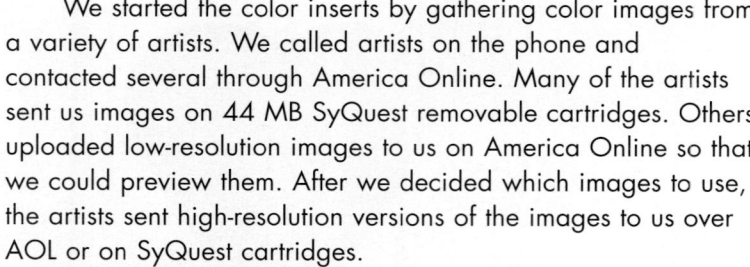

How we put it all together!

We started the color inserts by gathering color images from a variety of artists. We called artists on the phone and contacted several through America Online. Many of the artists sent us images on 44 MB SyQuest removable cartridges. Others uploaded low-resolution images to us on America Online so that we could preview them. After we decided which images to use, the artists sent high-resolution versions of the images to us over AOL or on SyQuest cartridges.

After SYBEX sent us the page size and margin sizes needed for the color insert pages, we began to create the layout in QuarkXPress on our Macintosh. Each page was created in a separate file. After we designed the layout and began placing the images in it, we sent SYBEX a color proof that we printed on a Tektronix dye sublimation printer. After SYBEX approved the pages, its production department sent them to the prepress house, Color Response of Charlotte, NC, to obtain an IRIS proof.

In order to view a proof that would provide better color accuracy than the IRIS, we had Color Response output a proof from their Kodak Approval Digital Color proofing system. This helped assure us that the conversion from RGB to CMYK would yield accurate colors. When all of the color pages were finalized, we sent them to Color Response on one 270 MB SyQuest cartridge. Color Response separated all of the RGB color images on a Scitex workstation. Then Color Response RIPed all of the QuarkXPress files from the Macintosh to a Scitex workstation. The color images were then placed into the layout and output to film using a Scitex Dolev at 150 lpi, emulsion down. After the film was output, Color Response created color 3M Matchprints—proofs from the film.

The production process for the text pages was slightly different than that used for the color pages. The black-and-white text pages were laid out in QuarkXPress. The illustrations were created using Image Club ArtRoom clip art that was altered in Adobe Illustrator. These illustrations were later imported into the QuarkXPress layout. When the text was completed, we sent a printout from our laser printer to SYBEX to proofread and approve. Next, we sent the Adobe Illustrator illustrations and the QuarkXPress layout on floppy disks to Color Response. The prepress house output the text layout with the illustrations from a Mac to a Dolev to produce the film for the text and illustrations. Next Color Response created bluelines and sent the bluelines and film to SYBEX. Finally, SYBEX sent the film from the color and black-and-white pages to its commercial printer, Art Print in Taylor, PA, to be printed.

To use Motion blur, first select the portion of your image that you wish to apply the blur to. If you wish to apply the blur to the entire image, you need not make a selection.

To open the Motion blur dialog box, choose Effects ➤ Focus ➤ Motion Blur.

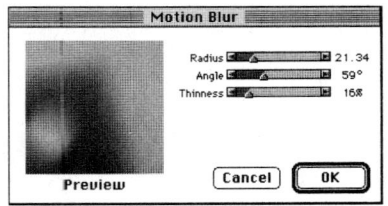

To adjust the blurring effect, Painter provides three sliders:

- ◆ **Radius**—Drag this slider to the right to increase the blurring effect.

- ◆ **Angle**—Use this slider to control the direction of the blur motion.

- ◆ **Thinness**—Dragging this slider to the right enables you to blur the image perpendicularly to the angle specified by the Angle slider.

When you are happy with the preview, click OK to apply the effect to your image.

Working with the Esoterica Commands

The Esoterica commands are a collection of diverse commands which apply a variety of unusual, startling, and fun effects. The Esoterica commands include Apply Marbling, Auto Clone, Auto Van Gogh, Blobs, Grid Paper, Growth, and Highpass. In Chapter 6 you learned how to use the Auto Clone and Auto Van Gogh commands. In the following sections, you'll learn how to use the Apply Marbling, Blobs, Growth, Grid Paper, and Highpass commands.

Using the Apply Marbling Command

Painter's Apply Marbling command is based on a marbling method in which ink floating in a liquid is dragged in different directions by a rake. Using Apply Marbling, you can create unusual backgrounds as shown in Figure 9.19. This figure was created by using the Apply Marbling command on a file with the Stripes 7 gradation.

FIGURE 9.19: An interesting image created by using the Apply Marbling command on a Painter gradation

To use Apply Marbling, create a new file and fill it with a color or gradient. To create the effect shown in Figure 9.19, use Painter's Stripes 7 gradient.

After you've filled the canvas with this gradient, choose Apply Marbling from the Effects ➤ Esoterica submenu. The sliders in the dialog box are used to adjust the marbling effect by simulating dragging a rake through a liquid with floating ink.

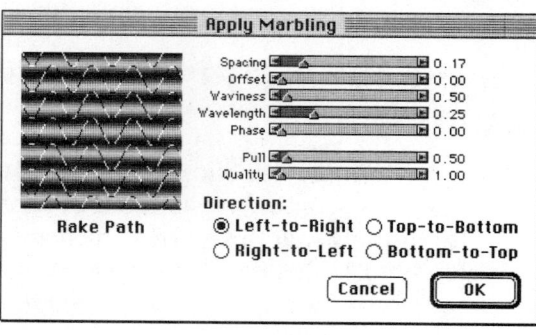

In the preview area, Painter provides a simulation of the wavelength created by dragging the rake.

◆ **Spacing**—Click and drag to the right to widen the space between the rake teeth. The greater the spacing the more spread-out the marbling effect.

◆ **Offset**—Simulates shifting the rake every time it rakes over an image. Clicking and dragging right adds more marbling complexity.

◆ **Waviness**—Controls the height of the wave's curve. Dragging to the right creates higher curves, to the left creates lower curves.

◆ **Wavelength**—Controls the distance of the wave. Dragging to the right creates a longer wavelength.

◆ **Phase**—Controls at what point on the curve the wave starts.

◆ **Pull**—Adjusts the amount of ink dragged by the rake. Drag the slider to the right to create a more intense dragging effect. (This effect is not shown in the preview box.)

◆ **Quality**—Dragging to the right creates a smoother effect created by anti-aliasing. (Dragging to the right also lengthens the processing time of the effect.)

In the Apply Marbling dialog box you can experiment with the sliders to fine-tune the effect you wish to produce, then click OK to apply the effect to your image.

Using the Blobs Command

The Blobs command is certainly one of the most unusual of Painter's special effects commands—it's also one of the most fun to use. The Blobs command works by transforming your image into blobs based upon whatever is in the Clipboard. If nothing is in your Clipboard, Painter uses the current primary color. Figure 9.20 shows the image of a clock that was copied to the clipboard before the Blobs command was applied. Figure 9.21 shows the liquefying effects of applying the Blobs command to a canvas filled with Painter's Colorburst gradient (Figure 9.22).

> **Note** *If you're not using a PowerMac, your computer must have an FPU (floating point unit), sometimes called a coprocessor, for the Blobs command to work.*

FIGURE 9.20: Image of clock that was used to create the blob effect of Figure 9.21

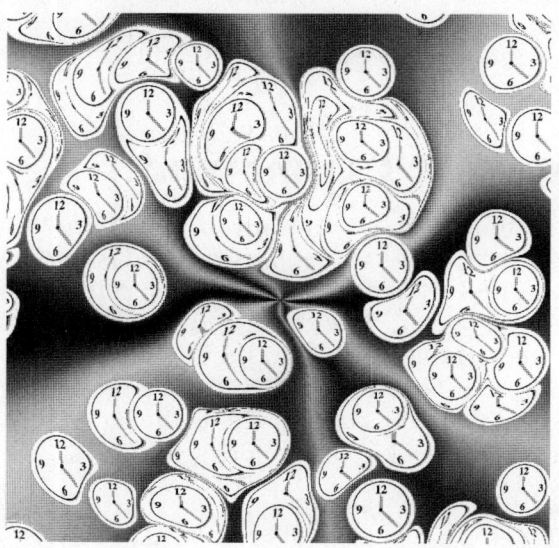

FIGURE 9.21: Image after applying the Blobs command to a Painter gradient.

FIGURE 9.22: Painter's Colorburst gradient

1. To use the Blobs command, start by creating a new file. For this example, fill the file with either a gradient or a weave. In Figure 9.21 Painter's Colorburst gradient was used.

2. Next either create an image (in another file) to use as the basis for your blobs, or open a file with an image in it to use as blobs.

Note To create the clock in Figure 9.20, use the Oval selection tool, Text Selection tool, and Outline Selection tool.

3. Now select the image you want to blob by choosing Select All or by using the Oval or Rectangular Selection tool. If you created the clock, select it now. To place the image into the Clipboard, choose Copy from the Edit menu, then close the file.

4. Once the image is selected and copied to the Clipboard, use the File ➤ Open command to load the file you want to apply the blobs to (if it is not already opened). Next, Choose Blobs from the Effects ➤ Esoterica submenu.

Create Marbling "Stone" Pattern

Number of blobs: 40 blobs
Minimum size: 50.0 pixels
Maximum size: 70.0 pixels
Subsample: 4 to 1

Cancel   OK

5. In the Blobs dialog box, Painter provides many options for creating just the right blob. You enter how many blobs you want, their maximum and minimum size in pixels, and how the edge of the blobs should appear. After you've entered numbers in the fields, click OK to create some blobs.

Using the Grid Paper Command

The Grid Paper command fills your canvas with a grid, as shown in Figure 9.23. The command allows you to pick the thickness and color of the grid lines. After your canvas is filled with a grid you can paint over it using one of the brushes. Although the Grid Paper command is certainly not as exciting as the Blobs command, it can be helpful when creating backgrounds, and, when used in conjunction with other commands, it can create interesting effects, as shown in Figure 9.24. In this figure, the Image Warp command was applied to the grid. Figure 9.25 shows the Image Warp dialog box used to create the effect.

FIGURE 9.23: A canvas after the Grid Paper command was applied

FIGURE 9.24: Grid after applying the Image Warp command

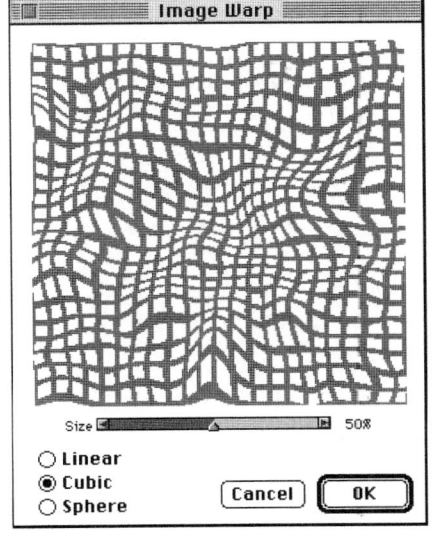

FIGURE 9.25: The Image Warp dialog box used to warp the grid

To use the Grid Paper command, create a new file. Then choose Grid Paper from the Effects ➤ Esoterica submenu.

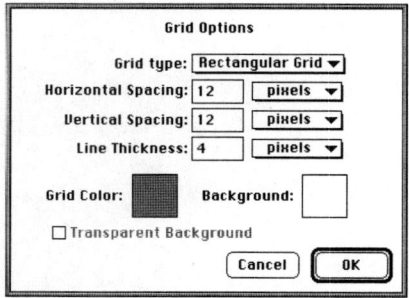

The Grid Options dialog box allows you to control the spacing, thickness and color of the grid. Here's a review of the choices.

◆ **Grid Type**—Choose whether you wish a rectangular grid, vertical or horizontal lines, or a dotted grid.

◆ **Horizontal Spacing**—Controls the space between horizontal lines.

◆ **Vertical Spacing**—Controls the space between vertical lines.

◆ **Line Thickness**—Controls the thickness of lines, measured in pixels. Remember there are more pixels per inch in a high-resolution document; thus, when using high-resolution images, you may need to enter a higher pixel value than when using a low-resolution image.

◆ **Grid Color**—Controls the color of the grid. Click on the color swatch to open the Apple Color Picker or Windows Color dialog box. After choosing a color, close the color picker dialog box.

◆ **Background**—Controls the color of the grid's background. Click on the color swatch to open the Apple Color Picker or Windows Color dialog box by clicking OK. After choosing a color, close the Color Picker dialog box by clicking OK.

Using the Growth Command

The Growth command allows you to create a wide variety of unusual branch shapes, as shown in Figure 9.26.

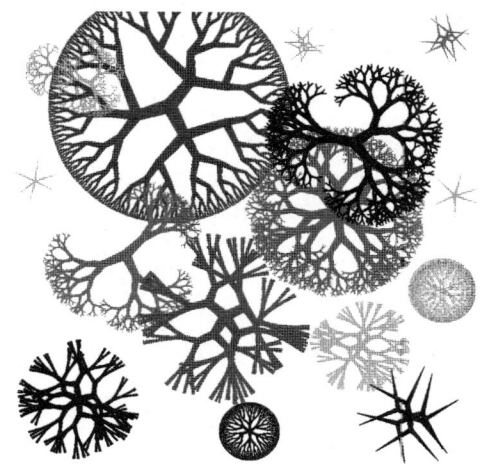

FIGURE 9.26: A variety of fractal and nonfractal growths

The following Growth dialog boxes show you some of the different shapes you can create.

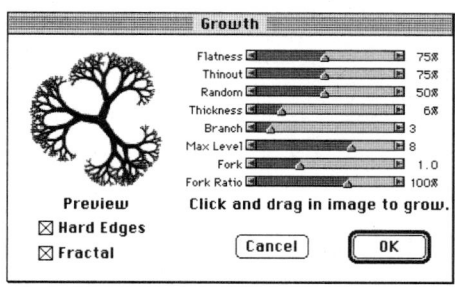

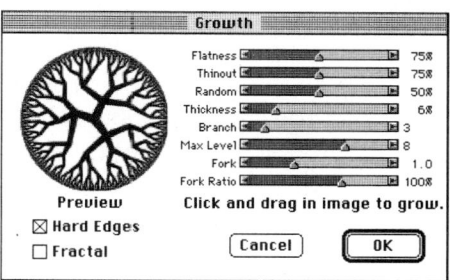

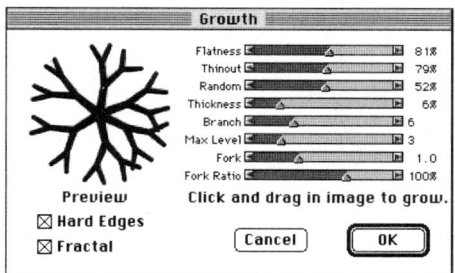

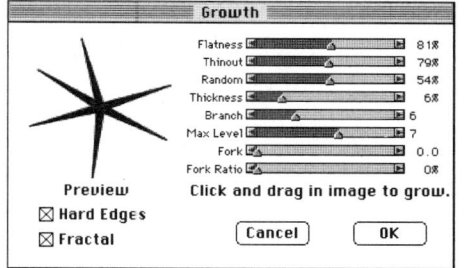

If you would like to try out the Growth command, create a new file in which to work. Next, make sure that the Art Materials :Colors palette is open, so that you can change the colors of the growths you create. Now, choose Growth from the Effects ➤ Esoterica submenu.

To start creating growths, click and drag on screen to create a growth. To make larger growths, you can click and drag in large arcs. A growth appears in the active primary painting color based upon the settings chosen in the dialog box. To create another growth in another color, change the primary painting color in the Colors palette.

If you want to change the shape of the growths you create, the Growth dialog box provides numerous options:

◆ **Hard Edges**—Select this check box if you wish the growths to have hard edges; otherwise they will be created with soft edges.

◆ **Fractal**—The Growth dialog box features two branchlike shapes. The Fractal shape creates shapes that are more like tree branches. If the Fractal check box is deselected, the growths are enclosed in a circular outline.

◆ **Flatness**—Drag this slider to the left to make the growths more concave. Drag to the right to create a rounded "fish-eye" effect.

◆ **Thinout**—Use this slider to control whether growth edges are thick or fine. Dragging the slider to over 100% causes the growth edges to become thicker. As you drag to the right, more of the growth pattern becomes distributed towards the edges of the growth. Dragging to the left produces the opposite effect, making the growth edges finer.

◆ **Random**—Drag this slider to the right to create more distorted growth patterns. Dragging to the left makes the growths straighter and more symmetrical.

◆ **Thickness**—Drag this slider to the right to thicken growth patterns uniformly; drag to the left to make them thinner uniformly.

◆ **Branch**—This slider controls the number of branches emanating from the center of the growth. The branch range is from 1 to 20.

◆ **Max Level**—Use this slider to specify the number of sub-branches in a growth.

◆ **Fork**—Drag this slider to the right to make the outside branches more intricate; drag to the left to make them less intricate.

◆ **Fork Ratio**—Drag this slider to the right to make the outside branch tips more intricate, drag to the left to make them less intricate.

Click OK to activate the changes.

Using the Highpass Command

The Highpass command creates special effects by accentuating image areas that contain sharp transitions in brightness levels (called high-frequency areas) and ignoring areas that contain smooth transitions (low-frequency areas). Figure 9.27 provides you with an idea of how the Highpass command can alter an image. This figure was created by applying the Highpass command to Figure 9.1.

FIGURE 9.27:   Image after applying the Highpass command

Before you apply the Highpass command, you might wish to use either the Effects ➤ Tonal Control ➤ Equalize command or the Effects ➤ Tonal Control ➤ Brightness & Contrast commands to create more contrast in the image. This causes the Highpass command to create a more dramatic effect.

To open the Highpass dialog box, choose Highpass from the Effects ➤ Esoterica submenu.

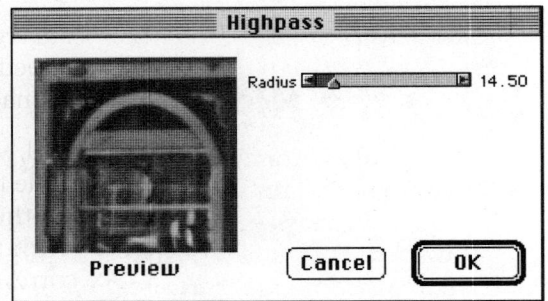

The Highpass dialog box features a Radius slider which allows you to control how Painter analyzes low-frequency image areas. (Low-frequency image areas exhibit little transition in brightness levels). When you click and drag the slider to the left, fewer low-frequency areas are allowed into the image. Drag the slider to the right and Highpass allows more low-frequency areas into the final image.

● Creating Other Painter Effects

Besides using the commands in the Effects ➤ Surface Control, Focus, and Esoterica submenus to create special effects, you can also use many other Painter commands to create special effects, and to combine special effects. For instance, don't forget about the Effects ➤ Objects ➤ Drop Shadow command covered in Chapter 8.

Remember to use the Cloners brushes (Chapter 6) to transform digital images into paintings. In Chapter 7 you feathered a selection to create a vignette. In Chapter 8 you also used floaters to create effects and to create an Image Hose from a group. In the following sections you'll learn to create an Image Hose using a grid; you'll also learn how to create and use patterns.

Creating an Image Hose in a Grid

The Image Hose brush paints with image elements from the contents of a nozzle file. For example, Figure 9.28 was created by painting with the Image Hose brush with a nozzle file composed of four different stock images from CMCD's Visual Symbols Sampler CD-ROM.

Although creating a nozzle file from a grid is a bit more complicated than creating one from floaters (as described in Chapter 8), it provides you with the ability to create more complex Image Hose effects.

Before creating a nozzle file on a grid, you should first determine the size of the individual objects in the nozzle file, and how you want the grid set up. Using this information, you can then determine the dimensions of your nozzle file. When you paint with the Image Hose brush, the size of the elements in the brush stroke correspond exactly to the size of the elements in the nozzle file.

FIGURE 9.28: A brush stroke created with the Image Hose brush

Here are the steps for creating a very simple nozzle file from a grid. In this example a 2 by 2 grid will be created. Each section in the grid will be 100 by 100 pixels. Thus the file size in pixels will be 200 by 200 pixels.

1. Create a new 75-ppi file. Set the image dimensions to 200 by 200 pixels.

Note *If you wish to create high-resolution Image Hose brush strokes, you should increase the resolution of your nozzle file.*

2. Once the file opens, create a grid size by choosing Canvas ➤ Grid Options. Set the horizontal width of the grid to 100 pixels and the vertical width of the grid to 100 pixels. Leave the Grid type pop-up menu set to Rectangular Grid and the Line Thickness set to 1 pixel. Click OK to activate the settings.

3. To view the grid on screen, click on the Grid icon at the top of the vertical scroll bar in the document window.

Note *If you are working in a high-resolution file, you will need to increase the width and height of the grid in pixels.*

4. In each cell of the grid, create an object or paint a color. Figure 9.29 shows the figures from CMCD's Visual Symbols Sampler laid out on the grid. To place the images on the grid, we copied and pasted them from the CD-ROM onto the grid. After repositioning the images in each cell of the grid, as shown in Figure 9.29, we clicked on the Drop All button in the Floater List palette to drop the floaters.

5. After you have an object in each cell of the grid, you must create a mask over them. Before you create the mask, set the Mask Drawing button (in the Objects :Path List palette) to Mask Outside (the second icon). Set the Mask Visibility button to Color Overlay (the second icon in the Visibility row). Figure 9.30 shows the mask created around each CD-ROM image. We did this in order to silhouette the images and remove the background white areas.

6. Before creating the mask, set the primary color to black in the Art Materials :Colors palette. Then choose a Masking brush and paint over the areas you wish to include when your Image Hose brush paints. If your mask spills over your images into the background, you can remove the Masking brush strokes by painting with white.

FIGURE 9.29: CMCD Images laid out on the grid

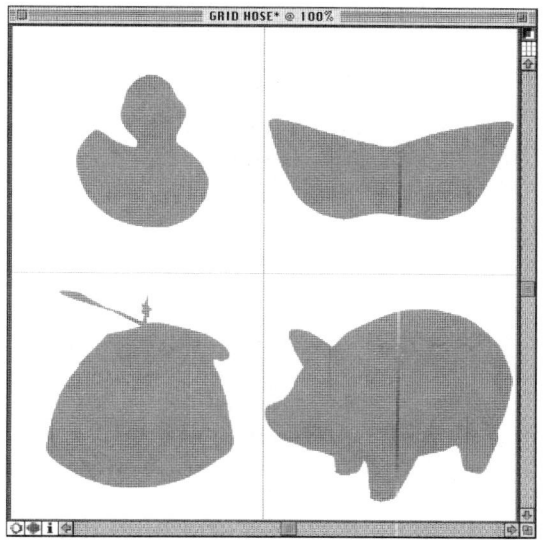

FIGURE 9.30: Mask overlaying images

Creating Special Effects

If your objects contain straight edges, you may wish to choose the Straight Lines option in the Controls :Brushes palette. Figure 9.30 shows the mask around the images from Figure 9.29.

7. When you've completed masking out the image, save the file in RIFF format.

Now you're ready to use the nozzle file. First you must load the RIFF file by using the Tools ➤ Load Nozzle command or by loading the nozzle file from the Brush Controls :Nozzle palette.

8. To load the file from the Nozzle palette, click on the Load button. When a dialog box appears, locate your nozzle file and open it.

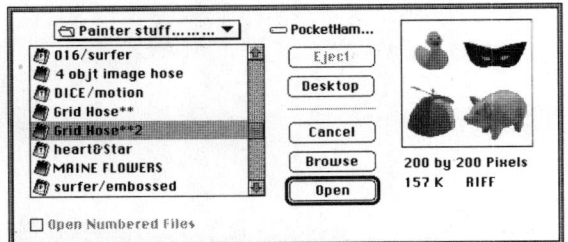

9. The first time you load the nozzle file, the Nozzle Definition dialog box appears. This is where you must specify the grid size, and how many items are in the nozzle file.

If you've been following the steps in this example, enter **100** in both the Item Width and Item Height fields. If you created the grid elements at a different size, enter the size in the Width and Height fields. Leave the Rank field set to 1 because you are creating a one-rank nozzle file (nozzle file ranking will be discussed later). Enter **4** in the Rank 1 field because you have 4 elements in your Rank 1 nozzle file. Click OK to close the dialog box.

10. Now choose the Image Hose brush in the Brushes palette, and start to paint—the elements from your nozzle file flow from the Image Hose brush. As you paint, you might wish to adjust the

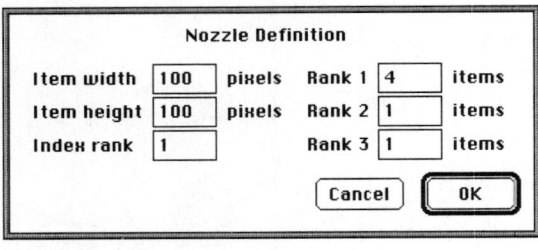

Rank 1 slider in the Nozzle palette to change the effects of the brush strokes. (See Chapter 3 for more information about using the Nozzle

palette). You might also wish to try clicking on the Add To Mask check box in the palette. This creates a series of masks on screen based upon the elements in your nozzle file. (To see the mask, you may need to change mask visibility icons). Try filling the masks with patterns, colors, and weaves to create more special effects. Also, don't forget to try painting with different Image Hose brush variants.

Creating Nozzle File Ranks

The Nozzle Definition dialog box allows you to divide your nozzle file into rankings. Different ranks allow you to use the Rank slider controls in the Brush Controls :Nozzle palettes to adjust how the Image Hose paints.

To create a multi-rank nozzle file, you can set up the columns and rows of your nozzle file as described in the previous section. When you first load your nozzle file, the Nozzle Definition dialog box will open. In the Nozzle Definition's Index Rank field, enter the number of ranks you wish to have. For instance, if you were setting up a two-rank nozzle file, you would enter **2** in the Index rank field. Next, you need to enter the grid dimensions in the Rank Items fields. For instance, if your grid contains four items in three rows, you could enter **4** in the Rank 1 field and **3** in the Rank 2 field.

If you are setting up a three-rank nozzle file, you would enter **3** in the Index rank field. If you had five items in three rows, you could enter **5** in the Rank 1 field, **1** in the Rank 2 field, and **3** in the Rank 3 field. If you were setting up a three-rank file with five items in six rows, you could enter **5**, **1**, and **6** in the fields—but **5**, **2**, and **3** would work as well. No matter how you divide up your rank items, when the numbers in the Rank Item fields are multiplied together, the total should equal the total number of grid elements in your nozzle file.

If you wish to change the nozzle file setup, you can later load the nozzle file, and choose Get Info from the File menu. In the File Information dialog box you will see a description of your nozzle file. For instance, you might see: "Image hose 2 by 3 items (height 100, width 100)." In the dialog box, you can edit this information to change how the nozzle file is applied when the Image Hose brush paints with it.

Note *If you create a nozzle file using floaters (as described in Chapter 8), Painter automatically inserts the correct text in the Get Info dialog box. If you wish to change information in this dialog box to alter the ranking of a nozzle file, make sure you follow the syntax described in the preceding section. You might also wish to review the discussion on ranking in Chapter 3.*

Creating and Using Patterns

Painter allows you to create numerous special effects from patterns. Once you create a tile for your pattern, you can paint the screen with it or fill the screen to use as a background. You can create a pattern from a section of a photograph or from a painted image. Figure 9.31 shows a photograph of a violin (photograph courtesy of ADC Image Vault). Figure 9.32 is a pattern created from the violin photograph. Figure 9.33 shows a saxophone image (clipart image courtesy of Image Club). Figure 9.34 is a pattern created from the saxophone image.

To create a pattern, either load a digitized image or create a new file and paint the image you wish to use as your pattern in the new file. If you are going to be creating a new file for your pattern, make sure that the image size is not too large, because if you apply a large pattern in a small canvas, you probably won't see the pattern repeat.

After you've created your image or loaded a photograph, you need to capture your image and define it as a *tile*.

To capture an image, you first need to select an image or part of a photograph. Use the Rectangular Selection tool to select an area. Don't deselect.

After you've selected an area, choose Capture Pattern from the Tools ➤ Pattern submenu.

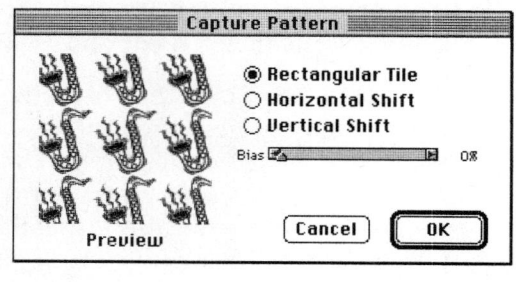

Instantly the Capture Pattern dialog box appears. The dialog box previews your pattern and allows you to shift the tiles. If you wish to shift the tiles horizontally or vertically, click either the Horizontal Shift or Vertical Shift option. To adjust tile shift, click and drag on the Bias slider. If you don't want to shift the tiles of your

FIGURE 9.31: The original violin photograph (Courtesy of ADC ImageVault)

FIGURE 9.32: A pattern created from a section of the violin photograph

FIGURE 9.33: The original saxophone image (Clipart image courtesy of Image Club)

FIGURE 9.34: A pattern created from the saxophone image

pattern, make sure that the Rectangular Tile option is selected. Click OK to create the pattern.

After you click OK, the tile is captured and placed in a new file. Save the new file, so that you can reuse it at a later date.

Now create a new file large enough to accommodate several repetitions of your pattern.

To apply the pattern, you can use the Fill command, a brush, or the Paint Bucket.

To apply a pattern using the Fill command, choose Effects ➤ Fill. In the Fill dialog box, the word *Pattern* has been substituted for the words *Clone Source*. Choose Pattern and then adjust the opacity, as desired. Click OK to apply the pattern. To apply a pattern with the Paint Bucket, first activate the Paint Bucket tool. In the Controls :Paint Bucket palette, choose Clone Source in the Fill group before clicking (or clicking and dragging) in your image. To paint with the pattern color, first pick a brush from the Brushes palette, then select the Use Clone Colors check box in the Art Materials :Colors palette. When you paint, the pattern colors are applied to your canvas according to the Brush settings and the settings in the Controls :Brushes palette. To apply a grainy effect, choose a grainy Method Subcategory in the Brushes palette, and adjust the Grain slider in the Controls :Brushes palette.

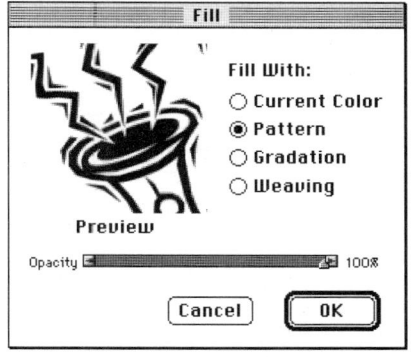

The Make Fractal Pattern Command

The Make Fractal Pattern command creates a new file filled with a texture based upon the options selected in the Make Fractal Pattern dialog box. The pattern created is based upon *fractal geometry*, in which shapes are created from mathematical rules. In general, fractals are created from a starting shape, then a set of rules is applied to generate other shapes.

Painter's Make Fractal Pattern command can be used to create anything from tiny bumpy textures to billowy cloudlike ones. Once you've created the pattern you can use it as a background for an image, or you can create a pattern out of it with the Capture Pattern command. To create a colored effect out of the pattern, use the Fill command to fill a color or gradation over it, then lower the Opacity setting in the Fill dialog box. You can also tint the pattern with a color by using the Color Overlay command.

Since the Make Fractal Pattern command creates a new file, you can conserve memory by closing all files before you execute the command. To use the command, choose Tools ➤ Pattern ➤ Make Fractal Pattern.

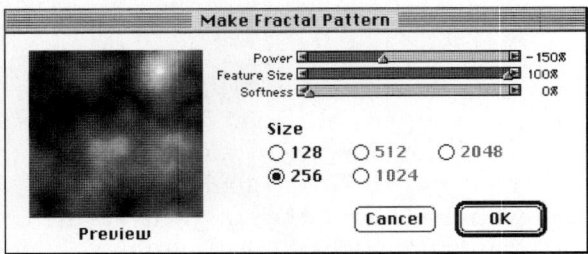

In the Make Fractal Pattern dialog box, the Size radio buttons determine the size in pixels of the file that will be created. For instance, a size of 128 means that the new file will be 128 by 128 pixels at 72 ppi. When the dialog box opens, Painter has already calculated the possible file sizes based upon memory available. Thus, one or several Size radio buttons may be grayed out because your system does not have enough memory to create the file.

In the Make Fractal Pattern dialog box, the sliders control the effect of the fractal pattern. As you adjust the sliders, pay close attention to the preview. This will help you understand how the three sliders interact to create texture.

The Power slider controls the roughness of the fractal features. If you drag the slider to the left, rougher fractals will be more prominent. If you drag to the right, smaller bumps are more pronounced in the texture. Use the Feature Size slider to control how repetitive the prominent areas are within the pattern. Drag to the right to increase the number of repetitions, drag to the left to decrease the repetitions. If you wish to make the edges of the pattern softer, drag the Softness slider to the right.

After you click OK, Painter will create a new file filled with the Fractal pattern. Beware, though: unless you have a fast computer, you may be in for a long wait.

Working with Third-Party Plug-ins

Third-party plug-ins add to Painter's ability to create special effects. As you'll see in this chapter, plug-ins are capable of many diverse effects. Some add to Painter's ability to create paintings out of digital images, many create surrealistic gradients and textures, and others create fantastic three-dimensional effects.

As discussed in Chapter 4, plug-ins are programs that can be loaded directly from within Painter. Most plug-ins were written for use with Adobe Photoshop, but virtually all are compatible with Painter. You'll often hear plug-ins referred to as *filters* or *special-effects filters*. The reason why they're called filters is that many plug-ins create effects similar to filters used in photography.

Electronic filters have many advantages over photographic filters. You can see the results immediately, you can apply them repeatedly, and they are quite simple to use. In the following sections, you'll learn about some of the more well-known and popular filters: Alien Skin Black Box, Andromeda Software Series 1 and 2, Adobe Gallery Effects, Kai's Power Tools, KPT Convolver, Alien Skin Textureshop by Virtus, Xaos Tools' Paint Alchemy and Terrazzo, MicroFrontier Pattern Workshop, and The Human Software Company's Squizz and Swap.

Effects	
Apply Surface Texture...	⌘/
Fill...	⌘;
Orientation	▶
Fill...	⌘F
Tonal Control	▶
Surface Control	▶
Focus	▶
Esoterica	▶
Objects	▶
Alien Skin	▶
Andromeda	▶
Blur	▶
Distort	▶
Gallery Effects: Classic Art 1	▶
Gallery Effects: Classic Art 2	▶
Gallery Effects: Classic Art 3	▶
HUMAN SOFTWARE	▶
KPT 2.1	▶
KPT Convolver	▶
Noise	▶
Other	▶
Pattern Workshop	▶
Sharpen	▶
Stylize	▶
Video	▶
Virtus	▶
Xaos Tools	▶

In order to access these filters, you must first install them onto your hard drive. If you have Adobe Photoshop, some of these might even be on your hard drive already, in Photoshop's Plug-ins folder. To access these plug-ins in Painter, you may wish to place all of your filters into one folder. Then you must use the

Edit ➤ Preferences ➤ Plug-ins command to direct Painter to the folder. Next, you'll need to restart Painter for the plug-ins to be accessible. When Painter restarts, it will load the plug-ins. They can all be accessed from the Effects menu.

The following section should provide you with an idea of the diversity and power of third party plug-ins. Remember that these filters are not sold with Painter; you need to purchase them separately.

> **Tip** *After you apply a filter, you can use Painter's Fade command to reduce the amount of the filter effect. Try setting the Fade slider to 50%—the effect will be as if you applied the filter at a 50% opacity. If you don't like the effects of the Fade or of a filter, you can always use Painter's Undo command to undo the effects.*

Using Alien Skin's Black Box Filters

Alien Skin's Black Box includes six different filters: Drop Shadow, Glass, Glow, HSB Noise, Swirl, and The Boss. Each creates an unusual effect. The Glass filter creates effects similar to Painter's Glass distortion command. Boss creates embossing effects. The HSB Noise allows you to create a colored mezzotint.

Figure 9.35 shows a landscape image before using a filter. Figure 9.36 shows the image after applying the Swirl filter. Figure 9.37 shows the Swirl settings used to create the effect in Figure 9.36.

FIGURE 9.35:   Image before applying a filter

FIGURE 9.36:   Image after applying Swirl filter

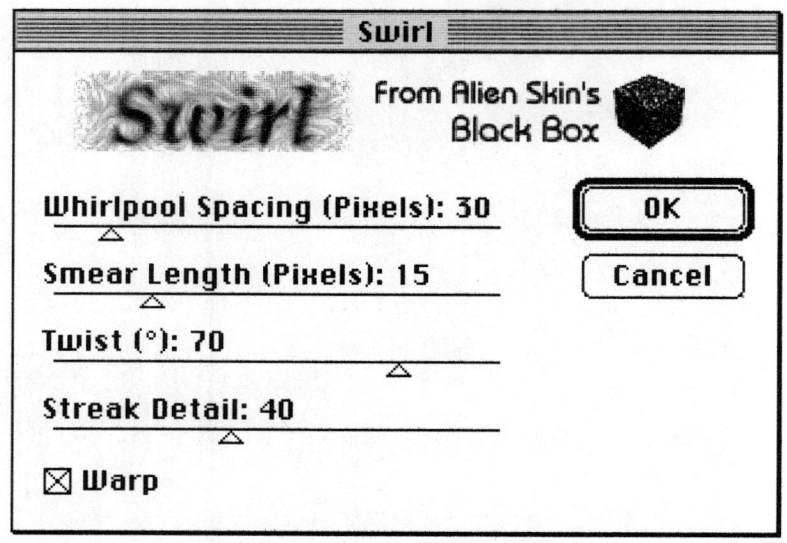

FIGURE 9.37: The Swirl settings used to create the effect seen in Figure 9.36

Using Andromeda Series 1 and 2 Filters

Andromeda's Series 1 includes ten filters and allows you to create reflections and add velocity to an image. Some create halos, rainbows, and stars. Others, such as cMulti and sMulti, create psychedelic effects.

Andromeda's Series 2 allows you to create three-dimensional images. Andromeda's 3-D filter allows you to wrap images around a sphere, cylinder, or cube. Figure 9.38 shows the effect of applying Andromeda's 3-D filter to an image of a field of flowers (which is shown in Figure 9.39). Figure 9.40 shows the dialog box that allows you to wrap images onto 3-D shapes.

FIGURE 9.38: 3-D effect from an Andromeda Series 2 filter

FIGURE 9.39: Image of flowers that were wrapped around a cube to create Figure 9.38

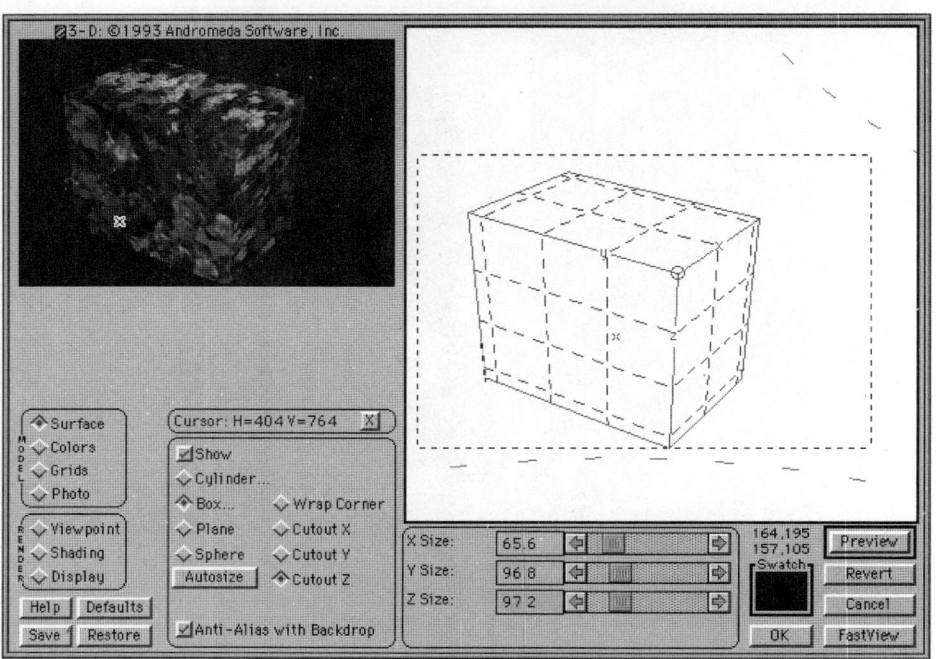

FIGURE 9.40: Settings used for the effect seen in Figure 9.38

Using Adobe Gallery Effects Filters

Adobe's Gallery Effects Volumes 1, 2, and 3 allow you to add painterly effects to photographs. Each volume has 16 filters. The filters vary from creating Charcoal to Sumi type effects out of digital images.

Figure 9.41 shows the effect of applying the Gallery Effects, Volume 3 Sumi-e filter to the image used back in Figure 9.35. Figure 9.42 shows the Sumi-e dialog box and settings used to create the image in Figure 9.41.

FIGURE 9.41: Image from Figure 9.35 after applying the Gallery Effects Sumi-e filter

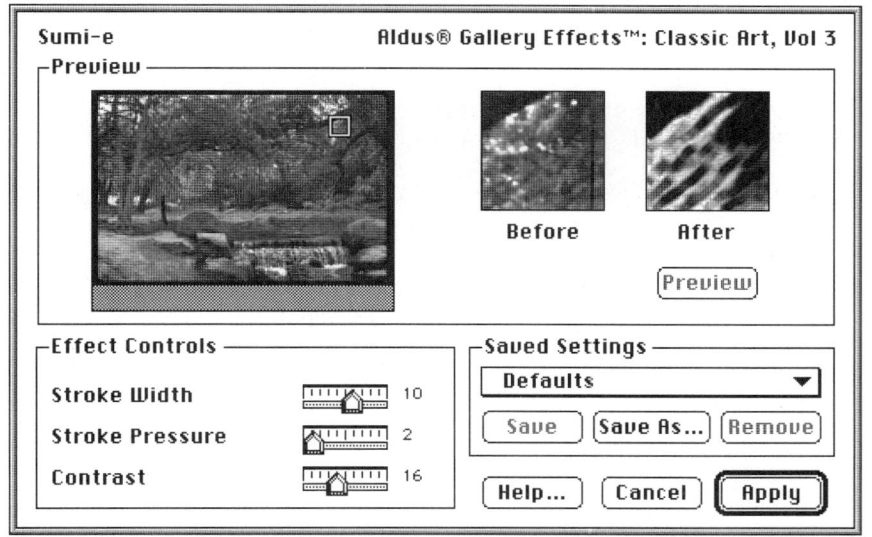

FIGURE 9.42: The Gallery Effects Sumi-e filter dialog box

Using HSC Software's KPT and KPT Convolver Filters

HSC Software's filters—Kai's Power Tools (KPT) and KPT Convolver—allow you to create a wide variety of effects such as textures, gradients, fractals, and page turns.

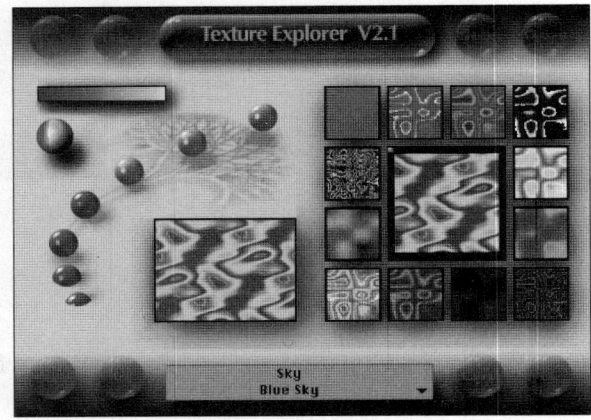

If you are in search of an interesting background, you might want to use KPT Texture Explorer, which is part of Kai's Power Tools. When you load Texture Explorer, a dialog box appears in which you can pick an option from the pop-up menu. The choices in the pop-up menu include sky, fabrics, liquids, marble, metal, nature, wood, and fire. After you've chosen an option you can vary its effect by clicking on swatches surrounding the preview. To pick more options you can click on the different spheres.

Figure 9.43 shows a texture created with the Sky/Blue Sky option in KPT Texture Explorer after changing settings in the swatches and spheres.

After you've created a texture, you can add a three-dimensional effect to it by using the Translucent option in the KPT Gradient Designer dialog box. You can also use the KPT Gradient Designer to apply translucent gradients over images. You access the KPT Gradient Designer dialog box from the KPT Gradient Designer command found in Painter's Effects ➤ KPT submenu.

To create a three-dimensional effect, you can click on a pop-up menu in the KPT Gradient Designer, and choose one of the following options from the Translucent category: Floating Doughnut, Floating Doughnut With Shadow, Moiré Shadows, Shadow Tube diagonal, and Bulgarian Bulges. Notice that the dialog box displays a preview of the current option. Figure 9.44 shows the Gradient Designer dialog box with a preview of the Translucent Bulgarian Bulges option.

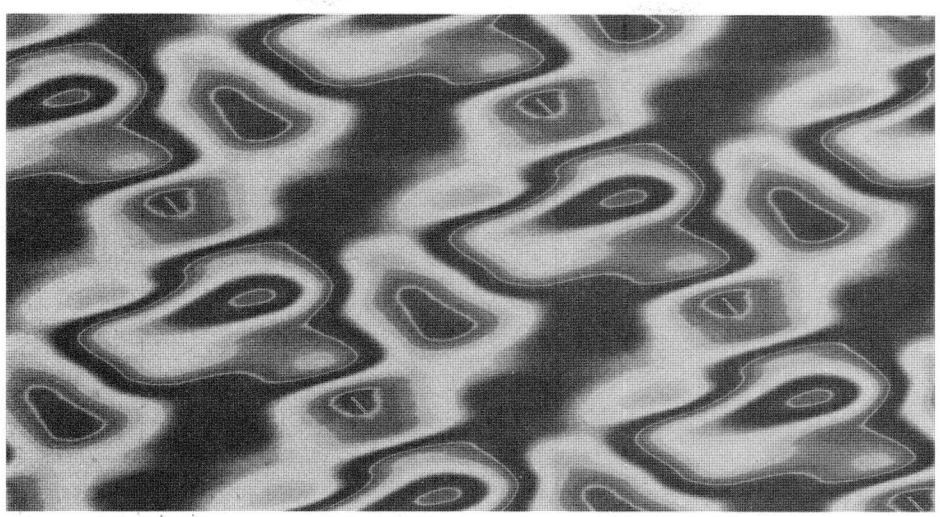

FIGURE 9.43: Texture created using KPT's Texture Explorer filter

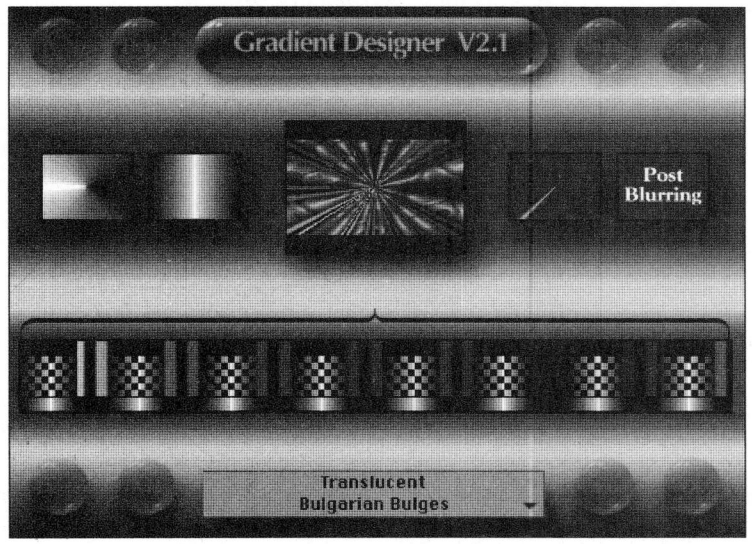

FIGURE 9.44: The KPT Gradient Designer dialog box

Figure 9.45 shows the Translucent Bulgarian Bulges option applied to Figure 9.43, created with the Gradient Explorer. Figure 9.46 shows the Translucent Floating Doughnut option applied to Figure 9.43.

FIGURE 9.45: The effect of the Translucent Bulgarian Bulges option applied to the texture in Figure 9.43

FIGURE 9.46: The effect of the Translucent Floating Doughnut option applied to the texture in Figure 9.43

Figure 9.47 shows the KPT Page Curl filter applied to Figure 9.43. Figure 9.48 shows the KPT Vortex Tiling filter applied to a background (Figure 9.49) created in Painter. The background was created in Painter by first creating two oval selections and filling them with a gradient. Then a pattern was created and applied to the canvas at a 50% opacity.

FIGURE 9.47: KPT Page Curl filter applied to texture

FIGURE 9.48: KPT Vortex Tiling, applied to a background image created in Painter

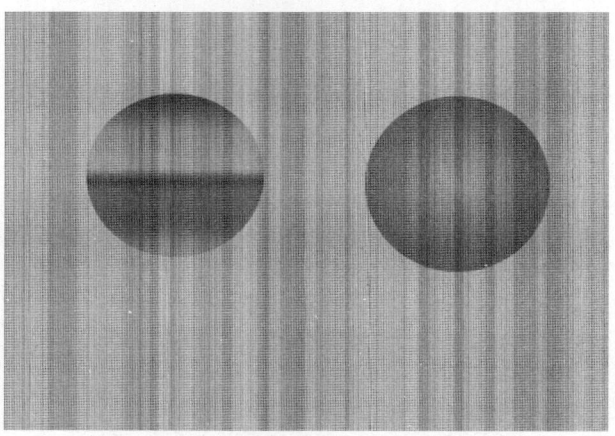

FIGURE 9.49: Background image for Figure 9.48 created in Painter

KPT Convolver is another HSC Software filter package that encourages you to experiment with a variety of digital effects. To access the KPT Convolver dialog box, choose KPT Convolver from the Effects menu.

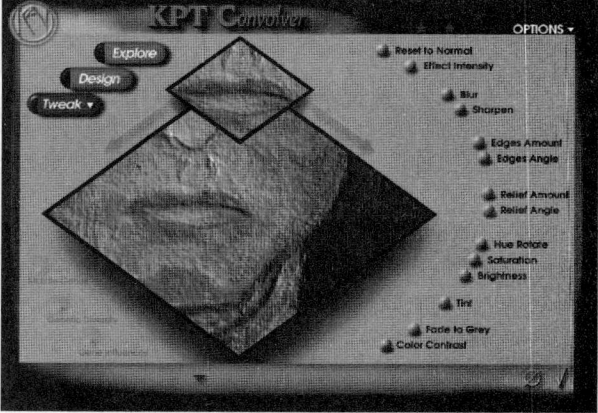

In the KPT Convolver dialog box you can blur and sharpen an image, change the hue, saturation, and brightness, or add a tint or relief effect. In Figure 9.50, the relief option was applied to certain image areas to apply more texture. To create the image in Figure 9.50, a sketch of a sculpture on slightly grainy paper was scanned, then painted in Painter. The background textures were created using Adobe Photoshop's layer options and KPT Texture Explorer. Then, KPT Convolver was applied to add a relief effect to the image. To see the image in color, turn to the color insert.

FIGURE 9.50: An image created with Painter, Photoshop, KPT, and KPT Convolver. (To see the image in color, turn to the color insert.)

Using Virtus's Alien Skin Textureshop Filter

Alien Skin Textureshop by Virtus allows you to create seamless two-dimensional and three-dimensional textures. Textureshop can be used as a stand-alone product or as a plug-in module. When you choose the Textureshop filter, a dialog box appears.

Creating Special Effects

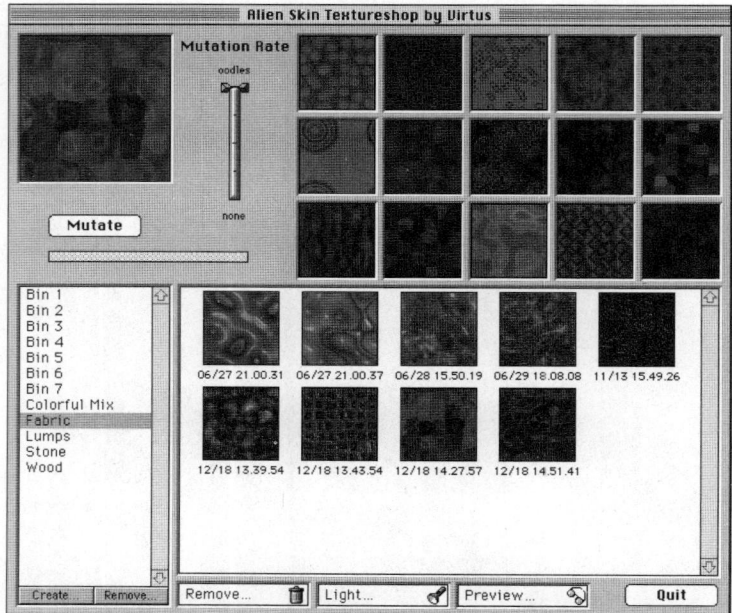

In the dialog box, you can pick a texture and then mutate it to create different versions of the texture. In the same dialog box, you can click on the Light button to access another dialog box that allows you to change the light color and direction.

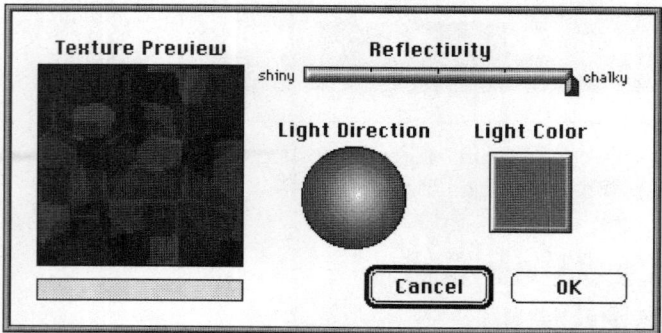

If you double-click on a texture in the Textureshop dialog box, another dialog box appears allowing you to change the Texture map, Height map, Color map, and tile size.

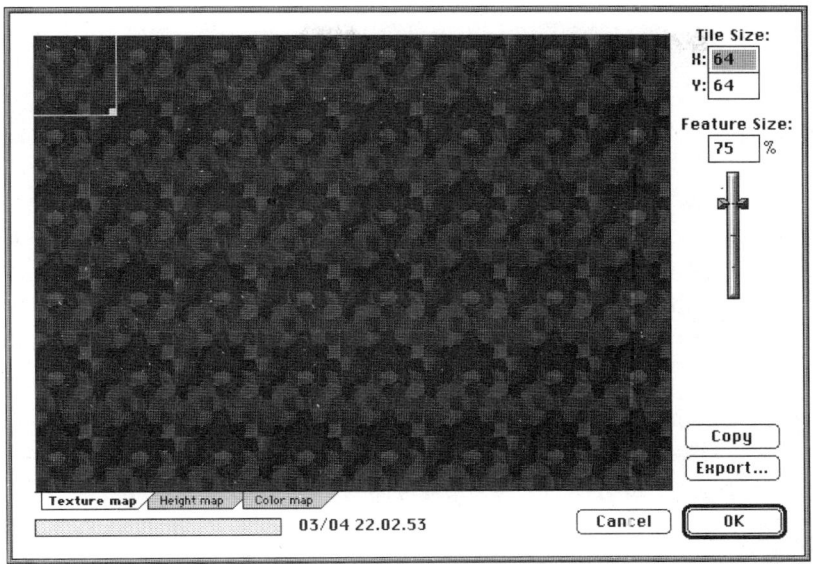

Using Xaos Tools' Filters

Xaos Tools' Paint Alchemy and Terrazzo are both very diverse and unusual filters. Paint Alchemy allows you to add painterly effects to images. Terrazzo allows you to create kaleidoscopic images.

Paint Alchemy is accessed by choosing Paint Alchemy from Painter's Effects ➤ Xaos Tools submenu.

In the Paint Alchemy dialog box you can pick a brush, color, size, angle, coverage, opacity, and style. Some of the styles that can be added

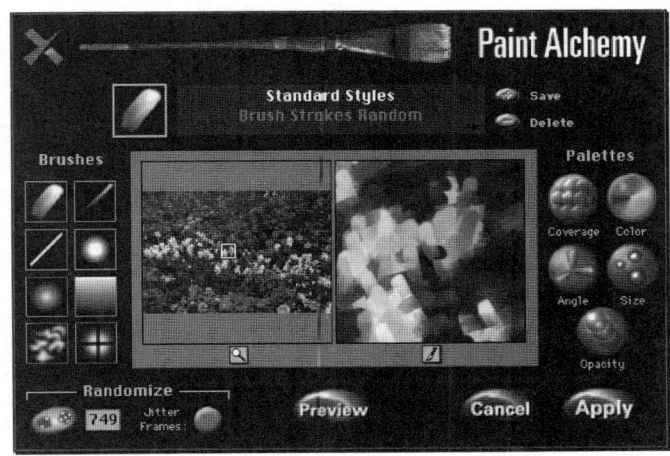

to your image include Smoke, Bubbles, Teardrops, Mosaic, Molecules, Canvas, and Oil Tip. To see a preview of the effect on a magnified portion of the image, you click on the Preview button. To apply the effect, you click on the Apply button.

Xaos Tools' Terrazzo can make it look like you're viewing your image through a kaleidoscope. Before you load Terrazzo you need to select a portion of your image. Once Terrazzo is loaded, you can choose different Symmetry options. The different options create different kaleidoscope tiles. Figure 9.51 shows the Terrazzo dialog box creating a tile out of a selection of flowers. Figure 9.52 shows the tile used to create a pattern.

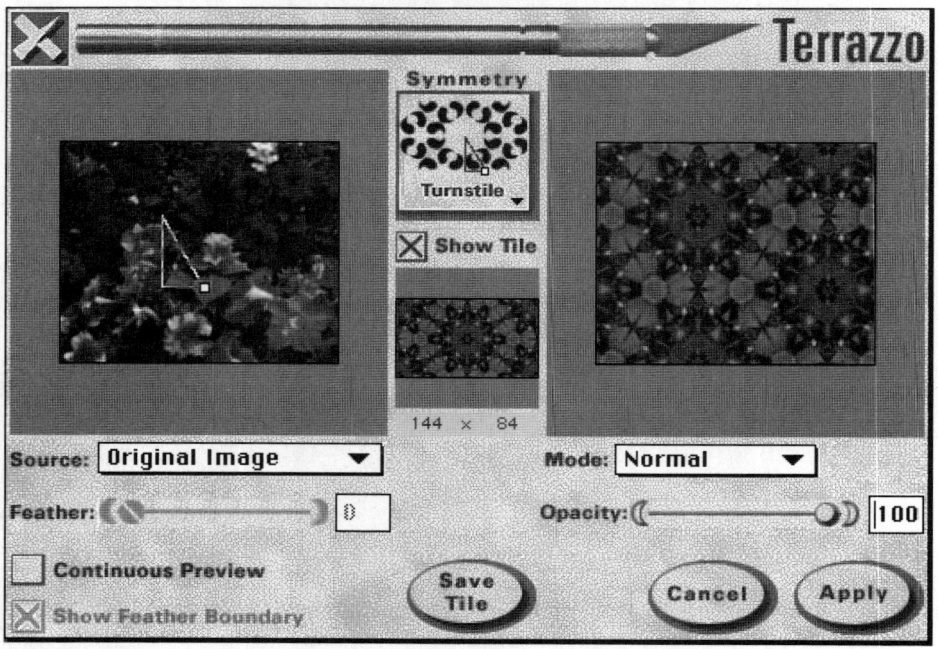

FIGURE 9.51: The Terrazzo dialog box displays a preview of your selected image and the resulting tile.

FIGURE 9.52: A pattern created from the tile in Figure 9.51

Using Other Filters

The list of filters that can be plugged in to Painter seems to grow larger every day. MicroFrontier's Pattern Workshop filter allows you to select an area in an image and capture it as a pattern. You can also save the patterns so that you can fill different images or image areas with them at any time. Pattern Workshop provides patterns already created for you to use. These include bricks, flowers, patriotic scenes, and many colored textures.

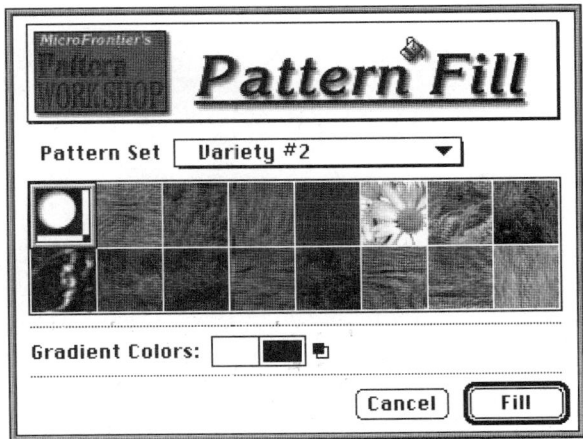

Creating Special Effects

The Human Software Company's Swap filter allows you to adjust the colors in your image by swapping red, green, and blue color components. The Human Software Company's Squizz filter allows you to warp an image using a brush or a grid.

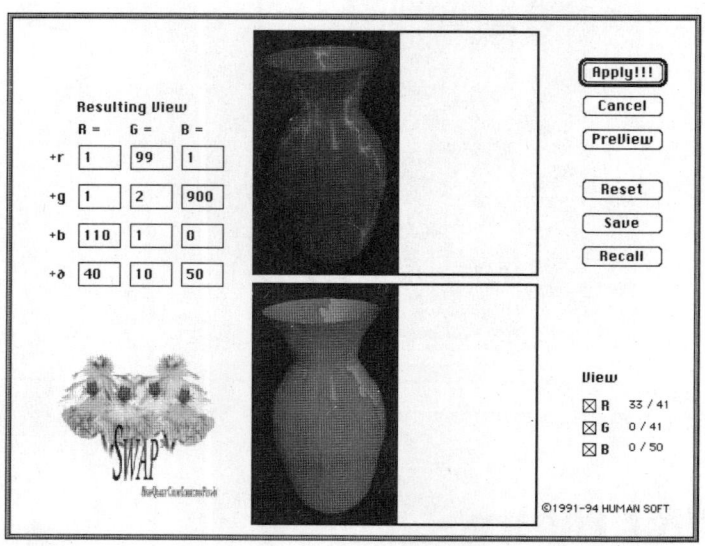

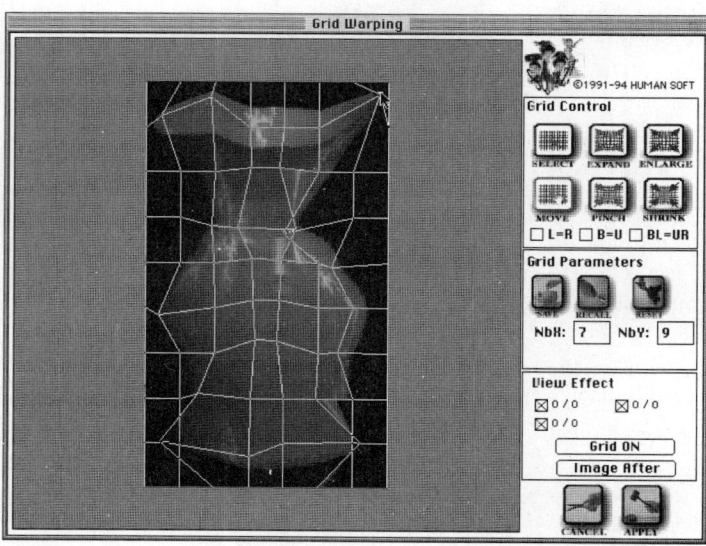

Creating Special Effects Using Other Programs

You can either place your Painter files into other programs to create special effects that aren't possible in Painter or create special effects in other programs and then place them into Painter.

Sometimes, using just one program won't allow you the freedom you need to create your artistic vision. Figure 9.53 is an image created using Adobe Illustrator, Fractal Design Painter, and Adobe Photoshop. To create the image, a sketch was scanned. Then the paths of the basic shapes were created in Illustrator using the Pen tool. The paths were loaded into Painter, where they were painted using the brushes and Paint Bucket.

FIGURE 9.53: Image created using Adobe Illustrator, Fractal Design Painter, and Adobe Photoshop. Turn to the color insert to see the image in color.

After the image was painted, it was brought into Photoshop. Adobe Photoshop offers a vast number of filters. Some allow you to distort, others can add more painterly effects, and still others are used to enhance an image. The filters used in the image in Figure 9.53 were the Tiles, Spherize, and Emboss filters. To see the final image in color, turn to the color insert.

To create amazing three-dimensional landscapes you might want to use KPT Bryce. Figure 9.54 is an image created by using both Fractal Design Painter and KPT Bryce, by artist Gary Clark. To create this image, Gary created the mountainscape in KPT Bryce. The telescope was grabbed from videotape and placed into the image. In Painter, Gary used the Water tools to create the sky and smooth edges.

FIGURE 9.54: Image created by Gary Clark using both Fractal Design Painter and KPT Bryce

To create three-dimensional type you might want to use Adobe Dimensions, Ray Dream Add Depth, Pixar Typestry, Specular LogoMotion, or Crystal Flying Fonts. Figure 9.55 shows 3-D type created in Adobe Dimensions. First, two-dimensional text was created, then the type was extruded into three dimensions.

If you're interested in creating 3-D images to integrate with Painter, you might want to use a program that includes 3-D modeling and/or rendering and/or animation features. Here's a list of some of the more well-known 3-D programs: Strata Vision 3d, Strata Studio Pro, Alias Sketch,

FIGURE 9.55: 3-D text created in Adobe Dimensions

Specular Infini-D, Ray Dream Designer, Macromedia MacroModel, Macromedia Swivel 3D, Macromedia Three-D, Pixar Showplace and Renderman, Caligari trueSpace, Crystal Topas, The Electric Image Animation System, Autodesk 3-D Studio, Crystal Designer, and Visual Simply 3D. If you want to create 3-D human life forms, you might want to investigate Fractal Design's Poser.

Figure 9.56 shows a 3-D shape created with Alias Sketch. Figure 9.57 shows a 3-D shape created with Strata StudioPro.

FIGURE 9.56: 3-D shape created using Alias Sketch

FIGURE 9.57: 3-D shape created using Strata StudioPro

You can also use Painter to create textures for your 3-D shapes and images. Figure 9.58 shows an image created in Macromedia MacroModel and rendered in Strata StudioPro using Painter's Shadow 1 weave as a texture map. To create the image, the MacroModel image was imported into StudioPro; then the Painter file was saved in PICT format, and imported into StudioPro as a texture map. Finally, the texture and model were rendered using StudioPro's ray tracing rendering mode.

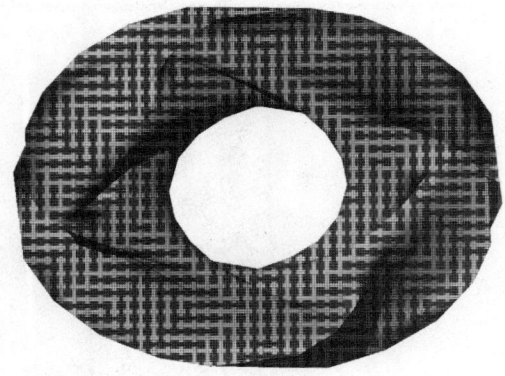

FIGURE 9.58: 3-D shape created in Macromedia MacroModel, rendered in Strata StudioPro using a Painter weave as the texture

Tip *You can import shapes and objects created in 3-D programs into Painter to use as elements in nozzle files. After loading the nozzle file, you can paint with the 3-D elements using the Image Hose brush.*

To create morphing effects you might want to use Gryphon Morph, Elastic Reality, or HSC Morph. To create 3-D virtual walkthroughs you might want to use Strata Virtual 3D, Virtus Walkthrough Pro, Virtus VR, and Visual Reality.

Note *When importing or exporting Painter files, you will need to use other file formats besides RIFF. To learn about file formats, see the appendix.*

● Wrapping It Up

In this chapter you've learned how to create a vast amount of special effects. In the next two chapters you'll learn how to create more interesting effects. In Chapter 10, you'll learn how create movies out of the steps you take when you paint an image in Painter. In Chapter 11 you'll learn how to create, edit, and save animations.

Recording and Playing Back Strokes and Sessions

Using Painter's Record and Playback functions is like having a camcorder connected to your computer. Painter allows you to record your work one stroke at a time, or even a session at a time, so that you can sit back later and watch the strokes or sessions replay. You can use these features to demonstrate how artwork is created, to create new artwork, and to play back artwork at a higher resolution than the one at which it was recorded. Thus, if you'd like to have Painter relieve some of your work load, this chapter is for you. You'll learn how to record one brush stroke and have Painter automatically fill your canvas with that brush stroke. You'll also learn how to record and playback an entire Painter session, and even turn it into a movie.

Recording a Stroke

Undoubtedly the easiest way to get started using Painter's recording features is to record a brush stroke, using the Record Stroke command. Once you record a brush stroke, you can have Painter play it back again and again so you can use the strokes as a background pattern for your images.

Note *If you want to record more than one brush stroke you need to record a session, discussed in the next section.*

In order to use the Record Stroke command, you must have a canvas on screen. Create one now as a practice file. Make the file 4″ by 4″ with the resolution set to 75 ppi. Next, choose a brush and variant from the Brushes palette. Then pick a color in the Art Materials palette. If you want the stroke to vary in color, drag the Color Variability sliders to the right. You are now ready to record a stroke. From the Tools menu choose Record Stroke.

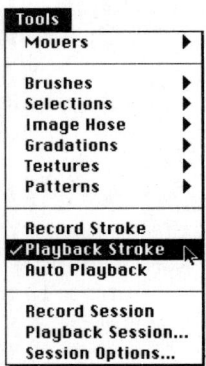

Now click and drag in your canvas to create a brush stroke. As you create the brush stroke, Painter records it. To quickly fill your canvas with the stroke you just recorded, choose Auto Playback from the Tools menu. Instantly, the recorded stroke is applied again and again to your canvas. When you want the strokes to stop, just click on the canvas. Figure 10.1 shows the recorded stroke (top) and the brush stroke applied using the Auto Playback command (bottom). The Chalk brush with the Oil Pastel variant was used to create the brush stroke.

If you'd like, you can change brushes or colors before playing back a stroke, then reapply the stroke with the new color and brush using the Auto Playback command. If you don't want Painter to paint your screen again and again with your brush stroke, you can have it play back one brush stroke in a specific area of your canvas.

To do this, choose Tools ➤ Playback Stroke, then click on the canvas to apply one recorded stroke at the position where you click on the canvas.

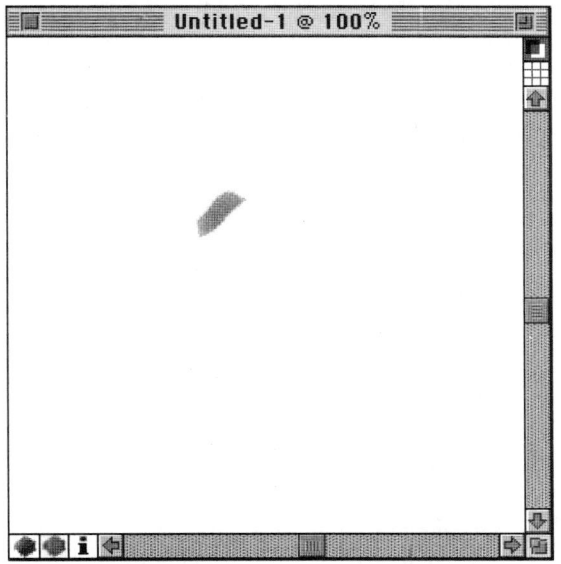

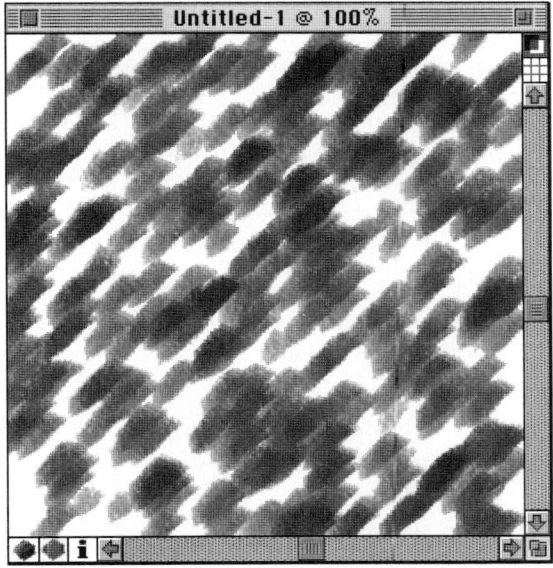

FIGURE 10.1: Top: Brush stroke recorded with Record Stroke command.
Bottom: Canvas after brush strokes played back.

Recording a Session

Painter allows you to record all brush strokes, tool choices, menu commands, and dialog box choices that comprise a painting session. Later you can play back your session at a higher resolution, or play back the session as a demonstration of painting techniques.

Before you start creating a painting, choose Tools ➤ Session Options.

In the Session Options dialog box, leave the Record Initial State check box selected if you wish Painter to play back using the exact same brushes, colors, and textures that you used when recording. If you deselect this option, Painter uses the brushes or other tools and art materials selected at the time of playback. Thus, the Record Initial State option allows you to experiment with different colors and brush variants without having to manually repaint your image. The Save Frames On Playback option is used when playing back a session (and is covered in the next section). Click OK to close the dialog box.

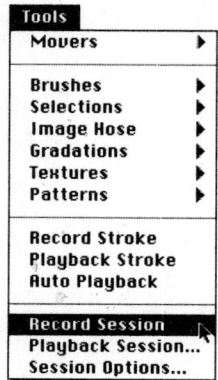

To record a session you can use either the Sessions palette or choose the Record Session command. Later in this chapter, you'll learn how to use the Session palette. For now, Choose Tools ➤ Record Session to start recording a session.

After executing Record Session, start painting. Feel free to use any number of brushes, colors, or menu commands. When you're finished, choose Tools ➤ Stop Recording Session.

After you choose the Stop Recording Session command, a dialog box opens allowing you to name and save your session. Type **MySession** in the Save As field, then click on OK to save your session.

To see an icon representing your session, open the Objects palette, then click on the Sessions palette. Not only does your session's icon appear at the top of the palette, but its name appears in the pop-up menu in the Objects :Sessions palette's drawer.

Playing Back a Session

You can play back a session by using the Playback Session command in the Tools menu or by clicking on the Playback button in the Objects :Sessions palette.

> **Note** *Before playing back a session, you may wish to create a new file.*

To play back using the menu command, choose Tools ➤ Playback Session.

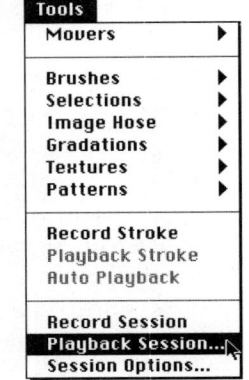

When the Recorded Sessions dialog appears, click on the name of the session that you want to play back. Then click the Playback button to play back the session. The session starts playing back. To stop the session, click Command+period (Windows users: Ctrl+Break) on your keyboard.

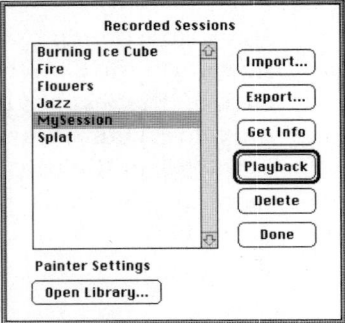

Figure 10.2 shows a few strokes of the session called MySession (top) and the completed session of MySession (bottom).

> **Note** *In the Recorded Sessions dialog you can click on the Get Info button to see the date the session was recorded and how much disk space the session consumes.*

FIGURE 10.2: Top: First few strokes of Session playback. Bottom: Completed playback of sessions.

Exporting and Editing Session Scripts

If you'd like to see a list of your recorded brushstrokes and keystrokes, or if you'd like to edit the recording you've made, you can also export a session as a *script*. This creates a text file, which you can open in a word processor and edit. To export a session and create a script file, click the Export button in the Recorded Sessions dialog box. In the dialog box that appears, enter a name for your script, then click Save.

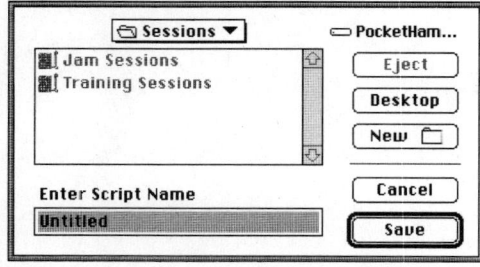

Once the script file is created, you can open it in a word processing program and edit it. The following text is an example of part of a Painter script:

```
is_painter_3
artist_name "Adele"
start_time date Fri, Feb 24, 1995 time 8:27 PM
start_random 1215718250
variant "Painter Brushes" "Chalk" "Oil Pastel"
texture "Paper Textures" "Basic Paper"
grain_inverted unchecked
scale_slider     1.00000
portfolio_change "Painter Portfolio"
gradation "Painter Settings" "gold 1"
weaving "Painter Settings" "Buchanan 14"
use_brush_grid unchecked
add_to_mask unchecked
color red 0 green 0 blue 0
background_color red 255 green 255 blue 255
stroke_start
pnt x    54.00 y    25.50 time 666595
```

After you've edited the script, save the changes in the word processor. To reimport the edited script into Painter, click the Import button in the Recorded Sessions dialog box (accessed by choosing Playback Session from the Tools menu). Another dialog box appears, allowing you to locate the edited script you want to import. Click on the script, then click on the Open button. Next, the Name The Session dialog box appears, allowing you to name the edited script. Name the script and then click on the OK button.

Note *For more information on editing a script, review the Session Script Tech Note that comes on the Painter CD-ROM.*

Playing Back a Session in a High-Resolution File

If you record your artwork at a low resolution, you can play it back at a higher resolution. As mentioned in Chapter 4, you may need to create high-resolution files for output on a printing press. If you do wish to re-cord a session at a low resolution, it's advisable to choose Edit ➤ Select All to select the entire screen before recording your session. This gives Painter a reference area for playing the session back in a high-resolution file. When your session is played back, the selection ensures that your artwork is played back in the same canvas position in which it was recorded.

After you've recorded a session, open a new high-resolution file. When the high-resolution file opens, select the entire canvas by choosing Edit ➤ Select All. Then play back the session by choosing Tools ➤ Playback Session. In the Playback Session dialog box, select the session, then click on the Playback button.

Working with the Sessions Palette

The Sessions palette is used to quickly record and play back a session. To display the Objects :Sessions palette, choose Window ➤ Objects Palette to open the Objects palette, then click on the Session icon in the Objects palette. The palette drawer must be closed in order to see the various but-tons that are available to help you record and play back a session (see Fig-ure 10.3). In order to start recording a session, click the Record button (the button with a circle). When you finish recording, click the Stop button (the button with a rectangle). When you stop recording, a dialog box ap-pears, allowing you to save and name your session. To play back a session, click on the Play button (the button with a sideways triangle).

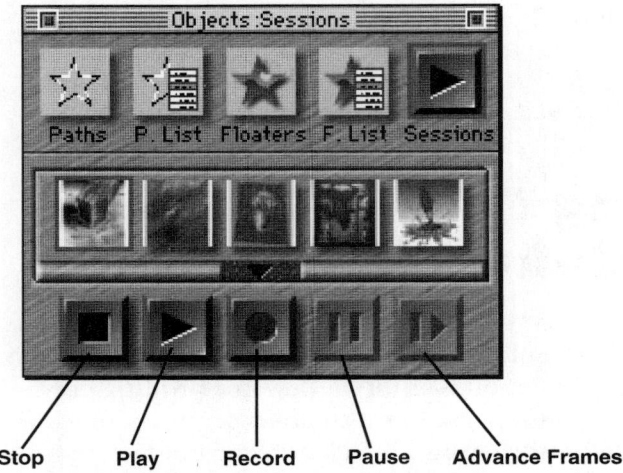

FIGURE 10.3:   The buttons in the Objects :Sessions palette

Working with Session Libraries

You can store your sessions in different libraries. You create session libraries similar to the way you create libraries of brushes, weavings, gradations, etc. To create a new session library, choose Session Mover from the Tools ➤Movers submenu.

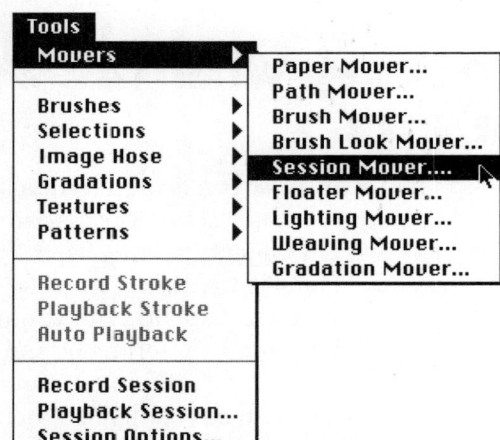

When the Sessions Mover dialog box appears, click on the New button to create a new session library.

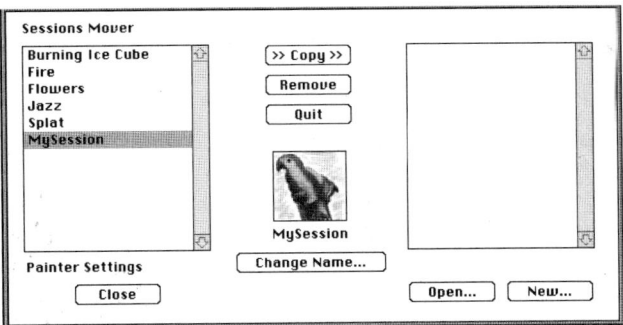

In the dialog box that appears, name your session. You might want to save your session library in the Sessions folder in Painter. Click Save to create a new session library.

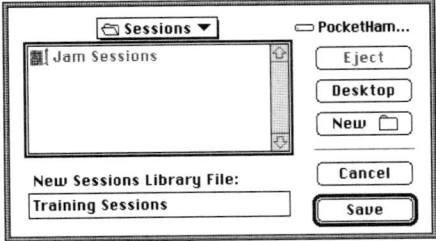

To copy a session from one library to another, click on the session name, then choose Copy. To remove the session from the old library, click on the session and click on the Remove button. When you're done, click Quit to exit the Sessions Mover dialog box.

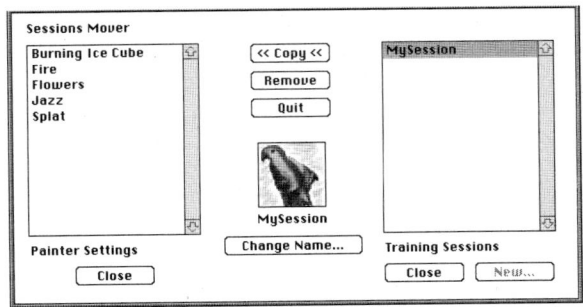

To open a session library, you need to first open the Sessions palette drawer. When the drawer is open, click on the Library button. Locate the Sessions folder and click on the session you want to open. The sessions in the Session palette will change to reflect the session in the library you have opened.

You can also access a session library through the Recorded Sessions dialog box (accessed by choosing Tools ➤ Playback Session). In the Recorded Sessions dialog box, click on the Open Library button. In the next dialog box that appears, locate the session you want to open, then choose Open. The sessions in the session library appear in the Recorded Sessions dialog box. If you only wanted to change libraries, click the Done button. If you want to play back a session in the library you just opened, click on the session, then click on the Playback button.

● Saving a Session as a Movie

After you've created a session, you can convert it into a Painter *frame stack* movie. By converting a session to a movie, you can edit individual frames so the playback looks exactly the way you want it to.

To save a session as a movie, first open a new canvas large enough to play back your session. To convert a session into a movie you first need to open the Session Options dialog box and select the Save Frames On Playback check box.

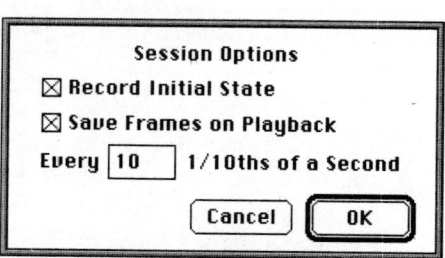

This check box allows you to specify how many tenths of a second you want a frame recorded. If you type **1**, Painter will record every tenth of a second; if you leave the default set to **10**, Painter records a frame every second. Obviously, the lower the number you enter, the more fluid the playback. The downside of entering small numbers, though, is that your movie consumes more disk space. Click OK to activate the changes.

To play back a session and have it recorded as a movie, click on the session you want to convert into a movie and then either click on the Play button in the Sessions palette or choose Playback Session from the Tools menu. A dialog box appears allowing you to name and save your session as a movie. Name your session. If you wish, save your movie in Painter's Movie folder. Click the Save button to name and save your session as a frame stack movie.

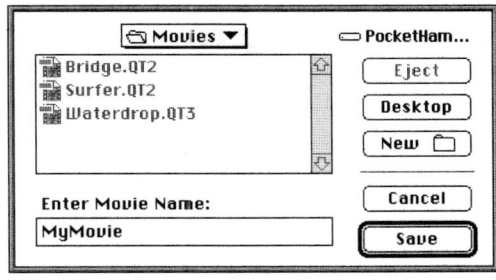

In the New Frame Stack dialog box that appears, you can choose how many layers of *onion skin* you desire and a *storage type*. For this session, leave the settings at their defaults and click OK. You'll learn more about frame stack movies, onion skin and other movie options in Chapter 11.

The session is played back into a movie. While the movie is being played on the canvas on screen, it is also being "built" in the Frame Stacks palette, which also appears on screen. After the movie is built, you can use the different buttons in the Frame Stacks palette (see Figure 10.4) to play back the movie.

If you wish to save the current frame in your movie as an individual image, save the entire movie in QuickTime format, or save the movie as a separate numbered file, choose File ➤ Save As. In the Save Movie dialog box, specify the desired option. You'll learn more about options for saving movies in Chapter 11.

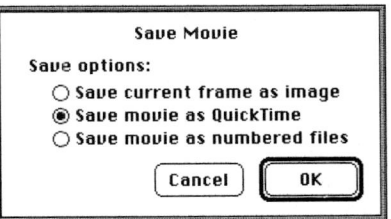

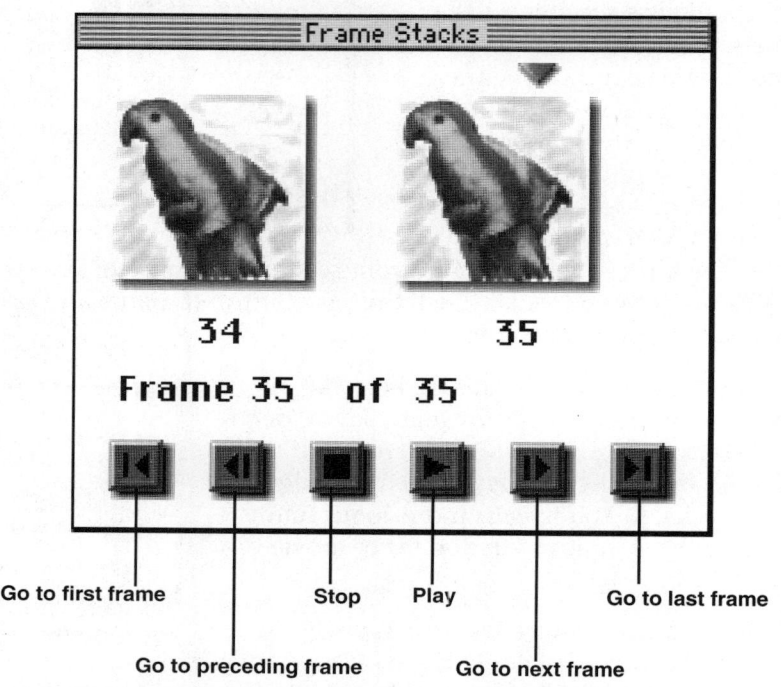

Go to first frame

Go to preceding frame

Stop

Play

Go to next frame

Go to last frame

FIGURE 10.4:   Frame Stack palette

● Wrapping It Up

Recording and playing back sessions should give you an idea of some of the animation options available in Painter. In the next chapter, you'll move deeper into the world of animation as you learn how to create and edit movies in Painter.

All about Making Movies

Lights! Camera! Action! Painter's moviemaking magic can make your Painter images come to life.

When you create a movie in Painter, you open up a new world—where even a once placid still-life can shake, rattle, and roll, or perhaps dance to the light of a painted moon. If you'd like, you can even make the moon do a jitterbug dance. All of this animation magic is possible because Painter allows you to record painted images frame by frame and play them back sequentially as movies.

Not only can Painter's movie capabilities allow you to create cartoon-type animations, but corporate presentations as well. You can even send an animated art portfolio to prospective clients. Once a movie is saved it can be exported to programs such as Macromedia Director, Macromedia Authorware, Adobe Premiere, or Adobe After Effects for inclusion in multimedia projects.

● How Painter Creates Movies

When you create a movie in Painter the process is very similar to painting on separate pages in a flip book. You start the process by picking the dimensions and number of frames you want in your production. The frames in your production are called a *frame stack*. Each frame is accessed through the Frame Stacks palette.

When you create a frame stack movie in Painter, you simply paint in a movie canvas. As you move from frame to frame in the Frame Stacks palette, and paint in the movie canvas, Painter automatically saves your work.

To help you create your animation, Painter provides onion skin layers. Onion skin layers allow you to see a specific number of previous frames to help you perfectly align your animation.

To run your movie, you can use controls very similar to a VCR. You click the play button, and Painter flashes each frame on screen.

● Animating a Bouncing Ball

Creating movies and animating images in Painter is easy and fun, once you are familiar with the basics. In this section you'll learn how to create a simple animation of a bouncing ball. In doing so, you will also learn the basics of creating a movie *frame stack* using onion skin layers.

Creating your First Frame Stack Movie

Creating a new movie file is slightly different than creating a normal image file. To create a new movie, choose New from the File menu. In the New Picture dialog box, you must first type the dimensions and resolution for your movie.

Since your movie will probably be displayed on a computer screen, there is generally no reason to make the resolution any greater than the resolution of your computer monitor. Most Macintosh monitors display images at 75 ppi, many PC monitors display images at 96 ppi. On a 14" VGA monitor a 640-by-480-pixels image will consume the entire screen. If you want to create a movie at this size, make sure you've got lots of hard disk space free. The larger the screen dimensions and the more frames in your movie, the more disk space your movie will consume. To start out, make your movie half the screen size, for example, at a resolution of 320 by 240 pixels at 75 ppi. If you want to change the paper color of your movie, click on the Paper Color swatch and pick a color.

Next, choose the Movie radio button from the Picture Type group. Enter the number of frames you want to use. Note that you can always add more frames later, if you want. For the bouncing ball exercise, type in **10** frames, since you'll be bouncing the ball for five frames from the top left to

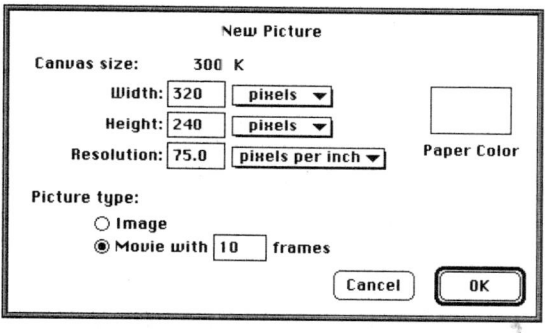

the bottom center and then bouncing the ball for five more frames from the bottom center to the top right of the canvas. Click OK to proceed.

After you click OK, a dialog box appears asking you to name the movie frame stack. Type **Bouncing ball** (Windows users: **ball**) in the name field. Locate the folder into which you wish to save the file. You may want to save it inside Painter's Movie folder. Click OK to name and save your first movie frame stack.

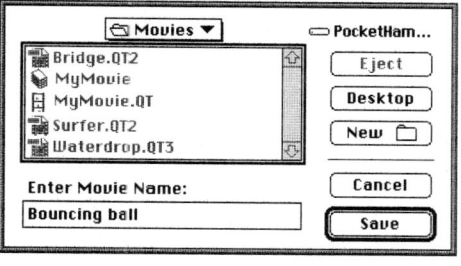

Next, the New Frame Stack dialog box appears. In this dialog box you can choose from two to five layers of Onion Skin to use. Onion Skin layers allow you to see the image in the previous frames. If you choose 5, you can see the images from the previous four frames in the canvas window. For the bouncing ball exercise set the Onion Skin layers to 5. In this dialog box you can also

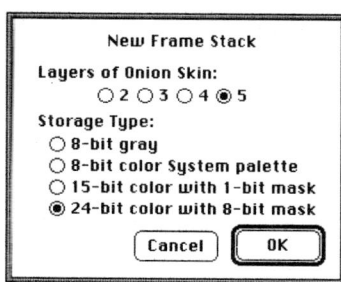

set the storage type. The Storage Type group allows to pick the number of gray levels or colors in your image. It also allows you to include a mask which can be used to create superimposition effects if you export the movie into a digital video editing program such as Adobe Premiere.

The 8-bit gray choice provides 256 levels of gray. *8-bit color* provides 256 colors, using the Mac or Windows color palette. *15-bit Color with 1-bit Mask* provides over 32,000 colors with a black-and-white mask layer. 24-bit Color provides you with millions of colors and a mask layer capable of 256 levels of gray. (This mask is often called an *alpha channel.*)

For the bouncing ball exercise, set the storage type to 24-bit Color with 8-bit Mask, but only if you have a 24-bit color board on your computer and lots of memory. Otherwise, you can pick the 8-bit color choice, since the simple ball will not require many colors. Click OK to close the dialog box and continue.

In a few moments the Frame Stacks palette and a blank canvas appear on screen. Before proceeding, take a look at the title bar of the blank canvas on screen. Notice the fraction 1/10 appears. This means that you are on frame 1 of 10.

In the Frame Stacks palette (Figure 11.1) you will notice an arrow over frame 1. This means you are in frame 1. The arrow always appears above the frame you are on. Also, notice that the frame is blank. After you create an image in the canvas area on screen, and move to another frame, the frame in the Frame Stacks palette displays a miniature version of the image created in the canvas area.

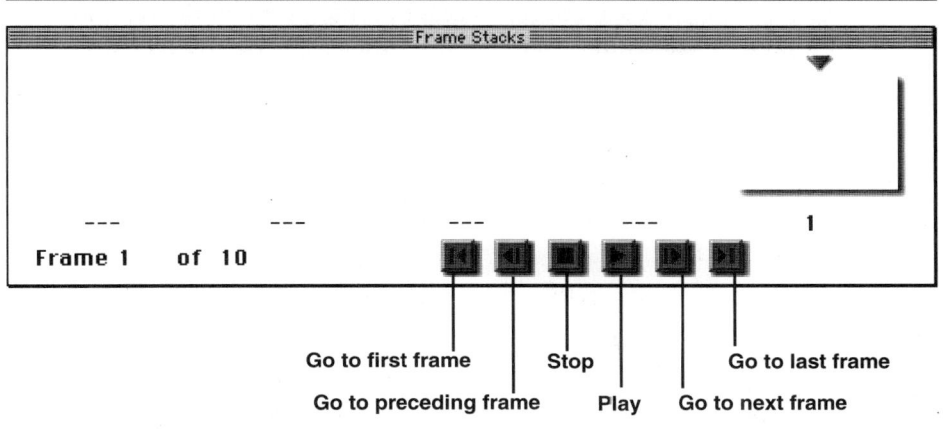

FIGURE 11.1: The Frame Stacks palette

The Frame Stacks palette allows you to play, stop, rewind, or fast-forward a movie, as shown in Figure 11.1. In conjunction with the Frame Stacks palette you can use the Movie menu to add, delete, erase, clear, and go to a particular frame.

Now you are ready to create the bouncing ball and begin animating it.

Using Onion Skin Layers to Animate

In order to begin creating and animating a bouncing ball, you must have a new blank movie on screen with five onion skins. If you don't, follow the steps in the previous section to create one. Before starting the exercise, make sure that the Objects :Path List palette is open on screen. You'll use this palette to keep reactivating an oval selection (that you'll use to create the ball) so that you don't need to keep redrawing it in each frame.

With canvas 1/10 (frame 1) activated on screen, your first step is to start creating the ball with the Oval Selection tool.

1. Activate the Oval Selection tool and create a small oval selection in the canvas. If you'd like, use the Path Adjuster tool (arrow) to resize the selection. (See Chapter 7 to review using the Oval Selection and Path Adjuster tools.) Don't

make the oval selection too big, because you will be duplicating it in the different frames to make it look like it is bouncing. After you've adjusted the oval, use the Path Adjuster tool to drag it to the top left-hand corner of the canvas.

2. Next, pick a gradient from the Art Materials :Grads palette, then use the Effects ➤ Fill command to fill the ball with a gradient. For best results, don't fill the ball with a linear gradient. Otherwise the ball will look too flat.

After you've created the ball, you need to activate the onion skin feature in order to see part of the ball's path as you create the animation.

3. To take advantage of the five onion skins, you must activate Painter's Tracing Paper mode. To turn it on, click on the tracing paper icon at the top right-hand corner of the canvas. To make sure that Tracing Paper is on, click on the Canvas menu. If there isn't a check mark next to the words Tracing Paper, then Tracing Paper is off.

Once the onion skin option is activated, you are ready to begin making your ball bounce.

4. Next, advance to frame 2 by either clicking on the Go To Next Frame button in the Frame Stacks palette, or by choosing the Go To Frame command from the Movies menu and typing **2** in the dialog box.

When you move to frame 2, the title bar in the canvas reads 2/10 (frame 2 of 10). Notice that the ball in frame 1 is still displayed in the canvas, but that it is dimmed. This is the tracing paper mode in action.

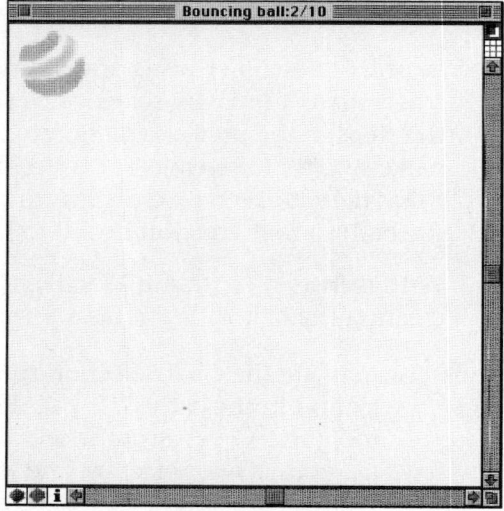

5. In frame 2, move the oval path selection, using the Path Adjuster tool so that it is offset diagonally down and to the right from the ball in frame 1. Next, turn it into a selection, by clicking on the oval icon next to the path name in the Path List palette. When the oval path is a selection, fill it with the same gradient as before.

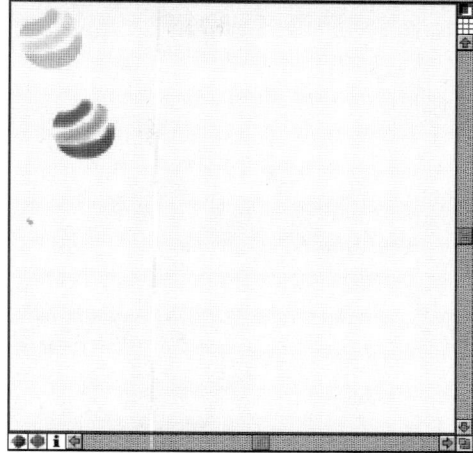

6. Advance to the next frame. Then move the oval path using the Path Adjuster tool, so that it is offset down and to the right from the ball in the previous frame. Now, convert the path to a selection by clicking on the oval icon next to the path name in the Path List palette. When the oval path is a selection, fill it with the same gradient as before.

7. Repeat step 6 for frames 4 and 5. Each time you recreate the ball, make sure that you are in a different frame and that you change its position in the canvas. Compare the first five frames in the Frame Stacks palette to canvas 5/10, which shows the five balls of the first five frames in one canvas (see Figure 11.2). Notice that you can see a dimmed version of the balls from frames 1 through 4 in the canvas of frame 5. This is because the tracing paper is on and because the onion skin option was set to 5.

Tip *You can add special effects to the ball by rotating and/or scaling it as you progress from one frame to another. To Rotate or Scale, use the commands in the Effects* ➤ *Orientation submenu.*

8. Repeat step 6 for frames 6 through 9, but instead of offsetting the oval path diagonally down to the right, offset it so that it is diagonally up and to the right. Leave frame 10 blank. Notice that the ball is on a V path, bouncing down and then up. If you wish, you can also create a W path. Figure 11.3 shows the ball in frames 5-9 in the Frame Stacks palette. Figure 11.4 shows the five balls from frames 5-9 in the canvas 9/10.

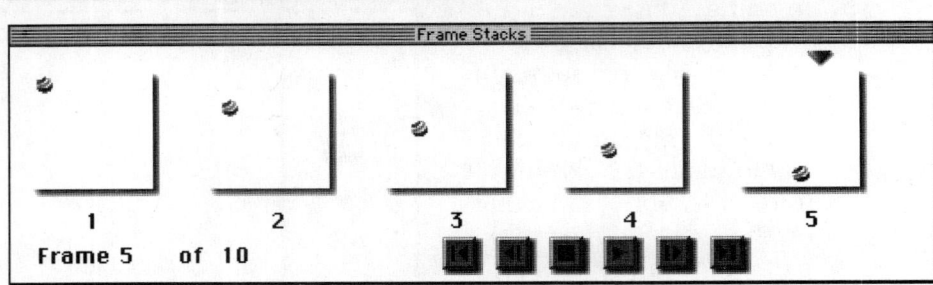

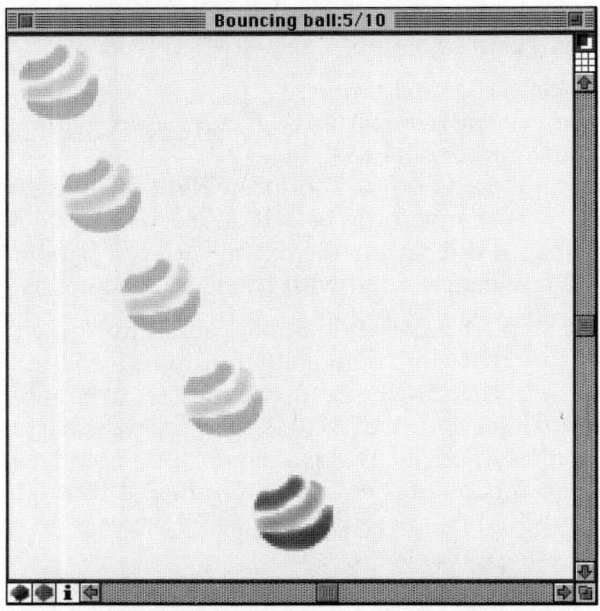

FIGURE 11.2: Frames 1 through 5 in the Frame Stacks palette compared to Canvas 5/10, showing the onion skin effect on frames 1 through 5

> ***Note*** *Instead of filling an oval selection with a gradient you could also paint a brush inside of it and then copy and paste it into different frames, instead of dragging the oval path and filling it. Be aware, though, every time you paste a selection, Painter turns it into a floater. Before you move from frame to frame, drop the floater. To drop a floater, click on the Drop button in the Floater List palette. You'll learn more about creating movies using floaters later in this chapter.*

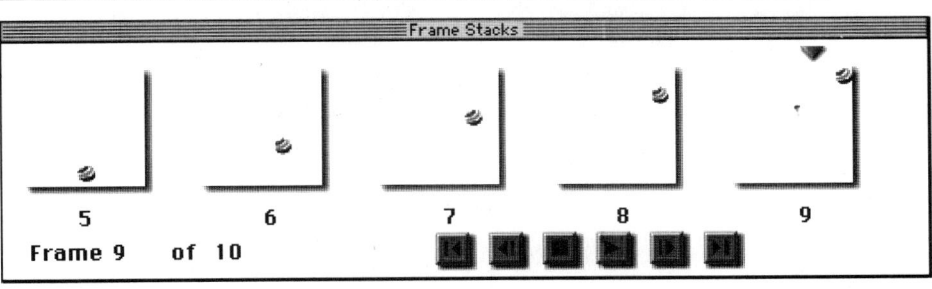

FIGURE 11.3: Frames 5 through 9

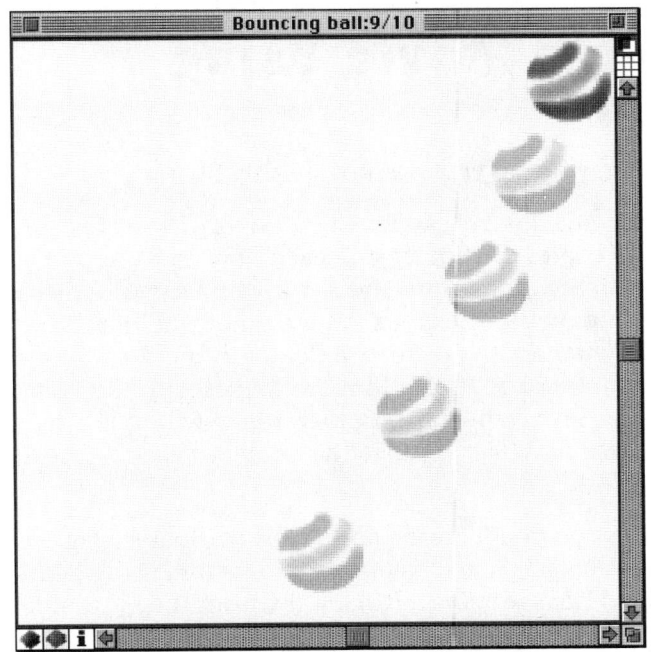

FIGURE 11.4: Frame 9, showing the onion skin effect on frames 5 through 9

Playing a Movie

To play a movie, click on the Play button in the Frame Stacks palette. Alternatively, you can choose Play from the Movie menu.

After you've played your movie, close it and proceed to the next section to learn how floaters can help you create a movie.

> **Note** *Any changes you make to the frame stack will automatically be updated in the file that you originally named when you created your movie. You only need to press File ➤ Save if you want to save your movie frame stack as a QuickTime movie (Windows users: Video For Windows) or as numbered files. You'll learn how to do this later in this chapter.*

 # Creating a Movie Using Floaters

In Painter, you can create a movie using floaters.

Working with floaters can save you hours of work because Painter automatically copies the floater into each new frame as you create the frame. This is a tremendous convenience: If you needed to place the same image in 12 frames without using a floater, you would have to copy and paste it into every frame. If you create a floater in the first frame of a movie with only one frame and then add more frames with the floater active using the Go To Next Frame button, each frame will be created with that floater in it. If desired, you can move the floater in each frame to create an animated effect.

In this section you'll create a movie using floaters. Figure 11.5 shows a few frames (frames 3, 5, and 7) of a movie created using floaters. The balloon in Figure 11.5 is moving against a sky from the bottom left-hand corner to the top right-hand corner. Up, up, and away!

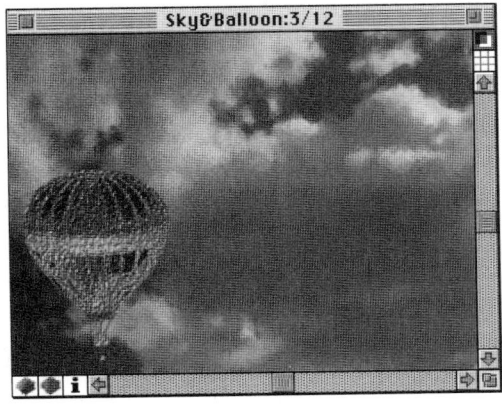

FIGURE 11.5: Up, up, and away—animation created with a balloon floater

Here's a short exercise that will lead you through the steps of creating a movie with floaters.

1. To get started, create a new movie, by choosing File ➤ New. In the New Picture dialog box make the canvas size 320 × 240 pixels at 75 ppi. Make sure that the Movie radio button is selected and that there is a 1 in the frames

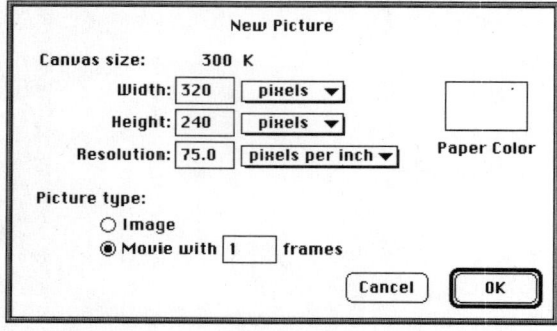

field. This will create only one frame in the movie. Then click OK to create a frame stack movie.

2. When a dialog box appears, name the frame stack, then click Save.

3. When the New Frame Stacks dialog box appears, set the layers of onion skin to 2. Set the Storage type to 8-bit color, 15-bit color, or 24-bit color depending upon your system.

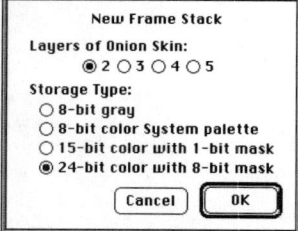

In a few moments, the Frame Stacks palette and a blank canvas appear. Notice that the title bar of the blank canvas includes the name of the file and 1/1. This means you are on frame 1 of 1. In the Frame Stacks palette, notice an arrow over frame 1. This means you are in frame 1. The arrow moves as you move through frames. Also, notice that the frame is blank.

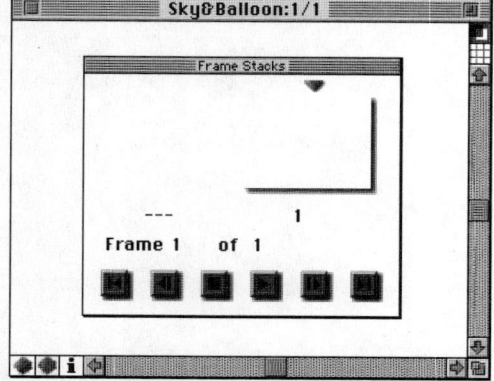

4. In frame 1 you are going to create the background that will appear throughout the movie.

You can either paint an image from scratch using one of the brushes or apply a few special-effects commands to a digitized photograph to make it look more painterly. If you want to create a painting from scratch, start painting. To turn a photograph into a painting, or add painterly effects to one, you first need to open the image you want to use. If you don't have an image, either use one of Painter's tutorial images or use a stock image from a CD-ROM.

Figure 11.6 shows the image of the sky before it was edited. The image of the sky is a selection from an image in Image Club's Photogear Volume Six: Skyscapes CD-ROM. Figure 11.7 shows a portion of the image after it was altered in Painter.

FIGURE 11.6: The sky image before altering. (Image courtesy of The Image Club)

FIGURE 11.7: A portion of the sky image after altering

After you have an image on screen, you can either use one of the commands in Painter's Effects menu or a third-party filter to add a painterly effect. You might want to review Chapter 9 for more information on how to create special effects. To create the effect in Figure 11.7, the image was Auto Cloned using the Colored Pencils brush, with the Method Category set to Cover, the Method Subcategory set to Soft Cover, and the Use Clone Color option selected.

After you have perfected the image and are happy with the effect, you need to make the image a floater in the first frame. If you created the background image from scratch in frame 1, change the image into a floater by first selecting the entire image, then clicking in it with the Floating Selection tool. Remember: you can double-click on the Rectangular Selection tool in the Tools palette to select the entire canvas.

To verify that you've created a floater, open the Objects :Floater List palette. You should see the floater listed and selected in the palette. Keep the floater selected.

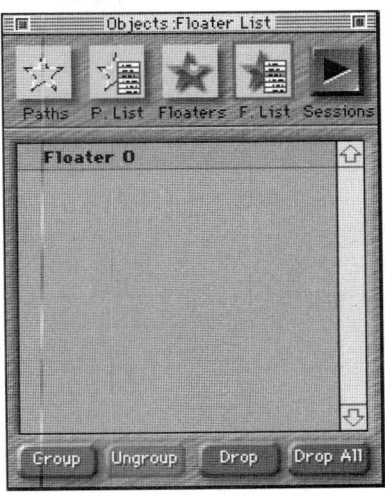

If you opened a photographic image and made it more painterly in a separate file, you might need to resize the image before you paste it into frame 1 of the movie canvas. Check the size of the photographic image by clicking on the **i** at the bottom left-hand corner of the canvas. If the image is larger than the movie you'll need to resize it or it may be cropped when you paste it into the movie canvas. Use the Canvas ➤ Resize command to resize your image. (See Chapter 4 to review using the Resize command). Next, you need to select the entire image, then copy it by choosing Edit ➤ Copy. Once it's been copied you can close the file. Save it if you want. Now, activate frame 1 of the movie stack and choose Edit ➤ Paste to paste the image. (Every time you paste an image, Painter makes that image a floater.) Open the Objects :Floater List palette to see the floater listed in the palette.

5. After you've made the background image a floater, you are ready to add more frames to your movie. You can add more frames by using the Go To Next Frame button in the Frame Stack palette. Don't use the Add Frames command, because it will add frames, but will not add the image in the floater to each frame.

Create at least 12 frames. Notice that as you create new frames, the image in the floater is added to every frame.

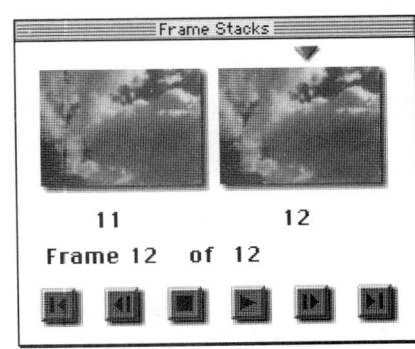

6. After you've created all the frames you'll need, you can drop the floater. To drop the floater, choose Drop from the Floater List palette. There should no longer be a floater in the Floater List palette.

Tip If you want to change the background in all the frames after you've already created them, first return to frame 1. Then choose Delete Frames from the Movie menu. In the Delete Frames dialog box, type 2 through 12, then click OK to delete the frames. Now, paste or paint your new movie background in frame 1. If it is not a floater, turn it into a floater by selecting it and then clicking on it with the Floating Selection tool. Now create new frames using the Go To Next Frame button. As you create new frames, Painter fills each frame with the image in your floater.

Now it's time to animate an object or character using a floater. In the next few steps, you'll see another advantage of using floaters when creating movies. Painter copies the image in the floater into each frame after you reposition the floater and move to a new frame. For instance, assume you are in frame 1 and have a floater in the movie canvas. If you go to frame 2 and move the floater to a new position in the movie canvas, Painter copies the object in the floater into frame 2. You see the change when you move to frame 3.

7. Press the Go To First Frame button in the Frame Stacks palette to return to frame 1. Now move to frame 2 by pressing the Go To Next Frame button. You'll start creating an animated sequence with a floater in frame 2.

8. Your next step is to paste or drag a floater onto the canvas to use as the object or image you wish to animate. If you wish to drag a floater into your movie canvas, simply pick one from the Objects :Floaters palette. Alternatively, you can create an object or character in a new file, mask it, and then paste it into the canvas. After you paste the object on screen, Painter automatically converts it into a floater. You can also select an object or character from a photograph, edit it to make it more painterly, and paste it into your movie canvas.

Figure 11.8 shows an image of a balloon from Digital Stock's Active Lifestyles CD-ROM. The image was first silhouetted using the Outline Selection tool and the Masking brushes. Then the Glass Distortion, Equalize, Highpass, and Apply Surface Texture commands were applied.

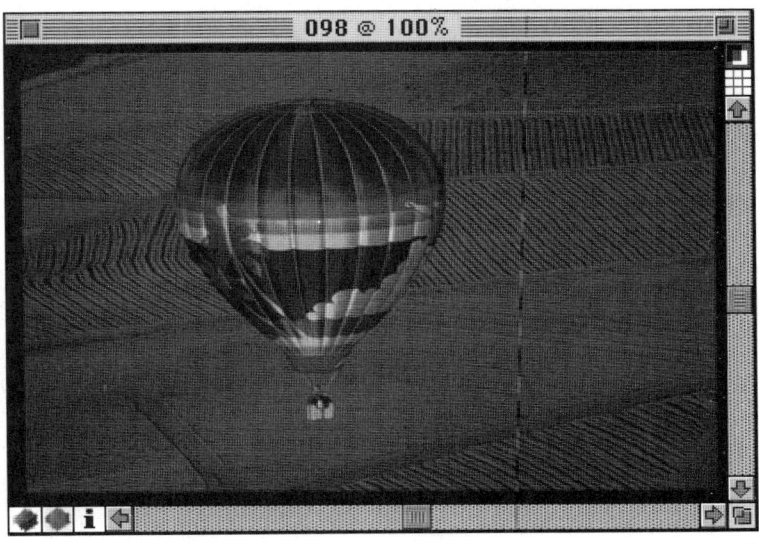

FIGURE 11.8: Balloon image before adding special effects. Image courtesy of Digital Stock.

After painterly effects were added to the image (Figure 11.9), it was copied and pasted into the second frame of the frame stack. Then it was scaled using the Canvas ➤ Orientation ➤ Scale command.

9. After you've copied and pasted your object or character in frame 2, move it into position. Since the balloon is going to move up from the bottom left, it was moved into the bottom of the left corner of the canvas.

10. Go to frame 3. Notice that the floater from frame 2 appears in frame 3. If you have an active floater in a movie frame and move to the next frame after

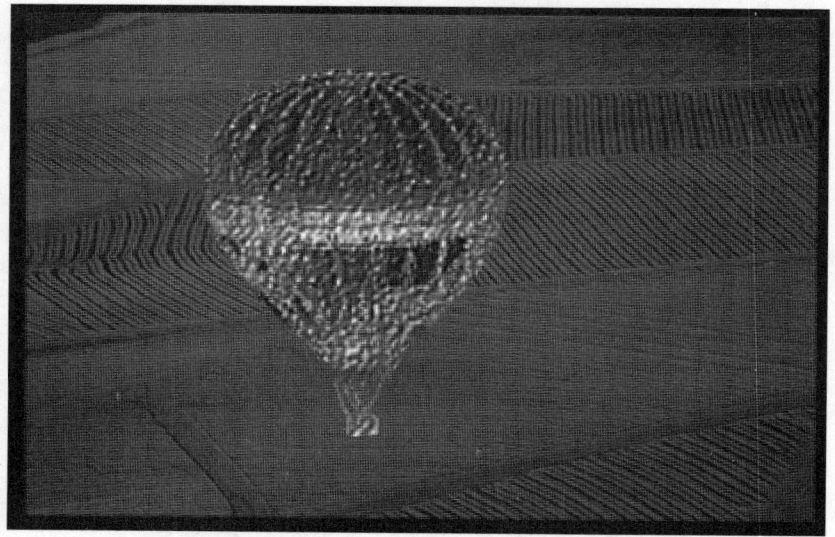

FIGURE 11.9: Balloon image after adding special effects

repositioning the floater, Painter automatically copies the floater into the frame. This means that you don't need to keep copying and pasting objects in order to animate them. All you need to do is reposition a floater in a frame and then go to the next frame. Now, click and drag on the floater in frame 3 to reposition it.

11. Now move to the next frame, then move the floater that appears in the frame. Continue this procedure until you have filled 11 frames of your movie.

12. After you've completed the animation process, delete the floater by pressing Delete on the keyboard.

To play the movie, click on the Play button in the Frame Stacks palette.

Tip You can make a movie play behind an object, shape, or character. To do this, first create a movie, then place a floater in the middle frame of your movie frame stack. Play the movie. You will see that the movie will play behind the floater.

Modifying a Movie

Once you've created a movie, Painter allows you to return to any frame and edit it. To move to a frame, you can simply click on it in the Frame Stacks palette. Alternatively, you can choose Go To Frame from the Edit menu. In the Go To Frame dialog box, enter the frame you wish to return to, then click OK. The canvas on screen will now contain the image from the frame on the frame stack. You can then use any of Painter's brushes or commands to paint and edit.

Rotoscoping

Painter allows you to paint or edit any frame. Editing an image one frame at a time is called *Rotoscoping*. You can easily edit any image by painting over it. For precise control, use Painter's Masking brushes to create masks over the image areas you wish to paint over. You can also create masks in floaters and use the Floater Mask Visibility buttons in the Objects :Floater List palette to allow the area behind the floater mask to appear through the floater. For more information about creating masks, see Chapter 7. For more information about creating masks in floaters, see Chapter 8.

Applying a Session to a Movie

Painter allows you to apply a recorded session to any frame stack. As discussed in Chapter 10, recorded sessions allow you to record brush strokes and Painter commands, then play them back. By applying a recorded session to a movie, you can quickly create effects that appear in every frame in a movie. For instance, you could record a session which uses Painter's Dye Concentration or Glass Distortion command to change the texture of an entire image. When you apply the session to the movie, the special effects appear in every frame.

To apply a session to a movie, choose Movie ➤ Apply Session To Movie. This opens the Recorded Sessions dialog box, where a list of all recorded sessions appear. Click on a session and choose Playback. You can apply as many sessions as you'd like to a movie.

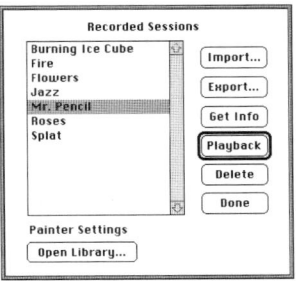

Applying Grain Textures to Frames

Painter provides an extremely efficient technique for changing the texture of each frame in a movie. To apply unusual surface effects to a movie, you must first record a session that applies the Effects ➤ Surface Control ➤ Dye Concentration or Effects ➤ Surface Control ➤ Surface Texture command. When you start recording your session, choose Tools ➤ Session ➤ Options. In the Options dialog box deselect Record Initial State. This ensures that you can have your grain change randomly, if desired.

After your session is recorded, and you've opened your movie, choose Move ➤ Set Grain Position. In the Frame-to-Frame Grain Position dialog box, choose whether you wish to have the grain remain unchanged, move randomly, or move linearly. If you choose the Grain Moves Linearly option, you can enter the distance in pixels that the grain moves vertically or horizontally.

```
┌─────────────────────────────────────┐
│  Frame-to-Frame Grain Position       │
│  Grain movement:                     │
│    ○ Grain Stays Still               │
│    ○ Grain Moves Randomly            │
│    ◉ Grain Moves Linearly            │
│  Per-frame distance:                 │
│    Move: [3  ]  pixels horizontally  │
│    Move: [0  ]  pixels vertically    │
│              ( Cancel )   [  OK  ]   │
└─────────────────────────────────────┘
```

Once you set the dialog box options click OK. Now you can apply the grain effect to your movie by choosing Movie ➤ Apply Session To Movie.

Cloning a Movie

Painter's cloning commands can be used to clone images from one movie into another. The steps for cloning two movies together are quite similar to cloning image areas from one file into another. In order to clone two movies together, though, both movies must be created at the same resolution, with the same dimensions, and the same number of frames. Here are the steps to cloning two movies together:

1. Open two movies that have the same resolution, dimensions, and number of frames.

2. Activate the movie that you wish to serve as the image source for the second movie, then choose Movie ➤ Set Movie Clone Source.

Note *Painter's File ➤ Clone command will not create a clone of the entire movie. If you execute this command while in a movie, Painter only clones the currently active frame.*

3. Activate the movie that you wish to clone into. Select a Cloners brush. Once you've selected a Cloners brush, click on any frame and begin painting. As you paint, you'll see the image from the clone source movie appear.

Tracing One Movie into Another

Painter allows you to trace over the images of one movie while you're in another movie. The steps are very similar to those described in Chapter 4 where you used Tracing Paper to trace one image over another. To trace one movie over another movie:

1. Open two movies that have the same resolution, dimensions, and number of frames.

2. Activate the movie that you wish to be the image source for the second movie, then choose Movie ➤ Set Clone Source.

3. Activate the movie you that you wish to trace in. Turn on Painter's tracing paper by choosing Canvas ➤ Tracing Paper. A ghosted version of the first frame of your original movie appears in the active movie.

4. You can now trace over the original movie using any of Painter's brushes. After you've completed tracing one frame, click the Next button in the Frame Stacks palette to move to the next frame.

Applying an Image Hose to a Movie

Painter allows you to apply any brush stroke to a movie, including an Image Hose brush stroke. By applying an Image Hose brush stroke to every frame in a movie, you can create interesting, unusual, and whimsical effects.

In order to apply elements from an Image Hose's nozzle file to every frame in a movie, you must first record an Image Hose brush stroke. Start by creating a new small picture file in which to create your brush stroke. Then choose the Image Hose brush from the Brushes palette. Now load a nozzle by choosing Tools ➤ Load Nozzle. You can either use one of your own nozzle files or one of the nozzles in Painter's Nozzle folder. For a whimsical effect, you might want to use Painter's Plants nozzle.

Before you start making a brush stroke, choose the Tools ➤ Record Stroke command. After you execute the Tools ➤ Record Stroke command, start painting a brush stroke with the Image Hose. Try drawing in a circular motion. That way when you play back the brush stroke it will be played back in a circular motion.

To apply the Image Hose brush stroke or any other recorded brush stroke to a movie, create a new movie or open a movie. If you create a new movie, you might want to fill it with a color, gradient, or weave. If you created your brush strokes in a circular motion you might want to use a radial gradient, such as Tree Rings, as the background. Next, choose Movie ➤ Apply Brush Stroke To Movie. To add more brush strokes, you can reapply the brush stroke by choosing Movie ➤ Apply Brush Stroke To Movie. Figure 11.10 shows a few frames of a movie created using the Tree Rings gradient as the background and an Image Hose stroke with the Plants nozzle applied a few times to the movie.

If you are applying a nozzle file to a movie, Painter paints one or more images from the nozzle file onto each frame of your movie. If you apply another type of brush stroke to a movie, Painter applies elements of the stroke to each frame in the movie.

Making an Image Hose Nozzle File from a Movie

Nozzle files for Painter's Image Hose brush can easily be created from a Painter movie. To create a nozzle file from a movie, choose the Make Nozzle From Movie command from the Tools ➤ Image Hose submenu. After you execute the command, Painter opens a new file containing each frame of your movie laid out in a grid. Now save the file in RIFF format so that it can be used as a nozzle file.

When you wish to use the nozzle file, choose Tools ➤ Load Nozzle, then load the nozzle from the disk. Alternatively, you can load the nozzle file from the Brush Controls :Nozzle palette. To learn how to use the features in the Nozzle palette, see Chapter 3. To use the currently selected nozzle file, select the Image Hose brush from the Brushes palette.

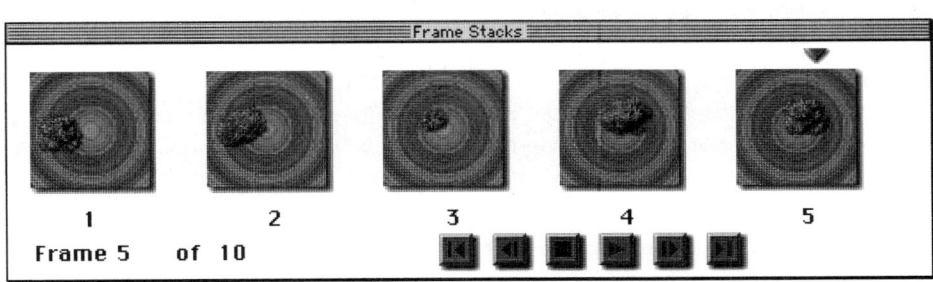

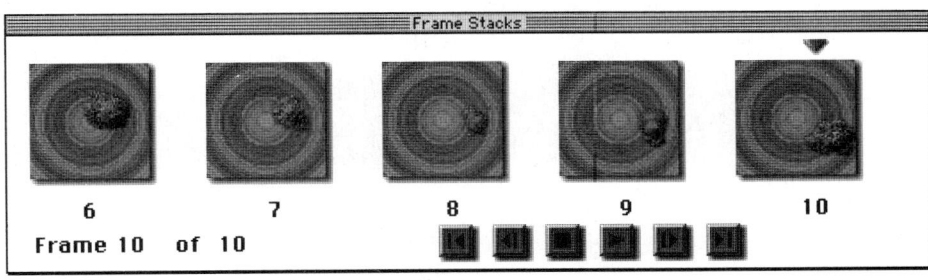

FIGURE 11.10: Movie created by applying a gradient and an Image Hose brush stroke

Inserting a Movie

You can use the Movie ➤ Insert Movie command to insert a movie into a pre-existing movie as long as the two movies are the same dimensions and resolution. To do so, you must first have a movie on screen. Next choose Movie ➤ Insert Movie.

In the Insert Movie dialog box you can choose to insert the movie before or after a frame, or at the start or end of a movie. Choose either option, then click OK. When a dialog box appears, choose a movie to insert. Remember that the two movies must have the same dimensions and resolution. Instantly, the movie is inserted.

Saving a Movie

You don't have to worry about saving a movie in Painter's own movie frame stack format, because Painter automatically saves the changes you make. You can save a movie in a variety of other formats. You can save it as a series of sequentially numbered files. Mac users can save movies in Apple Computer's QuickTime format. Windows users can save a file in Microsoft's Video For Windows format.

Saving in QuickTime Format

Painter's Mac version allows you to save frame stack files as QuickTime movies. QuickTime is a system extension that allows computers without video boards to play movies in QuickTime compatible programs. For instance, you could save your Painter movie as a QuickTime movie, then open it up in Macromedia Director or Macromedia Authorware, Macromedia Action, Adobe Premiere, or Adobe After Effects.

1. To save a movie as a QuickTime movie, choose Save As from the File menu. In the Save Movie dialog box choose Save Movie As QuickTime. Click OK.

2. In the dialog box that appears, enter a movie file name. Click on Save.

3. In the Compression Settings dialog box (this is the standard QuickTime save dialog box which also appears in other programs) you can choose a compression option and setting and motion option. If you're not familiar with QuickTime, the choice can be bewildering.

Here's a brief discussion of the options QuickTime provides.

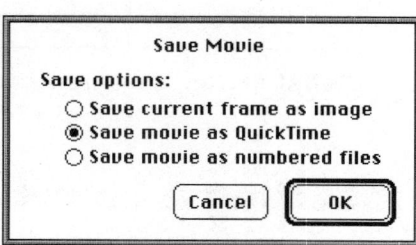

Compressor

The choices that appear in the first pop-up menu in the Compressor group are known as CODECs (Compression/Decompression standards). They are described below. The second pop-up menu in the Compressor group allows you to choose the number of colors you wish your image to contain.

The following list describes the different CODECs available in the first pop-up menu. Choose the most appropriate one for your work. (Several are not necessary when simply saving movie files created in Painter.)

◆ **Animation**—This CODEC is recommended for most computer animation. The compression is lossless, so image quality does not suffer from the compression process. It's not recommended for use with images captured from videotape. Using this CODEC, you can play back images at 30 frames per second (fps) using 24-bit color.

◆ **CinePak**—This is recommended when you wish to compress 16 and 24-bit images that will be played on CD-ROMS.

◆ **Graphics**—Use for compressing video for high-quality playback on systems displaying 256 colors This CODEC is suitable for playing back images from hard disks, but generally not from CD-ROMs.

◆ **None**—This option is used if you are recording video images directly to your hard disk without any compression.

◆ **Photo JPEG**—JPEG stands for Joint Photographers Experts Group. It is a commonly used standard for compressing digital images. This CODEC can be used for storing video clips, but is considered too slow for playing back animation.

◆ **Video**—The video CODEC is used to capture and compress video. It yields high-quality playback from hard disks.

Note *If you're using a video recording and playback system such as Raster-Ops MoviePak or MoviePak2, you may see options for these packages in the pop-up menu.*

Quality

Use the Quality slider to set the quality of your movie when it is compressed in QuickTime format. The higher the quality the larger the disk file.

Motion

The motion field allows you to set the number of frames per second for movie playback. QuickTime allows you to choose playback rates from 1 to 30 frames per second. The greater the number of frames per second, the better the playback. Note that if your computer and hard disk are slow, you may be picking a playback rate that is faster than your computer can handle efficiently.

◆ **Key Frames**—When QuickTime records your movie, it doesn't actually need to record every frame. It can compress the image better if it records one key frame, and then record only the image data that is different from that key frame. A higher key frame rate results in smoother movies. If you don't select the Key Frame option, Quick-Time simply records every frame.

◆ **Limit Data Rate To**—This field is only selectable when the Cinepak choice is selected in the Compressor pop-up menu. The option allows you to set the playback speed for CD-ROMs. For instance, to play back a movie on a double-speed CD-ROM, enter 200 to set the Playback speed to 200,000 bytes per second.

Pick an option and click OK to save your movie as a QuickTime movie.

At any time you can open a QuickTime movie in Painter and play it.

Exporting Painter QuickTime Movies into Other Programs

If you wish, you can export your Painter QuickTime movies into Adobe Premiere, Adobe After Effects, Macromedia Director and Macromedia Authorware, and then play them.

To open a Painter QuickTime movie in Adobe Premiere, choose File ➤ Open and open the file. When the movie appears you can play it.

To import your Painter QuickTime movies into Macromedia Director, choose Import from Director's File menu. In the Type pop-up menu, choose QuickTime movie. Select the movie from the file list, then click the Import button. Once the movie is imported it appears in Director as a "cast member." You can then drag the movie cast member into the Score window or Stage window to place it in your Director presentation. You can use the Tempo channel in the Score window to have your Director animation pause until the QuickTime movie stops playing. If you wish to preview or edit your movie in Director, choose Digital Video from the Window menu. (If you are using Video For Windows movies, you can follow the same basic steps as those described for QuickTime movies.) To play your movie, click on the Play button in Director's Control Panel. Figure 11.11 shows the balloon movie (described earlier in the chapter), ready to be played in Director.

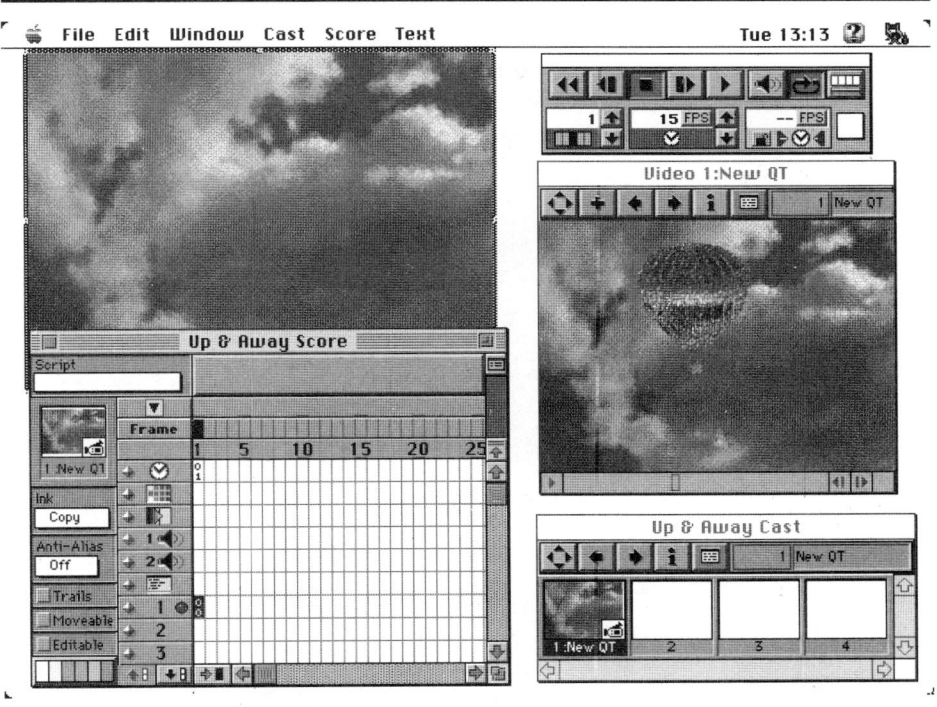

FIGURE 11.11:   Balloon movie loaded into Macromedia Director

Saving a Movie as Numbered Files

If you'd like to export movies you created in Painter into Adobe Premiere, in order to add transitional effects, you might want to save your Painter movie as numbered files.

All about Making Movies

1. To save a movie as numbered PICT or BMP files, choose File ➤ Save As.

2. In the Save Movie dialog box, choose Save Movie As Numbered Files. Click OK.

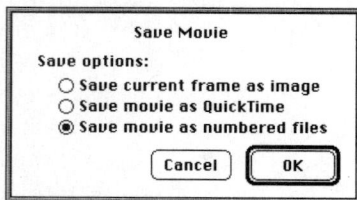

3. In the dialog box that appears, enter a short name for your movie. (Mac users must then add **.000** to the end of the name.) This will start the number-ing process when you save the file. To open a movie editing program such as Premiere, Macintosh users should choose PICT and Windows users should choose BMP. Before you press the Save button, Mac users can create a new folder in which to save the file. That way all the files are saved into one folder. Next, click Save. Painter instantly starts writing the numbered files and saves them into the folder you choose.

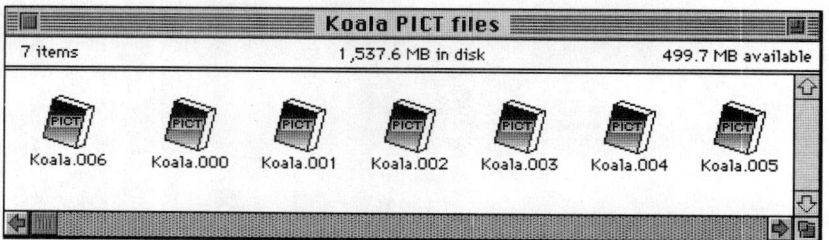

Now you can open the numbered files in a video editing program and add transitional effects.

Importing Numbered Files into Adobe Premiere

To import a folder containing numbered files into Adobe Premiere you must first have a new project on screen. If you don't, choose File ➤ New ➤ New Project. In the New Project Presets dialog box choose a preset, then click OK. Next, choose File ➤ Import ➤ Folder. Select the folder you want to import. Instantly the folder with the numbered files appears in the Pro-ject palette. Drag the folder to video track A in the Construction window. Now, you can add a transition by dragging one of the transitions from the Transition palette to the construction track, T. For more interesting effects you can import Painter PICT files and add them to the B or S1 video tracks. If you'd like you can even add sound to your presentation.

To play the Premiere movie, choose Project ➤ Preview. Premiere will ask you to save the movie before it builds a preview. Save the movie, then wait till it builds so that you can see it in motion.

Figure 11.12 shows a Premiere movie created using Painter numbered files. Notice the transitions in track T and the Painter images in tracks A and B.

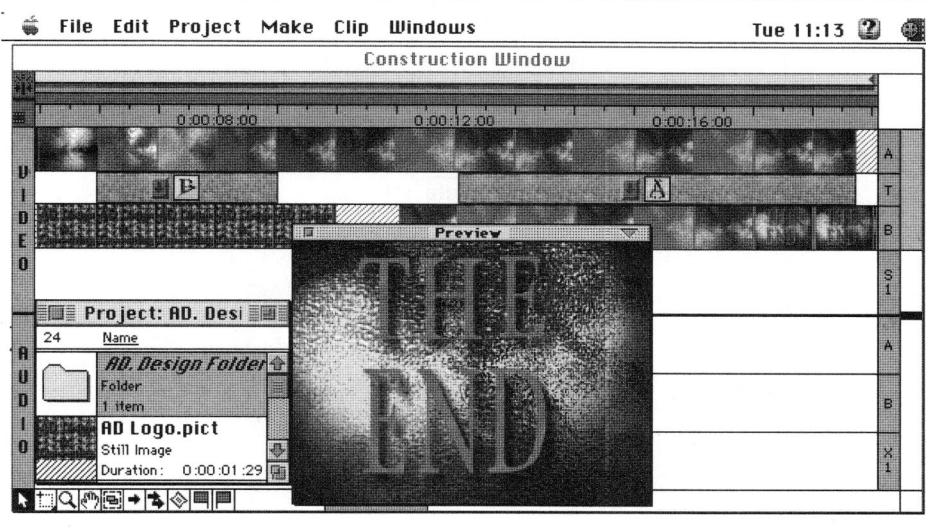

FIGURE 11.12:   Painter PICT images imported into Adobe Premiere

Opening Numbered Files in Painter

You can open a few frames from a movie that you grabbed using a video capture board and create a frame stack or QuickTime movie out of it. (See Chapter 4 to review how to capture images from video.) When you save them in order to open them as numbered files, the captured frames need

All about Making Movies

to be saved in the same format and numbered sequentially. To help keep your work organized, save all the numbered files in the same folder.

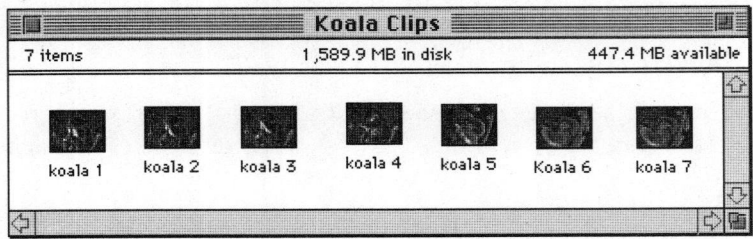

To open sequentially numbered files, choose File ➤ Open. In the dialog box that appears, choose the Open Numbered Files option in the bottom left-hand corner of the dialog box. Notice that below the Open button the words "Choose First Numbered File" appear. Click on the first numbered file and click Open.

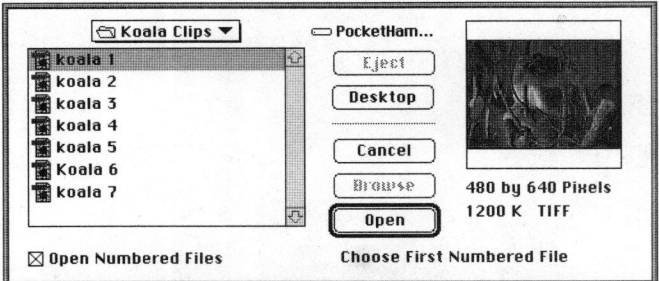

The Open dialog box reappears, but this time the words "Choose Last Numbered File" appear below the Open button. Click on the last numbered file and click Open.

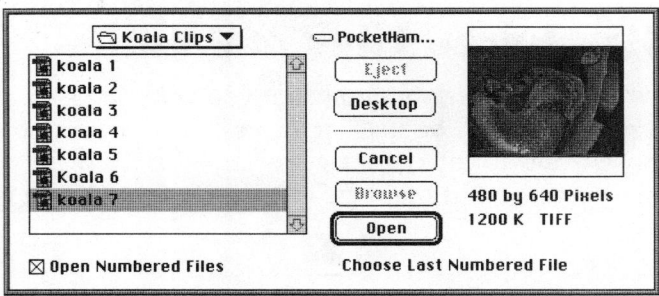

Next, a dialog box asking you to enter a Movie name appears. Enter a name and click Save.

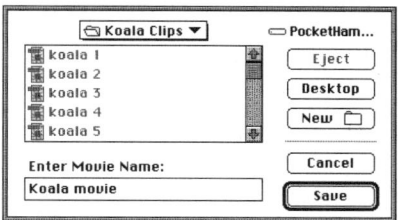

When the New Frame Stack palette appears, make your selections and choose OK.

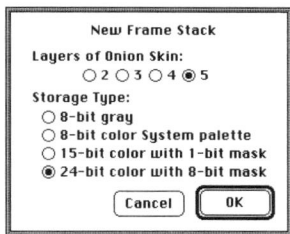

In a few moments, the numbered files appear in the Frame Stacks palette.

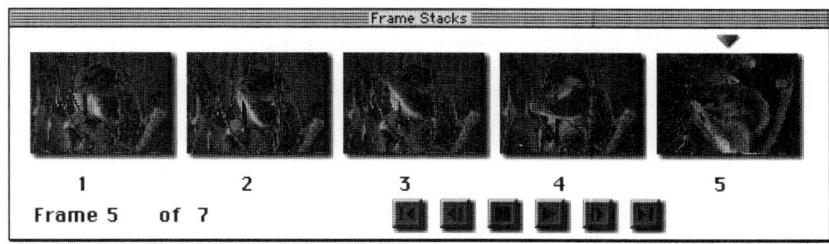

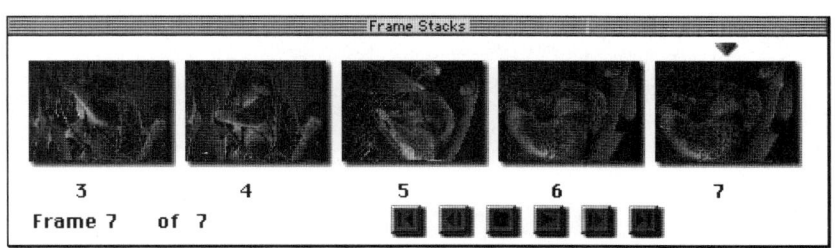

When the movie is on screen, add painterly effects using Painter's different tools and commands.

Saving a Current Frame as an Image

Painter allows you to save a frame from your movie as an image. To do so, go to the frame you want to save as an image. Next, choose the frame, then choose File ➤ Save As. In the Save Movie dialog box, choose Save Current Frame As Image. Click OK to save the frame as an image.

⬤ Wrapping It Up

This chapter has introduced you to the magical world of moving images. Keep working at it—and who knows, you may soon be nominated for an Academy Award for Best Animated Short of the Year. In your acceptance speech, don't forget to mention Painter.

Outputting Your Painter Work

There's no reason to hide away your fantastic Painter artwork behind the bits and bytes of your computer's hard disk. Painter artwork should be seen, not just stored away on digital media. If you'd like to see your Painter artwork without having to load it from your hard disk every time you want to view it, you have several choices.

Undoubtedly, the easiest and most obvious way to output your work is to simply print your Painter images on a printer connected to your computer. Painter images can also be output to a printing press, to slides, and to video. You can pay fine arts digital printmakers to print Painter files on canvas, rice paper, and even metal. But no matter how you output your images, it's important to understand the digital production process. Otherwise, the printed versions of your files may never match the exquisite images you see on screen.

In order to help you learn how to output Painter images, this chapter provides an overview of the different output options available. You'll learn how Painter images can be converted to CMYK color files so that they can be output on a printing press or to a Scitex IRIS to create fine art prints. You'll also explore the various options in Painter's Page Setup

(Windows users: PostScript Setup) and Print dialog boxes. The chapter concludes with a look at outputting images to slides and to video.

The Importance of Calibration

Before you begin the process of outputting your images, it's important to remember that the colors you see on a computer screen won't always match the colors of an image when output.

As discussed in Chapter 3, your monitor outputs color by emitting light. Colors that appear on the printed page appear as a result of light waves absorbed by and reflected from ink on the printed page. The difference between these two systems of creating colors often means that a color on screen appears brighter and more saturated than it does when printed. Furthermore, images on screen may look lighter or darker simply because of the type of monitor that you are using (not to mention the brightness and contrast levels set on your monitor).

In order to help insure that the colors on screen match printed output, several companies such as Daystar, Radius, and RasterOps sell monitor calibration devices. Some programs, such as Adobe Photoshop, include utilities to help calibrate your monitor. Painter does not provide any calibration utilities, but it does provide a gamma setting for your monitor's brightness. This setting is found in the Page Setup dialog box, and is discussed later in this chapter.

Outputting to a Printing Press

One of the most common destinations of Painter images is a printing press. Before a Painter image can be printed on a printing press, it must be converted into a CMYK color file. As discussed in Chapter 2, CMYK is the color system used to print continuous-tone color images. Although you can convert a Painter image to CMYK by saving it into EPS format, many users pay a service bureau or prepress house to handle the conversion. Others convert to CMYK using Adobe Photoshop, or they can convert when outputting in their page layout program, such as Quark XPress.

Note *If you convert a Painter image to CMYK using Photoshop, you can control many aspects of the separation process, and you can also edit the final CMYK color image using CMYK colors.*

After conversion to CMYK, the next stop for the Painter file is often a page layout program. Once the final layout is determined, it is then output on an imagesetter. Imagesetters are high-end devices capable of outputting images on photographic paper or film. During the output process, the imagesetter re-creates the Painter image on four negatives, one for each of the CMYK process colors, often at a resolution of 2,540 dpi. The negatives that are created are not produced in color; instead, they are grayscale representations of the CMYK color components of the image.

The commercial printer then uses the four negatives to create plates for the printing press. When the image is printed on the press, different-sized cyan, magenta, yellow, and black ink dots combine to create the countless colors in the final image.

Understanding Digital Halftones

The different-size dots that blend together to produce colors in the printing process are called *halftones*. These tiny dots are produced by combinations of smaller dots, often called pixels, created by the imagesetter. The number of halftones per inch constitutes the image's printing screen frequency (measured in lines per inch, or lpi). The relationship between a halftone dot, imagesetter pixels, and screen frequency is depicted in Figure 12.1.

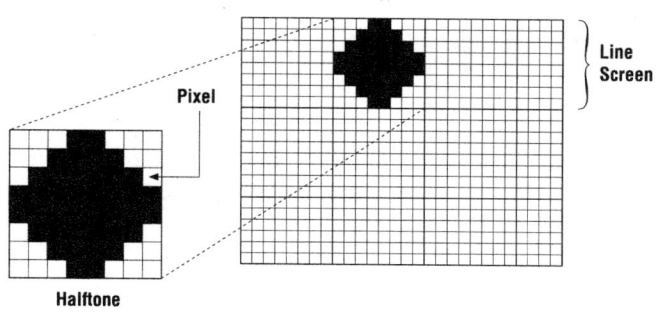

FIGURE 12.1: A halftone dot is made up of imagesetter pixels.

Usually the determination of screen frequency is based on the paper and printing press. The greater the screen frequency, the sharper the images and the better the color reproduction. Newspapers are often output at a screen frequency between 80 and 100 lpi; magazines are often output at a screen frequency between 133 and 150. The screen frequency, as well as the angles at which the halftones are created, all affect the quality of the final printed image.

The Proofing Process

The journey from Painter file to printed page is long, and often fraught with some degree of uncertainty. For instance, the conversion from RGB to CMYK might produce an image darker than desired. Or the printed image may exhibit a color cast, an overall tint produced by unbalanced colors. An image output at the wrong screen angles could produce moiré patterns, an undesirable mottled pattern over the image. To help reduce the uncertainly, a *proof*, a sample printout, should be output as often as possible.

By printing a proof you can correct color problems before it is too late—that is, before you spend the money to print the image on a printing press. During the proofing process, you may find that you need to lighten, sharpen, or color-correct various parts of your image. If the image has already been converted to a CMYK file, you may wish to correct your image in a program like Photoshop (which allows you to edit CMYK color files), or ask the prepress house to handle the final color corrections.

Proofs are often divided into three categories: digital proofs, off-press proofs, and press proofs.

Digital Proofs

A digital proof is a proof created directly from a digital file. Thus, a printout created from a black-and-white laser printer can be considered a digital proof, though it would be considered a low-end digital proof.

Digital proofs are usually created on thermal wax printers, dye sublimation printers, or high-end inkjet printers, such as the Scitex IRIS.

Thermal wax printers create color images from ribbons coated with cyan, magenta, yellow, and black wax. The colored waxes are heated and transferred to paper. Dye sublimation printers create colors with dyes that *sublimate* (turn into gas) when a colored ribbon makes contact with a heated printhead. Most dye sublimation printers provide near-photographic images superior to images created on thermal wax printers. High-end inkjet printers, such as the Scitex IRIS, create colors by combining millions of tiny ink dots sprayed from nozzles. An IRIS produces photorealistic images that can often closely match final printed output.

Although high-end digital proofs such as those created by the IRIS are often very accurate, most graphics professionals demand off-press proofs to insure color accuracy.

Off-Press proofs

Off-press proofs are created from the four CMYK film negatives output from an imagesetter. Since the proof and printing plates are both created from the film negatives, off-press proofs are considered a reliable indicator of how the image will look when output on a printing press. The two main types of off-press proofs are overlay proofs and laminated proofs.

In an overlay proof, four exposed images are overlaid on acetates. Laminated proofs, such as Dupont's Chromalin, 3M's Matchprint, and Agfa's Agfaproof, are usually considered more reliable than overlay proofs. In the laminated proofing process, four different colored layers are developed and laminated to the base material of the proof.

If you do obtain a Matchprint, be aware that the colors of a Matchprint can be more intense than the final colors created on a printing press. Before printing a job, many commercial printers will actually require you to obtain a laminated proof. The proof will be used as *contract proof*, one that the print shop is expected to match.

Press Proofs

Press proofs are proofs that are created on a printing press using the same paper and ink that will be used in the print run. Although press proofs are highly accurate, they are often considered too expensive for many print jobs.

 # Fine Art IRIS Printing

Many Painter artists do not need their images printed on printing presses, yet desire high-quality fine art prints of their work. To satisfy the demand for high-quality digital output, several digital printmaker studios have pioneered outputting digital images using long-lasting inks and printmaking papers. Cone Editions Press of East Topsham, Vermont (with subsidiaries in New York and London); Digital Pond in San Francisco; and Nash Editions in Manhattan Beach, California are probably the most well-known providers of fine art digital prints. Each company can output a Painter image on a variety of exotic substrates such as canvas, rice paper, linen, silk, leather, and even mylar and metal.

> **Note** *If you wish to contact Cone Editions Press, call 802-439-5751. If you wish to contact Digital Pond call 415-495-POND. If you wish to contact Nash Editions, call 310-545-4352.*

All three of the aforementioned fine art studios create high-quality prints by outputting images on an Scitex IRIS printer. The IRIS printers capable of outputting on art paper cost from $85,000 to $100,000. An IRIS can output images as large as 34 by 46 inches. In the printing process, the IRIS's four inkjet nozzles spray millions of droplets of cyan, magenta, yellow, and black inks to create continuous-tone images.

The IRIS can output at resolutions of 300, 150, and 100 ppi (although, visually, high-resolution printing actually resembles 1800 ppi). Working at 300 ppi in Painter produces the best images for outputting to an IRIS; however, high-quality images can also be obtained from lower-resolution images. If you can't work at a high resolution, discuss your artwork with your fine arts service bureau.

Since the IRIS uses CMYK inks, a Painter image must be converted to a CMYK color file before it is output. Thus if you are working on a Painter image that will be output on an IRIS, you should paint with the Printable Colors options selected in the Art Materials palette (See Chapter 3 for more details). Although you can convert a Painter file to CMYK when you save it in EPS format or you can convert it to CMYK in Adobe Photoshop, your best bet is to let your fine arts studio handle the separation. If you work with Cone Editions Press, you can ask for separation tables to be used in Adobe Photoshop.

To give you an idea of the difference between using a standard service bureau and one dedicated to outputting fine art prints, here is a quote from a fact sheet provided by Cone Editions Press:

> *In order to insure that images are printed with great saturation, we use software that we developed which increases the ink output of the Iris printer by nearly a third. We print to unusual materials and thick papers without stray ink spots and misting because of the alterations we performed to the Iris printing head and its electronics. Our fine art IRIS prints have from 5 to 40 times more permanency than typical service bureau prints due to the high-gamut fine arts inks we use in conjunction with the HALS/UVA overcoat we developed. Finally, the papers, canvas and linen that we developed or produce are far superior to commercially available products.*

Printing to Large Canvases

If you'd like to see your Painter images framed on large canvases, you might wish to have your images printed to canvas by Noble & Company of Alamo, California.

Noble & Company can output your images on canvases four feet wide by any length. The process was pioneered by Richard Noble, a California artist who developed the system with VuTek of New Hampshire, a company that manufactures large printers for outputting outdoor billboards on large vinyl sheets. When Richard Noble learned that VuTek could output large vinyl sheets from the computer, he encouraged the company to try outputting Painter images to canvas. Once the process was perfected, Richard began offering the service to other artists.

In the printing process, images are created on canvas by four separate jets spraying cyan, magenta, yellow, and black acrylic-based inks. Since the pigments are the same ones used for outdoor signs, the process produces highly saturated and long-lasting colors. One of the most fascinating aspects of the process is that the VuTek printer sprays pigments at 18 dpi. Since the spraying creates a soft painterly effect, no dots are visible on the canvas. The result is a high-quality image that does not need to be generated by a high-resolution Painter file.

The setup charge for printing images is $35, with an additional charge of $12 per square foot. For information contact Richard Noble, Noble & Company, 510-838-5524.

Low-Cost Color Printing Options

If you can't afford high-quality fine art prints, or just want to produce inexpensive reproductions of your artwork, you should contact a local service bureau or copy shop. For a fee, many service bureaus and copy shops will output your work on color laser printers or dye sublimation printers. Although the colors may not be perfect, at least you'll have a printed version of your artwork. Before paying for output, ask to see a sample from the color laser printer or dye sublimation printer so that you have an idea of the final print quality. In many cities, you can also rent computer workstations and output color images on color laser printers.

If you can't find a location to output your images, call a local computer store that specializes in Macintosh computers. There's a good chance the computer store will know of a service bureau that can meet your needs. If nothing else, you may even be convinced to purchase your own color printer.

Using Painter's Printing Options

If you wish to output your Painter images to a printer or imagesetter, you'll need to learn how to use the options in Painter's Print and Page Setup (Windows users: PostScript Setup) dialog boxes.

If you don't have a color printer and wish to output your color images, you'll probably need to pay a service bureau to output your work. If you are sending large color files to a service bureau, you'll probably need to save your image or images on a removable hard drive cartridge. The industry standard cartridges are manufactured by SyQuest Technology, who make cartridges that hold 44 MB, 88 MB, 105 MB, 200 MB, and 270 MB of data. For the color insert of this book, we saved all of the color images on one 3½" SyQuest 270 MB cartridge and sent it to the prepress house.

If a service bureau or prepress house does output your image, you won't need to worry about most of the choices in Painter's Print and Page Setup dialog boxes. Nevertheless, understanding the different options can help you better understand the print production process, and perhaps better communicate with your service bureau.

Note *Prepress and service bureaus may require you to save your images in TIFF or EPS formats. To learn how to use these formats, see the appendix.*

Using the Page Setup Dialog Box

Most of Painter's printing setup commands are handled through its Page Setup dialog box (Windows users: PostScript Setup dialog box), available from the File menu. The dialog box, shown in Figure 12.2, provides the following choices specific to Painter.

◆ **Size to Fit Page**—(Macintosh only) Choose this option if your image is larger than your paper size. This causes Painter to resize your image to fit on the printed page. If your image is larger than your paper, and you don't choose this option, an alert box will appear with the message: "Printer bed not big enough for whole image." If you click the Continue button, Painter prints the image, but clips the portion that won't fit on the page.

◆ **Printer/Press Dot Gain**—During the printing process, ink from the tiny dots that create the image can spread. This phenomenon is known as *dot gain*. The degree of dot gain is usually determined by the paper used for printing, the printing press, and the inks. Normally dot gain is most apparent in midtone areas of an image, which may print darker due to dot gain. Dot gain is measured in percentages. Thus, a 30 percent dot gain would cause a 50 percent dot to print at 80 percent.

The Printer/Press Dot Gain option compensates for dot gain by allowing you to enter the estimated percentage of dot gain. When Painter prints, it reduces the size of the halftone dots to compensate for dot gain. Before changing dot gain settings, check with your commercial printer.

◆ **Monitor Gamma**—This setting controls monitor brightness. The correct gamma setting is important if you want your onscreen image to match the printed image. If you will be outputting your image to

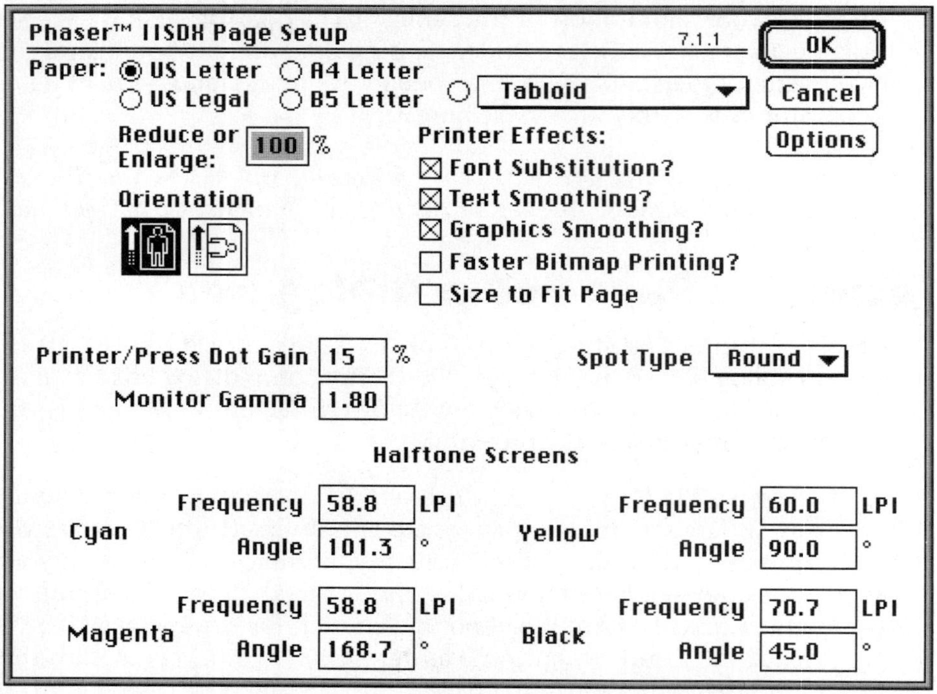

FIGURE 12.2: The Page Setup dialog box. The output device is a Tektronix dye sublimation color printer.

a printing press or printing your image on PostScript printers, leave Monitor Gamma set to 1.8. If you will be outputting your image to slides, you may wish to change this setting to 2.2, since this is the gamma used for most film recorders (check with your service bureau first). The 2.2 setting is also used when outputting to video.

◆ **Screen Frequency**—This option is only used if you are outputting color separations. Each field allows you to enter the output screen frequency in lines per inch for each of the four process colors: cyan, magenta, yellow, and black. As discussed earlier in this chapter, screen frequency is the number of halftones per inch in an image. The greater the number the sharper the image. (For more information about outputting color separations in Painter, see the "Using the Print Dialog Box" section later in this chapter.)

◆ **Angle**—When printing separations, the halftone dots for each of the four CMYK colors must be printed at the correct angle. Otherwise, when the CMYK colors are overlaid, output may look blurry and moiré patterns may appear. Do not change the default settings in the angle fields without the advice of your prepress house or commercial printer.

◆ **Spot Type**—Use this option if you wish to change the shape of halftone dots. Changing the dot shape from round to another shape can produce interesting effects. The choices in the pop-up menu are Round, Line, Ellipse, and Custom. If you wish to see the effects of changing the halftone shape, try choosing Line, then printing out a black-and-white print on a laser printer. To learn how to create custom shapes when saving images in EPS format, see the appendix.

Using the Print Dialog Box

After you've completed your artwork, and changed any necessary settings in the Page Setup dialog box, you're ready to print your image. To start the printing process, you need to use Painter's Print dialog box, which is shown in Figure 12.3. To access the dialog box, choose File ➤ Print.

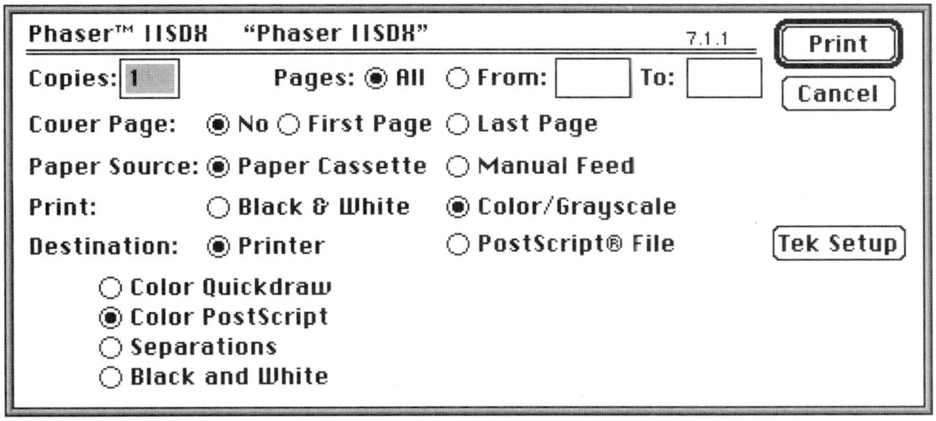

Phaser™ IISDX "Phaser IISDX" 7.1.1	Print
Copies: 1 Pages: ⦿ All ○ From: [ ] To: [ ]	Cancel
Cover Page: ⦿ No ○ First Page ○ Last Page	
Paper Source: ⦿ Paper Cassette ○ Manual Feed	
Print: ○ Black & White ⦿ Color/Grayscale	
Destination: ⦿ Printer ○ PostScript® File	Tek Setup
○ Color Quickdraw ⦿ Color PostScript ○ Separations ○ Black and White	

FIGURE 12.3: The Print dialog box. The output device is a Tektronix dye sublimation color printer.

Once the dialog box opens, notice that it resembles the standard Print dialog box for Macintosh and Windows applications. Here is a review of the print options specific to Painter.

◆ **Color QuickDraw**—(Macintosh only) QuickDraw is the Macintosh's internal language for creating text, lines, and graphic objects on screen. Most lower-priced laser and inkjet printers that are not PostScript printers are QuickDraw printers. Choose this option if you have a black-and-white or color QuickDraw printer.

QuickDraw printers cannot print separations. Changing the screen frequency, dot gain, or spot settings in the Page Setup dialog box will not change output on a QuickDraw printer.

◆ **GDI Printing**—(Windows version only) GDI stands for Windows Graphic Device Interface. If you have a printer that is not a PostScript printer, check this option. Most Bubblejet, Inkjet, and Paintjet printers are not PostScript printers.

GDI printers cannot print separations. Changing the screen frequency, dot gain, or spot settings in the PostScript Settings dialog box will not change output on a GDI printer.

◆ **Color PostScript**—PostScript is a page description language created by Adobe Systems. When a PostScript printer prints, it uses its RIP (Raster Image Processor) to convert the PostScript code to create an image. If you own a color PostScript printer such as a Tektronix dye sublimation or 3M Rainbow printer, choose this option.

◆ **Separations**—When a commercial printer prints images with many colors, the print shop must create four printing plates, one for each of the four process colors (cyan, magenta, yellow, black). When you choose this option, Painter breaks down an image into its CMYK color components, outputting four pages (or negatives), one for each of the four process-color components. As discussed earlier in this chapter, the different-size cyan, magenta, yellow, and black dots overlaying each other create countless colors.

When Painter outputs separations, it places the color name on each separation page, along with color bars and registration marks. When you print separations, be aware that the quality depends on the screen frequency, dot gain, and spot type settings in the Page Setup dialog box.

If you are outputting to negative film, make sure you click on the Options button (Windows users: Windows Advanced Options). This will open an Options dialog box where you can select the Negative check box, if your printer can output negatives.

Normally, color separations are output on imagesetters on negative film. Nevertheless, if you own a PostScript laser printer, you might wish to try printing separations. Even though you won't be able to use the separations, printing them on your own printer can help you understand the four-color printing process.

Note *Painter can create color separation files if you save your file in EPS format. To learn how to do this, see the appendix.*

♦ **Black & White PostScript**—If you are outputting to a black-and-white PostScript laser printer, choose this option. When your printer outputs your image, it will print a grayscale version of your color image.

Other Output Formats

Painter images can be output to video, to slides, and to chromes, (4-by-5 and 8-by-10-inch transparencies). Many of the issues raised by outputting to a printing press do not apply when outputting to slides or to video.

Outputting to Slides

A film recorder is used to output Painter images to slides or larger transparencies. Since film recorders use RGB colors, there's no need to work in Painter with the Printable Colors Only option set in the Art Materials dialog box. However, many service bureaus recommend setting your monitor gamma to 2.2 when creating images that will be output to slides. (See the "Using the Page Setup Dialog Box" section of this chapter to learn how to change monitor gamma).

Different film recorders output images in lines composed of different numbers of pixels. For instance, one file recorder could output using 2000 pixels, another at 4000 pixels. The more pixels a film recorder uses, the better the quality of transparency.

When outputting to a film recorder, the Painter image must fit within the grid of pixels that the film recorder outputs. To insure the highest-quality images, discuss image resolution with your service bureau.

Outputting to Video

If you will be outputting your Painter images or Painter QuickTime movies to video, you should change the monitor gamma in the Page Setup (Windows users: PostScript Setup) dialog box to 2.2. This will set the monitor brightness to the level used by television monitors.

Since the gamut of video colors is smaller than the gamut of RGB computer-generated colors, use Painter's Effects ➤ Tonal Control ➤ Legal Video Colors command to insure that the colors on screen fall within the colors used in video. When you activate Painter's Video Legal Colors command, you can choose whether to use colors based on the NTSC (American) television system or the PAL system (European standard). If you wish to output Painter images to video you will need a video board installed in your computer. Both RasterOps and Radius sell video systems that allow you to save video images to your computer and output to video from your computer.

● Wrapping It Up

We hope you've enjoyed *The Ultimate Guide to Painter*. By now, we're sure you're on your way to creating artistic masterpieces. If you would like to contact us, please write to the following address:

> The Ultimate Guide to Painter
> PO BOX 3117
> Westport, CT 06880

————Adele and Seth

Appendix

Using File Formats

If you will be outputting your Painter images to page layout, image editing, and multimedia programs, you will need to save your files in other formats besides Painter's native file format, RIFF. Other file formats are necessary so that programs like Quark XPress, Adobe PageMaker, Adobe Photoshop, Adobe Illustrator, Adobe Premiere, and Macromedia Director can read your Painter files. You may also need to save Painter files in other formats so that a prepress house or service bureau can output your files.

As you work on a Painter project, you may need to load images saved in other file formats by other programs. For instance, you might wish to import an image created in Photoshop into Painter, or you may simply wish to load a digitized stock image into Painter.

The following sections review all of the different file formats supported by Painter.

> **Warning** *Before you begin using other file formats, it's important to understand that only Painter's native format (RIFF) and Photoshop 3.0 format support floaters. If you create an image with floaters and then save the file in any format other than RIFF or Photoshop 3.0, you will lose your floaters.*

Saving in Another File Format

When you wish to save a file in another file format, choose File ➤ Save if the document has not previously been saved. If the document already has a file name, choose File ➤ Save As instead. In the Save As dialog box, choose a file format from the Type pop-up as shown in Figure A.1. Painter supports the following File formats: RIFF, TIFF, PICT, Photoshop 3.0, Photoshop 2.0, BMP, PCX, Targa, GIF, JPEG, and EPS.

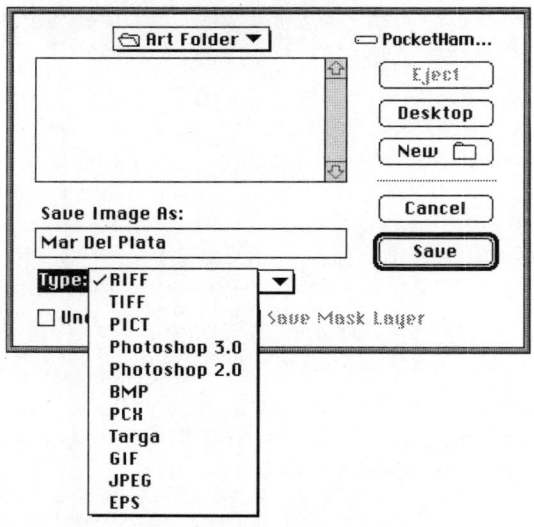

FIGURE A.1: File formats chosen from Painter's Save As dialog box

EPS File Format

EPS (Encapsulated PostScript) is a file format commonly used by drawing programs and supported by most page layout programs. Painter's EPS option allows you to save your file in EPS-DCS format, which is used to export color separations (DCS stands for Document Separation format). This format creates five different files: a preview file for viewing in a page lay-out program, and four color-component files (one for each of the four CMYK color components). When you save a file in this format, you create a color separation on disk from Painter.

> **Note** *Painter cannot read files saved in EPS-DCS format. Always make a backup of your file in RIFF format before saving in EPS-DCS.*

After you name your file, choose the EPS format from the Type pop-up menu, and then click Save. Painter opens the EPS Options dialog box (Figure A.2).

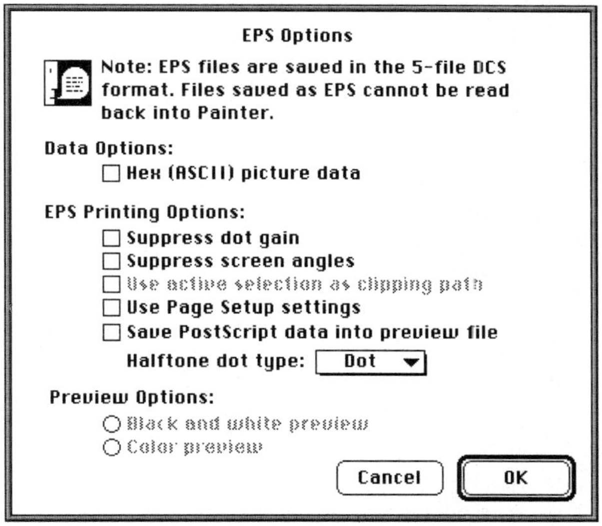

EPS Options

Note: EPS files are saved in the 5-file DCS format. Files saved as EPS cannot be read back into Painter.

Data Options:
☐ Hex (ASCII) picture data

EPS Printing Options:
☐ Suppress dot gain
☐ Suppress screen angles
☐ Use active selection as clipping path
☐ Use Page Setup settings
☐ Save PostScript data into preview file
Halftone dot type: [Dot ▼]

Preview Options:
○ Black and white preview
○ Color preview

[Cancel] [OK]

FIGURE A.2: The EPS Options dialog box

The EPS Options dialog box provides the following choices:

◆ **Hex (ASCII) Picture Data**—Some programs, such as Adobe Page-Maker, can only read EPS data in text format (often called ASCII). Since this option creates large data files, do not choose it unless absolutely necessary. Programs that do not need ASCII data accept Binary files, which are half the size of ASCII files.

◆ **Suppress Dot Gain**—If you are outputting an image in another program, such as a page layout program, you may prefer to use the dot gain settings in that program rather than those set in Painter. By selecting Suppress Dot Gain, any dot gain settings in Painter's Page Setup dialog box are ignored. See Chapter 12 for more information about dot gain.

◆ **Suppress Screen Angles**—This option is similar to the Suppress Dot Gain option. If you are outputting an image in another program, you will probably prefer to use the output settings in that program rather than Painter's. By selecting Suppress Screen angles, the Screen Angles settings in Painter's Page Setup dialog box are ignored. See Chapter 12 for more information about screen angles.

◆ **Use Page Setup Settings**—If you wish to output your EPS File using your own custom settings specified in the Page Setup (Windows users: PostScript Settings) dialog box, select this option. Otherwise Painter will use the settings in its Printer Settings file. In this file, screen frequency is set to 133 lpi with standard screen angles, and dot gain is set to 16%. For more information about using the Page Setup (Windows users: PostScript Settings) dialog box, see Chapter 12.

◆ **Save PostScript Data into Main File**—If you wish Painter to include a preview of the EPS file for use by another application, select this option. This activates the two radio buttons in the Preview Options section. Select either the Black-and-White preview or Color preview radio button.

◆ **Spot Type**—Use this pop-up menu if you wish to change the shape of the dots that create the halftones output by an imagesetter. If you wish to create a custom halftone shape, you must write it using the PostScript page-description language. After you write the program code, save it as a text file in the Painter directory using the name **Custom Screen** (Windows users: **CUSTOM.SCN**). Then choose this file name in the Spot Type pop-up menu.

● TIFF File Format

TIFF (Tag image file format) is a standard graphics data file format used primarily for saving digitized images from scanners and other devices. Stock images distributed on CD-ROM disks are also often saved in this format. Painter can load and save in TIFF (Windows users: TIF) file format. When you save in TIFF format, you can save a mask from Painter's mask layer by clicking on the Save Mask Layer check box in the Save As dialog box.

PICT File Format

PICT is a standard graphics file format developed by Apple for Macintosh computers. PICT files can be read by most Macintosh graphics programs and many PC Packages. If you wish to save your files for export into the Mac versions of multimedia programs such as Macromedia Director, Macromedia Authorware, or Adobe Premiere, save your images in PICT Format.

Photoshop 3.0 File Format

Painter can read Photoshop 3.0 files and save in this format so Painter images can be loaded into Photoshop 3.0.

Floaters and Layers

When you save a file with floaters in Photoshop 3.0 format, Painter's floaters appear in separate Photoshop layers. If you name your floaters in Painter, the names appear in Photoshop's Layers palette. When you load a Photoshop file that includes layers, they are loaded into Painter as floaters. The names of the Photoshop layers appear in the Objects :Floater List palette. When a Photoshop layer is converted into a floater, Painter trims the layer to create the smallest rectangular border possible around the Photoshop image data.

Photoshop Layer Masks

"Layer masks" created in Photoshop will be converted to a mask in a floater's mask layer. If the image is exported back to Photoshop, the mask will appear as part of the Photoshop layer, not as a separate layer mask.

Paths

Paths created in Photoshop are compatible with Painter's paths. Thus, paths created in Photoshop appear in Painter as paths in the Objects :Path List palette. Photoshop path names retain their names when loaded into

Painter. Depending upon how the path was created, the paths will either appear as one path or several paths. When loading a path from Painter into Photoshop, Painter's paths will automatically be converted to Photoshop paths. Painter's grouped paths will appear as individual paths. Painter's Negative paths will appear as subpaths.

> ***Note*** *Photoshop's clipping paths are not supported by Painter.*

Alpha Channels

If you load a Photoshop file that has alpha channels into Painter, Painter converts the first alpha channel into a mask. Use Painter's Mask Visibility icons to view the mask. When you save a Painter image that includes a mask in a Photoshop format, it is saved as an alpha channel in Photoshop.

Photoshop 2.0 Format

Painter can load files created in Photoshop 2.0 and save files in Photoshop 2.0 format.

BMP File Format

BMP (Windows Bit Map) format is a graphics file format popularized by Windows Paint. Painter can read BMP files and save files using this format.

PCX File Format

PCX (PC Paintbrush) is a graphics file format originally created by zSoft for its PC Paintbrush program. The file format is commonly used by many PC graphics programs. Painter can load files created in PCX format and save files using this format.

Targa (TGA) File Format

Targa is a PC file format created by TrueVision. It is used by many PC programs. Painter can load files created in Targa format and save files using this format.

GIF File Format

GIF (Graphics Interchange Format) is a compressed file format created by CompuServe Information Services. It was created to provide an efficient means of sending files over the telephone. The format is also used to save files on the Internet. Painter can read GIF files and write files in this format. If you are using this format, it's important to remember that it only supports up to 256 colors.

When you save a file in GIF Format, the GIF dialog box appears (Figure A.3).

The following options are available:

◆ **Number of Colors**—This option converts your 24-bit (16.7 million) color file to a 2-to-8-bit color file. Click the appropriate radio button to set the optimum number of colors for the GIF file.

◆ **Imaging Method**—This option controls how Painter handles the reduction of color in the GIF File. If you choose Quantize To Nearest Color, Painter will analyze each pixel and choose the closest match it can from the reduced color palette. If you choose Dither Colors,

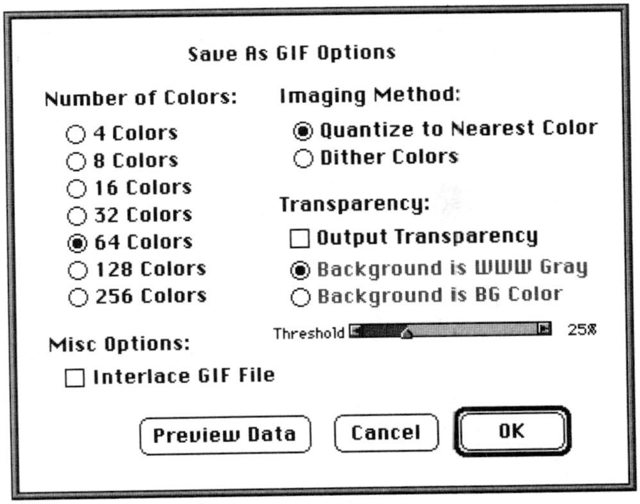

FIGURE A.3: The Save As GIF Options dialog box

Painter creates the colors in a dot pattern, which helps smooth transitions and avoid abrupt color changes.

◆ **Output Transparency**—The value of Painter's mask layer controls which areas are transparent in the GIF file. Check this option to make Painter's masked layer control transparency areas in the GIF file. If your image will be viewed on the Internet's World Wide Web, you may wish to choose Background Is WWW Gray. This makes transparent areas gray. If you wish to use the background paper color as the background for your GIF document, choose Background Is BG Color.

◆ **Threshold**—Drag the Threshold slider to control the point at which the mask layer becomes transparent. When using the slider, click on the Preview Data button to see how the slider affects your image. In the Preview window that opens, a shaded grid overlay indicates the transparent area.

◆ **Misc Options**—If your image will appear as a World Wide Web Page on the Internet, click on the Interlace GIF File option to help ensure that your image will be displayed faster.

JPEG File Format

JPEG (Joint Photographers Expert Group) is a file format used to compress large graphics files. Since JPEG is a "lossy" file format, some image data is discarded when you save in this format.

Painter can read files in JPEG format and save in this format. When you save in JPEG format, a dialog box appears (Figure A.4) allowing you to choose the quality of the format. The higher the quality the larger the file; the lower the quality the smaller the file.

Opening and Saving QuickTime and Video For Windows Movies

Painter allows Mac users to open and play QuickTime movies, and allows Windows users to open and play Video For Windows movies.

```
┌─────────────────────────────────────┐
│   ┌─────────────────────────────┐    │
│   │  JPEG Encoding Quality      │    │
│   │     ○ Excellent             │    │
│   │     ○ High                  │    │
│   │     ◉ Good                  │    │
│   │     ○ Fair                  │    │
│   │                             │    │
│   │   [ Cancel ]    [  OK  ]    │    │
│   └─────────────────────────────┘    │
└─────────────────────────────────────┘
```

FIGURE A.4:   The JPEG Encoding Quality dialog box

When you are working with a frame stack movie, Mac users can save it as a QuickTime movie, and Windows users can save it as a Video For Windows movie. QuickTime provides several different file compression options. To learn more about movies, and saving in QuickTime format, see Chapter 11.

Opening and Saving Numbered Files

Painter allows you to open and save groups of numbered files for use when working with frame stack movies. If you wish to open a numbered file, click on the Open Numbered File check box in Painter's Open File dialog box. After you create a frame stack movie, you can save it as a numbered file. For more information about opening and saving numbered files, see Chapter 11.

> **Note** *If Painter's many file formats do not satisfy your file translation needs, try one of these other programs for their file translation features: Mac users might wish to investigate Equilibrium's DeBabelizer—one of the most powerful file translation programs available—and PC users should check out Ulead ImagePals, a popular file translation program.*

Index

Note to the Reader:

Boldfaced numbers indicate pages where you will find the principal discussion of a topic or the definition of a term. *Italic* numbers indicate pages where topics are illustrated in figures.

FOR EVERY COMPUTER QUESTION,
THERE IS A SYBEX BOOK THAT HAS THE ANSWER

Each computer user learns in a different way. Some need thorough, methodical explanations, while others are too busy for details. At Sybex we bring nearly 20 years of experience to developing the book that's right for you. Whatever your needs, we can help you get the most from your software and hardware, at a pace that's comfortable for you.

We start beginners out right. You will learn by seeing and doing with our **Quick & Easy** series: friendly, colorful guidebooks with screen-by-screen illustrations. For hardware novices, the **Your First** series offers valuable purchasing advice and installation support.

Often recognized for excellence in national book reviews, our **Mastering** titles are designed for the intermediate to advanced user, without leaving the beginner behind. A **Mastering** book provides the most detailed reference available. Add our pocket-sized **Instant Reference** titles for a complete guidance system. Programmers will find that the new **Developer's Handbook** series provides a more advanced perspective on developing innovative and original code.

With the breathtaking advances common in computing today comes an ever increasing demand to remain technologically up-to-date. In many of our books, we provide the added value of software, on disks or CDs. Sybex remains your source for information on software development, operating systems, networking, and every kind of desktop application. We even have books for kids. Sybex can help smooth your travels on the **Internet** and provide **Strategies and Secrets** to your favorite computer games.

As you read this book, take note of its quality. Sybex publishes books written by experts—authors chosen for their extensive topical knowledge. In fact, many are professionals working in the computer software field. In addition, each manuscript is thoroughly reviewed by our technical, editorial, and production personnel for accuracy and ease-of-use before you ever see it—our guarantee that you'll buy a quality Sybex book every time.

To manage your hardware headaches and optimize your software potential, ask for a Sybex book.

FOR MORE INFORMATION, PLEASE CONTACT:

Sybex Inc.
2021 Challenger Drive
Alameda, CA 94501
Tel: (510) 523-8233 • (800) 227-2346
Fax: (510) 523-2373

Sybex is committed to using natural resources wisely to preserve and improve our environment. As a leader in the computer books publishing industry, we are aware that over 40% of America's solid waste is paper. This is why we have been printing our books on recycled paper since 1982.

This year our use of recycled paper will result in the saving of more than 153,000 trees. We will lower air pollution effluents by 54,000 pounds, save 6,300,000 gallons of water, and reduce landfill by 27,000 cubic yards.

In choosing a Sybex book you are not only making a choice for the best in skills and information, you are also choosing to enhance the quality of life for all of us.

Let us hear from you.

Painter's Brushes palette includes 18 brushes. Each brush is discussed in Chapter 3:

Here are the brushes in the Brushes palette:

Pencils

Eraser

Water

Chalk

Charcoal

Pens

Image Hose

Felt Pens

Crayons

Airbrush

Liquid

Brush

Artists

Cloners

Water Color

Masking

Burn

Dodge